The American
Deists

The American Deists
Voices of Reason and Dissent
in the Early Republic

Kerry S. Walters

University Press of Kansas

For source notes and additional copyright
information see page 369

Published by the University Press of Kansas (Lawrence, Kansas
66049), which was organized by the Kansas Board of Regents and is
operated and funded by Emporia State University, Fort Hays State
University, Kansas State University, Pittsburg State University, the
University of Kansas, and Wichita State University

Library of Congress Cataloging-in-Publication Data
Walters, Kerry S.
    The American deists : voices of reason and dissent in the early
republic / Kerry S. Walters.
        p.   cm.
    Includes bibliographical references and index.
    ISBN 0–7006–0540–1
    1. Deism.   2. Deism—United States—History—18th century.
I. Title.
BL2747.4.W33   1992   92–2827
211'.5'097309033—dc20

British Library Cataloging in Publication Data is available.

Printed in the United States of America
10 9 8 7 6 5 4 3 2 1
The paper used in this publication meets the
minimum requirements of the American National Standard
for Permanence of Paper for Printed Library Materials
Z39.48–1984.

For
Chan Coulter
Lou Hammann
and
Lisa Portmess
Colleagues and Friends

And
of course
for Kim

Contents

Preface
ix

Introduction
1

Benjamin Franklin
I Believe in One God, Creator of the Universe
51

Thomas Jefferson
Reason and Free Inquiry Are the Only Effectual Agents against Errors
106

Ethan Allen
Nature Is God's Revelation
141

Constantin François Chasseboeuf, Comte de Volney
Let Man Study Nature's Laws!
182

Thomas Paine
My Own Mind Is My Own Church
209

Elihu Palmer
Reason, the Glory of Our Nature
240

Philip Freneau
The Reasoning Power, Celestial Guest, the Stamp upon the Soul Impress'd
278

The Temple of Reason
In Defence of Pure Religion
306

Prospect; or, View of the Moral World
Virtue, the Highest Dignity of Man
332

The Theophilanthropist
The Love of God and Man
358

Sources and Permissions
369

Bibliographic Essay
375

Index
391

Preface

The deistic movement in eighteenth-century America is a fascinating but sadly neglected chapter in the history of American thought. In this anthology, I have collected and commented on the most pertinent deistic texts, many of them long out of print, and prefaced the whole with an introductory essay that examines the historical and intellectual background to the curious career of American rational religion as well as its influence on subsequent theological and philosophical thought. Selections have been gleaned from the major books and periodicals of the deistic movement, and this necessarily means that important but less central sources—such as selections from the writings of Joel Barlow or articles from the Newburgh *Mirror*—have been omitted. In dealing with a tradition that has as rich and extensive a literature as American deism, certain sacrifices must be made, however reluctantly.

I make no pretense of providing in this volume a social or political history of the American Enlightenment. Instead, I focus squarely on an examination and interpretation of deism in order to unravel its philosophical, theological, and ethical tenets. Those readers who wish to supplement this intellectual history with broader and more concrete treatments may consult the titles listed in the bibliographical essay, including my own *Rational Infidels: The American Deists* (1992).

Two editorial comments are in order here, one structural and the other stylistic. First, chapters 3 through 10 are introduced by short essays in which I provide summaries and pertinent historical information. The first two chapters, containing selections from Benjamin Franklin and Thomas Jefferson respectively, employ a slightly more complicated format. In addition to the usual preliminary essays, I also preface each of the selections in the Franklin chapter, and many in the Jefferson one, with individual introductions that focus on their specific historical backgrounds and underscore their thematic continuity. Most of the Franklin and Jefferson selections are taken from private correspondence and journal memoranda rather than from systematic treatises or books. As a consequence, it seemed important that the reader have some idea of the two men's correspondents as well as the context of their remarks. Given the number of readings in each of the first two chapters, the least confusing (although perhaps slightly cumbersome) strategy seemed to begin each selection with short explanatory prefaces.

Second, in preparing material for each of the ten chapters, I have corrected obvious misprints and idiosyncratic spellings that found their way into the

x   eighteenth-century sources from which I worked. At times I have also altered punctuation to facilitate comprehension of more convoluted passages. In most instances, however, I have retained typical eighteenth-century stylisms, spelling, and grammar.

I wish to extend my thanks to the staff members of the following libraries who aided me in my research: Andover Library, Harvard Divinity School; Houghton Library, Harvard University; Lamont Library, Harvard University, Musselman Library, Gettysburg College; and Ellen Clarke Bertrand Library, Bucknell University.

The comments of Professors Roderick S. French (George Washington University) and Mark A. Noll (Wheaton College) on an earlier draft of this book rescued it from a number of ambiguities and downright gaffes, and I wish to take this opportunity both to thank them for their painstaking advice and to absolve them from responsibility for any errors of fact or interpretation that may remain. Professor Jeffrey Turner (Bucknell University) graciously and expertly helped me translate the quotations from classical sources in the Thomas Jefferson chapter. Cynthia Miller, my editor at the University Press of Kansas, has been a constant source of good humor and support. Cynthia Ingham, my copyeditor, has been especially helpful. Her patient and meticulous reading of the manuscript both amazed and humbled me. My colleagues at Gettysburg College—Lisa Portmess and Chan Coulter (Philosophy) and Lou Hammann (Religious Studies)—sustained me with generous measures of gracious patience, encouragement, and wit. As partial recompense, I dedicate this volume to them.

Finally, Kim Daubman has been my mainstay in this and past projects. *The American Deists* is also dedicated to her as an inadequate but heartfelt tribute.

Introduction

An Age of Infidelity

On 6 August 1759, an alarmed Ezra Stiles of Newport, Rhode Island, wrote the following note to Thomas Clap, president of Yale College: "Deism has got such Head in this Age of Licentious Liberty that it would be in vain to try to stop it by hiding the Deistical Writings: and the only Way left to conquer & demolish it, is to come forth into the open Field & Dispute this matter on even Footing—the evidences of Revelation in my opinion are nearly as demonstrative as Newton's Principia, & these are the Weapons he used."[1]

If upset in 1759 over what he feared was an age of infidelity, Stiles was positively distraught nineteen years later when he succeeded Clap as Yale's president. Efforts by him and other Christians in the intervening period to quell the influence of "Deistical Writings" by arguing for the reasonableness of revealed religion had failed miserably. In fact, deistic rebuttals of such attempts proved so persuasive that toward the end of Stiles's administration Yale was perceived as a hotbed of what the orthodox establishment of the day indiscriminately labeled "infidelity." Lyman Beecher, who entered Yale in 1793, later recalled that the "college was in a most ungodly state. The college church was almost extinct. Most of the students were skeptical . . . . That was the day of the infidelity of the Tom Paine school. Boys that dressed flax in the barn, as I used to, read Tom Paine and believed him. . . . Most of the class before me were infidels, and called each other Voltaire, Rousseau, D'Alembert."[2] Beecher almost certainly exaggerated the extent to which infidelity infected the Yale of his youth. But even if his recollections are not completely trustworthy, they shed interesting light on a belief that was widely held in late eighteenth-century America: Deism was alive and well in the colleges.[3]

The perception of Yale's apostasy was not unique. A 1789 alumnus of Dartmouth College recalled that his fellow students were "very unruly, lawless, and without the fear of God" and lamented that ten years later "but a single member of the class of 1799 was publicly known as a professing Christian."[4] Virginia's College of William and Mary acquired the dubious reputation toward century's end as a training ground for "infidelity and . . . the wild politics of France."[5] By 1799, the College of New Jersey (Princeton) had "only three or four [students] who made any pretensions to piety."[6] Even conservative Boston's Harvard had succumbed. William Ellery Channing, describing his years (1794–98) there as a student, ruefully recalled that the college "was never in a worse state than when I entered. . . . The French Revolution had diseased

2   the imagination and unsettled the understanding of men everywhere. . . . The tone of books and conversation was presumptuous and daring. The tendency of all classes was to scepticism."[7] Officials at Harvard obviously shared Channing's concern. In 1791 they had banned and publicly burned Edward Gibbon's *Decline and Fall of the Roman Empire* on the grounds that its thesis was uncomplimentary to the Christian faith. Three years later, when young William Channing matriculated, each incoming student was presented with a copy of Richard Watson's *Apology for the Bible*. The hope was that this treatise, a polemic against Thomas Paine that accused him of employing "Railing for reasoning, vulgar and illiberal sarcasm in the room of argument,"[8] would exercise a salutary influence on Harvard's young scholars. That hope was not met. The wave of deistic infidelity that Ezra Stiles had deplored as far back as 1759 continued to swell throughout the academy for the rest of the century. Its pervasiveness may not have been as entrenched as popular and horrified piety contended, but there was a good amount of fire behind the smoke.

Nor were colleges the only breeding grounds of deistic "Licentious Liberty." In the second half of the eighteenth century, its presence also became increasingly obvious—and, to the Christian churches, increasingly worrisome —in the society at large. Newspapers, journals, and magazines published article after article on deism, most of which spawned scores of furious or delighted responses. Urban tradesmen gleefully discussed the uproar in public houses over pipes and tankards, even though only a handful of them probably bothered to read any of the debate's broadsides. Hundreds of city dwellers flocked to meetinghouses, out of either curiosity or conviction, to listen to addresses defending deism's religion of nature. Moreover, such "lowbrow" interest was mirrored in "high" society. The artist John Trumbull recalled attending a dinner party hosted by Thomas Jefferson in 1793 at which "free-thinking" sentiments dominated the table talk. The final straw for Trumbull was when Senator Giles of Virginia "proceeded so far at last, as to ridicule the character, conduct and doctrines of the divine founder of our religion—Jefferson, in the mean time, smiling and nodding approbation."[9] Individuals who had no access to genteel salon conversation organized fraternal clubs in which to debate and promulgate deism's principles, while others founded societies to stem its odious influence. And a sizable portion of the period's private correspondence was devoted to either outraged denunciations or fervent defenses of it.

Predictably, the churches observed the growing popularity of deism with horror. Men of the cloth blasted infidelity from their pulpits, titillating their parishioners' imaginations with lurid (and largely fictional) accounts of the deists' debauched lifestyles. A favorite clerical strategy was to associate, if not to outright identify, the movement with the Antichrist. As one clergyman gloomily predicted, "Our Zion must die without an helper" while deistic infidels laugh at her "dying groans." When it became obvious that such individual broadsides were relatively ineffective, the churches moved to a more collective and militant offensive. The Methodist Episcopal church urged a national day of fasting and prayer in 1796 to stem the tide of deism. The General Assembly of the Presbyterian church followed suit two years later—adding, with typical Calvinist earnestness, that divine wrath would descend on America unless she turned away from deism.[10]

Ironically, the Christian establishment's rather hysterical campaign against deism drew attention to the movement it otherwise might not have received. Deism's challenge to Christian hegemony was real but probably not as grave as the orthodox community supposed. In launching a full-scale attack on the new infidelity, churchmen shoved it center stage, thereby increasing its audience and its converts. Philip Freneau was more correct than not when he said Paine's *Age of Reason* would never have enjoyed the popular notoriety it did without the Christian establishment's constant and virulent bombardment of it.[11] When Elihu Palmer boasted toward century's end that there were "thousands and tens of thousands of deists" in America,[12] he might have added a note of gratitude to Christian leaders for their unwitting assistance in recruitment.

In short, the period in which the deistic controversy raged in the Early Republic was an exciting one. As Charles Dickens later said of the French Revolution, it was the best of times and the worst of times, depending on which side of the debate one's allegiance fell. There was an electricity in the air. It painfully shocked some, such as Uzal Ogden, who thundered that deism "more became a lunatick, than a person in the enjoyment of his rational faculties!" and then clenched his point by asking: "When the restraints of religion are dissolved, what can be expected, but that men should *abandon* themselves to the impulse of their passions?"[13] Yet that same electricity stimulated others to see in deism the dawning of a new age—the age of rational religion and freedom of conscience—in which universal benevolence and justice would prevail. Then, in the words of Tunis Wortman of New York, "we can only expect to arrive at that ultimate state of perfection of which the human character is susceptible. . . . Persecution and superstition, vice, prejudice and cruelty will take their eternal departure from the earth. National animosities and distinctions will be buried in eternal oblivion."[14] Verbal volleys such as these were hurled back and forth across the barricades, often bursting with much flash but little damage. One thing, however, is clear. Regardless of whether the issue scorched or inflamed, its heat generated one of the first large-scale intellectual controversies in the young Republic, embroiling clerics, literati, statesmen, students, and laypersons alike. The debate between deism and Christianity even-

4 tually extended far beyond the purely religious sphere, touching political, ethical, social, and philosophical nerves along the way. And although the controversy's intellectual and emotional fury burnt itself out for all practical purposes by 1811, its legacy remained. After the deistic challenge, Christian sensibility in the United States would never be quite the same.

What was the nature of this movement which so horrified some and enraptured others? Although there is no simple answer to this question, the following laudatory description of deism, written in 1801 by Elihu Palmer, the chief of the American deists, provides a starting point.

> Deism declares to intelligent man the existence of one perfect God, Creator and Preserver of the Universe; that the laws by which he governs the world, are like himself immutable, and of course, that violations of these laws, or miraculous interference in the movements of nature, must be necessarily excluded from the grand system of universal existence; that the Creator is justly entitled to the adoration of every intellectual agent throughout the regions of infinite space; and that he alone is entitled to it, having no copartners who have a right to share with him the homage of the intelligent world. Deism also declares, that the practice of a pure, natural, and uncorrupted virtue, is the essential duty, and constitutes the highest dignity of man; that the powers of man are competent to all the great purposes of human existence; that science, virtue, and happiness, are the great objects which ought to awake the mental energies, and draw forth the moral affections of the human race."[15]

This preliminary statement of deism's tenets provokes a number of questions. Why did conservative churchmen condemn as a tool of the Antichrist such a seemingly inoffensive system, while liberal ones as well as non-Christians welcomed it as the harbinger of a new age of reason and emancipation? Why did orthodoxy see deism, "the practice of a pure, natural, and uncorrupted virtue," as the vehicle by which individuals abandoned themselves, in Uzal Ogden's words, "to the impulse of their passions"? How did those who fervently declared the existence of "one perfect God" acquire reputations for atheism and infidelity? Moreover, despite the burden of such calumny, why did the ranks of self-proclaimed deists swell throughout the eighteenth and early nineteenth centuries? Finally, how is it that American deism, a widespread and militant movement, suddenly fizzled out, almost overnight, by 1811? In order to answer these and other questions, it is necessary to examine American deism against its broader social and intellectual backdrop.

Enlightenment and the New Learning

Deism was a child of the Enlightenment—that period in Western thought roughly coterminous with the eighteenth century, which is often somewhat misleadingly labeled the "Age of Reason." The Enlightenment as an intellectual and popular movement accommodated a wide diversity of perspectives as well as personalities and hence resists airtight, comprehensive definition. It is better understood as an interpretive way of looking at the world than an intransigent body of beliefs and doctrines. As Carl Becker argued, the Enlightenment ethos was a "climate of opinion," not a chiseled-in-stone dogma.[16] Still, despite divergence of opinion among Enlightenment savants, there is enough family resemblance between their ideas to allow for the postulation of five general tendencies that capture the movement's *überhaupt* orientation. The extent to which individual thinkers emphasized each of them certainly differed, but as a matter of degree rather than kind.

First, Enlightenment savants systematically defended experience and reason, rather than aprioristic speculation, as the twin foundations of human knowledge. They were, as Charles Taylor put it, "epistemological innovators,"[17] breaking with the traditional Aristotelian model of deduction from inherited first principles and relying instead on observation and induction. Their primary reason for rejecting Aristotelianism was what they saw as its unwarranted and impractical appeal to such mysterious categories as substance, final causation, and innate ideas. (Curiously, many Enlightened authors failed to see that they themselves often resorted to analogous explanations in their own writings—proof that each generation of intellectuals has its own blindspot.) In place of such arcane standards, the Enlightenment savants argued that human experience and rational analysis were the only barometers of legitimate knowledge. Scrutiny of experience supplied the raw material from which reason's logical operations could infer meaningful generalizations. Armchair speculations that spun elaborate a priori schema without benefit of empirical grounding were, at best, pleasant diversions. But they were not to be taken seriously.

Second, this epistemic appeal to empirical reason catapulted the study of nature—or "natural philosophy"—into the spotlight. Close study of physical phenomena became obligatory in the Enlightenment intellectual's search for universal lawlike patterns and explanations. Moreover, the methodology of the natural sciences was accepted as both a necessary and sufficient standard in *any* arena of investigation. Nature and nature's laws were uniform and all-encompassing, incorporating human and social relations as well as physical ones. To understand the realm of nature, then, was to understand everything, at least in principle. Consequently, to master the natural sciences was to command all disciplines.

Third, the new empiricism's reliance on experience and nature encouraged a deep-seated suspicion of authority. Savants were quick to challenge traditional answers and received models, whether they were philosophical, ethical, theological, or political. The book of nature, not the dusty tomes of either the church or the Scholastics, were the first and final court of appeal. This disencumbrance from authority and hidebound tradition was seen, as Immanuel Kant put it, as "man's release from self-imposed tutelage. Tutelage is the inability to use one's natural powers without direction from another. This tutelage is called 'self-imposed' because its cause is not any absence of rational competence but simply a lack of courage and resolution to use one's reason without direction from another. *Sapere aude*!—Dare to reason! Have the courage to use your own minds!—is the motto of enlightenment."[18]

Fourth, the Enlightenment's distrust of authority, as well as its optimistic faith in the liberating power of human reason, focused its attention on social, political, and normative issues. This in turn led to a humanitarian espousal of the primacy of individual freedom and political equality, most often expressed in the "social contract" model of society endorsed by reform-minded figures such as John Locke, Jean-Jacques Rousseau, and Denis Diderot. The basic assumption behind this championing of individual liberty was that greater understanding of social laws would inevitably lead to the rationalization of human behavior, just as a fuller comprehension of physical laws would result in the conquest of nature.

Finally, this confidence in reason's ability to eliminate political evils as well as ignorance encouraged a deep faith in the eventual and inevitable perfection of both society and human knowledge. As Ernst Cassirer correctly pointed out, "No other century is so completely permeated by the idea of intellectual progress as that of the Enlightenment."[19] This exuberant confidence colored all areas of human inquiry and endeavor, and thinkers such as Jean Le Rond d'Alembert presumed that enlightenment would continue to extend the penetrating beam of reason until all facets of existence were illuminated.

> The discovery and application of a new method of philosophizing, the kind of enthusiasm which accompanies discoveries, a certain exaltation of ideas which the spectacle of the universe produces in us—all these causes have brought about a lively fermentation of minds. Spreading through nature in all directions like a river which has burst its dams, this fermentation has swept with a sort of violence everything along with it which stood in its way.

The upshot? "Natural science from day to day accumulates new riches. . . . The true system of the world has been recognized, developed, and perfected."[20] The golden age, in short, was at hand.

The immediate intellectual sires of the Enlightenment's exuberant advocacy of empirical reason, natural philosophy, and reform were three seventeenth-century Englishmen: Francis Bacon (1561–1626), John Locke (1632–704), and Isaac Newton (1642–1727). Their influence on eighteenth-century thought (and, by association, deism) can hardly be exaggerated. They defended and legitimized a new way of perceiving the world which was often referred to by Enlightenment thinkers as the "New Learning."

Bacon set the stage in *The Great Instauration* (1603) and *Novum Organum* (1620) by advocating what he took to be a revolutionary system of inductive logic that broke with the Aristotelian model of "syllogistic" reasoning. The old model, according to Bacon, was methodologically inadequate because it ignored the lessons of experience and concentrated exclusively on the deduction of logical implications from abstract first principles. True, such deductions often resulted in logically impeccable inferences. But because the first principles or "notions" on which the system was built were a priori and untested, the syllogistic arguments generated from them reduced to little more than vapid speculations possessing neither explanatory power nor utility. As Bacon remarked, "The syllogism consists of propositions, propositions of words; words are the signs of notions. If, therefore, the notions (which form the basis of the whole) be confused . . . there is no solidity in the superstructure."[21] And since the first principles usually *were* "confused," given their complete detachment from the realm of experience, Bacon concluded that "demonstration by syllogism" lets "nature skip out of its hands."[22]

In place of the traditional deductive model, Bacon proposed a method that took as its starting point not abstract first principles but concrete data gleaned from experience. This data in turn was manipulated—experimented on—and refined, until the observer was able to discern patterns or functional correlations in nature's operations, which then were used to generate hypothetical explanations and lawlike principles. The old deductive logic, in sum, dealt only with words and propositions, thereby shutting itself off from the real world of experience. Bacon's new system proceeded inductively, by examining experience and then inferring rational generalizations from it, and so firmly grounding itself in reality. This concentration on nature and experience, Bacon assured his readers, not only provided a more solid foundation for human knowledge than the Aristotelian model, but also imbued reasoning with an instrumentality—a practical calculus by which to manipulate and subdue nature—that syllogistic logic failed to supply. And for Bacon, as for his eighteenth-century intellectual descendants, knowledge and utility were synonymous. This switch in emphasis from idle speculation to instrumental reason is apparent in the following passage from *The Great Instauration*:

> The art which I introduce . . . is a kind of logic; though the difference between it and the ordinary [or syllogistic logic] is great; indeed im-

mense. For the ordinary logic professes to contrive and prepare helps and guards for the understanding, as mine does; and in this one point they agree. But mine differs from it in three points especially; viz., in the end aimed at; in the order of demonstration; and in the starting point of the inquiry. For the end which this science of mine proposes is the invention not of arguments but of works; not of things in accordance with principles, but of principles themselves; and not of probable reasons, but of designations and directions for works. And as the intention is different, so accordingly is the effect; the effect of the one being to overcome an opponent in argument, of the other to command nature in action.[23]

Bacon's call for a scientific methodology that took experience rather than abstract speculation as its raw material struck a responsive chord in his contemporaries. The specifics of his proposed system were not without their detractors: Thomas Hobbes, for example, was one of the new logic's harshest critics. But even if the intellectual world declined to endorse Bacon's method unanimously, it did applaud the spirit of his efforts. His championing of empirical reason, as well as his insistence that knowledge should properly aim for the "invention of arts," inspired the seventeenth and eighteenth centuries with a heady vision of continuous scientific progress.

The perceived merits of Bacon's condemnation of syllogistic logic were underscored by the appearance of Isaac Newton's *Philosophiae Naturalis Principia Mathematica* (1687) and *Optics* (1704). These works provided the eighteenth century with a theory of physical reality that demonstrated to everyone's satisfaction the superiority of observation, experiment, and mathematical calculation to abstract speculation. As Newton himself proudly asserted in describing his methodology, "*Hypotheses non fingo*" ["I do not feign hypotheses"]. This claim, in retrospect, may be too strong. But as far as the Enlightenment's advocates of the New Learning were concerned, Newton's model dramatically embodied the empiricist method earlier outlined by Bacon.

In the preface to his *Principia*, Newton carefully delineated the empiricist boundaries of his methodology: "The whole burden of [natural] philosophy seems to consist in this: from the phenomena of motions to investigate the forces of nature, and then from these forces to demonstrate the other phenomena."[24] Beginning, then, with a careful observation of the phenomenon of motion, Newton constructed a systematic model of physical reality that comprehensively and mathematically showed the material order to be rational and explicable in terms of incontrovertible and uniform laws. Mystery and caprice were thereby expunged from nature, by means of "principles . . . deduced from phenomena and made general by induction, which is the highest evidence that a proposition can have."[25] Physical reality revealed itself to be a clockwork mechanism of intricate and fail-safe precision. Material bodies, regardless of their location or level of complexity, could be explained by the laws of inertia, change of motion, and reaction. Moreover, given the demonstrated fact that "Nature is very consonant and conformable to her self," human manipulation of nature's laws became an actual as well as a logical possibility.

Certainly Newton's mechanistic model did not claim to unriddle all of physical reality. The origin of the "Attractions" of "Gravity, Magnetism and Electricity," he conceded, "may be perform'd by impulse, or by some other means unknown to me."[26] But regardless of the ultimate impetus for the rational operations definitive of physical reality, two things were obvious to Newton: first, that the material order displayed rationality and design; second, that "this most beautiful system of the sun, planets, and comets could only proceed from the counsel and domination of an intelligent and powerful Being."[27] This Primordial Mover, whose presence was deducible from the apparent orderliness of nature, was removed from physical events, serving as their first cause but only indirectly operating through unvarying natural law. But its existence was indisputable—although the Marquis de Laplace, working from a Newtonian framework a century later, would triumphantly assert that *his* astronomical schema had no need of the "God hypothesis."

Newton, in short, provided the eighteenth century with a dramatic verification of the soundness of Bacon's empiricist method. He also bequeathed to it the intellectual assurance that reality was lawlike and that its orderly uniformity pointed to the existence of a rational deity. Alexander Pope thus spoke for his entire generation when he later celebrated Newton and the New Learning with the famous couplet: "Nature and Nature's laws lay hid in night;/ God said, Let Newton be, and all was light."

While Newton charted nature's laws, thereby demystifying the cosmos, John Locke did the same for the laws of reason, undertaking no less a task than the elucidation of "the original, certainty, and extent of *human knowledge*, together with the grounds and degrees of *belief, opinion*, and *assent*." Moreover, he did so in good New Learning fashion, proceeding from the "historical, plain method" of inquiring into "the original of those ideas . . . which a man observes."[28] In his *Essay Concerning Human Understanding* (1690), Locke claimed that the "ground of belief" was experience. The five senses provided the human intellect—which itself was a potentiality (the famous *tabula rasa*) for the absorption or imprinting of experience—with the raw material of thought and reflection. Sense data, or "simple ideas," were consequently the basis of all human knowledge. Complex ideas were generated from simple ones by the mental function of association: The intellect compared simple ideas, noting their similarities and differences, and then abstracted from them to make lawlike principles.

The mind makes the particular [or simple] ideas, received from particular objects, to become general; which is done by considering them as they are in the mind, such appearances, separate from all other existences, and the circumstances of real existence, as time, place, or any other concomitant ideas. This is called *abstraction*, whereby ideas, taken from particular beings, become general representatives of all of the same kind, and their names general names, applicable to whatever exists conformable to such abstract ideas."[29]

Inductive generalization from sensory experience, then, was the origin of abstract, scientific postulations. The truth value of any knowledge claim could be established either by appealing to sensory experience or by testing for the logical coherency of associations of simple ideas. Meaningful speculation and reliable discourse, for Locke, never strayed from these twin epistemic foundations. Appeals to "mysterious" standards such as innate ideas or subjective, psychological certainty were unnecessary.

In formulating the grounds of legitimate belief, Locke described what soon came to be regarded as mental laws, which were just as immutable as Newton's physical ones. They were also deemed universal in application, cutting across the entire range of human beliefs. Even the knowledge supposedly furnished by divine revelation was answerable to the standards of experience and reason. If pronouncements that posed as revelatory proved upon reflection to be irrational or counterintuitive, they were prima facie candidates for rejection. Locke, a more or less orthodox Christian, saw the theological import of his thesis and awkwardly hedged his bet by insisting that "genuine" instances of revelation were "above," not "contrary to," reason.[30] But his empiricist analysis of the nature and extent of human knowledge cast grave doubts in the minds of many on the verisimilitude of beliefs that claimed divine origin.

The New Learning's emphasis on experience and nature, then, was founded on Bacon's advocacy of instrumental reason, Newton's demonstration that physical nature conforms to universal laws, and Locke's analogous claim in the realm of human psychology. Their work served as the basis for the Enlightenment's confidence that reality was rational and hence capable of being understood by rational human minds. The study of nature provided evidence of order, harmony, and regularity in the physical cosmos. The study of reason revealed the same attributes in the human faculty of understanding. Reality more and more appeared as a vast continuum whose laws applied with clocklike precision to all facets of existence. And the meticulous charting of the lawful operations of the cosmic clockwork, all felt assured, would inevitably lead to perfection in human knowledge, virtue, and happiness.

Liberal Christianity and British Deism

The influence of Bacon, Newton, and Locke was soon apparent in all areas of intellectual endeavor, and religion was no exception.[31] Some churchmen were horrified at the theological implications of the New Learning. Although Newton did not reject the possibility of divine intervention (or miracles) and Locke retained faith in Christian revelation, their respective systems undercut the likelihood of rational belief in either. Similarly, although Bacon characterized his new logic as a reinforcement of the scriptural primacy assigned to humans, his strident denunciations of a priori first principles cut at the heart of many orthodox doctrines. This tension became increasingly obvious to the trio's defenders as well as their critics and often prompted the latter to reject the New Learning outright. Such a dismissal, however, was rare. Most clerics saw Baconian logic, Newtonian physics, and Lockean psychology as supporting evidence for the existence of the Christian God. The lawlike orderliness of the cosmos as well as the mind, in their estimations, clearly pointed to the necessity of an intelligent and benevolent Supreme Architect.

Moreover, Bacon's claim that legitimate reasoning was inductive rather than aprioristic convinced them that knowledge of God's existence was attainable through an investigation of nature. Consequently, many churchmen, particularly in Britain, accommodated the new Learning in their writings by positing a distinction between "natural" and "revealed" theology. The former generally focused on naturalistic design arguments for the existence and attributes of God. The latter concentrated on distinctively Christian dogmas— the Trinity, the divinity of Jesus, miracles, and scriptural revelation—which were incapable of being discovered by the light of experience or understood by human reason. Following Locke's suggestion in the *Essay*, the liberal or "latitudinarian" theologians of the eighteenth century insisted that Christian dogma was above rather than contrary to reason and complemented rather than contradicted natural theology's claims. Thus Samuel Clarke (1675–1729), one of Newton's close associates, argued that Christianity's supernatural revelation was congruent with natural theology, even if its dictums were necessarily faith-based and hence outside the purview of rational analysis.[32] Similarly, George Cheyne (1671–1743), physician and fellow of the Royal Society, argued that the inherited taint of original sin hindered human reason from acquiring on its own an adequate knowledge of God. Therefore, natural religion needed the aid of divine revelation.[33]

In spite of its self-assuredness, liberal theology's marriage of natural reason and supernatural revelation was an uneasy one. Apologists such as Clarke and Cheyne who enthusiastically absorbed the New Learning while retaining their faith in Christian doctrine tended to give away with their left hand what they took with their right. They embraced the assumption that reality was an im-

12 mense mechanism operating in accordance with rational and immutable laws of nature and hence capable of being fully understood through experience and human reason. But they pulled back—arbitrarily, some thought—when it came to traditional Christian dogma, thereby suggesting that the postulated lawlike character of reality was not so immutable or rational after all.

This tension sparked the emergence of British deism, a movement that attempted to formulate a "pure" religion of nature by expunging from it elements of Christian supernaturalism. The campaign was launched by John Toland (1670–1722), who published his *Christianity Not Mysterious* (1696) one year after the appearance of Locke's liberal tract *The Reasonableness of Christianity.* Toland claimed—much to the embarrassment of Locke, who publicly disassociated himself from Toland's deism—to base his arguments on the New Learning's empiricist model of knowing. Toland asserted that a credible natural religion must display logical consistency, even at the expense of traditional Christian articles of faith. He therefore discounted the possibility of miracles and divine revelation, the former because they were contrary to experience, the latter because it was beyond the reach of reason and therefore not bona fide knowledge. The deistic Supreme Craftsman was as rational as his creation, and Toland considered it unworthy as well as illogical of the Architect of Reason to communicate in less than rational ways or to violate the system of natural laws he had established.

Anthony Collins (1676–1729) agreed with Toland and surpassed him in his attack on supernatural religion. Arguing that the pure religion of nature and reason had been perverted by superstitious priestcraft, Collins's *Discourse on the Grounds and Reasons of the Christian Religion* (1724) indirectly challenged ecclesiastical authority by describing sacred Scripture, the basis of that authority, as irrational and incomprehensible. While Collins directed his attack specifically against biblical prophecy, his contemporary Thomas Woolston (1669–1733) took on the doctrine of miracles. In his *Discourses on the Miracles of Our Saviour* (1727–29), he concluded that the New Testament's account of Jesus's miracles was as "broken, elliptical and absurd" as any tale "told of any imposter . . . in religion" and that even the early church fathers interpreted scriptural miracles in only a figurative, allegorical way.[34]

A rash of deistic treatises denouncing the claims of revealed Christianity appeared in subsequent years.[35] Although they were not especially acute from a philosophical or theological perspective, they stirred up enough controversy to keep the movement in the public eye. Undoubtedly the most influential was one written by Matthew Tindal (1657–1733). His *Christianity as Old as the Creation* (1730) quickly became known as the "Deist Bible" and was, of all the British deistic works, the best reasoned and most comprehensive defense of the religion of nature. Tindal argued that revealed as opposed to natural theology was not based on the "Nature and Reason of things" but rather on superstition and wishful thinking. He offered as an antidote to supernaturalist confusion the following rule: If any putatively revealed truth differs in even the slightest detail from experience or reason, it is to be condemned and rejected.[36] This represented a radical break with Locke's liberal attempt to salvage Christian revelation. For Tindal, there was no appreciable distinction between a proposition "above" and a proposition "contrary to" reason. One was perhaps a bit less mysterious than the other, but neither ultimately proved satisfactory to a rational mind. In addition, Tindal denied the divinity of Jesus, claiming that the notion was an invention of priestcraft; held that the Scriptures demanded veneration of an ethically unworthy deity who displayed capriciousness, jealousy, and arbitrary cruelty in his dealings with humans; and concluded that true religion—the religion of nature, stripped of all priestly superstitious embellishment—was both logically and ethically superior to Christianity.

The deistic movement in Britain carried to its logical theological conclusion the New Learning initiated by Bacon, Newton, and Locke. It rejected revealed religion as contrary to human as well as divine reason and insisted that the "Great Book of Nature" and the "Light of Reason" were better guides to a knowledge of both God and morality than scriptural or priestly dogma. Although frequently accused of atheism by their contemporaries, the British deists were not disbelievers so much as religious and ethical reformers. They accepted the existence of a Supreme Architect and argued that his presence was demonstrable through reason and experience. They took as their task the methodical critique of an ideology—supernaturalist Christianity—which they believed had subverted the original reasonableness and purity of religious sentiment. In doing so, they posed a sweeping threat to orthodox religion's hegemony, which far surpassed the liberalizing tendencies of latitudinarian Christianity. An indignant Jonathan Edwards accurately captured the deists' radical point of departure in his *History of the Work of Redemption* (1773), when he said they

> wholly cast off the Christian religion, and are professed infidels. They are not like the Heretics, Arians, Socinians, and others, who own the Scriptures to be the word of God, and hold the Christian religion to be the true religion, but only deny these and these fundamental doctrines of the Christian religion: they deny the whole Christian religion. Indeed, they own the being of a God; but deny that Christ was the son of God, and say he was a mere cheat; and so they say all the prophets and apostles were: and they deny the whole Scripture. They deny that any of it is the word of God. They deny any revealed religion, or any word of God at all; and say that God has given mankind no other light to walk by but their own reason.[37]

14

Deism Comes to America

New ideas that arise from and agitate cosmopolitan settings trickle down only gradually, if at all, to provincial societies—especially colonial ones. People who settle a frontier are understandably more concerned with adapting to their environment and establishing a foothold than with philosophizing. Such was the case with the American colonies in the early eighteenth century. Although urban growth and native culture were on the rise, the colonies in the first half of the eighteenth century still tended to import their books and ideas from Britain and, to a lesser extent, France. As a result, there was generally a lag between the emergence of new thought on the Continent and its arrival in America.

American exposure to the New Learning was no exception to this rule. The works of Newton, Locke, and Bacon arrived only in 1714, as part of an excellent collection dispatched from England to Yale by Jeremiah Dummer. Before that date (and for some time afterward) Yale students were taught an undiluted Aristotelian physics, learning that the earth was at the center of the universe and that the four elements were the basic constituents of reality.[38] Harvard was somewhat more progressive, having taught Copernicanism since the mid-seventeenth century; even so, Newton's system was introduced there only in the late 1720s.[39] Moreover, all colonial colleges relied on a Scholastic model of logic, particularly as defended by the Puritan divine William Ames, which stressed Aristotelian deduction from abstract first principles.[40] After the Dummer gift, however, the New Learning quickly caught fire and spread throughout the American schools. Princeton's curriculum reflected it by 1746,[41] and by midcentury students as well as a handful of reading laypersons were familiar with, even if somewhat still confused by, the new way of thinking.

Locke, Bacon, and Newton may have been too rich a diet for many in the colonies to digest comfortably. But by the 1750s, the more accessible works of the Scottish common sense philosophers had arrived on the scene, and they exerted a profound impact on American Enlightenment thought. (The American deists proper, with the notable exceptions of Benjamin Franklin and especially Thomas Jefferson, appear to have been slightly less influenced by them.) The members of the Scottish school, particularly Francis Hutcheson and Thomas Reid, discussed the implications of empiricism in language that was usually more easily understandable than that of the Enlightenment's three luminaries. They also argued that ordinary experience was trustworthy, providing knowledge of the objective world that was, if not absolutely certain, at least probable and testable. Even before David Hume raised the specter of skepticism, perceptive critics had voiced unease over Locke's insistence that the *idea* of reality is all that the human mind immediately knows. If this was the case, these critics concluded, the knower could never be confident that his or her ideas of the objective realm actually corresponded to it. The Scottish philosophers countered these early winds of skepticism by arguing that commonplace ideas derived from sense perception were reliable because the mind possessed certain "necessary" or "self-evident" intuitive faculties by which knowledge could be safely appraised and the sciences, moral as well as physical, established. Such a defense of common sense empiricism, regardless of its philosophical strength, provided the American Enlightenment with the foundation for the empiricist method it sought.[42]

Britain's legacy of liberal Christianity likewise arrived in the colonies during the first half of the eighteenth century. John Tillotson's *Principles of Natural Religion* (1675) and William Wollaston's *Religion of Nature Delineated* (1722) were the two most widely read of the many liberal attempts to reconcile the New Learning with Christian revelation, although Clarke and Cheyne were also known. As in Britain, liberal theology became popular with all but the most conservative representatives of organized Christianity in colonial America (including even that redoubtable exemplar of Puritanism, Cotton Mather).[43] Its influence was so far-reaching that Harvard College founded the Dudleian Lectures in 1755 for the express purpose of "the proving, explaining, and proper use and improvement of the principles of Natural Religion."[44]

Less welcomed by the religious establishment was the colonial importation of British deism. Members of the upper class and intelligentsia read Toland, Collins, and Tindal. Alexander Pope and Joseph Addison, with their watered-down versions of deism, were two of the colonists' favorite authors. More accessible to the general reading public than actual deistic works were scores of antideistic tracts, such as Charles Leslie's *Short and Easy Method with the Deists* (1697) and John Leland's *View of the Principal Deistical Writers* (1754). These and similar apologetics, dipped into by laypersons whose curiosity had been piqued by clerical denunciations of deism, often had the disconcerting effect of converting their readers to the religion of nature. Sometimes the lapse into "infidelity" was only temporary. Joseph Hawley (1723–88), a cousin of Jonathan Edwards's, became so infected while studying at Harvard that he soon refused to countenance "any Doctrine upon the mere authority of God's word,"[45] but he returned to the fold in 1762. Similarly, the Reverend William Bliss (1728–1808) "was deeply plunged in their system for many years" after a youthful encounter with antideistic polemics.[46]

But for others, including the young Benjamin Franklin, deism took hold. Initially intrigued by writers such as Leland and Leslie, Franklin graduated to Collins and Tindal and by the age of seventeen was a convinced deist. Although later in life he moderated his earlier enthusiastic advocacy of deism, he never abandoned his regard for natural religion nor his distrust of Christian dogma. In any case, whether the individual commitment to deism was short-

16   lived or permanent, it is clear that its radical critique of supernatural religion was well known in the colonies by midcentury. The reading public imbibed it directly from antideistic tracts or deistic texts themselves, and the illiterate or nonreading layperson absorbed it indirectly from pulpit denunciations. It is little wonder that in 1759 a scandalized Ezra Stiles (who in his own youth had briefly flirted with deism)[47] called the period an "Age of Licentious Liberty."

The New Learning's emphasis on empirical reason and natural philosophy prompted different forms of "infidelity" in different countries, depending on the specific social and intellectual climate. In England, for example, where the Church of England had at least tacitly endorsed a relatively liberal Christianity since the days of Archbishop Laud, Enlightenment criticisms of orthodoxy assumed the shape of a mild deism that was sometimes scarcely discernible from latitudinarianism. France's autocratic political structure, as well as the entrenched and oppressive dominance of its Catholic establishment, often pushed disgruntled Enlightenment savants into outright atheism. But American infidelity avoided both of these extremes. More militant than British rational religion but less radical than French atheism, American deism can be seen in retrospect as falling between the two in both its concrete tenets and its general mood. Although there are any number of reasons why deism on the American shore adopted this character, the three primary ones are: the Calvinist tradition against which it reacted; the steady infiltration into North America of French Enlightenment ideals; and the experience of national independence.

Calvinism

Aspects of the theology associated with John Calvin (1509–64) were embodied in the Church of England's Thirty-nine Articles. But the seventeenth-century English Puritan movement, which called for drastic doctrinal reformation and a return to spiritual, ecclesial, and ethical purity, wholeheartedly endorsed what has since come to be known as "Calvinism" proper. Puritan dissenters who eventually found their way to the Massachusetts Bay Colony did so with the express goal of creating a society—the "New Jerusalem"—in which church and state, Moses and Aaron, "were coordinate authorities, strengthening each other jointly to enforce the moral law."[48] Early New England, inspired by what it saw as its mission to build a Zion in the wilderness, became for all practical purposes a social and political theocracy. Nor was the Calvinist ethos limited to New England. It also extended, although not as ubiquitously, to the middle Atlantic and southern colonies. Regardless of whether the denomination was Congregational or Anglican, Presbyterian or even Quaker, the unrelenting presence of Calvinist theology was a staple, to one extent or another, in most colonial Christian sects.

American Calvinism's doctrinal beliefs and style of theologizing were neither static nor monolithic. New England Congregationalism focused on issues and adopted an ecclesial structure that differed, for example, from its Presbyterian counterpart in the middle colonies, and there was a certain degree of theological pluralism among the clergy.[49] Despite such diversity, Calvinism in the colonial period tended to revolve around the "Five Points" defined by the Synod of Dort in 1618–19. This statement originally had been hammered out as a response to Arminianism, a "heretical" offshoot which held that human beings are capable of freely accepting the divine gift of grace and therefore play an important cooperative role in their salvation.[50] In opposition, the authors of the Five Points followed Calvin by insisting that God chooses whom to save and whom to condemn; that Christ's sacrifice guarantees the salvation of some—the "elect"—but not all; that all individuals are utterly reliant for their salvation on Christ's atonement because of their innate depravity; that selection by God for spiritual regeneration is irresistible; and that those individuals redeemed by divine grace are incapable of falling from it—that is, they "persevere" in grace.

But the Five Points were not simply a reaction to a seventeenth-century heresy. In the Calvinist mind, they were also a codification of the theological consequences of two historical "covenantal" invitations extended to humanity by God, as described in Scripture. The first of these was known as the "covenant of works"; the second, the "covenant of grace."

The details of the first invitation are recounted in Genesis. God placed the parents of the race, Adam and Eve, in the Garden of Eden and promised them a paradisiacal existence as well as dominion over creation. In return, he asked for their obedience to his will, as symbolized by his injunction against their partaking of the Tree of the Knowledge of Good and Evil. The quid pro quo was simple: In exchange for God's blessings, humans need only perform the meritorious actions or works entailed by the divine request for obedience. Thus the primordial contract between God and humans became known as the covenant of works.

The outcome of this invitation is, of course, familiar. According to Scripture, Adam and Eve succumbed to temptation, violated their end of the agreement by disobeying the divine command, and hence nullified the original contract. In just retribution, God rescinded his blessings and punished the aboriginal couple's sinful disobedience with death—physical and, more significantly, eternal, the never-ending torment of irrevocable separation from God. In addition, according to the logic of spiritual genetics defended by St. Augustine in the fifth century and accepted by Calvinists, all of Adam's offspring inherited the taint as well as the consequences of this first act of disobedience. Human beings, initially created pure and good, were forever cursed with the blemish of original sin and hence were utterly depraved, morally as well as rationally. Try as they might to walk the straight and narrow, their acquired

18   corruption would inevitably lead to willful disobedience to God's laws. Their works would fall short of the mark.

The utter failure of the first covenant, then, left the human race adrift on a horizonless ocean of hopeless and inescapable wickedness. But, as foretold by the prophets and revealed in the New Testament, God bestowed on suffering humanity a way out, a second chance, as it were, for spiritual regeneration. This new opportunity was provided by the sacrifice of Christ. Adam's original transgression was paid for through the Son of God's vicarious atonement. This merciful divine action extended a second invitation to humanity: the covenant of grace. Although individuals remained tainted after the atonement, utterly corrupt in mind and will, its occurrence ensured that those who humbled themselves, recognized and confessed their complete depravity, and accepted Christ as their Savior would be spared the eternal death with which Adam's iniquity had burdened his descendants. There was no question of such a salvation being *earned* by the sinner; rather, it was freely given without regard to individual works. However, the elect could prepare themselves for God's irresistible infusion of grace by acknowledging their impotence to save themselves and throwing themselves on the undeserved capital of Christ's sacrifice.

The Synod of Dort's Five Points were an attempt to express in credal terms this scripturally based covenantal history. It is understandable why it so vigorously opposed Arminian tendencies: The Calvinist scheme of salvation could in no way countenance the suggestion that humans were capable of freely effecting their redemption through works. Such a presumption flew in the face of the historical "fact" of Adam's disobedience and the consequent nullification of the first covenant. Even more to the point, it trivialized the crucial significance of Christ's atonement and its instauration of the new covenant of grace.

Regardless of its sectarian differences, American Calvinism in the eighteenth century accepted the plan of salvation suggested by scriptural accounts of the two covenants and canonized by the Synod of Dort. In particular, as one recent commentator has pointed out, Calvinist divines in America especially focused on "the problem raised by the absolute responsibility of individuals for their behavior even when they were evil by nature and could not resist grace."[51] The immediacy of this dilemma preoccupied Calvinist clergy as well as laypersons, nudging them in the direction of incessant introspection and soul-searching. That God's power, knowledge, and goodness were absolute was unquestionable. Attention consequently turned from God to man in the search for a way to understand the precarious human condition as well as for psychological signs of a regenerative infusion of undeserved grace. The central question was how to know if one was elected for salvation. The answer was simple in theory but arduous in practice: Search within, humble the passionate and self-asserting ego, cultivate patience, and cling to Christ. As the Puritan divine Jonathan

Mitchell succinctly put it: "Pursue and follow home in self-examination, by applying and considering the Scripture-evidences of a state of Salvation, and searching whether they be found in thee."[52]

This preoccupation with introspective delvings into the psyche in the hope of fully realizing one's inherent corruption and possibly discerning evidences of grace gave rise to a curious internal dialectic peculiar to Calvinism. If receptivity to God's invitation entailed humbling oneself to his majesty by acknowledging utter depravity, the proper course for an individual was a no-holds-barred declaration of war on the self and all of its necessarily wicked pretensions and vanities. But the primary weapon in this struggle consisted precisely of the self's ability to burrow into its own depths. The goal was to abase the self to the extent that Christ's love could enter within, but the way to achieve this end was through unceasing meditation on the self and its vileness. The bizarre nature of this quest was not lost on early Calvinists. In his 1607 *Auto-Machia*, a didactic poem immensely popular in both British and colonial Calvinist circles, George Goodwin spelled out in uncompromising terms the implications of the struggle:

I sing my SELFE: my *Civil Warrs* within;
The *Victories* I howrely lose and win;
The dayly *Duel*, the continuall Strife,
The *Warr* that ends not, till I end my life.[53]

The dialectic of self recruited in the war against self, generated by the demands of Calvinism's scheme of salvation, was complemented and exacerbated by yet another paradoxical aspect of the struggle for grace: the war of reason against reason. Calvinism in America enjoyed a long tradition of emphasizing the cultivation of the intellect. Calvinist clergy were noteworthy among American clerics for their training in languages, theology, and natural philosophy. Their sermons were often learned discourses which aimed to educate as much as edify congregations. The theological impetus for this intellectual inquiry was linked to the demand for incessant self-examination. Just as there were observable psychological signs of God's workings in the human soul, so the natural realm was imbued with evidences of divine presence and intention, apparent to anyone with the skill to discern them. But since Adam's fall had corrupted the self, it likewise had depraved the reason. Consequently, in the intellectual pursuit of God, the Calvinist searcher had to employ a faculty that again was ultimately untrustworthy. Its limits had to be tested and ascertained, and the way to do this was through its exercise. When coupled with the demand to wage an unceasing war against the self, this injunction to discover the limitations of reason through rational inquiry gave rise to a sometimes incompatible mixture of anti-intellectual piety and meticulous rationalism. As Perry Miller writes, in certain aspects the Puritan appears an antirationalist, but in others he is exceedingly rational; he attacks with fury those misguided zealots who jump to the conclusion that religion can dispense with learning, ministers with education, saints with knowledge, or converts with the fullest possible understanding, not only of theology, but of science and philosophy. Puritan writers can pity the insignificance of human reason, and in the next breath sing the praises of the human mind.[54]

For many orthodox Calvinists, these unsettling conflicts gave salvation a bleak but hopeful nature. After all, as one recent commentator has insightfully noted, the worshipper's confusion and despair over his or her ambiguous situation was inextricably linked to a complementary "ecstasy about Christ's atonement and the bliss of the saved."[55] The "Civil Warr" of self against self and reason against reason was, by virtue of human depravity, ultimately doomed to defeat. But, in the context of Calvinism's peculiar dialectic, such inevitable defeat was a necessary condition for occasional victory.

However, for other Calvinists, the tensions generated by their religion's bifurcated attitude toward self and reason were psychologically overwhelming. This painful situation only worsened with the arrival in America of the New Learning, with its accent on clarity and its championship of the mind's ability to fathom reality as well as freely pursue the good. Caught between these two antithetical worldviews, it was inevitable that the more liberal segments of the Calvinist community would begin to veer toward the New Learning by stressing the rationalist strain in their religion at the expense of the pietistic one. Calvinist divines gravitated from revealed to natural theology and so emphasized the role of human rationality that many of them, such as Ebenezer Gay (1696–1787) and Ezra Stiles (1727–95), came dangerously close to affirming Arminian doctrine—that humans, by the use of unaided reason, could come to know God's will and save themselves through their own efforts.[56] This obviously entailed the denial (if only tacit) that reason and self were as utterly depraved as orthodox Calvinism had it. Such rationalist challenges to Calvinism's dialectic even prompted some clergy to renounce their Puritan heritage and return to the more liberal Anglican church. (Yale College was especially scandalized by such a denominational exodus in the 1720s.) But most of them remained in the Calvinist fold and attempted, sometimes awkwardly, sometimes masterfully, to accommodate the New Learning to the theology of the Five Points.

American Calvinism's uneasy acceptance of both piety and rationalism propelled it toward a crisis, which came in the 1740s with the intercolonial religious revival now known as the "Great Awakening."[57] Sparked by "enthusiasts" such as George Whitefield (1714–70), Gilbert Tennent (1703–64), and Jonathan Edwards (1703–58), the Great Awakening was in many respects an effort on the part of orthodox Calvinists to derail Arminian and rationalist challenges to the traditional Puritan scheme of salvation. Insisting that the Christian faith had been poisoned by ungodly defenses of human reason and freedom of determination, the leaders of the revival called for a return to a religion of the heart that stressed the traditional pietistic standards of acknowledgement of complete depravity and introspective preparation for regeneration. Soul-searching, fear, and self-abasement, not reason or works, were the necessary conditions for salvation. The inherent corruption of human nature, the inability of individuals to save themselves through either good intentions or efforts, and the irremediable inefficacy of reason to fathom the ways of God were expounded in fire-and-brimstone sermons calculated to whip listeners into a frenzy of horror and submission that would draw them back to traditional piety. As Tennent thunderously warned in a 1741 sermon, the misguided advocates of Arminianism and liberal Christianity

> keep Driving, Driving, to Duty, Duty, under this Notion, That it will recommend natural Men to the Favour of GOD, or entitle them to the Promises of Grace and Salvation: And thus those blind Guides fix a deluded World upon the false Foundation of their own Righteousness; and so exclude them from the dear Redeemer. All the Doings of unconverted Men, not proceeding from the Principles of Faith, Love, and a new Nature, nor being directed to the divine Glory as their highest End, but flowing from, and tending to Self, as their Principle and End; are doubtless damnably Wicked in their Manner of Performance, and do deserve the Wrath and Curse of a Sin-avenging GOD.[58]

Embroiling New England as well as the middle and southern colonies, the Great Awakening seemed just the antidote to liberal tendencies longed for by the faithful. And, in fact, it did restore, at least for a while, widespread religious fervor. But it failed in the long run to stem the tide of either liberal Christianity or natural religion. Even more to the point, it had the ironic effect of actually nurturing the growth of deism in America.

There are two reasons for this unintended and undesired consequence of the Awakeners' efforts. First, their revivalist message inadvertently encouraged the very Arminian tendencies they hoped to forestall. Even as Edwards in his pulpit and Whitefield in his open meadow preached the orthodox doctrines of utter depravity and salvation of the elect, they also, in keeping with the Calvinist dialectic, exhorted their listeners to try to throw off sloth, open themselves to divine grace, and work toward their own conversion and ultimate regeneration. It is difficult to see how the Awakeners could have avoided this mixed signal, since the very purpose of a revival is to encourage sinners to mend their evil ways and return to a godly state. But it is precisely this message of spiritual self-determination, conveyed with gripping eloquence and fiery passion, that sank in—especially since many in the Awakeners' audiences were already leaning toward Arminianism from sheer weariness with traditional Calvinism. The Awakeners' unintentional espousal of Arminian autonomy undercut the very fidelity to doctrinal literalness they hoped to revive.

Moreover, the Great Awakening polarized and brought to the foreground the conflict between rationalism and traditional piety which had been brewing for the last few decades. Many colonials, attracted to the New Learning but bound by emotional ties to Calvinism, had tried to keep a foot in both camps by explaining away fundamental differences between the two worldviews. After the Great Awakening—despite its unwitting bow to Arminianism—such compromises became increasingly difficult. Battle lines were clearly established between orthodoxy and liberalism, pietism and natural theology, and they split what had hitherto been a more or less solid Calvinist hegemony into several doctrinal splinter groups. The Great Awakening, then, paradoxically ended the Puritan ideal of a theologically homogeneous Zion in the wilderness. As Alan Heimert has noted, the Awakening was not so much a successful revival of Calvinism as "the dying shudder of a Puritanism that refused to see itself as an anachronism."[59]

The almost suicidal theological convulsions of the Great Awakening were among the factors that prepared the way for the subsequent popularization of deism in America. First, the splintering and dissolution of the earlier Calvinist hegemony created a climate of theological and speculative ambivalence, which rescued American deism from the need to protect itself by adopting the harsh and uncompromising infidelity of the French savants. True, deistic sensibilities were savaged by the American Christian establishment, and secular penalties for heresy remained on the law books well into the first years of the Republic. Yet for all that, American deists were spared the relentless secular and ecclesial persecution their continental counterparts endured. Colonial and Early Republic deism certainly was angry and militant, but the demise on the American short of orthodox hegemony for the most part prevented it from sliding into paranoiac hysteria.

Second, the legitimization of liberal theology that the Great Awakening unwittingly helped to foster enhanced receptivity to the later defense of a religion of nature. Many observers of the emotional frenzy fanned by the revival were horrified and disgusted by such displays of passionate enthusiasm (even if, like Benjamin Franklin, they were also reluctantly stirred by them at times). The perceived irrationality of such episodes only underscored an Enlightenment-tinctured conviction in the superiority of reason as an arbiter in both secular and theological beliefs. Moreover, the revival's renewed emphasis on the increasingly distasteful doctrines of human depravity and elected salvation highlighted in their estimations the merits of the New Learning's humanistic alternative of self-determination and rationality—especially since Calvinism's own injunction about cultivation of the mind had uncomfortably prepared the way for acceptance of these ideals.

Finally, the spiritual and philosophical vacuum created by the erosion of widespread fidelity to Calvinism's orthodox worldview provided a point of entry for new religious perspectives. Since the climate of opinion was already sympathetic to the claims of rationalism and liberal religion, the uncompromising naturalism of deism, which stressed reason, human dignity, and ethical responsibility, was seen by many as a logical and saving foundation on which to construct a new religious system. The deistic Temple of Reason and Humanity, in short, arose from the rubble of the orthodox New Jerusalem.

The French Influence and the Spirit of Independence

Colonial and Early Republic deism was primarily an outgrowth of British New Learning. Bacon, Newton, and Locke represented the triune court of authority to which American liberal religionists most often appealed, along with, to a lesser extent, the common sense philosophy of Reid and Hutcheson. Still, the mood of French Enlightenment thought was not unfamiliar to the colonists. Its influence was admittedly less pervasive than that of British rationalism, if for no other reason than the obstacle of language. But the gradual importation of French ideals affected American infidelity in at least two ways.

First, the harsh anticlericalism of the French savants provided an exhilarating example to many American thinkers chafing under what they took to be an unjustified degree of ecclesial influence. Men of the cloth in the American colonies (particularly in New England) traditionally had enjoyed what today is an almost unimaginable scope of spiritual and moral authority. They were not simply the religious and intellectual leaders of their communities. They also often assumed the roles of social and political watchdogs, condoning or condemning lifestyles and mores from the vantage point of a spiritual wisdom difficult for the layperson to gainsay. Even after the overt Calvinist hegemony began to crumble in the early eighteenth century, the clergy as a class was still endowed in the popular mind with a patina of almost inviolable authority. French anticlericism, with its mocking denunciations of priestly venery and ecclesiastical corruption, helped break the sacrosanct aura surrounding the clergy, just as the British New Learning eroded the indisputability of orthodox dogma. Both tendencies encouraged the bold criticisms of institutionalized Christianity hurled by the American deists.

Second, and more significant, the ideals of the French Enlightenment bequeathed to American deism a radical ethical and political flavor that British deism by and large lacked. The republican orientation of French thought, with its emphasis on the brotherhood of humanity, natural and inalienable rights, and social equality, was imbibed by colonial thinkers long before the American

24   Revolution. Exposure to French radicalism began as early as the French and Indian War, which brought American soldiers into contact with French officers familiar with and sympathetic to political liberalism. Although orthodox American churchmen deplored the religious infidelity that many of the Gallic officers championed, most were still captured by the latter's visions of political equality and fraternity. In 1759, for example, Ezra Stiles condemned the "vitiated morals of Deism" disseminated through colonial exposure to French Enlightenment thought.[60] But just one year later, he preached to his Newport congregation a sermon whose radical political tone clearly mirrored the very French influence he had earlier castigated.

> We are planting an Empire of better Laws and Religion. Everyone that has any acquaintance with the Laws must be sensible that so many have been retained at home from the catholic Times, so many of contrary Import and Decision, . . . and lastly so many by no means adapted to the Circumstances of this country, not to observe that many are obsolete, that it is almost infinitely difficult for Lawyers themselves to decide what is true law. In short, the Law is so voluminous and indecisive that it is high Time to throw it up and assume an Institute de novo, more intelligible and adapted to the state of the British Nation in the present age.[61]

These were heady words in 1760, but they reflected a growing dissatisfaction on the part of Americans for "obsolete" laws and sociopolitical structures that to some degree was prompted by exposure to the republican ideals of the French Enlightenment. These ideals transformed many American thinkers, including Franklin, Ethan Allen, and Jefferson, into unabashed Francophiles. Inspired by the savants' claim that reason and equality were the twin pillars of both individual felicity and social justice, they and other colonial figures looked to French radicalism as an exemplar for their own political development.

    The American Revolution and the subsequent formation of the Republic impressed on the minds of many the fundamental correctness of the French goals of liberty, equality, and universal emancipation. Moreover, the rousing example of the subsequent French Revolution only underscored that conviction. It is little wonder that Yale students in 1793 proudly called one another Voltaire, Rousseau, and d'Alembert. For them, as for many other Americans, the French Enlightenment's philosophical defenses of personal and intellectual freedom were dramatically vindicated by the turn of political events in both the United States and Europe. Human reason had been tried and tested against the ramparts of civil and ecclesial despotism and had prevailed.

    Although American enthusiasm for French thought began to wane after the horrible excesses of the Terror, Early Republic deists for the most part remained sympathetic with its radical ideals. They were convinced that complete freedom of conscience depended on sweeping political and social changes. Like the French thinkers whom they so admired, deists such as Jefferson, Allen, Paine, Philip Freneau, and Elihu Palmer believed that ignorance, fear, poverty, and superstition had their roots in political and ecclesial authority. To eliminate the one without likewise destroying the other, they reasoned, was merely to cut off one of the Hydra's heads. Consequently, American deism, particularly in its final, overtly militant stage, championed social as well as religious reform, calling for the complete separation of church and state, universal education, and a free press. Some supporters also advocated an end to slavery and equal legal rights for women. Deism's political radicalism came to be viewed—and correctly so—as posing as much of a danger as its denunciations of revealed religion, and critics were quick to point out that deistic sentiments, if left unchecked, could destroy social stability as well as Christian faith. The Reverend Robert Hall, in his *Modern Infidelity Considered with respect to Its Influence on Society* (1801), was one of those who saw that the French-inspired political radicalism of American deism had moved it away from the earlier mild and intellectual British variety.

> The effort of [American] infidels, to diffuse the principles of infidelity among the common people, is another alarming symptom peculiar to the present time. *Hume, Bolingbroke*, and *Gibbon* addressed themselves solely to the more polished classes of the community, and would have thought their refined speculations debased by an attempt to enlist disciples from among the populace. Infidelity has lately grown condescending: bred in the cloisters of the learned and afterwards nursed in the lap of voluptuousness and of courts; having at length reached its full maturity, it boldly ventures to challenge the suffrages of the people, solicits the acquaintance of peasants and mechanics, and draws whole nations to its standards.[62]

Although Hall's sarcasm was heavy-handed, it nonetheless accurately captured the distinctively egalitarian nature of American deism. It was a movement that sought to push the exercise of reason out of the confines of the scholar's study and the aristocrat's salon into the street, tavern, and household. It took the ideal of intellectual freedom more seriously than did its British counterpart, insisting that the emancipation of the mind from superstition and fear ultimately depended on the establishment of an educated and politically free populace. But this conviction, although borrowed from French radicalism, stopped short of advocating the wholesale destruction that characterized the French Revolution. Part of the reason for this moderation was the atmosphere of relative civil and religious freedom in which American deism flourished. But

26   another factor was the deep-seated belief shared by American deists that changes in attitudes, values, and social structure could not be coerced through violence and intimidation. "Reason, righteous and immortal reason," as Elihu Palmer put it, was the key to the liberation of the human spirit from poverty, oppression, and ignorance. The sword might eventually have to replace the printing press as a weapon of emancipation, but only as a final resort.[63]

The Maturing of American Deism

Edmund Burke, the British champion of Christian orthodoxy as well as American independence, triumphantly asked in 1790: "Who, born within the last forty years, has read one word of Colins [*sic*], and Toland, and Tindal, and Chubb, and Morgan, and that whole race who called themselves Freethinkers? Who now reads Bolingbroke? Who ever read him through?"[64] This rhetorical snort, so typical of Burke, was partly justified. By 1790 British deism which Burke conventionally styled "free thought," had run its course. Still, Burke's victory cry was premature. Had he known, the great orator would have been shocked and grieved that deism, while relatively moribund in England, was alive and well in the American republic he so admired.

In fact, it was just coming into its own, entering that stage of maturity from which it would play a major role in the next two decades of the young Republic's intellectual and religious life. Although isolated advocates of deism had resided in the American colonies since the first quarter of the eighteenth century, the steady proliferation of the New Learning, the breakup of Calvinist hegemony, the osmosis of French radicalism, and the exuberantly optimistic examples of the American and French revolutions had created by the 1790s a climate of opinion in which deistic sensibilities were popularly cultivated and publicly proclaimed. Contrary to Burke, Americans not only read Tindal and Toland; they absorbed their deistic messages and elaborated on them. "Free thought" was in the air, and orthodoxy was troubled. The "Age of Licentious Liberty" Ezra Stiles bemoaned in 1759 had arrived with a vengeance.

Several historians of ideas have distinguished between a "moderate" and a "militant" stage in American deism, with the former falling roughly in the first three-quarters of the eighteenth century and the latter finishing it out and extending into the first decade of the next.[65] This division, although convenient, is somewhat misleading. Those individuals in the first part of the century who considered themselves deists instead of orthodox or liberal Christians usually subscribed to most of the "radical" religious beliefs of a Collins, Toland, or Tindal. They rejected (or at least were extremely dubious of) such traditional Christian doctrines as revealed knowledge, the divinity of Jesus, original sin, miracles, eternal damnation, and the Trinity. Their concept of God was that of a Supreme Architect who served as the original cause of uniform physical laws and whose existence and nature could be inferred rationally from an examination of those laws. Like their British counterparts, they argued that natural philosophy was the highest form of worship as well as the best avenue for knowledge of things divine. If the American deists of this period are appraised in terms of their philosophical distance from the tenets of orthodox Christianity, they clearly were anything but "moderate." Instead, they were intellectual and theological radicals.

Still, it is undeniable that American deism toward century's end took on a harsher tone and was more vocal than it had been in earlier periods. Pre-Republic deists, as a general rule, *were* less apt to openly acknowledge allegiance to rational religion. Indeed, they displayed a marked aversion to trumpeting their disagreement with (and in some cases contempt of) Christianity's worldview. They shied away from proselytizing and only rarely allowed themselves to even hint in public their heterodox leanings. Individual confessions of infidelity, when made, were normally confined to safe circles—salon conversations with select acquaintances or private correspondence. This functional difference in tone and public expression is what separated moderate from militant deists more than any disagreements in their orientation or worldview.

There are three primary reasons for the diffident tone of the early American deists. The first is that many of the older converts, such as Benjamin Franklin, in fact were somewhat ambivalent in their private endorsements of heterodox theological beliefs. They were too close in age and temperament to the heyday of American Calvinism, too immersed in its cultural and intellectual milieu, to forsake it easily or entirely. Although they intellectually rejected most if not all of its five essential doctrines, they often found themselves torn in their religious persuasions between the claims of the enlightened mind and those of tradition's heart. Franklin, for instance, never quite reconciled his deistic conviction that physical reality was explicable in terms of immutable and absolute mechanistic laws with his Calvinist-inspired suspicion that providential or miraculous interventions in the cosmic machinery's functions were both logical and actual possibilities. Still, the ambivalence of American deists in the first part of the eighteenth century should not be overstated. Although they sometimes were uncomfortably caught between two competing worldviews, their primary allegiance was to the deistic one.

A second and more substantial reason for American deism's early reticence can be traced to a concern for social and economic stability. Many colonial intellectuals who privately professed the tenets of deism were both suspicious and contemptuous of what they considered to be the "mob." They recognized all too well that deism's call for the exercise of reason and its promotion of egalitarianism struck at the roots of class privilege as well as political and ecclesiastical authority. It was but a short step, in their estimation, from calling into question traditional scriptural and clerical authority to doing the same with economic and social relations. And this in turn could open the floodgates to

28   social upheaval, sweeping away the established political structures of the day. Christianity seemed a necessary check against the unruly and leveling tendencies of "King Mob." Deism was a rational person's religion; but the general populace—illiterate, passionate, and envious of their social betters—was anything but rational. Better to allow the mob to retain its faith in conventional Christian beliefs until such time as it was better educated and less unpredictable. Even if those beliefs were false, they at least had the social utility of controlling the destructive tendencies of the rabble (through the threat of eternal damnation) and encouraging its members to be content with their social and economic lot (through the promise of eternal and conveniently otherworldly bliss). As late as 1786, Benjamin Franklin disingenuously expressed this sentiment when he cautioned an unknown correspondent (possibly Tom Paine) against the publication of a popular tract on deism: "I would advise you, therefore, not to attempt unchaining the Tyger, but to burn the Piece before it is seen by any other Person; whereby you will save yourself a great deal of Mortification from the enemies it may raise against you, and perhaps a good deal of Regret and Repentence. If men are so wicked as we see them *with religion*, what would they be *if without it*."[66]

Franklin's advice is interesting because it reflects the extent to which American deists of an older generation adopted the nonpolitical flavor of earlier British deism. But it is also interesting in that it hints at the third major reason for American deism's early moderation: the threat of "Mortification from the enemies" of deism. In this Franklin was quite correct. Loyalty to orthodox Christianity was still strong in America even in 1786, and those who set themselves against it could expect social opprobrium. But during the first half of the eighteenth century, when deism was just beginning to gain a foothold, the risks of open "infidelity" were even greater. Although the theocratic hegemony of Puritan New England began to break apart following the Great Awakening, the influence of Calvinism remained strong. It is not surprising that early sympathizers with deism adopted a cautious, moderate tone. They had too much to lose in bucking the entrenched, even if partially declawed, Christian establishment. Dissenters had little to fear in the way of actual legal persecution by midcentury from the surviving Calvinist community, but they were still susceptible to a loss of reputation, a diminution of the likelihood of professional advancement, and public scorn.

The shift in tone between early and late eighteenth-century American deism notwithstanding, there is an obvious philosophical continuity running throughout the entire movement. This is not to suggest that all deists agreed on all points. Like the overall Enlightenment ethos, American deism was a general orientation rather than a unanimously endorsed set of doctrines. As an editorial in the *Prospect*, a leading deistic newspaper, observed in 1803, the deists had "no intention to impose a creed upon men . . . we know that among those who believe that the religion of nature is the only true religion, there are shades of difference in their opinions." But, "these differences are inconsiderable—less, much less, than those which are every day exhibited in every part of the christian world." Consequently, the *Prospect* claimed, it is possible "to state with simplicity, and delineate with correctness the prominent features" of American deism.[67] An examination of the writings of the deistic authors collected in this anthology—Franklin, Jefferson, Allen, Volney, Paine, Palmer, and Freneau—as well as the articles in *The Temple of Reason*, the *Prospect*, and *The Theophilanthropist*, reveals that these "prominent features" include the critique of Christianity; reflections on reason, nature, and God; and ethical theory.

Deism's Critique of Christianity

American deism's crusade against Christianity attacked on two fronts. First, it charged that the supernaturalistic worldview advocated by Christianity was illogical because it mandated belief in propositions that violated both the lessons of experience and the principles of reason. Second, it normatively condemned Christian orthodoxy for its historical record of intolerance and persecution as well as its scriptural depiction of the deity as a capricious and wicked celestial tyrant.

Regardless of the extent to which they differed on finer points of analysis, the American deists unanimously rejected the triune concept of God and the divinity of Jesus. The former was dismissed because it struck the deists as an obvious logical impossibility. The notion of a God who is simultaneously three substances yet one substance violated, in their estimation, one of the very foundations of rational thought and discourse: the principle of noncontradiction. As such, it could not even be classified as one of those mysterious Lockean truths "above but not contrary to" reason. It was meaningless, so nonsensically paradoxical that no rational person could assent to it.

Similarly, the orthodox dogmas of the incarnation and resurrection were dismissed by the deists as irrational superstitions. The infinite and eternal could not possibly embody itself as a finite and historical man and still remain fully divine. Such a suggestion, once again, did violence to the principle of noncontradiction: How could an entity be fully human and yet fully divine at the same time? Moreover, the claim that a dead man could reanimate after three days in the grave ran contrary to the lessons of experience. The perceived uniformity of nature cried out against such an egregious rupture of the fabric of universal law.

The deistic denial of the resurrection extended to a disbelief in all other orthodox accounts of miracles. For the deists, a miracle by definition constituted an infraction of the regular and predictable operations of physical reality. If God occasionally intervened in the mechanistic orderliness of nature by miraculously suspending its lawlike operations, only one of two conclusions

30   could be drawn. Either the deity was playing an ad hoc game of patch-up, trying by supernatural intervention to mend weaknesses or disfunctions in the cosmic machine; or physical reality, despite its apparent uniformity and mathematical regularity, did not in fact possess these attributes but was instead manipulated in mysterious ways by a whimsical and arbitrary God. The first conclusion, the deists reasoned, was unacceptable because it reduced God to a less-than-perfect entity—to a faulty or careless Architect who so botched the original design and execution of reality that endless repairs were necessary to bolster the structure. The second conclusion was equally unacceptable, insofar as it violated ordinary experience as well as the more sophisticated discoveries of natural philosophers such as Newton. There was no compelling evidence whatsoever to suggest that reality did not operate solely according to the dictates of immutable and rational laws. Anecdotal accounts of miraculous intervention, then, when weighed against empirical data and mathematical demonstration, lacked credibility. The deists thus were in complete agreement with the analysis of miracles David Hume offered in his *Enquiry Concerning Human Understanding* (1748): "A miracle is a violation of the laws of nature; and as a firm and unalterable experience has established these laws, the proof against a miracle, from the very nature of the fact, is as entire as any argument from experience can possibly be imagined."[68]

Nor did the American deists confine their skepticism to the doctrine of miracles. They also criticized and rejected another of Christianity's central tenets: revealed knowledge. Sectarian beliefs supposedly originating from divine revelation, according to the deists, were ultimately untestable by any nonsectarian standard of truth, such as reason or experience. The orthodox community nonetheless argued for the reliability of "revealed" truths on two grounds: that they were recorded in sacred Scripture, which itself was deemed inspired and inerrant, and that a believer who accepted revelatory precepts was psychologically convinced of their truth. But Scripture, the deists countered, was internally inconsistent as well as intrinsically unbelievable in places. Jefferson, Paine, and Palmer went to great pains to expose what they took to be the textual errancy of Scripture. Moreover, Volney, in his masterful comparative study of the world's religious traditions, showed that each sect claimed infallible revelation as its foundation and that these revelations often contradicted one another. Finally, the justification of revelation on the basis of the certainty with which it was accepted likewise was rejected. As Locke had argued in his *Essay on Human Understanding*, subjective conviction was no guarantee of the truth of a proposition. Such certainty revealed information about the mind of the believer but in no way shed light upon the truth value of his or her belief.

In challenging the authority of revelation and Scripture, the American deists obviously rejected the orthodox Christian notion of faith. For the deists, faith-based propositions were nothing more than the probable conclusions of inferential arguments, inductively arrived at through the observation and analysis of empirical data. Hence orthodoxy's claim that faith is a nonrational, grace-inspired assent to supernatural tenets was dismissed as a needless obfuscation of a transparently logical process.

Just as the illogical nature of orthodox Christianity offended the deists' sense of rational propriety, so its perceived immorality violated their strong sense of justice. There were two standard normative objections to Christianity to which its deistic opponents most often appealed. The first was that its sectarian dogmatism bred intolerance of dissenting perspectives and outright persecution of those who maintained their right to a free conscience. Franklin, Jefferson, and Paine were particularly angered and disgusted by what they saw as historical Christianity's narrow-minded unwillingness to countenance heterodoxy in religious persuasion.

Moreover, most deistic critics argued that Christianity's insistence on scriptural inerrancy forced it into the position of mandating belief in a capricious and vindictive deity, who practiced with impunity all the destructive passions that surely would have been condemned in a human agent. Such a double standard was unjustifiable and unworthy of the Author of nature. Nor did the moral character of Jesus escape criticism. Some deists, such as Jefferson and Franklin, considered the Galilean to be the paragon of human virtue, even though they denied his divinity. But others, including Palmer, disagreed. As they saw it, the Jesus portrayed in Scripture performed numerous acts of pettiness and spite and defended as virtuous such human weaknesses as humility and meekness. True, he occasionally espoused ethical proverbs that were normatively praiseworthy and rational, but there was no system to his moralizing. Nor was there anything especially original, much less divinely inspired, about it. The maxims New Testament writers attributed to Jesus had been expounded earlier—and, for the deists, much more cogently—by the Greek and Roman philosophers.

Reason, Nature, and God

In many ways, the American deists were more empiricist in their epistemology than Locke and more mechanistic in their natural philosophy than Newton. Locke, a liberal Christian, had allowed for the legitimacy of divinely revealed knowledge that was nonrational (although not irrational). Newton, mystic that he privately was, left open the possibility that the Supreme Designer periodically intervened in a miraculous, nonmechanistic way in the otherwise lawlike operations of the cosmic machine. But neither of these possibilities was acceptable to the American deists.

Reason, experience, orderliness, lawlike functionality—these were the primary characteristics of the worldview of American deism. Ordinary experience disclosed an orderliness in physical reality that abstract, mathematical analysis afterward demonstrated beyond a reasonable doubt. That the human intellect was capable of discerning the rational nature of physical reality in turn pointed to the fact that humans themselves were preeminently rational creatures. This only made sense, inasmuch as they were but an aspect of the larger physical whole, and the parts reflected the nature of the whole. Besides, Locke clearly revealed the laws of thought by which the human intellect operated, laws as objectively verifiable as Newton's natural ones. The human intellect, then, was a microcosm of the rational universe. As such, it was excellently qualified to elucidate and describe reality.

The American deists interpreted the perceived orderliness and rationality of human and physical reality as a clear demonstration of the existence of an equally orderly and rational deity. Most of them concurred with Ethan Allen's claim that the observed lawlike nature of reality demanded that it be the deliberate and intelligent product of a First Cause. This standard deistic appeal to a combination of causal and design arguments for the existence of God was not an especially strong claim. After all, David Hume had persuasively argued that the mere appearance of orderliness in nature in no way entailed intelligent, purposeful design by a rational First Cause and that to assume otherwise was to indulge in question-begging.[69] But this was a logical point the deists were either ignorant of or chose to ignore. For them, the existence of God was demonstrable, in a posteriori fashion, from an examination of and reflection on the world of experience. The Book of Nature, not sectarian "holy" writings, was God's true revelation. The study of nature was consequently one of the highest forms of worship and veneration.

Although the American deists fervently believed in the existence of a deity—they were not atheists, contrary to their orthodox critics' favorite charge—they maintained an agnosticism regarding the divine nature. True, certain insights into God's essence could be gleaned by observing and inferring from his creation. Since reality was rational, for example, God must likewise be rational. Since the lawlike operations of nature were conducive to the well-being of humans, God was also benevolent. But little else could be known about God's character. It is important to note, however, that this assumption of divine unknowability was based not so much on mysterious dogma or supernaturalistic awe as on what the deists took to be a very rational principle: The finitude of the human intellect was incapable of fully comprehending divine infinitude. Humans were imbued with a spark of the divine reason and so were privy to a limited knowledge of the divine. Ultimately, however, awareness of God's essence was beyond the race's ken.

The American deists recognized abstract, speculative reason, but they, like other Enlightenment figures, assigned to it a relatively minor role. Far more important to them was the Baconian notion of reason as instrumental, utility-laden, and promotive of good works rather than merely of elaborate argumentations. Reason, according to the American deists, was capable of liberating humanity from superstition as well as political oppression, from ignorance as well as material want. Its instrumental character necessarily laid open the promise of continuous progress in the natural and human sciences. This identity between reason and utility only underscored, in the minds of the deists, the importance of technological knowledge. Some of them, such as Franklin and the authors of *The Theophilanthropist*, became ardent cheerleaders of Enlightenment science, seeing in it the salvation of humankind. Other deists, such as Freneau, were less sanguine. But all of them, from the moderate to the more militant, were equally convinced that reason was and ought to be the vehicle of concrete instrumentality. A priori speculation and arid syllogizing were at best useless, at worst dogmatic and conducive to supernaturalistic bigotry.

Ethics

American deism from first to last focused attention on ethical issues. It reflected on the nature of virtue and vice, as well as the necessary conditions for the good life, and argued that the most appropriate way of showing reverence for the God of nature was by living virtuously. In keeping with its instrumentalist orientation, American deism's emphasis on ethical issues had a pragmatic agenda: the clarification of the means by which to maximize individual and social felicity. The assumption was that eliminating those factors that breed exploitation, oppression, ignorance, and superstitious fear would make room for the practical and spiritual perfection of society. Just as important, because virtuous behavior in the eyes of the deists was rational behavior, it was the natural and ultimate goal of human beings.

The ideal of moral perfection, on a social as well as individual level, occupied the American deists more than any other single issue. Franklin, with almost mathematical precision, worked out a moral calculus and argued that human virtue, as Aristotle had suggested, was a matter of habituation to good works. Jefferson considered the primary end of religious belief to be the promotion of virtue and admired Jesus (although not institutionalized Christianity) because of what he took to be the purity of the Nazarene's ethical principles. Allen, Paine, and Volney all declared that virtuous behavior was the highest form of worship and the chief duty of humankind. Freneau argued that the light of divine reason within each individual was, if harkened to, a sufficient guide for moral perfection. And Elihu Palmer, the greatest of the American deists, provided the movement with a systematic ethical theory based on the principles of "reciprocal justice" and "universal benevolence." He contended that ethical principle was independent of the will or even command of a deity but was instead grounded in human reason and psychobiological principles. This represented the first major naturalistic ethical theory defended by an American thinker, and both its postulates and conclusions were deistic to the core.

But American deists were more than just theoretical ethicists. They were also, to one degree or another, reformers, actively disseminating their moral conviction that reason and tolerance were the cornerstones of a free society and a happy individual existence. In their writings and speeches they campaigned for freedom of conscience, separation of church and state, the elimination of slavery, the emancipation of women, universal education, an end to economic, political, and ecclesiastical privilege, and the decentralization of government. Their ardent republican sympathies and their fearless opposition to Federalist sentiments probably earned them almost as much hatred as did their unabashed religious heterodoxy. But public censure and even occasional legal persecution were relatively ineffective as impediments to deistic activism. The movement continued as an outspoken and often strident conscience of the nation—particularly through the gadfly stings of *The Temple of Reason*, the *Prospect*, and *The Theophilanthropist*—until the beginning of the nineteenth century.

Deism's Demise

The deistic movement in America did not long survive the eighteenth century. *The Theophilanthropist* came to a dismal conclusion in 1811. Paine had died two years earlier, Palmer five. Jefferson would linger on until 1826, but he remained as reluctant to publicize his religious views as ever. Philip Freneau, deism's bard, whose eloquence celebrated the God of nature, had the unhappy distinction of being the last of the American Enlightenment deists. By the time he died in 1832, deism as an influential and aggressively outspoken movement had been finished for two decades.

The demise of American deism is partly attributable to the fact that its leading spokesmen died out as the eighteenth century turned into the nineteenth. Without the direction of firebrands such as Paine and Palmer, the militancy that characterized the movement in its heyday was impossible to sustain. But it is equally true that the "temple of reason" laboriously constructed by rational religionists began to collapse under its own weight. Conceptual weaknesses in its Enlightenment-based foundation became increasingly apparent as the years progressed—structural cracks that not even a Paine or a Palmer could have adequately patched. American deism ultimately lost currency because the New Learning that served as its philosophical base ceased to exercise the intellectual authority it once had. The deistic worldview, fixed squarely on the Enlightenment's allegiance to mechanism and rationalism, began to be perceived as simplistic to the point of distortion. This increasingly negative appraisal of deism's basic assumptions proceeded along two parallel paths: a critique of the immaculately rational system it defended, and the charge that its account of God was inadequate.

Hume's Challenge to Mechanism[70]

The fundamental conceptual prism through which the American deists interpreted reality was the Newtonian mechanistic model. For them, the universe was analogous if not identical to a cosmic machine whose various parts causally interacted with mathematically predictable precision. The algorithmic key to understanding the cosmic machine was the system of natural laws ordained and set in motion by the supremely rational First Cause. These immutable and uniform laws governed the material realm in such a way that there was no possibility of physical phenomena deviating from the preordained blueprint. This meant that causal relations within the universe were necessary ones: The cosmic machine *must* operate in the way it does. Even the slightest deviation from the set chain of causal relations would shatter the rational integrity of the system as a whole. Given this cosmological assumption, it is not surprising that the American deists denied the possibility of miraculous interventions in the established nexus of physical causation. Such supernatural ruptures would violate the mechanistic harmony of creation as well as the majestic omnirationality of God. It would also destroy the possibility of natural philosophy.

To the eighteenth-century deists, exhilarated as they were by a heady diet of scientific discoveries and inventions that seemed to corroborate Newton's system, the validity of the mechanistic model was self-evident. It was also a clear advance over traditional cosmologies, such as Aristotle's, which obfuscated more than clarified the nature of reality. Finally, the pristinely simple cosmos of Enlightenment mechanism possessed an austere beauty that appealed to the neoclassical aesthetic and intellectual sensibilities of a generation that valued clarity above all else. But as the eighteenth century waned, the earlier confidence in a mechanistic universe began to crumble.

David Hume's devastating critique of the assumption that the idea of causation actually corresponded to objective "fact" was the first hammer-blow to the cosmic machine. Hume originally launched his attack in his 1739 *Treatise of Human Nature*. But, as he later admitted, the book's first edition "fell deadborn from the press," and as a consequence his examination of the concept of causation attracted little attention for a generation. Subsequent editions, however, hit the mark and succeeded in casting doubt on one of the fundamental tenets of Enlightenment deism.

In his *Treatise*, Hume granted that humans have an idea of causation, and he likewise conceded that it was the keystone of the natural sciences. He also acknowledged, in good empiricist fashion, that this concept, like all ideas, originated in experience. Considering the nature of the concept of causation, the experience that gave rise to it must have been one of a relationship between objects or events. So far, so good. Neither Newton nor his American followers would have disagreed.

36   But then Hume dropped his philosophical bombshell. An unprejudiced examination of the experience of physical relationships, he claimed, revealed but three kinds: contiguity, priority in time, and constant conjunction. In other words, objects or events were experienced as proximate to one another, temporally related to one another such that one always preceded the other, or inevitably conjoined. What experience did not and could not convey was any "necessary connexion" between the objects or events related in any of these ways. Instead, causation was merely inferred on the basis of "association," which in turn arose from repeated experience of the three types of relations. Necessary causal connections, then, were neither empirically observable nor logically deducible from the scrutiny of physical relations. This conclusion obviously struck at the very heart of Newtonian mechanism, grounded as it was in the assumption that necessary causal relations were both self-evident and the objective foundation on which natural philosophy based its cosmological case.[71] Hume's assault on the deterministic integrity of the Newtonian machine may not have been as dramatic as a supernaturalist defense of divine intervention, but it was much more damaging. It denied that reality was as lucidly explicable as the deists maintained and, in doing so, called into question the reach of human reason as well as the trustworthiness of natural philosophy.

It would be misleading to suggest that Hume's argument devastated late eighteenth-century advocates of the Newtonian worldview. Many of them—particularly the American deists—were too dazzled by mechanism's totalizing vision to pay much attention to Hume's rather arcane analysis of causation. Even Hume himself admitted that his philosophical skepticism was best confined to the intellectual's library and that a practical person would do well to act as if necessary causation was an objective fact. But his denial of necessary causation contributed to new winds that began to blow across the Enlightenment landscape, eventually stirring the dust enough to expose a fault in the deterministic machine defended by rational religionists.

Mechanism and Alienation

Hume's attack on the notion of necessary causation, despite his woeful claim, was not completely deadborn. It did exercise a few of the more discerning thinkers of his generation; Kant, for one, graciously acknowledged that it awoke him from his "dogmatic slumber." Still, Hume's philosophical skepticism failed to reverberate immediately throughout the wider community. But a second crack appeared in the mechanistic model of reality which, although more psychological than philosophical in nature, did make its presence felt.

The abstractly immaculate model defended by the American deists and enthusiastically appealed to as a self-evident demonstration of both the clocklike regularity of physical law and the omnirationality of God began to grate on early nineteenth-century sensibilities. What had earlier been regarded as an awe-inspiring cosmos rich with scientific potentiality increasingly came to be viewed as a forlorn and lifeless desert. In the minds of many, the mechanistic universe was an austere, impersonal, and forbidding place whose mute expanses, in spite of the deistic insistence on providential design, remained indifferent to the human condition. How could a machine do otherwise? Blaise Pascal in the seventeenth century had anticipated this unease with his plaintive cry that the eternal silence of infinite space filled him with terror, but for the most part the eighteenth century's Enlightenment-bred optimism drowned out his voice. It was not until the advent of the nineteenth century, when the cosmic machine's impersonal perfection began to alienate more than enrapture, that Pascal's prophetic warning was taken seriously. Edwin Burtt expressed the nature of this alienation when he wrote that its overpowering presence tended to reduce humanity's self-image to that of a

> puny irrelevant spectator (so far as a being wholly imprisoned in a dark room can be called such) of the vast mathematical system whose regular motions according to mechanical principles constituted the world of nature. . . . The world that people had thought themselves living in— a world rich with color and sound, redolent with fragrance, filled with gladness, love and beauty, speaking everywhere of purposive harmony and creative ideals—was crowded now into minute corners of the brains of scattered organic beings. The really important world outside was a world hard, colorless, silent and dead.[72]

Burtt has nicely captured the sense of displacement that Enlightenment mechanism came to inflict on nineteenth-century intellectuals and reading laypersons alike. In their minds, the Newtonian system not only reduced humans to cogs in the machine; it also, as Burtt pointed out, rendered them irrelevant. The nagging, protoexistentialist forlornness bred by such an impersonal cosmology had bothered even some of the deists themselves. Franklin attempted to inject more warmth into the clockwork universe by clinging to the notion of special providences. Freneau, at the other end of the historical line of American deism, tried to ameliorate the detached coldness of mechanism by infusing it with elements of romanticism that smack of the later transcendentalist movement. Each of the other American deists had insisted, although usually rather vaguely, that the divine First Cause, in spite of his aloof, impassable nature, looked upon humankind with a benign benevolence. But the mathematically abstract worldview that served as the underlying assumption of their rational religion tended to belie such claims, and this became increasingly apparent as well as oppressive to the early nineteenth-century mind.

Closely linked to the psychological sense of alienation bred by mechanism's sterile cosmos was the unsettling suspicion, which later matured to a cardinal

38   tenet of American romanticism, that humans were not the austerely rational creatures portrayed by either deism or the Enlightenment's New Learning. Hume, of course, had already cast philosophical shadows on the adequacy of human reason with his epistemic skepticism. But as the nineteenth century unfolded, a different impetus to skepticism, this time sparked by Kant and the German Idealists, began to emerge. The conviction that reason was a sure guide to the nature of both physical and human reality was dismissed as an extravagant presumption. There were depths within the human soul impervious to rational investigation, depths that could only be dimly fathomed by harkening to one's moods, intuitions, and passions. To ignore this darker side of the human condition was to run the risk of stifling one's nature, of retarding one's potential for insight. It encouraged a smug complacency and false optimism, dividing subject from self and providing a falsely simplistic blueprint of humanity and the universe. Once again, it was Pascal who had anticipated this change of direction two centuries before. "What will become of you then, O man," he had asked, "who try by your natural reason to discover what is your true condition? . . . Know then, proud creature, what a paradox you are to yourself. Be humble, impotent reason; be quiet, imbecile nature: *know that man surpasses man infinitely.*"[73]

Pascal's contemptuous dismissal of reason as "impotent" was a far cry from Elihu Palmer's enraptured "righteous and immortal reason," but it better suited the mood of the early nineteenth century. It also pointed to what in retrospect can be seen as one of the fundamental weaknesses of the deistic worldview. For all the sincerity of their humanistic ideals, the American deists endorsed a philosophical anthropology that simplistically objectified the human spirit. Given their fidelity to mechanistic Newtonianism and its accompanying rationalism, such a view of human nature was perfectly consistent; it was also shallow. In their efforts to extend the domain of scientific method to all arenas of investigation, they tended to ignore or dismiss those elements in experience that resisted such incorporation. In the case of their analysis of what it meant to be human, this resulted in a radical desubjectivization of persons: Humans were little more than animated physical objects which, like all other objects, necessarily conformed to immutable natural laws. The sole obstacles to humanity's recognizing its determined place in the vast scheme of things were superstition and ignorance. Remove these hindrances, and individuals would naturally accommodate their thoughts and actions to the rational order of which they were a part. The cosmic machine would then operate perfectly at the human level, and individual felicity as well as social progress would inevitably ensue.[74]

But this type of humanism, very much like the cosmological mechanism that served as its foundation, in fact was rather lifeless and flew in the face of ordinary experience. Humans are not predictably rational cogs in a complex world machine, and this became more and more apparent to critics of Enlightenment deism. Instead, as Kant asserted in his *Critique of Pure Reason*, humans occupied a unique place in the scheme of things. They were, to some degree, bound by the same rational laws as all other elements of nature. But, Kant continued, humans also possessed freedom and an interior existence that distinguished them from the physical system of bodies in motion. They were in one respect akin to the "starry heavens above," but they were also to a certain extent unpredictably free of mechanistic restraints. This paradoxical combination of disparate dimensions filled Kant with "ever new and increasing admiration and awe," as well it should have. It also echoed Pascal's point when he said of humans, "What a paradox you are to yourself." But the fact that humans cannot and should not be regarded as just another class of rationally analyzable material bodies by and large escaped the American deists. In their zeal to liberate individuals from the burdens of superstition and the shackles of irrationality, they unwittingly reified them into exclusively rational entities reminiscent of René Descartes's description of humans as embodied thinking substances.

Deism in America, then, revolved around an Enlightenment view of reality as well as reason that began to crack under its own weight at the beginning of the nineteenth century. Its mechanistic cosmology, based as it was on the assumption of the objective existence of necessary causal connections, was called into question—on empiricist grounds—by David Hume. Less technically, mechanism's portrayal of reality as an impersonal system of deterministic relations bred an uneasy sense of alienation, in which the individual felt adrift in a world, as Burtt put it, devoid of "color and sound, . . . gladness, love and beauty." Similarly, its Baconian-inspired belief that reason was a sufficient instrument for the complete illumination of both physical and human nature grew increasingly unacceptable as early nineteenth-century transcendentalists promoted the existential as well as epistemic centrality of moods, affections, and intuitions. In short, the twin principles on which the deistic worldview rested tended to oversimplify reality, reason, and the human condition, reducing each of them to a limpid but unidimensional set of explanations. The richness of experience, in all its bewildering diversity, was sacrificed for the sake of a deceptive lucidity, and such an unfortunate trade-off eventually served to undermine American deism's credibility.

The Eclipse of the God of Nature

The Enlightenment ethos, with its optimistic confidence that reality was preeminently rational and hence susceptible to human exploration and manipulation, reflected what one recent commentator has styled the "profound human need for a manageable universe."[75] The savants of the Enlightenment, fired by the promise of Newtonian mechanism and Baconian logic, were confident that

40   reality could be systematized, that the realm of phenomena was reducible to easily classifiable categories and explanations, and they pursued this vision with zeal. All of reality, physical as well as human, psychological as well as social, was subsumable in their minds to a single set of scientific principles which, once discovered, would reveal to the inquirer both the inner workings of nature as well as the means of managing it. Ambiguity and open-endedness, not to mention mystery, were antithetical to this fervent will to systematize. The presence of such elements pointed to a lapse of reasoning or a gap in the data, not to any intrinsic aspect of reality itself. Clarity in knowledge of the world was an obtainable goal, because the universe itself was manifestly rational. And clarity was valuable because it served as the necessary condition for manageability. True, the Enlightenment savants exulted in the discovery of new insights and delighted in the pursuit of knowledge for its own sake. But abstract inquiry into the secrets of nature was never their ultimate aim. The final goal of all natural philosophy, as Bacon had insisted, was the promulgation of arts and inventions. Only in this way could nature be subdued and individual felicity as well as social progress ensured.[76]

This urge to manage reality was inherited by the American deists. All of them, even the protoromantic Freneau, were captivated by the promise of science and technology, seeing both as markers on the highroad to a golden age of reason and plenty. This desire, this "profound need" to control reality by eliminating from its descriptions the final vestiges of ambiguity and uncertainty, also influenced the deists' reflections on God.

Like so many other Enlightenment thinkers, the American deists modestly claimed that a full understanding of divine nature was beyond the ken of humans, even though the divine's existence was logically deducible from an observation of the workings of natural law. This agnosticism was in principle grounded in the a priori assumption that God possessed such unbounded attributes as absolute power, absolute knowledge, and timelessness and that the finitude of human reason prevented it from fully comprehending these infinite qualities. They could be safely posited as abstractions but never understood in and of themselves.

Even so, the God of the deists was a quite nonmysterious entity whose essence consisted of the same rationally ascertainable and predictable features as those encountered in the natural realm. This is not to say that the deists rather cynically regarded their God as nothing more than a convenient deus ex machina. But it is the case that, despite their agnostic protestations, God for them was an uncomplicated being whose nature and operations were transparent to the rational inquirer. In the reified atmosphere of the temple of reason, the divine became the First Cause *simpliciter*, the sustainer of the universe whose essential traits were reflected in the bountiful order mapped by natural philosophy. He was purely rational and hence unambiguous; supremely benevolent and consequently trustworthy; unable or unwilling to intervene supernaturally in the established physical order and therefore predictable. The deistic God, in short, was a manageable deity, the fail-safe engine of an immaculate cosmic machine. For the deist eager to eliminate disorder from the universe, such a deity was a vast improvement over earlier anthropomorphic descriptions of God as passionate and unpredictable.

But there was a price to be paid for this flawlessly rational and comfortably manageable God. He ascended to ethereal heights, taking on a metaphysical abstractness that carved an unbridgeable gulf between his austere rationality and the religious needs of human beings. The God of nature, for all the deistic rhetoric about his benevolence and providential design, assumed the aloof character of an absentee landlord, so far removed from the everyday existence of ordinary people as to be completely indifferent to their petitions and worship. For the Enlightenment savant primarily concerned with charting the uniform workings of physical reality, such a distant God was convenient. It meant a rationally grounded universe as well as a God who would not interfere with the uniformity essential to the success of natural philosophy and technology. For the deist, this concept of an absentee God made perfect sense. However, for an increasing number of laypersons and intellectuals at the beginning of the nineteenth century, such a manageable deity was anything but fulfilling. God as the distant, inaccessible, almost mathematical First Principle was perhaps capable of engendering an awed, intellectual appreciation. But his abstract and nonmysterious character utterly failed to encourage the affective adoration or trust so vital to the religious temperament. The God of nature was not a *mysterium tremendum et fascinans.*[77] Instead, he—or more appropriately, it—was a formula, a cosmological premise, incapable of arousing empathy, love, or fear.

The manageable God of the American deists was thus too transcendent, too removed from the realm of ordinary human needs and aspirations, to provide individuals with either an experience of religious communion or emotional sustenance. It was increasingly difficult for the post-Enlightenment mind to take him seriously. His majestic aloofness, far from inspiring confidence in the immutability of the divine plan, began to strike many as disconcerting impotence. To invoke Pascal once more, the religion of nature's Supreme Architect was the God of the philosophers, not of Abraham, Isaac, or Jacob. An awareness of such a God might satisfy the intellect, but it left the passions cold and the heart heavy. He was every bit as alienating as the closed, deterministic cosmos he had set in motion.

Even more damaging, he was really rather superfluous. As Baron d'Holbach, the French atheist, contemptuously said in his *System of Nature*, the deistic concept of God was a "useless" one.[78] It was increasingly unnecessary to explain how the system of natural laws operated, since continuing investiga-

42   tion suggested that the cosmic system was self-regulating, and hence it dismally fell short of the emotional comfort demanded by popular religiosity. The American deists, of course, would have disagreed with both these points. But by the time Paine died in 1809, the intellectual climate as well as popular opinion was against them.

One immediate upshot of American deism's fall was that new, post-Enlightenment forms of infidelity took its place. American transcendentalism, championed by figures such as Ralph Waldo Emerson, Bronson Alcott, Margaret Fuller, and Henry David Thoreau, challenged Christian orthodoxy as well as Enlightenment rationalism with its unique blend of German idealism, nature mysticism, and Yankee pragmatism. Just as eighteenth-century college students had devoured the works of Voltaire and Paine, so their successors eagerly read and discussed Emerson's essay on nature and transcripts of his revolutionary address to the Harvard Divinity School. Social reformers such as Robert Owen and Frances Wright, excited by the liberal visions of European utopian socialists, assailed the tenets of supernaturalist religion but did so from a conceptual and temperamental basis different from that of the American deists. Wright and Owen were more interested in emancipating the individual from social irrationalities and injustices than in exploring the natural realm and deducing from it a rational alternative to Christian orthodoxy. Their religious infidelity was corollary to their social agenda—not, as was the case with American deism, the nucleus around which reformist zeal revolved.[79]

A second outcome was that Christian orthodoxy, sensitive to the spiritual vacuum created by the aridity of the deistic worldview, hurled itself into the frenzied excesses of what has come to be known as the "Second Great Awakening." This nationwide revivalist movement, lasting from roughly 1780 to 1830, was characterized by its emphasis on personal piety, salvationism and anti-intellectualism.[80] Its success in consolidating and extending "popular religion"—which, like its twentieth-century counterpart, stressed biblical fundamentalism and political conservatism—was dramatic. Between 1820 and 1830, for example, Methodist membership doubled. By the first decade of the nineteenth century, Baptist membership had increased tenfold, and the number of Baptist congregations mushroomed from five hundred to over twenty-five hundred. The number of evangelical preachers exploded in the same period, swelling from some eighteen hundred in 1775 to almost forty thousand by 1845.[81] In short, religious populism in the early nineteenth century overwhelmed the nation, eclipsing the deistic threat that had so effectively challenged eighteenth-century orthodoxy. As the century progressed, both transcendentalism and utopian socialism would be replaced by Darwinian-inspired forms of infidelity, and the fires fanned by the Second Great Awakening would cool. But before their own deaths, each in its own way buried the remains of Enlightenment deism once and for all. There would be other challenges to orthodoxy in the United States, but none as widespread or militant as the one launched by eighteenth-century rational religionists.

The Legacy of Deism in America

For all its weaknesses and what in retrospect can be seen as occasional naiveté, deism bequeathed a lasting legacy to American thought. It failed to endure as either a national movement or a religious alternative to Christianity, but it did succeed in functioning as a catalyst for change in both the theological and social arenas.

Rant and rave as eighteenth- and early nineteenth-century orthodox ministers might against the religion of nature, they learned a valuable lesson from it: Theological speculation could not ignore the discoveries and methodology of the natural and human sciences. True, the immediate reaction of orthodoxy to deism—the Second Great Awakening—was a besieged retreat into biblical fundamentalism and religious enthusiasm. But the more reflective men of the cloth realized that the way to counter this new form of infidelity was to speak its language and face it on its own turf. As Ezra Stiles had suggested in the mid-eighteenth century, natural philosophy was a double-edged sword that could be drawn as easily in defense of Christianity as against it, and many American clergy later took this point to heart.

In the years that followed the deistic challenge, Christian theologians increasingly stressed the importance of rational inquiry in their apologetics. They still insisted, of course, on the primary role of supernatural revelation, but their style as well as arguments reflected a newly discovered awareness that a viable religious perspective must speak to both the intellect and the passions. This led to a new theological method that, as one twentieth-century historian noted, "gravitated toward the connotation it had for the Deists: intellectual assent to a definable proposition."[82] Leonard Woods of Harvard's Andover Seminary proclaimed in 1830 that the ultimate test for the formulation of Christian beliefs was that they be expressed in "language which shall carry them to the mind of every enlightened Christian and philosopher with perfect clearness." Lyman Beecher, who had been a stalwart foe of deism in his youth, was later so convinced of the importance of reason in Christian belief that he rather intemperately dismissed mysticism as irrational and rebuked those enthusiastic Christians who "love to dream amid the repetition of beautiful uncertain sounds, and glittering undefined images."[83] And the very orthodox Reverend Alexander Campbell, in a notorious 1829 debate with Robert Owen over the evidences of Christianity, chided American Christians for their failure to invoke rational apologetics, using phrases that might have been lifted from a deistic tract.

Scepticism and infidelity are certainly on the increase in this and other countries. Not, indeed, because of the mildness of our laws, but because

44   of the lives of our professors, and a very general inattention to the evidences of our religion. The sectarian spirit, the rage of rivalry in the various denominations, together with many absurd tenets and opinions propagated, afford more relevant reasons for the prevalence of scepticism than most of our professors are able to offer for their faith.[84]

American theologians, then, tended to absorb certain elements of the rational religion they sought to refute. What was initially a forensic strategy gradually matured into a spirit of rational inquiry that gained widespread acceptance, at least among the clergy. There remained, of course, influential segments in the Christian community that refused to compromise. But notwithstanding their resistance, eighteenth-century deism had set in motion a new approach to theological questions that could not be denied. John Macquarrie, a twentieth-century Anglican theologian, has expressed this point well. Although he is specifically referring to the Enlightenment impact on contemporary theology, his words could just as well apply to deism's influence on nineteenth-century American Christianity. "In . . . important respects," Macquarrie says, "we remain inevitably children of the Enlightenment. Some of its lessons can never be unlearned. We cannot go back to the mythology of a former age, or to its supernaturalism, or to the spiritual authoritarianism of an infallible church or an infallible Bible."[85] At least in the American context, the impossibility of such a regression is partly due to the influence of the eighteenth-century American deists. They failed to replace Christianity with the religion of nature, but their example served to ameliorate the extremism and refine the sensibility and methods of American theology. Deism, in short, helped to awaken Christianity in the United States from its dogmatic slumber.

But American deism was not just a religious movement. On a more fundamental level, it attempted a comprehensive worldview, which sought to construct on an Enlightenment base a systematic defense of certain ethical, political, and social principles that stemmed from and complemented its theological ones. Influenced by the liberalism of thinkers such as Locke and the French savants, the American deists were strident republicans and ardent defenders of a humanism that stressed freedom of conscience and expression, separation of church and state, and universal public education. Their social agenda correlated with their underlying conviction that reality was rational and that humans were capable of fully comprehending its mysteries. The advance of free inquiry, unchecked by state or ecclesial oppression and unintimidated by public sanction, was the necessary condition for the fulfillment of reason's promise and the emancipation of the human spirit. Thus Franklin, ambivalent though his relationship to deism was, tirelessly campaigned for doctrinal toleration. Jefferson's many projects included writing legislation that promoted freedom of conscience and public education as well as attempting to fashion a coherent ethical system that ensured equality of treatment under the law for all individuals. Paine and Palmer never tired of condemning church and state alliances as viper's nests of oppression, and Palmer went so far as to call for the abolition of slavery, the emancipation of women, and an end to the brutal abuse of Native Americans. Volney suggested in his *Ruins* that a nation that refused to encourage free and rational inquiry doomed itself to extinction, and Ethan Allen thundered in his *Oracles* that the only legitimate standard of appraisal or action was reason. Finally, Freneau's poetry time and again returned to the themes of freedom of conscience and the insidious consequences on both individual and society of superstition, doctrinal exclusivity, and social elitism.

Convinced as they were that the full exercise of reason and the inauguration of a golden age of scientific progress as well as social prosperity could only be nurtured in an environment that respected diversity of opinion and freedom of thought, the American deists assumed the role of reform agitators. Their aim was to emancipate the individual from obstacles to the full development of his or her rational potentiality, and such an enterprise, in their eyes, included the elimination of political as well as religious shackles. As suggested earlier, the deists' militant championship of republican and humanistic ideas probably earned them as many enemies as did their assault on traditional Christianity. But for these advocates of the religion of nature, the two were inseparable. Repression was repression, regardless of whether it was ecclesial or political in origin.

The deistic movement in America, then, functioned as a goad that continuously irritated and occasionally thumped the public conscience. In fulfilling this purpose, it helped to consolidate those social and political ideas that, whether lived up to in actual practice or not, have become associated with the American ethos. It is too much to claim that the humanistic social agenda advocated by the deists was solely or even primarily responsible for subsequent reforms in education, that their campaign for freedom of conscience directly resulted in the establishment of the federal constitutional separation clause, or that their advocacy of the rights of slaves produced ameliorating legislation. Too many other social, economic, and political factors were at work in each of these areas to confirm a direct causal link between deistic agitation and eventual reform. But the humanistic ideals touted by late eighteenth-century deism contributed to a climate of opinion that, along with other factors, set the republican mood of the young nation. As is the case with deism's influence on subsequent American theology, its primary function in the social arena was catalytic. It continuously hammered home the need for reform, for emancipation, and for respect of individual differences and, in so doing, stirred discussion and debate about the proper relationship of the individual to society. The deistic challenge enraged some and delighted others, but few politicians or private citizens remained indifferent to its demands for social justice and freedom of conscience.

46   American deism both failed and succeeded. As a movement that sought to supplant supernaturalist orthodoxy with rational religion, to build shining temples of reason on the crumbling ruins of Christian churches, it fell short of the mark. But as a catalyst for reform in theological method as well as social and political practices, deism left to the young Republic a lasting and far-reaching bequest. Such an accomplishment would hardly have satisfied many of the rational religionists, particularly the more militant Paine and Palmer, but it was no small achievement. Their campaign for free and rational religion and social justice—notwithstanding modern dismissal of their overly simplistic assumptions about reality and the human spirit—was a grand and noble experiment. The reader today may not agree with the optimistic rationalism of a Franklin, Palmer, or Freneau, but he or she can scarcely escape being challenged by it. In the final analysis, such an accomplishment is a victory, for readers as well as the deists.

Notes

1. Folio volume of Stiles MSS, Yale University, p. 460. Quoted in I. Woodbridge Riley, *American Philosophy: The Early Schools* (New York: Dodd, Mead, 1907), 217.

2. Lyman Beecher, *Autobiography and Correspondence*, edited by Charles Beecher (New York: Harper & Brothers, 1866), 1:43.

3. Edmund Morgan has argued that Beecher deliberately blew up his accounts of infidelity at Yale to put forth himself and Timothy Dwight, Stiles's successor, as the twin champions of orthodoxy who valiantly pulled the college back from the brink of apostasy. "Ezra Stiles and Timothy Dwight," *Proceedings of the Massachusetts Historical Society* 72 (October 1957–December 1960): 101–17. For a more sympathetic account of Beecher's battle against deism, see Stuart C. Henry, *Unvanquished Puritan: A Portrait of Lyman Beecher* (Grand Rapids, Mich.: William B. Eerdmans, 1973).

4. Quoted in G. Adolf Koch, *Republican Religion: The American Revolution and the Cult of Reason* (New York: Henry Holt, 1933), 242.

5. William Meade, *Old Churches, Ministers, and Families of Virginia* (Philadelphia: Lippincott, 1910), 1:175.

6. John Johnston, *The Autobiography and Ministerial Life of the Rev. John Johnston, D.D.*, edited by James Carnahan (New York: M. W. Dodd, 1856), 30.

7. W. H. Channing, *Life of William Ellery Channing* (Boston: American Unitarian Association, 1880), 30.

8. Richard Watson, *An Apology for the Bible in a Series of Letters, Addressed to Thomas Paine* (Cambridge, Mass.: Hilliard and Brown, 1828), 15.

9. John Trumbull, *Autobiography, Reminiscences, and Letters of John Trumbull* (New Haven, Conn.: B. L. Hamlin, 1841), 170–71.

10. Koch, *Republican Religion,* 275–82.

11. "His *Age of Reason*, would never have been much known in this country if the Clergy had suffered it to rest; but they dragged it into publicity—let the text be what it would, animadversions on Paine made a part of the sermon. The Clergy wrote—the people read." Philip Freneau, *Letters on Various Interesting and Important Subjects . . . by Robert Slender* (Philadelphia: D. Hogan, 1799), 37–38.

12. *Prospect; Or View of the Modern World,* 16 June 1804. It is likely that Palmer's count here is exaggerated, but probably not by much.

13. Uzal Ogden, *An Antidote to Deism* (Newark: John Woods, 1795), 2:280; 1:17.

14. Tunis R. Wortman, *An Oration on the Influence of Social Institutions upon Human Morals and Happiness* (New York: C. C. Van Alen & Co., 1796), 24, 25.

15. Elihu Palmer, *Principles of Nature; or, A Development of the Moral Causes of Happiness and Misery among the Human Species* (New York, 1806), chapter 25.

16. Carl Becker, *The Heavenly City of the Eighteenth-Century Philosophers* (New Haven, Conn.: Yale University Press, 1932).

17. Taylor defends this conclusion in the first chapter of his *Hegel* (Cambridge: Cambridge University Press, 1975).

18. "Beantwortung der Frage: Was Ist Aufklärung?" in *Immanuel Kants Werke*, edited by Ernst Cassirer and Hermann Cohen (Berlin: Bruno Cassirer, 1912), 4:174.

19. Ernst Cassirer, *The Philosophy of the Enlightenment*, translated by Fritz C. A. Koelln and James P. Pettegrove (Boston: Beacon Press, 1965), 5.

20. Quoted in ibid., 2–4.

21. *Novum Organum*, vol. 1, paragraph 14, in Francis Bacon, *Advancement of Learning and Novum Organum*, edited by James Edward Creighton (New York: Willey Book Co., 1944).

22. *The Great Instauration*, in *The Works of Francis Bacon*, vol. 1, *Philosophical Writings*, edited by James Spedding, R. L. Ellis, and D. D. Heath (Boston: Houghton Mifflin, n.d.), 41.

23. Ibid., 40–41.

24. In Newton's *Philosophy of Nature: Selections from His Writings*, edited by H. S. Thayer (New York: Hafner, 1974), 10.

25. Newton to Cotes, 1713, in ibid., 6.

26. *Optics*, query 23, quoted in Alexandre Koyre, *From the Closed World to the Infinite Universe* (Baltimore, Md.: Johns Hopkins University Press, 1979), 209.

27. *Principia*, book 3, in Newton's *Philosophy of Nature*, 42.

28. John Locke, *An Essay Concerning Human Understanding*, edited by Peter H. Nidditch (Oxford: Oxford University Press, 1979), book 1, chapter 1.

29. Ibid., book 2, chapter 11.

30. Ibid., book 4, chapter 18.

31. Parts of this section and the next ("Deism Comes to America") are adapted from the introduction to my *Elihu Palmer's "Principles of Nature": Text and Commentary* (Wolfeboro, N.H.: Longwood, 1990).

32. Samuel Clarke, *A Discourse concerning the Unchangeable Obligations of Natural Religion, and the Truth and Certainty of the Christian Revelation*, in *A Collection of Theological Tracts*, edited by R. Watson (London, 1791), 4:109–295. See also Clarke's *Discourse on Natural Religion*, in *British Moralists, Being Selections from Writers Principally of the Eighteenth Century*, edited by L. A. Selby-Biggs (Oxford: Clarendon Press, 1897), 2:3–56.

33. George Cheyne, *Philosophical Principles of Religion: Natural and Revealed* (London, 1715).

34. Thomas Woolston, *Discourses on the Miracles of Our Saviour* (London, 1728), 2:48.

35. Leslie Stephen provides an insightful and exhaustive treatment of the lesser British deists in the first volume of his *History of English Thought in the Eighteenth Century* (New York: G. P. Putnam's Sons, 1908).

36. Matthew Tindal, *Christianity as Old as the Creation; or, The Gospel a Republication of the Religion of Nature* (London, 1730), 52, 60.

37. Jonathan Edwards, *History of the Work of Redemption,* in *The Works of Jonathan Edwards,* edited by Edward Hickman (Boston, 1834), 1:599.

38. Theodore Hornberger, *Scientific Thought in the American Colleges, 1638–1800* (New York: Octagon Books, 1968), chapter 4.

39. Samuel Eliot Morison, *Harvard College in the Seventeenth Century* (Cambridge, Mass.: Harvard University Press, 1936), 1:214–51.

40. The most widely used work by Ames was his *Medulla Theologica* (1629).

41. Francis L. Broderick, "Pulpit, Physics, and Politics: The Curriculum of the College of New Jersey, 1746–1794," *William and Mary Quarterly* 6 (1949): 42–68.

42. The influence of Scottish common sense philosophy on eighteenth-century American thought is discussed, *inter alia,* in Elizabeth Flower and Murray G. Murphey, *A History of Philosophy in America* (New York: G. P. Putnam's Sons, 1977), volume 1; Henry May, *The Enlightenment in America* (New York: Oxford University Press, 1976); Donald H. Meyer, *The Democratic Enlightenment* (New York: G. P. Putnam's Sons, 1976); Morton White, *The Philosophy of the American Revolution* (New York: Oxford University Press, 1978); and Garry Wills, *Inventing America: Jefferson's Declaration of Independence* (Garden City, N.Y.: Doubleday, 1978). These and other studies deal with the impact of Scottish philosophy on the broader American Enlightenment, not on deism per se. The connections there remain to be fully explored.

43. For an excellent treatment of Mather's interest in and contributions to the New Learning, see Kenneth Silverman, *The Life and Times of Cotton Mather* (New York: Columbia University Press, 1985), especially 40–42, 243–54, 405–10.

44. Josiah Quincy, *The History of Harvard College* (Cambridge, Mass., 1840), 2:139.

45. Joseph Hawley, *Confessions of His Belief in Arminianism,* quoted from the unpublished manuscript by Herbert A. Morais, *Deism in Eighteenth-Century America* (New York: Russell & Russell, 1960), 67.

46. Ezra Stiles, *Literary Diary,* edited by R. B. Dexter (New York: C. Scribner's Sons, 1901), 1:566.

47. For a detailed account of Stiles's youthful dalliance with deism, see Edmund S. Morgan, *The Gentle Puritan: A Life of Ezra Stiles, 1727–1795* (New York: W. W. Norton, 1983).

48. Silverman, *The Life and Times of Cotton Mather,* 60.

49. For discussions of the doctrinal and stylistic permutations of Calvinist theology in America, see Richard L. Bushman, *From Puritan to Yankee: Character and the Social Order in Connecticut, 1690–1765* (Cambridge, Mass.: Harvard University Press, 1967); Frank Hugh Foster, *A Genetic History of the New England Theology* (New York: Russell & Russell, 1963); James Hoopes, *Consciousness in New England: From Puritanism and Ideas to Psychoanalysis and Semiotic* (Baltimore, Md.: Johns Hopkins University Press, 1989), especially chapters 1–5; Perry Miller, *The New England Mind: The Seventeenth Century* (Cambridge, Mass.: Harvard University Press, 1982); Harry Stout, *The New England Soul: Preaching and Religious Culture in Colonial New England* (New York: Oxford University Press, 1986); and Teresa Toulouse, *The Art of Prophesying: New England Sermons and the Shaping of Belief* (Athens: University of Georgia Press, 1987), especially chapters 1–3.

50. Arminianism is so called after the Dutch theologian Jacobus Arminius (1560–1609), who was the leading champion of the "heretical" view associated with his name.

51. Bruce Kuklick, *Churchmen and Philosophers: From Jonathan Edwards to John Dewey* (New Haven, Conn.: Yale University Press, 1985), 6.

52. Quoted in Miller, *The New England Mind,* 53.

53. George Goodwin, *Auto-Machia,* translated by Joshua Sylvester (London, 1607),

no pagination. For interesting discussions of the "Civil Warrs" of self against self pre-cipitated by Calvinism, see Sacvan Bercovitch, *The Puritan Origins of the American Self* (New Haven, Conn.: Yale University Press, 1975), chapter 1, and Kuklick, *Churchmen and Philosophers*, 6–8.

54. Miller, *The New England Mind*, 66.

55. Kuklick, *Churchmen and Philosophers*, 8. Kuklick goes on to claim that "the Calvinists were, finally, extraordinary optimists." This contention, in my judgment, is much too strong, but Kuklick's warning against imputing to eighteenth-century Cal-vinists the same gloominess with which their doctrines strike twentieth-century readers is well-taken.

56. See Robert J. Wilson, *The Benevolent Deity: Ebenezer Gay and the Rise of Ratio-nal Religion in New England, 1696–1787* (Philadelphia: University of Pennsylvania Press, 1984), and Morgan, *The Gentle Puritan*.

57. The Great Awakening is a complicated and multifaceted historical event, involv-ing social, political, doctrinal, and philosophical factors. For the purpose of the present discussion, I have limited my remarks to the Awakening's relationship to the break-down of American Calvinism and the rise of American deism, but a full treatment of the Great Awakening extends, of course, beyond these specific issues. For more compre-hensive treatments, see Alan Heimert and Perry Miller, eds., *The Great Awakening: Documents Illustrating the Crisis and Its Consequences* (Indianapolis: Bobbs-Merrill, 1967). Alan Heimert's *Religion and the American Mind: From the Great Awakening to the Revolution* (Cambridge, Mass.: Harvard University Press, 1966) is a masterful analysis of the Great Awakening's impact on New England Congregationalism as well as Calvinist thought in general, as is Harry Stout's *New England Soul*.

58. Gilbert Tennent, "The Danger of an Unconverted Ministry, Considered in a Sermon on Mark vi.34," in Heimert and Miller, *The Great Awakening*, 79.

59. Heimert and Miller, *The Great Awakening*, xiv.

60. Quoted in Riley, *American Philosophy: The Early Schools*, 217.

61. Sermon delivered on 20 November 1760, quoted in Morgan, *The Gentle Puri-tan*, 213.

62. Robert Hall, *Modern Infidelity Considered with respect to Its Influences on Society* (Charlestown, Mass.: Samuel Etheridge, 1801), 44–45.

63. Palmer, *Principles of Nature*, chapter 25.

64. Edmund Burke, *Reflections on the Revolution in France* (London: J. Dodsley, 1790), 135.

65. This classification was originally popularized by Koch in his *Republican Religion*, continued by Morais in his *Deism in Eighteenth-Century America*, and recently used as a heuristic for the Enlightenment as a whole by May in his *Enlightenment in America*.

66. Franklin to ?, 3 July 1786(?), in *Benjamin Franklin: Representative Selections*, edited by Chester E. Jorgenson and Frank Luther Mott (New York: Hill and Wang, 1962), 485.

67. *Prospect*, 17 December 1803.

68. David Hume, *Enquiry Concerning Human Understanding* (LaSalle, Ill.: Open Court, 1988), section 10.

69. David Hume, *Dialogues Concerning Natural Religion* (Indianapolis: Hackett, 1985).

70. For a more detailed discussion of Hume's challenge to the mechanistic world-view, see chapter 8 of my *Rational Infidels: The American Deists* (Wolfeboro, N.H.: Longwood, 1992). In the pages that follow, I have borrowed four paragraphs from this earlier treatment.

50   71. Hume's analysis of causation is in *A Treatise on Human Nature,* book 1, part 3, sections 1–4, 12–15.

72. E. A. Burtt, *The Metaphysical Foundations of Modern Science* (Garden City, N.Y.: Doubleday, 1955), 238–39.

73. Pascal, *Pensées,* article 8, quoted in Ernst Cassirer, *The Philosophy of the Enlightenment,* 144.

74. For a fuller discussion of the Enlightenment ideal to "scientize" society and the behavioral sciences, see my *Sane Society Ideal in Modern Utopianism* (Lewiston, N.Y.: Edwin Mellen Press, 1989).

75. Rosemary Haughton, *The Passionate God* (New York: Paulist Press, 1981), 8.

76. Two insightful studies dealing with the Enlightenment's zeal to "manage" and manipulate nature are William Leiss, *The Domination of Nature* (Boston: Beacon Press, 1974), and Carolyn Merchant, *The Death of Nature: Women, Ecology, and the Scientific Revolution* (San Francisco: Harper and Row, 1980). For a full discussion of the Baconian background, see chapter 2 of my *Sane Society Ideal in Modern Utopianism.*

77. The phrase *mysterium tremendum et fascinans* is, of course, the coinage of Rudolf Otto in *The Idea of the Holy,* translated by John W. Harvey (New York: Oxford University Press, 1950).

78. Paul-Henri Thiery, baron d'Holbach, *Système de la nature, où des Lois du monde physique et du monde moral* (Paris, 1770), volume 3, chapter 5.

79. For treatments of post-Enlightenment infidelity, see Herbert Hovenkamp, *Science and Religion in America, 1800–1860* (Philadelphia: University of Pennsylvania Press, 1978); Albert Post, *Popular Freethought in America, 1825–1850* (New York: Columbia University Press, 1943); and James Turner's masterful *Without God, Without Creed: The Origins of Unbelief in America* (Baltimore, Md.: Johns Hopkins University Press, 1985). Although Enlightenment deism in America died out at the end of the eighteenth century, a few post-Enlightenment infidels arose whose apostasy had certain affinities with Enlightenment rationalism. Roderick S. French has made such a case for Abner Kneeland (1777–1844) in "The Trials of Abner Kneeland" (Ph.D. dissertation, George Washington University, 1971) and "Liberation from Man and God in Boston: Abner Kneeland's Free-Thought Campaign, 1830–1839," *American Quarterly* 32 (Summer 1980): 202–21. Kneeland was a renegade Universalist whose thought has been sadly neglected.

80. For excellent analyses of the Second Great Awakening, see John Butler, *Awash in a Sea of Faith: Christianizing the American People* (Cambridge, Mass.: Harvard University Press, 1990), chapter 9; Nathan O. Hatch, *The Democratization of American Christianity* (New Haven, Conn.: Yale University Press, 1989); and Donald G. Matthews, "The Second Great Awakening as an Organizing Process, 1780–1830," in *Religion in American History: Interpretive Essays,* edited by John Mulder and John F. Wilson (Englewood Cliffs, N.J.: Prentice-Hall, 1978), 199–218.

81. Hatch, *The Democratization of American Christianity,* 3.

82. Turner, *Without God, Without Creed,* 103.

83. Ibid., 146; Lyman Beecher, *Lectures,* Lecture 6, "The Attitudes and Character of God," 139, quoted in ibid., 103.

84. Robert Owen and Alexander Campbell, *Debate on the Evidences of Christianity* (Cincinnati, Ohio.: Robinson and Fairbanks, 1829), 13. Campbell was the founder of the Disciples of Christ and an ardent evangelist throughout his career.

85. John Macquarrie, *Jesus Christ in Modern Thought* (London: SCM Press, 1990), 26.

Benjamin Franklin
I Believe in One God, Creator of the Universe

As suggested in the Introduction, American deism is better understood as a general philosophical orientation that allowed for a certain amount of flexibility in individual belief than a set-in-stone catechism of infallible and obligatory doctrine. There was obviously a nucleus of belief shared by all deists, giving them a distinct intellectual identity: conviction in an orderly, rational universe, as well as a rational and benevolent deity; a distrust of metaphysical speculation and scriptural authority; and advocacy of empirical methodology and a concomitant scorn of such supernaturalist tenets as revelation; a denial of the divinity of Jesus and the triune God; confidence in human progress; and an emphasis on the utility of virtue. But integral to this core of deistic thought was the fact that it accommodated a great deal of interpretive leeway. Some deists, for example, applauded Jesus' ethical teachings so long as they were stripped of their supernaturalist and ecclesial "corruptions"; others deplored them. Most deists accepted the immortality of the soul, but a few denied the possibility. Yet others were convinced that the divine reveals itself only through the lawlike operations of the physical order, while some were willing to grant that God at least in principle is capable of "special" providences in the moral realm. In short, the credal tolerance deism so ardently advocated allowed for a wide latitude in personal belief among its proponents but did not result in the reduction of the movement to a laissez-faire hodgepodge of amorphously private opinion. This flexibility was especially apparent in deism's early stage, when some sympathizers attempted to straddle the traditional world of orthodoxy and the Enlightenment one of rationalism. Very often, in fact, it was (and is) difficult to distinguish a moderate deist from a liberal Christian.

Benjamin Franklin (1706–90), the first noteworthy American advocate of deism, was one of those caught in the middle. He clearly was not an orthodox Christian, but neither was he as unequivocally deistic in his thinking as Jefferson, Paine, or Palmer. Rooted in tradition but baptized in the New Learning of Bacon, Newton, and Locke, Franklin's religious orientation was a sometimes uneasy balance between the two, with the pendulum more to the rationalist than the Christian side. He is best characterized as an ambiguous deist.

The equivocalness of his religious thought emerged quite early. Although he tells us in the *Autobiography* that he was reared "piously in the Dissenting way" by Calvinist parents and "religiously educated as a Presbyterian," young

52   Franklin dropped whatever overt allegiance he might have had to the gloomy theology of the Westminster Confession by the time he was sixteen. Like so many other adolescents who rebel against an orthodox upbringing, he initially hurled himself in the opposite direction and at the age of nineteen wrote a precocious treatise, *A Dissertation on Liberty and Necessity, Pleasure and Pain*, defending dogmatic materialism. Two features about the *Dissertation* shed light upon the fundamental ambiguity of Franklin's religious perspective. In the first place, the essay, which claims to be a series of logical inferences from Newtonian mechanism, arrives at conclusions reminiscent of (although not identical to) the very Calvinist doctrine Franklin thought he had rejected: an insistence that physical events as well as human destinies are predetermined by divine power and knowledge. Moreover, Franklin soon rejected this Calvinist-cum-mechanistic treatise, correctly fearing that its reasoning posed a threat to moral rectitude, and eventually came to see the habituation of virtue as the centerpiece of an authentically religious life. But it is arguable that the change in philosophical direction had its distant origins in Franklin's youthful absorption of Cotton Mather's *Bonifacius* (1710), an essay that stressed the everyday utility of Christian virtue. As Franklin himself confesses in the *Autobiography*, Mather's work "gave me such a turn of thinking, as to have an influence on my conduct through life; for I have always set a greater value on the character of a *doer of good* than on any other kind of reputation."

The point is that the initial composition and the eventual repudiation of the *Dissertation* reflect the young Franklin's tense and at times conceptually unstable mixture of traditionally orthodox and radically Enlightened currents. The attraction and repulsion between the two reemerged time and again in most of his subsequent reflections on religion. This is not to say that Franklin was a confused or sloppy thinker, but only that he, like so many of his generation, mirrored the religious uncertainly of the day. Franklin grew to intellectual maturity during a conceptual watershed, in which Enlightenment rationalism challenged but did not yet supplant the traditional Calvinist ethos. It was perhaps inevitable that his thinking should reflect both.

Even so, Franklin was more deistic in his orientation than not. This is apparent from an examination of the three central assumptions around which his religious worldview revolved. First, he was convinced that all varieties of religious sentiment and all credal expressions contain some element of truth, and the rational person therefore should refrain from narrow-mindedly repudiating any of them. But he also believed that most religious systems had allowed doctrinal misconstructions and irrational bigotries to distort their intuitions on the truth. Consequently, it is equally unwarranted for a rational person to endorse any of them wholeheartedly. For Franklin, all systematic attempts to explain nature and God are prone to error, particularly when they indulge in a priori "metaphysical reasoning" (an approach that Franklin himself, except in his youthful and soon lamented *Dissertation*, always shunned). The wise individual, as Franklin points out in his 1738 letter to his parents, avoids the temptation of dogmatizing about religious questions and instead follows the dictates of reason in evaluating them.

But how does reason enable humans to separate doctrinal wheat from chaff? By directing the powers of understanding to an examination of experience and nature. Franklin early on had read Locke's defense of an empiricist epistemology, becoming convinced that all ideas originate from and can be judged according to sensate experience. In theological terms, this implied that the book of nature and the lessons of ordinary experience are capable of shedding light upon the existence as well as the character of the deity. For Franklin, the study of physical and human nature discloses an orderliness that cannot be gratuitous but instead is only explicable if the existence of a rational and all-powerful First Cause is posited. Moreover, as he argues in *On the Providence of God in the Government of the World* (1732), an examination of natural operations reveals that they are conducive to the well-being of humans, thereby leading to the assumption that the First Cause is also benevolent and compassionate. It is but a short step from the acknowledgement of divine benevolence to the postulate that the most appropriate way for humans to adore the deity is to imitate his goodness through the cultivation of virtuous behavior and that such behavior will be rewarded, in this life as well as the next. As Franklin has Poor Richard say, "What is serving God? 'Tis doing Good to Man." These three tenets—that a rational and omnipotent God exists, that he is benevolent, and that humans ought to imitate his goodness and will be judged in terms of their success in so doing—are supported by reason. Other specifically Christian doctrines—the divinity of Jesus, the resurrection of the body, divine revelation, miracles, and so on—are not and thus may or may not be correct. As Franklin said toward the end of his life, they are "questions I do not dogmatize upon" (letter to Ezra Stiles, 9 March 1790). But given his suspicion of "metaphysical reasoning" as well as his certitude that nature is uniformly lawlike and hence explicable in rational terms, it is understandable that Franklin was less sanguine about their truth.

The second fundamental assumption of Franklin's religious worldview is as deistic in tenor as the first: his insistence on the rationality as well as practicality of a virtuous life and his concomitant conviction that the noblest way of serving and worshipping the deity is in the regular performance of good works. All of the American deists concentrated on moral questions; Elihu Palmer even wrote one of the most sophisticated ethical treatises of the Early Republic. But Franklin's preoccupation with the ideal of moral perfection bordered on obsession. From his earliest to his final writings, regardless of the subject matter, Franklin rarely missed an opportunity to bring up the issues of virtue and moral progress. In fact, he seriously contemplated writing a tract on virtue, although

54   public and private responsibilities prevented him from doing more than outlining his thoughts in the *Autobiography* or distilling them, through Poor Richard, into the succinct moralistic maxims so familiar to schoolchildren.

Franklin's intoxication with moral perfection, as well as his no-nonsense, quasi-mathematical program for cultivating the virtues, has been the brunt of much subsequent criticism. The usual charge is that Franklin the ethicist is more of a bookkeeper than a reflective thinker, substituting an unimaginative calculus of ethical checks and balances for a genuinely sophisticated treatment of the moral life. This criticism has undeniable merit. Although there is a disarming quaintness to Franklin's famous plan for the daily exercise of virtues (such as temperance, silence, order, frugality, and industry), it can also be read as the facile musings of a self-satisfied and rather shallow moralist. But when examined against the backdrop of his deistic worldview, Franklin's remarks on moral perfection shed a good deal of their seeming flimsiness.

Franklin was convinced that moral progress is dependent on two necessary conditions: a rationally consistent attitude of benevolence and tolerance, and a single-minded fidelity to virtuous behavior. The first condition reflects the lawlike and predictable essence of both deity and nature, as well as Franklin's belief that error-prone humans have no logical or normative justification for dogmatic intractability. The second is based on the Aristotelian assumption that virtue is a learned behavior instead of an innate quality and that the most rational way to cultivate it is through concrete habituation to good works. Franklin did not discount the importance of good intentions, but, as in his *Self-Denial Not the Essence of Virtue* (1735), he insisted that the ultimate test of moral development is in the doing, not the contemplating. Otherwise, it is too easy for humans to succumb to lazy or self-indulgent behavior and weasel out of moral culpability by claiming that the spirit is willing, even if the flesh is weak. For Franklin, such a gross discrepancy between motive and act is too irrational to serve as an excuse for malfeasance. Since the private intentions of an individual can never be fully appraised by others, the only remaining criterion for ethical evaluation is ostensible behavior. Moreover, a methodical effort to perform virtuous actions, even if the deeds initially are done reluctantly or with an ill will, eventually conditions individuals to virtue in such a way that they ultimately come to desire what originally they merely endured: the consistent performance of good works.

In short, Franklin, like all the American deists, sought an objective, naturalistic means by which to nurture and gauge virtue, one that would be accessible to all rational humans because it was disabused of mysterious appeals to innate predispositions or supernaturalist entreaties to divine grace. Read in this light, his mathematical regimen for the cultivation of virtue appears more profound.

The third and final conviction around which Franklin the deist constructed his worldview was an Enlightenment-influenced faith in the perfectibility of society and individuals. In common with all American deists, Franklin had complete confidence that science was the vehicle through which both natural forces and human irrationality would be tamed. Unlike the other deists (except perhaps Jefferson), Franklin was also an accomplished scientist and so had first-hand experience on which to base his estimation. The scientific charting of natural and psychological laws would usher in the age of reason if society only learned to tolerate dissent and encourage the free interplay of ideas—or at least so Franklin believed in his more optimistic moments. In keeping with his fundamental ambiguity, he was not always so hopeful. For example, in a letter to Joseph Priestley (8 February 1780) which praises science's progress in technology and physics, Franklin also laments its apparent inability to foster equal advancement in morality: "O that moral Science were in as fair a way of Improvement, that Men would cease to be Wolves to one another, and that human Beings would at length learn what they now improperly call Humanity!" In an even more remarkable display of pessimism, Franklin advises an unknown correspondent (possibly Paine) to refrain from publishing a treatise on deism, on the grounds that the manuscript's critique of revealed religion might damage the inducements to morality contained in orthodox Christianity. And "if men are so wicked as we now see them *with religion*, what would they be *if without it*."

However, these occasional moments of cynicism are less characteristic of Franklin than his expressions of exuberant optimism. Instead, they are the cautionary remnants of a Calvinist background. More typical is Franklin's ardent defense of religious tolerance, as seen is his *Dialogue between Two Presbyterians* (1735), or the cool-headed, rationalistic faith evident in his *Articles of Belief and Acts of Religion* (1728) and *Doctrine to be Preached* (1731). Franklin's religious perspective may have uncomfortably waffled throughout the years between Calvinist gloom and enlightenment optimism, but when considered in its entirety, it is remarkably consistent for a thinker of his generation. As he reaffirmed at life's end, "I believe in one God, Creator of the Universe. That he governs it by his Providence. That he ought to be worshipped. That the most acceptable Service we render to him is doing good to his other Children. That the soul of Man is immortal, and well be treated with Justice in another Life respecting its Conduct in this. These I take to be the fundamental Principles of all sound Religion, and I regard them . . . in whatever Sect I meet with them." With only minor exceptions, few subsequent deists would have disagreed with this eloquent profession.

A Dissertation on Liberty and Necessity, Pleasure and Pain (1725)

The earliest (and, in many ways, the most philosophically ambitious) of Franklin's works, the Dissertation *was intended as a response to William Wollaston's (1660–*

56   *1724) liberal tract* The Religion of Nature Delineated. *Franklin was a young journeyman in a London printing house when he dashed off the* Dissertation, *and its strict defense of thoroughgoing mechanism reflects the youthful iconoclasm and intellectual self-assuredness with which it was written. But Franklin was soon to shed his exuberant confidence in the* Dissertation*'s thesis. Although one hundred copies of it were printed, Franklin quickly destroyed most of them, fearing that the dissemination of his treatise would "have an Ill Tendency." In later life he wrote an essay (now lost) repudiating the* Dissertation*'s conclusions, and in his* Autobiography, *he listed the early work as one of his life's "erratas."*

Considering Franklin's subsequent emphasis on the importance of "truth, sincerity and integrity, in dealings between man and man," it is obvious why he came to regret and reject this early venture into "metaphysical reasoning." Starting from the affirmation of an all-powerful and supremely good deity, Franklin's Dissertation *infers that reality is mechanistic in nature, that humans are thereby without free will, that desire for pleasure and aversion to pain are the ubiquitous sources of motivation and behavior, and that human actions, given their deterministic character, are morally indifferent. In sum, the* Dissertation *defends a dogmatic, quasi-Hobbesian materialism and concludes that everything is as it must be and that everything is good because ordained by an all-good God.*

The Dissertation*'s historical interest lies in the fact that it pushes deism's postulation of a perfectly lawlike deity as well as its endorsement of Newtonian mechanism into a radical denial of free will, ethical responsibility, and human progress. This was a step conventional deists obviously were unwilling to take, insofar as it undercut their Enlightenment faith in the progressively liberating effects, societal as well as normative, of reason. Franklin soon realized that his defense of a pervasive materialism was not so much a brief for deism as a* reductio ad absurdum *repudiation of it, and he consequently backed off. But his eventual renunciation of the* Dissertation*'s mechanistic conclusions never dampened his fundamental trust in basic deistic tenets.*

Sect. 1. Of Liberty and Necessity

I. *There is said to be a* First Mover, *who is called* GOD, *Maker of the Universe.*

II. *He is said to be all-wise, all-good, all powerful.*

These two Propositions being allow'd and asserted by People of almost every Sect and Opinion; I have here suppos'd them granted, and laid them down as the Foundation of my Argument; What follows then, being a Chain of Consequences truly drawn from them, will stand or fall as they are true or false.

III. *If He is all-good, whatsoever He doth must be good.*

IV. *If He is all-wise, whatsoever He doth must be wise.*

The Truth of these Propositions, with relation to the two first, I think may be justly call'd evident; since, either that infinite Goodness will act what is ill, or infinite Wisdom what is not wise, is too glaring a Contradiction not to be perceiv'd by any Man of common Sense, and deny'd as soon as understood.

V. *If He is all-powerful, there can be nothing either existing or acting in the Universe* against *or* without *his Consent; and what He consents to must be good, because He is good; therefore* Evil *doth not exist.*

Unde Malum? has been long a Question, and many of the Learned have perplex'd themselves and Readers to little Purpose in Answer to it. That there are both Things and Actions to which we give the Name of *Evil*, is not here deny'd, as *Pain, Sickness, Want, Theft, Murder*, &c. but that these and the like are not in reality *Evils, Ills*, or *Defects* in the Order of the Universe, is demonstrated in the next Section, as well as by this and the following Proposition. Indeed, to suppose any Thing to exist or be done, *contrary* to the Will of the Almighty, is to suppose him not almighty; or that Something (the Cause of *Evil*) is more mighty than the Almighty; an Inconsistence that I think no One will defend: And to deny any Thing or Action, which he consents to the existence of, to be good, is entirely to destroy his two Attributes of *Wisdom* and *Goodness*.

There is nothing done in the Universe, say the Philosophers, *but what God either does, or* permits *to be done.* This, as He is Almighty, is certainly true: But what need of this Distinction between *doing* and *permitting?* Why, first they take it for granted that many Things in the Universe exist in such a Manner as is not for the Best, and that many Actions are done which ought not to be done, or would be better undone; these Things or Actions they cannot ascribe to God as his, because they have already attributed to Him infinite Wisdom and Goodness; Here then is the Use of the Word *Permit;* He *permits* them to be done, *say they.* But we will reason thus: If God permits an Action to be done, it is because he wants either *Power* or *Inclination* to hinder it; in saying he wants *Power*, we deny Him to be *almighty;* and if we say He wants *Inclination* or *Will*, it must be, either because He is not Good, or the Action is not *evil*, (for all Evil is contrary to the Essence of *infinite Goodness.*) The former is inconsistent with his before-given Attribute of Goodness, therefore the latter must be true.

It will be said, perhaps, that *God permits evil Actions to be done, for* wise *Ends and Purposes.* But this Objection destroys itself; for whatever an infinitely good God hath wise Ends in suffering to *be*, must be good, is thereby made good, and cannot be otherwise.

VI. *If a Creature is made by God, it must depend upon God, and receive all its Power from Him; with which Power the Creature can do nothing contrary to the Will of God, because God is Almighty; what is not contrary to His Will, must be agreeable to it; what is agreeable to it, must be good, because He is Good; therefore a Creature can do nothing but what is good.*

This Proposition is much to the same Purpose with the former, but more

58 particular; and its Conclusion is as just and evident. Tho' a Creature may do many Actions which by his Fellow Creatures will be nam'd *Evil*, and which will naturally and necessarily cause or bring upon the Doer, certain *Pains* (which will likewise be call'd *Punishments*,) yet this Proposition proves, that he cannot act what will be in itself really Ill, or displeasing to God. And that the painful Consequences of his evil Actions (*so call'd*) are not, as indeed they ought not to be, *Punishments* or Unhappinesses, will be shewn hereafter.

Nevertheless, the late learned Author of *The Religion of Nature* . . . , has given us a Rule or Scheme, whereby to discover which of our Actions ought to be esteem'd and denominated *good*, and which *evil*: It is in short this, "Every Action which is done according to *Truth*, is good; and every Action contrary to Truth, is evil: To act according to Truth is to use and esteem every Thing as what it is, &c. Thus if *A* steals a Horse from *B*, and rides away upon him, he uses him not as what he is in Truth, viz. the Property of another, but as his own, which is contrary to Truth, and therefore *evil*." But, as this Gentleman himself says (Sect. 1. Prop. VI.) "In order to judge rightly what any Thing is, it must be consider'd, not only what it is in one Respect, but also what it may be in any other Respect; and the whole Description of the Thing ought to be taken in:" So in this Case it ought to be consider'd, that *A* is naturally a *covetous* Being, feeling an Uneasiness in the want of *B's* Horse, which produces an Inclination for stealing him, stronger than his Fear of Punishment for so doing. This is *Truth* likewise, and *A* acts according to it when he steals the Horse. Besides, if it is prov'd to be a *Truth*, that *A* has not Power over his own Actions, it will be indisputable that he acts according to Truth, and impossible he should do otherwise.

I would not be understood by this to encourage or defend Theft; 'tis only for the sake of the Argument, and will certainly have no *ill Effect*. The Order and Course of Things will not be affected by Reasoning of this Kind; and 'tis as just and necessary, and as much according to Truth, for *B* to dislike and punish the Theft of his Horse, as it is for *A* to steal him.

VII. *If the Creature is thus limited in his Actions, being able to do only such Things as God would have him to do, and not being able to refuse doing what God would have done; then he can have no such Thing as Liberty, Free-Will or Power to do or refrain an Action.*

By *Liberty* is sometimes understood the Absence of Opposition; and in this Sense, indeed, all our Actions may be said to be the Effects of our Liberty: but it is a Liberty of the same Nature with the Fall of a heavy Body to the Ground; it has Liberty to fall, that is, it meets with nothing to hinder its Fall, but at the same Time it is necessitated to fall, and has no Power or Liberty to remain suspended.

But let us take the Argument in another View, and suppose ourselves to be, in the common sense of the Word, *Free Agents*. As Man is a Part of this great

Machine, the Universe, his regular Acting is requisite to the regular moving of the whole. Among the many Things which lie before him to be done, he may, as he is at Liberty and his Choice influenc'd by nothing, (for so it must be, or he is not at Liberty) chuse any one, and refuse the rest. Now there is every Moment something *best* to be done, which is alone then *good*, and with respect to which, every Thing else is at that Time *evil*. In order to know which is best to be done, and which not, it is requisite that we should have at one View all the intricate Consequences of every Action with respect to the general Order and Scheme of the Universe, both present and future; but they are innumerable and incomprehensible by any Thing but Omniscience. As we cannot know these, we have but as one Chance to ten thousand, to hit on the right Action; we should then be perpetually blundering about in the Dark, and putting the Scheme in Disorder; for every wrong Action of a Part, is a Defect or Blemish in the Order of the Whole. Is it not necessary then, that our Actions should be over-rul'd and govern'd by an all-wise Providence? How exact and regular is every Thing in the *natural* World! How wisely in every Part contriv'd! We cannot here find the least Defect! Those who have study'd the mere animal and vegetable Creation, demonstrate that nothing can be more harmonious and beautiful! All the heavenly Bodies, the Stars and Planets, are regulated with the utmost Wisdom! And can we suppose less Care to be taken in the Order of the *moral* than in the *natural* System? It is as if an ingenious Artificer, having fram'd a curious Machine or Clock, and put its many intricate Wheels and Powers in such a Dependance on one another, that the whole might move in the most exact Order and Regularity, had nevertheless plac'd in it several other Wheels endu'd with an independent *Self-Motion*, but ignorant of the general Interest of the Clock; and these would every now and then be moving wrong, disordering the true Movement, and making continual Work for the Mender; which might better be prevented, by depriving them of that Power of Self-Motion, and placing them in a Dependance on the regular Part of the Clock.

VIII. *If there is no such Thing as Free-Will in Creatures, there can be neither Merit nor Demerit in Creatures.*

IX. *And therefore every Creature must be equally esteem'd by the Creator.*

These Propositions appear to be the necessary Consequences of the former. And certainly no Reason can be given, why the Creator should prefer in his Esteem one Part of His Works to another, if with equal Wisdom and Goodness he design'd and created them all, since all Ill or Defect, as contrary to his Nature, is excluded by his Power. We will sum up the Argument thus, When the Creator first design'd the Universe, either it was His Will and Intention that all Things should exist and be in the Manner they are at this Time; or it was his Will they should *be* otherwise i.e. in a different Manner: To say it was His Will Things should be otherwise than they are, is to say Somewhat hath contradicted His Will, and broken His Measures, which is impossible because inconsistent with his Power; therefore we must allow that all Things exist now in a Manner agreeable to His Will, and in consequence of that are all equally Good, and therefore equally esteemed by Him.

I proceed now to shew, that as all the Works of the Creator are equally esteem'd by Him, so they are, as in Justice they ought to be, equally us'd.

Sect. II. Of Pleasure and Pain

I. *When a Creature is form'd and endu'd with Life, 'tis suppos'd to receive a Capacity of the Sensation of* Uneasiness *or* Pain.

It is this distinguishes Life and Consciousness from unactive unconscious Matter. To know or be sensible of Suffering or being acted upon is *to live;* and whatsoever is not so, among created Things, is properly and truly *dead.*

All *Pain* and *Uneasiness* proceeds at first from and is caus'd by Somewhat without and distinct from the Mind itself. The Soul must first be acted upon before it can re-act. In the Beginning of Infancy it is as if it were not; it is not conscious of its own Existence, till it has receiv'd the first Sensation of *Pain;* then and not before, it begins to feel itself, is rous'd, and put into Action; then it discovers its Powers and Faculties, and exerts them to expel the Uneasiness. Thus is the Machine set on work; this is Life. We are first mov'd by *Pain,* and the whole succeeding Course of our Lives is but one continu'd Series of Action with a View to be freed from it. As fast as we have excluded one Uneasiness another appears, otherwise the Motion would cease. If a continual Weight is not apply'd, the Clock will stop. And as soon as the Avenues of Uneasiness to the Soul are choak'd up or cut off, we are dead, we think and act no more.

II. *This Uneasiness, Whenever felt, produces* Desire *to be freed from it, great in exact proportion to the Uneasiness.*

Thus it is *Uneasiness* the first Spring and Cause of all Action; for till we are uneasy in Rest, we can have no Desire to move, and without Desire of moving there can be no voluntary Motion. The Experience of every Man who has observ'd his own Actions will evince the Truth of this; and I think nothing need be said to prove that the *Desire* will be equal to the *Uneasiness,* for the very Thing implies as much: It is not *Uneasiness* unless we desire to be freed from it, nor a great *Uneasiness* unless the consequent Desire is great.

I might here observe, how necessary a Thing in the Order and Design of the Universe this *Pain* or *Uneasiness* is, and how beautiful in its Place! Let us but suppose it just now banish'd the World entirely, and consider the Consequence of it: All the Animal Creation would immediately stand stock still, exactly in the Posture they were in the Moment Uneasiness departed; not a Limb, not a Finger would henceforth move; we should all be reduc'd to the Condition of Statues, dull and unactive: Here I should continue to sit motionless with the Pen in my Hand thus—and neither leave my Seat nor write one Letter more. This may appear odd at first View, but a little Consideration will make it evident; for 'tis impossible to assign any other Cause for the voluntary

Motion of an Animal than its *uneasiness* in Rest. What a different Appearance then would the Face of Nature make, without it! How necessary is it! And how unlikely that the Inhabitants of the World ever were, or that the Creator ever design'd they should be, exempt from it!

I would likewise observe here, that the VIIIth Proposition, in the preceding Section, viz. *That there is neither Merit nor Demerit,* &c. is here again demonstrated, as infallibly, tho' in another manner: For since *Freedom from Uneasiness* is the End of all our Actions, how is it possible for us to do any Thing disinterested? How can any Action be meritorious of Praise or Dispraise, Reward or Punishment, when the natural Principle of *Self-Love* is the only and the irresistible Motive to it?

III. *This* Desire *is always fulfill'd or satisfy'd.*

In the *Design* or *End* of it, tho' not in the *Manner.* The first is requisite, the latter not. To exemplify this, let us make a Supposition; A Person is confin'd in a House which appears to be in imminent Danger of Falling, this, as soon as perceiv'd, creates a violent *Uneasiness,* and that instantly produces an equal strong *Desire,* the *End* of which is *freedom from the Uneasiness,* and the *Manner* or Way propos'd to gain this *End,* is *to get out of the House.* Now if he is convinc'd by any Means, that he is mistaken, and the House is not likely to fall, he is immediately freed from his *Uneasiness,* and the *End* of his Desire is attain'd as well as if it had been in the *Manner* desir'd, viz. *leaving the House.*

All our different Desires and Passions proceed from and are reducible to this one Point, *Uneasiness,* tho' the Means we propose to ourselves for expelling of it are infinite. One proposes *Fame,* another *Wealth,* a third *Power,* &c. as the Means to gain this *End*; but tho' these are never attain'd, if the Uneasiness be remov'd by some other Means, the *Desire* is satisfy'd. Now during the Course of Life we are ourselves continually removing successive Uneasinesses as they arise, and the *last* we suffer is remov'd by the *sweet Sleep* of Death.

IV. *The fulfilling or Satisfaction of this* Desire, *produces the Sensation of* Pleasure, *great or small in exact proportion to the* Desire.

Pleasure is that Satisfaction which arises in the Mind upon, and is caus'd by, the accomplishment of our *Desires,* and by no other Means at all; and those Desires being above shewn to be caus'd by our *Pains* or *Uneasinesses,* it follows that *Pleasure* is wholly caus'd by *Pain,* and by no other Thing at all.

V. *Therefore the Sensation of* Pleasure *is equal, or in exact proportion to the Sensation of* Pain. As the *Desire* of being freed from Uneasiness is equal to the *Uneasiness,* and the *Pleasure* of satisfying that Desire equal to the *Desire,* the *Pleasure* thereby produc'd must necessarily be equal to the *Uneasiness* or *Pain* which produces it: Of three Lines, *A, B,* and *C,* if *A* is equal to *B,* and *B* to *C, C* must be equal to *A.* And as our *Uneasinesses* are always remov'd by some Means or other, it follows that *Pleasure* and *Pain* are in their Nature insepa-rable: So many Degrees as one Scale of the Ballance descends, so many exactly

62   the other ascends; and one cannot rise or fall without the Fall or Rise of the other: 'Tis impossible to taste of *Pleasure*, without feeling its preceding proportionate *Pain*; or to be sensible of *Pain*, without having its necessary Consequent *Pleasure*: The *highest Pleasure* is only Consciousness of Freedom from the *deepest Pain*, and Pain is not Pain to us unless we ourselves are sensible of it. They go Hand in Hand; they cannot be divided.

You have a View of the whole Argument in a few familiar Examples: The *Pain* of Abstinence from Food, as it is greater or less, produces a greater or less *Desire* of Eating, the Accomplishment of this *Desire* produces a greater or less *Pleasure* proportionate to it. The *Pain* of Confinement causes the *Desire* of Liberty, which accomplish'd, yields a *Pleasure* equal to that *Pain* of Confinement. The *Pain* of Labour and Fatigue causes the *Pleasure* of Rest, equal to that *Pain*. The *Pain* of Absence from Friends, produces the *Pleasure* of Meeting in exact proportion. &c.

This is the *fixt Nature* of Pleasure and Pain, and will always be found to be so by those who examine it.

One of the most common Arguments for the future Existence of the Soul, is taken from the generally suppos'd Inequality of Pain and Pleasure in the present; and this, notwithstanding the Difficulty by outward Appearances to make a Judgment of another's Happiness, has been look'd upon as almost unanswerable: but since *Pain* naturally and infallibly produces a *Pleasure* in proportion to it, every individual Creature must, in any State of *Life*, have an equal Quantity of each, so that there is not, on that Account, any Occasion for a future Adjustment.

Thus are all the Works of the Creator *equally* us'd by him; And no Condition of Life or Being is in itself better or preferable to another: The Monarch is not more happy than the Slave, nor the Beggar more miserable than Croesus. Suppose *A, B,* and *C,* three distinct Beings; *A* and *B,* animate, capable of *Pleasure* and *Pain, C* an inanimate Piece of Matter, insensible of either. *A* receives ten Degrees of *Pain*, which are necessarily succeeded by ten Degrees of *Pleasure*: *B* receives fifteen of *Pain*, and the consequent equal Number of *Pleasure*: *C* all the while lies unconcern'd, and as he has not suffer'd the former, has no right to the latter. What can be more equal and just than this? When the Accounts come to be adjusted, *A* has no Reason to complain that his Portion of *Pleasure* was five Degrees less than that of *B,* for his Portion of *Pain* was five Degrees less likewise: Nor has *B* any Reason to boast that his *Pleasure* was five Degrees greater than that of *A,* for his *Pain* was proportionate: They are then both on the same Foot with *C,* that is, they are neither Gainers nor Losers.

It will possibly be objected here, that even common Experience shews us, there is not in Fact this Equality: "Some we see hearty, brisk and chearful perpetually, while others are constantly burden'd with a heavy Load of Maladies and Misfortunes, remaining for Years perhaps in Poverty, Disgrace, or

Pain, and die at last without any Appearance of Recompense." Now tho' 'tis not necessary, when a Proposition is demonstrated to be a general Truth, to shew in what manner it agrees with the particular Circumstances of Persons, and indeed ought not to be requir'd; yet, as this is a common Objection, some Notice may be taken of it: And here let it be observ'd, that we cannot be proper Judges of the good or bad Fortune of Others; we are apt to imagine, that what would give us a great Uneasiness or a great Satisfaction, has the same Effect upon others: we think, for Instance, those unhappy, who must depend upon Charity for a mean Subsistence, who go in Rags, fare hardly, and are despis'd and scorn'd by all; not considering that Custom renders all these Things easy, familiar, and even pleasant. When we see Riches, Grandeur and a chearful Countenance, we easily imagine Happiness accompanies them, when often-times 'tis quite otherwise: Nor is a constantly sorrowful Look, attended with continual Complaints, an infallible Indication of Unhappiness. In short, we can judge by nothing but Appearances, and they are very apt to deceive us. Some put on a gay chearful Outside, and appear to the World perfectly at Ease, tho' even then, some inward Sting, some secret Pain imbitters all their Joys, and makes the Ballance even: Others appear continually dejected and full of Sor-row; but even Grief itself is sometimes *pleasant*, and Tears are not always with-out their Sweetness: Besides, Some take a Satisfaction in being thought un-happy, (as others take a Pride in being thought humble,) these will paint their Misfortunes to others in the strongest Colours, and leave no Means unus'd to make you think them thoroughly miserable; so great a *Pleasure* it is to them *to be pitied*; Others retain the Form and outside Shew of Sorrow, long after the Thing itself, with its Cause, is remov'd from the Mind; it is a Habit they have acquir'd and cannot leave. These, with many others that might be given, are Reasons why we cannot make a true Estimate of the *Equality* of the Happiness and Unhappiness of others; and unless we could, Matter[s] of Fact cannot be opposed to this Hypothesis. Indeed, we are sometimes apt to think, that the Uneasinesses we ourselves have had, outweigh our Pleasures; but the Reason is this, the Mind takes no Account of the latter, they slip away unremark'd, when the former leave more lasting Impressions on the Memory. But suppose we pass the greatest part of Life in Pain and Sorrow, suppose we die by Tor-ments and *think no more*, 'tis no diminution to the Truth of what is here advanc'd; for the *Pain*, tho' exquisite, is not so to the *last* Moments of Life, the Senses are soon benumb'd, and render'd incapable of transmitting it so sharply to the Soul as at first; She perceives it cannot hold long, and 'tis an *exquisite Pleasure* to behold the immediate Approaches of Rest. This makes an Equivalent tho' Annihilation should follow: For the Quantity of *Pleasure* and *Pain* is not to be measur'd by its Duration, any more than the Quantity of Matter by its Extension; and as one cubic Inch may be made to contain, by Condensation, as much Matter as would fill ten thousand cubic Feet, being

64   more expanded, so one single Moment of *Pleasure* may outweigh and compensate an Age of *Pain*.

It was owing to their Ignorance of the Nature of Pleasure and Pain that the Antient Heathens believ'd the idle Fable of their Elizium, that State of uninterrupted Ease and Happiness! The Thing is intirely impossible in Nature! Are not the Pleasures of the Spring made such by the Disagreeableness of the Winter? Is not the Pleasure of fair Weather owing to the Unpleasantness of foul? Certainly. Were it then always Spring, were the Fields always green and flourishing, and the Weather constantly serene and fair, the Pleasure would pall and die upon our Hands; it would cease to be Pleasure to us, when it is not usher'd in by Uneasiness. Could the Philosopher visit, in reality, every Star and Planet with as much Ease and Swiftness as he can now visit their Ideas, and pass from one to another of them in the Imagination; it would be a *Pleasure* I grant; but it would be only in proportion to the *Desire* of accomplishing it, and that would be no greater than the *Uneasiness* suffer'd in the Want of it. The Accomplishment of a long and difficult Journey yields a great *Pleasure;* but if we could take a Trip to the Moon and back again, as frequently and with as much Ease as we can go and come from Market, the Satisfaction would be just the same.

The *Immateriality* of the Soul has been frequently made use of as an Argument for its *Immortality;* but let us consider, that tho' it should be allow'd to be immaterial, and consequently its Parts incapable of Separation or Destruction by any Thing material, yet by Experience we find, that it is not incapable of Cessation of *Thought,* which is its Action. When the Body is but a little indispos'd it has an evident Effect upon the Mind; and a right Disposition of the Organs is requisite to a right Manner of Thinking. In a sound Sleep sometimes, or in a Swoon, we cease to think at all; tho' the Soul is not therefore than annihilated, but *exists* all the while tho' it does not *act;* and may not this probably be the Case after Death? All our Ideas are first admitted by the Senses and imprinted on the Brain, increasing in Number by Observation and Experience; there they become the Subjects of the Soul's Action. The Soul is a mere Power or Faculty of *contemplating* on, and *comparing* those Ideas when it has them; hence springs Reason: But as it can *think* on nothing but Ideas, it must have them before it can *think* at all. Therefore as it may exist before it has receiv'd any Ideas, it may exist before it *thinks*. To remember a Thing, is to have the Idea of it still plainly imprinted on the Brain, which the Soul can turn to and contemplate on Occasion. To forget a Thing, is to have the Idea of it defac'd and destroy'd by some Accident, or the crouding in and imprinting of great variety of other Ideas upon it, so that the Soul cannot find out its Traces and distinguish it. When we have thus lost the Idea of any one Thing, we can *think* no more, or *cease to think*, on that Thing; and as we can lose the Idea of one Thing, so we may of ten, twenty, a hundred, &c. and even of all Things, because they are not in their Nature permanent; and often during Life we see that some Men, (by an Accident or Distemper affecting the Brain,) lose the greatest Part of their Ideas, and remember very little of their past Actions and Circumstances. Now upon *Death*, and the Destruction of the Body, the Ideas contain'd in the Brain, (which are alone the Subjects of the Soul's Action) being then likewise necessarily destroy'd, the Soul, tho' incapable of Destruction itself, must then necessarily *cease to think* or *act*, having nothing left to think or act upon. It is reduc'd to its first unconscious State before it receiv'd any Ideas. And to cease to *think* is but little different from *ceasing to be*.

Nevertheless, 'tis not impossible that this same *Faculty* of contemplating Ideas may be hereafter united to a new Body, and receive a new Set of Ideas; but that will no way concern us who are now living; for the Identity will be lost, it is no longer that same *Self* but a new Being.

I shall here subjoin a short Recapitulation of the Whole, that it may with all its Parts be comprehended at one View.

1. *It is suppos'd that God the Maker and Governour of the Universe, is infinitely wise, good, and powerful.*

2. *In consequence of his infinite Wisdom and Goodness, it is asserted, that whatever He doth must be infinitely wise and good.*

3. *Unless He be interrupted, and His Measures broken by some other Being, which is impossible because He is Almighty.*

4. *In consequence of His infinite Power, it is asserted, that nothing can exist or be done in the Universe which is not agreeable to His Will, and therefore good.*

5. *Evil is hereby excluded, with all Merit and Demerit; and likewise all preference in the Esteem of God, of one Part of the Creation to another.* This is the Summary of the first Part.

Now our common Notions of Justice will tell us, that if all created Things are equally esteem'd by the Creator, they ought to be equally us'd by Him; and that they are therefore equally us'd, we might embrace for Truth upon the Credit, and as the true Consequence of the foregoing Argument. Nevertheless we proceed to confirm it, by shewing *how* they are equally us'd, and that in the following Manner.

1. *A Creature when endu'd with Life or Consciousness, is made capable of Uneasiness or Pain.*

2. *This Pain produces Desire to be freed from it, in exact proportion to itself.*

3. *The Accomplishment of this Desire produces an equal pleasure.*

4. *Pleasure is consequently equal to Pain.*

From these Propositions it is observ'd,

1. *That every Creature hath as much Pleasure as Pain.*

2. *That Life is not preferable to Insensibility; for Pleasure and Pain destroy one another: That Being which has ten Degrees of Pain subtracted from ten of Pleasure, has nothing remaining, and is upon an equality with that Being which is insensible of both.*

3. *As the first Part proves that all Things must be equally us'd by the Creator because equally esteem'd; so this second Part demonstrates that they are equally esteem'd because equally us'd.*

4. *Since every Action is the Effect of Self-Uneasiness, the Distinction of Virtue and Vice is excluded; and* Prop. VIII. *in* Sect. I. *again demonstrated.*

5. *No State of Life can be happier than the present, because Pleasure and Pain are inseparable.*

Thus both Parts of this Argument agree with and confirm one another, and the Demonstration is reciprocal.

I am sensible that the Doctrine here advanc'd, if it were to be publish'd, would meet with but an indifferent Reception. Mankind naturally and generally love to be flatter'd: Whatever sooths our Pride, and tends to exalt our Species above the rest of the Creation, we are pleas'd with and easily believe, when ungrateful Truths shall be with the utmost Indignation rejected. "What! bring ourselves down to an Equality with the Beasts of the Field! with the *meanest* part of the Creation! 'Tis insufferable!" But, (to use a Piece of *common* Sense) our *Geese* are but *Geese* tho' we may think 'em *Swans*; and Truth will be Truth tho' it sometimes prove mortifying and distasteful.

Articles of Belief and Acts of Religion (1728)

Written just three short years after the Dissertation, *Franklin's* Articles of Belief and Acts of Religion *reflects his subsequent distrust of "metaphysical reasoning," his increasing preoccupation with ethical issues, his dissatisfaction with orthodox Christianity, and his faith in the deistic God of nature and reason. "Disgusted," as he tells us in the* Autobiography, *with the rigidly sectarian and exclusively scriptural sermons of Calvinist ministers, Franklin ceased his intermittent attendance of one of Philadelphia's Presbyterian churches and wrote the* Articles and Acts *as a guide for his own private worship and contemplation. As he laconically notes, "I [turn'd] to the Use of [the* Articles*], and went no more to the public Assemblies."*

While the Dissertation *is a dispassionate exercise in logical speculation, the* Articles and Acts *is a deeply personal statement of Franklin's deistic sympathies. It stresses a pragmatic religion of nature in which orderliness, moral rectitude, self-improvement, and rational devotion are the keynotes. Franklin deliberately avoids references to Christian dogma, instead substituting humanistic expressions of confidence in a lawlike and benevolent deity. The liturgical readings he selects are culled from poets and liberal theologians, not from Scripture or the Westminster Confession. The* Articles and Acts, *in short, is the catechism of a man who has renounced orthodox Christianity as well as dogmatic materialism. It is one of the most touching and succinct of all deistic creeds.*

One feature of Franklin's liturgy has especially exercised the imagination and ingenuity of subsequent commentators: its suggestion that the "Author and Fa-

ther" of all creation has "created many Beings or Gods," each having "for himself one glorious Sun, attended with a beautiful and admirable System of Planets." It is difficult and perhaps impossible at this point to determine how seriously Franklin took this polytheistic tenet or from where he might have derived it. The statement is reminiscent of Plato's account in the Timaeus of the Demiurge's creation of a plurality of lesser gods, but there is no conclusive evidence that Franklin was acquainted with this particular dialogue. A more likely explanation of the notion's source would be Franklin's familiarity with the works of thinkers such as John Ray, Richard Blackmore, and Archbishop Fénelon (mentioned in the Articles and Acts), all of whom theorized about the possibility of multiple gods corresponding to multiple worlds. At any rate, the polytheistic speculations in Franklin's private catechism rarely reemerge in his subsequent writings. Its expression of deistic belief in a "wise and good God, who is the Author of our [rational] System" is, on the other hand, a constant theme.

The Articles and Acts presumably consisted of two distinct sections. The second part, if Franklin ever actually wrote it, is now missing.

First Principles

I Believe there is one Supreme most perfect Being, Author and Father of the Gods themselves.

For I believe that Man is not the most perfect Being but One, rather that as there are many Degrees of Beings his Inferiors, so there are many Degrees of Beings superior to him.

Also, when I stretch my imagination thro' and beyond our System of Planets, beyond the visible fix'd Stars themselves, into that Space that is every Way infinite, and conceive it fill'd with Suns like ours, each with a Chorus of Worlds for ever moving round him, then this little Ball on which we move, seems, even in my narrow Imagination, to be almost Nothing, and my self less than nothing, and of no sort of Consequence.

When I think thus, I imagine it great Vanity in me to suppose that the *Supremely Perfect*, does in the least regard such an inconsiderable Nothing as Man. More especially, since it is impossible for me to have any positive clear Idea of that which is infinite and incomprehensible, I cannot conceive otherwise, than that He, *the infinite Father*, expects or requires no Worship or Praise from us, but that he is even INFINITELY ABOVE IT.

But since there is in all Men something like a natural Principle which enclines them to DEVOTION or the Worship of some unseen Power;

And since Men are endued with Reason superior to all other Animals that we are in our World acquainted with;

Therefore I think it seems required of me, and my Duty, as a Man, to pay Divine Regards to SOMETHING.

I CONCEIVE then, that the INFINITE has created many Beings or Gods, vastly

68 superior to Man, who can better conceive his Perfections than we, and return him a more rational and glorious Praise. As among Men, the Praise of the Ignorant or of Children, is not regarded by the ingenious Painter or Architect, who is honour'd and pleas'd with the Approbation of Wise men and Artists.

It may be that these created Gods, are immortal, or it may be that after many Ages, they are changed, and Others supply their Places.

Howbeit, I conceive that each of these is exceeding wise, and good, and very powerful; and that Each has made for himself, one glorious Sun, attended with a beautiful and admirable System of Planets.

It is that particular wise and good God, who is the Author and Owner of our System, that I propose for the Object of my Praise and Adoration.

For I conceive that he has in himself some of those Passions he has planted in us, and that, since he has given us Reason whereby we are capable of observing his Wisdom in the Creation, he is not above caring for us, being pleas'd with our Praise, and offended when we slight Him, or neglect his Glory.

I conceive for many Reasons that he is a *good Being*, and as I should be happy to have so wise, good and powerful a Being my Friend, let me consider in what Manner I shall make myself most acceptable to him.

Next to the Praise due to his Wisdom, I believe he is pleased and delights in the Happiness of those he has created; and since without Virtue Man can have no Happiness in this World, I firmly believe he delights to see me Virtuous, because he is pleas'd when he sees me Happy.

And since he has created many Things which seem purely design'd for the Delight of Man, I believe he is not offended when he sees his Children solace themselves in any manner of pleasant Exercises and innocent Delights, and I think no Pleasure innocent that is to Man hurtful.

I *love* him therefore for his Goodness and I *adore* him for his Wisdom.

Let me then not fail to praise my God continually, for it is his Due, and it is all I can return for his many Favours and great Goodness to me; and let me resolve to be virtuous, that I may be happy, that I may please Him, who is delighted to see me happy. Amen.

---

1. Adoration   2. Petition.   3. Thanks.

Prel. Being mindful that before I address the DEITY, my soul ought to be calm and Serene, free from Passion and Perturbation, or otherwise elevated with Rational Joy and Pleasure, I ought to use a Countenance that expresses a filial Respect, mixt with a kind of Smiling, that signifies inward Joy, and Satisfaction, and Admiration.

O wise God,
  My good Father,
Thou beholdest the Sincerity of my Heart,
  And of my Devotion;
Grant me a Continuance of thy Favour!

---

(1)

Powerful Goodness, &c.
O Creator, O Father, I believe that thou art Good, and that thou art *pleas'd with the Pleasure* of thy Children.

Praised be thy Name for ever.

(2)

By thy Power hast thou made the glorious Sun, with his attending Worlds; from the Energy of thy mighty Will they first received their prodigious Motion, and by the Wondrous Laws by which they move.

Praised be thy Name for ever.

(3)

By thy Wisdom hast thou formed all Things, Thou hast created Man, bestowing Life and Reason, and plac'd him in Dignity superior to thy other earthly Creatures.

Praised be thy Name for ever.

(4)

Thy wisdom, thy Power, and thy GOODNESS are every where clearly seen; in the Air and in the Water, in the Heavens and on the Earth; Thou providest for the various winged Fowl, and the innumerable Inhabitants of the Water; Thou givest Cold and heat, Rain and Sunshine in their Season, and to the Fruits of the Earth Increase.

Praised be thy Name for ever.

(5)

I believe thou hast given Life to thy Creatures that they might Live, and art not delighted with violent Death and bloody Sacrifices.

Praised be thy Name for ever.

(6)

Thou abhorrest in thy Creatures Treachery and Deceit, Malice, Revenge, Intemperance and every other hurtful Vice; but Thou art a Lover of Justice and Sincerity, of Friendship, Benevolence and every Virtue. Thou art my Friend, my Father, and my Benefactor.

Praised be thy Name, O God, for ever.
Amen.

After this, it will not be improper to read part of some such Book as Ray's Wisdom of God in the Creation or Blackmore on the Creation, or the Archbishop of Cambray's Demonstration of the Being of a God;* &c. or else spend some Minutes in a serious Silence, contemplating on those Subjects.

Then Sing
Milton's Hymn to the Creator**

These are thy Glorious Works, Parent of Good!
Almighty: Thine this Universal Frame,
Thus wondrous fair! Thy self how wondrous then!
Speak ye who best can tell, Ye Sons of Light,
Angels, for ye behold him, and with Songs,
And Choral Symphonies, Day without Night
Circle his Throne rejoicing. You in Heav'n,
On Earth, join all Ye Creatures to extol
Him first, him last, him midst and without End.
Fairest of Stars, last in the Train of Night,
If rather thou belong'st not to the Dawn,
Sure Pledge of Day! That crown'st the smiling Morn
With thy bright Circlet; Praise him in thy Sphere
While Day arises, that sweet Hour of Prime.
Thou Sun, of this Great World both Eye and Soul
Acknowledge Him thy Greater, Sound his Praise
In thy Eternal Course; both when thou climb'st,
And when high Noon hast gain'd, and when thou fall'st.
Moon! that now meet'st the orient Sun, now fly'st
With the fix'd Stars, fix'd in their Orb that flies,
And ye five other Wandering Fires, that move
In mystic Dance, not without Song, resound
His Praise, that out of Darkness call'd up Light.
Air! and ye Elements! the Eldest Birth
Of Nature's Womb, that in Quaternion run

---

*Ed.: John Ray, *The Wisdom of God Manifested in the Works of the Creation* (London, 1691); Richard Blackmore, *Creation: A Philosophical Poem* (London, 1712); and Fénelon, Archbishop of Cambrai, *A Demonstration of the Existence and Attributes of God, Drawn from the Knowledge of Nature, from Proofs Purely Intellectual, and from the Ideas of the Infinite Himself,* second edition (London, 1720).
**Ed.: From *Paradise Lost,* Book 5, vv. 153–56, 160–204.

Perpetual Circle, multiform; and mix
And nourish all Things, let your ceaseless Change
Vary to our great Maker still new Praise.
Ye Mists and Exhalations! that now rise
From Hill or steaming Lake, dusky or grey,
Till the Sun paint your fleecy Skirts with Gold,
In Honour to the World's Great Author rise.
Whether to deck with Clouds th' uncolour'd Sky
Or wet the thirsty Earth with falling show'rs,
Rising or falling still advance his Praise.
His Praise, ye Winds! that from 4 Quarters blow,
Breathe soft or loud; and wave your Tops ye Pines!
With every Plant, in Sign of Worship wave.
Fountains! and ye that warble as ye flow
Melodious Murmurs, warbling tune his Praise.
Join Voices all ye living Souls, ye Birds!
That singing, up to Heav'n's high Gate ascend,
Bear on your Wings, and in your Notes his Praise.
Ye that in Waters glide! and ye that walk
The Earth! and stately Tread, or lowly Creep;
Witness *if I be silent*, Ev'n or Morn,
To Hill or Valley, Fountain or Fresh Shade,
Made Vocal by my Song, and taught his Praise.

Here follows the Reading of some Book or part of a Book
Discoursing on and exciting to MORAL VIRTUE

Petition

Prel. In as much as by Reason of our Ignorance We cannot be Certain
that many Things Which we often hear mentioned in the Petitions
of Men to the Deity, would prove REAL GOODS if they were in our
Possession, and as I have Reason to hope and believe that the
Goodness of my Heavenly Father will not withhold from me a suitable Share of Temporal Blessings, if by a VIRTUOUS and HOLY Life I
merit his Favour and Kindness, Therefore I presume not to ask such
Things, but rather Humbly, and with a sincere Heart express my
earnest Desires that he would graciously assist my Continual
Endeavours and Resolutions of eschewing Vice and embracing Virtue; Which kind of Supplications will at least be thus far beneficial,
as they remind me in a solemn manner of my Extensive DUTY.

72 That I may be preserved from Atheism and Infidelity, Impiety and Profaneness, and in my Addresses to Thee carefully avoid Irreverence and Ostentation, Formality and odious Hypocrisy,

Help me, O Father

That I may be loyal to my Prince, and faithful to my Country, careful for its Good, valiant in its Defence, and Obedient to its Laws, abhorring Treason as much as Tyranny,

Help me, O Father

That I may to those above me be dutiful, humble, and submissive, avoiding Pride, disrespect and Contumacy,

Help me, O Father

That I may to those below me, be gracious, Condescending and Forgiving, using Clemency, protecting *Innocent Distress*, avoiding Cruelty, Harshness and Oppression, Insolence and unreasonable Severity,

Help me, O Father

That I may refrain from Calumny and Detraction; that I may avoid and abhor Deceit and Envy, Fraud, Flattery and Hatred, Malice, Lying and Ingratitude,

Help me, O Father

That I may be sincere in Friendship, faithful in Trust, and impartial in Judgment, watchful against Pride, and against Anger (that momentary Madness),

Help me, O Father

That I may be just in all my Dealings and temperate in my Pleasures, full of Candour and Ingenuity, Humanity and Benevolence,

Help me, O Father

That I may be grateful to my Benefactors and generous to my Friends, exerting Charity and Liberality to the Poor, and Pity to the Miserable,

Help me, O Father

That I may avoid Avarice, Ambition, and Intemperance, Luxury and Lasciviousness,

Help me, O Father

That I may possess Integrity and Evenness of Mind, Resolution in Difficulties, and Fortitude under Affliction; that I may be punctual in performing my Promises, peaceable and prudent in my Behaviour,

Help me, O Father

That I may have Tenderness for the Weak, and a reverent Respect for the Ancient; that I may be kind to my Neighbours, good-natured to my Companions, and hospitable to Strangers,

Help me, O Father

That I may be averse to Craft and Overreaching, abhor Extortion, Perjury, and every kind of Wickedness,

Help me, O Father

That I may be honest and Openhearted, gentle, merciful and Good, cheerful in Spirit, rejoicing in the Good of Others,

> Help me, O Father

That I may have a constant Regard to Honour and Probity; that I may possess a perfect Innocence and a good Conscience, and at length become Truly Virtuous and Magnanimous,

> Help me, Good God,
> Help me, O Father

And forasmuch as Ingratitude is one of the most odious of Vices, let me not be unmindful gratefully to acknowledge the Favours I receive from Heaven.

Thanks.

For Peace and Liberty, for Food and Raiment, for Corn and Wine, and Milk, and every kind of Healthful Nourishment,

> *Good God, I Thank thee.*

For the Common Benefits of Air and Light, for useful Fire and delicious Water,

> *Good God, I Thank thee.*

For Knowledge and Literature and every useful Art; for my Friends and their Prosperity, and for the fewness of my Enemies,

> *Good God, I Thank thee.*

For all thy innumerable Benefits; for Life and Reason, and the Use of Speech, for Health and Joy and every Pleasant Hour,

> *Good God, I Thank thee. . . .*

Doctrine to Be Preached (1731)

Franklin describes himself in his Autobiography *as an inveterate scribbler of private reflections, passing thoughts, and outlines of planned (but often never written) works. This selection, probably composed in 1731, appears to have been a memorandum Franklin intended to work up into a public discourse—possibly to be delivered at a meeting of the Philadelphia Junto Society, which Franklin had founded in 1727. It is not known whether he actually "preached" this doctrine at some time, but the memo reemerged some forty years later in abbreviated form in the* Autobiography *(see selections from the* Autobiography, *below).*

The piece is an encapsulated account of Franklin's deistic orientation, stressing the rational imperatives of virtue and knowledge.

That there is one God Father of the Universe.
That he [is] infinitely good, Powerful and wise.

That he is omnipresent.

That he ought to be worshipped, by Adoration Prayer and Thanksgiving both in publick and private.

That he loves such of his Creatures as love and do good to others: and will reward them either in this World or hereafter.

That Men's Minds do not die with their Bodies, but are made more happy or miserable after this Life according to their Actions.

That Virtuous Men ought to league together to strengthen the Interest of Virtue, in the World: and so strengthen themselves in Virtue.

That Knowledge and Learning is to be cultivated, and Ignorance dissipated.

That none but the Virtuous are wise.

That Man's Perfection is in Virtue.

On the Providence of God in the Government of the World (1732)

On the Providence of God, *which Franklin recorded in his Commonplace Book, appears to be the draft of a speech he delivered or intended to deliver to his "Pot Companions" of the Junto Society.*

The essay is interesting on several counts. First, it indicates how far Franklin had retreated by 1732 from his earlier denial in the Dissertation *of human freedom. In this piece, he still considers the deity to be all-powerful and supremely good, but he now thinks it reasonable to suppose that since God is also infinitely free— that is, totally unconstrained by externalities—he imparts a spark of divine freedom (along with power and goodness) to the creatures made in his image.*

Moreover, Franklin argues that the omnibenevolent nature of God is such that he neither arbitrarily predestines certain individuals to eternal damnation and others to eternal bliss—a clear jab at Calvinism—nor totally distances himself from creation by leaving humans to the whimsy of chance. Neither course of action would be worthy of a deity who is supremely wise, good, and powerful. Instead, Franklin concludes that, given the "Power of the Deity," the only rational account of his relationship to creation is that he occasionally "interferes by his particular Providence and sets aside the Effects which would otherwise have been produced."

It is not at all clear how we are to read this passage. If by "interferes by his particular Providence" Franklin means the deity directly intervenes in the system of physical laws he has established—thereby, for example, magically preventing otherwise inevitable natural disasters such as earthquakes—then he seems to have stepped out of character, offering a most undeistic and obviously Calvinist doctrine of miracles and special providences. But there is no reason to suppose this is what Franklin had in mind. Instead, it seems more plausible to interpret his argument as a defense of the assumption that divine providence can sway, without necessarily coercing, human sentiment away from evil and toward virtue. It is significant, for example, that the illustration with which Franklin highlights his point is a political rather than physical one: God's infinite goodness can prompt him to interfere with wicked ambitions in such a way as to "deliver" an oppressed but righteous nation from the grip of a "cruel Tyrant." This interpretation of providence allows Franklin, in typical deistic fashion, to salvage divine power and goodness without sacrificing either human freedom or the mechanistic orderliness of the physical realm. At any rate, his rather murky attempt to accentuate the benevolence of the deity, even to the extent of pushing himself into a corner possibly incompatible with his deism, only underscores Franklin's growing preoccupation with ethical matters.

Finally, it should be noted that Franklin's discussion of divine attributes as well as providence is based on inductive extrapolations from experience. Like all deists, he was intensely suspicious of a priori metaphysical speculation or ecclesial (and supposedly revealed) authority, believing instead that knowledge of the deity is best gleaned from an examination of the "book of nature." His analysis of divine providence, as he says, is not founded on "The Authority of any Books or Men how sacred soever; because I know that no Authority is more convincing to Men of Reason than the Authority of Reason itself."

When I consider my own Weakness, and the discerning Judgment of those who are to be my Audience, I cannot help blaming my self considerably, for this rash Undertaking of mine, it being a Thing I am altogether ill practis'd in and very much unqualified for; I am especially discouraged when I reflect that you are all my intimate Pot Companions who have heard me say a 1000 silly Things in Conversations, and therefore have not that laudable Partiality and Veneration for whatever I shall deliver that Good people commonly have for their Spiritual Guides; that You have no Reverence for my Habit, nor for the Sanctity of my Countenance; that you do not believe me inspir'd or divinely assisted, and therefore will think your Selves at Liberty to assent or dissent, agree or disagree, of any Thing I advance, canvassing and sifting it as the private Opinion of one of your Acquaintance. These are great Disadvantages and Discouragements but I am enter'd and must proceed, humbly requesting your Patience and Attention.

I propose at this Time to discourse on the Subject of our last Conversation: The Providence of God in the Government of the World. I shall not attempt to amuse you with Flourishes of Rhetorick, were I master of that deceitful Science because I know ye are Men of substantial Reason and can easily discern between sound Argument and the false Glosses of Oratory; nor shall I endeavor to impose on your Ears, by a musical Accent in delivery, in the Tone of one violently affected with what he says; for well I know that ye are far from

76 being superstitious [or] fond of unmeaning Noise, and that ye believe a Thing to be no more true for being sung than said. I intend to offer you nothing but plain Reasoning, devoid of Art and Ornament; unsupported by the Authority of any Books or Men how sacred soever; because I know that no Authority is more convincing to Men of Reason than the Authority of Reason itself. It might be judg'd an Affront to your Understandings should I go about to prove this first Principle, the Existence of a Deity and that he is the Creator of the Universe, for that would suppose you ignorant of what all Mankind in all Ages have agreed in. I shall therefore proceed to observe: 1. That he must be a Being of great Wisdom; 2. That he must be a Being of great Goodness and 3. That he must be a Being of great Power. That he must be a Being of infinite Wisdom, appears in his admirable Order and Disposition of Things, whether we consider the heavenly bodies, the Stars and Planets, and their wonderful regular Motions, or this Earth compounded of such an Excellent mixture of all the Elements; or the admirable Structure of Animal Bodies of such infinite Variety, and yet every one adapted to its Nature, and the Way of Life it is to be placed in, whether on Earth, in the Air or in the Waters, and so exactly that the highest and most exquisite human Reason, cannot find a fault and say this would have been better so or in another Manner, which whoever considers attentively and thoroughly will be astonish'd and swallow'd up in Admiration.

2. That the Deity is a Being of great Goodness, appears in his giving Life to so many Creatures, each of which acknowledge it a Benefit by their unwillingess to leave it; in his providing plentiful Sustenance for them all, and making those Things that are most useful, most common and easy to be had; such as Water necessary for almost every Creature's Drink; Air without which few could subsist, the inexpressible Benefits of Light and Sunshine to almost all Animals in general; and to Men the most useful Vegetables, such as Corn, the most useful of Metals as Iron, and the most useful Animals, as Horses, Oxen and Sheep, he has made easiest to raise, or procure in Quantity or Numbers: each of which particulars if considered seriously and carefully would fill us with the highest Love and Affection. 3. That he is a Being of infinite Power appears, in his being able to form and compound such Vast Masses of Matter as this Earth and the Sun and innumerable Planets and Stars, and give them such prodigious Motion, and yet so to govern them in their greatest Velocity as that they shall not flie off out of their appointed Bounds nor dash one against another, to their mutual Destruction; but 'tis easy to conceive his Power, when we are convinc'd of his infinite Knowledge and Wisdom; for if weak and foolish Creatures as we are, by knowing the Nature of a few Things can produce such wonderful Effects; such as for instance by knowing the Nature only of Nitre and Sea Salt mix'd we can make a Water which will dissolve the hardest Iron and by adding one Ingredient more, can make another Water which will dissolve Gold and render the most Solid Bodies fluid—and by knowing the Na-

ture of Salt Peter Sulphur and Charcoal those mean Ingredients mix'd we can shake the Air in the most terrible Manner, destroy Ships Houses and Men at a Distance and in an Instant, overthrow Cities, rend Rocks into a Thousand Pieces, and level the highest Mountains. What Power must he possess who not only knows the Nature of every Thing in the Universe, but can make Things of new Natures with the greatest Ease and at his Pleasure!

Agreeing then that the World was at first made by a Being of infinite Wisdom, Goodness and Power, which Being we call God; The State of Things ever since and at this Time must be in one of these four following manners, viz.

1. Either he unchangeably decreed and appointed every Thing that comes to pass; and left nothing to the Course [of] Nature, nor allow'd any Creature free agency, or

2. Without decreeing any thing, he left all to general Nature and the Events of Free Agency in his Creatures, which he never alters or interrupts, or

3. He decreed some Things unchangeable, and left others to general Nature and the Events of Free Agency, which also he never alters or interrupts; or

4. He sometimes interferes by his particular Providence and sets aside the Effects which would otherwise have been produced by any of the Above Causes.

I shall endeavour to shew the first 3 Suppositions to be inconsistent with the common Light of Reason; and that the 4th is most agreeable to it, and therefore most probably true.

In the 1. place. If you say he has in the Beginning unchangeably decreed all Things and left Nothing to Nature or free Agency. These Strange Conclusions will necessarily follow; 1. That he is now no more a God. 'Tis true indeed, before he had made such unchangeable Decree, he was a Being of Power, Almighty; but now having determin'd every Thing, he has divested himself of all further Power, he has done and has no more to do, he has ty'd up his Hands, and has now no greater Power than an Idol of Wood or Stone; nor can there be any more Reason for praying to him or worshipping of him, than of such an Idol for the Worshippers can never [be] the better for such Worship. Then 2. he has decreed some things contrary to the very Notion of a wise and good Being; Such as that some of his Creatures or Children shall do all Manner of Injury to others and bring every kind of Evil upon them without Cause; that some of them shall even blaspheme him their Creator in the most horrible manner; and, which is still more highly absurd that he has decreed the greatest Part of Mankind, shall in all Ages, put up their earnest Prayers to him both in private and publickly in great Assemblies, when all the while he had so determin'd their Fate that he could not possibly grant them any Benefits on that Account, nor could such Prayers be any way available. When then should he ordain them to make such Prayers? It cannot be imagined they are of any Service to him. Surely it is not more difficult to believe the World was made by a God of Wood or Stone, than that the God who made the World should be such a God as this.

In the 2. Place. If you say he has decreed nothing but left all things to general Nature, and the Events of Free Agency, which he never alters or interrupts. Then these Conclusions will follow; He must either utterly hide him self from the Works of his Hands, and take no Notice at all of their Proceedings natural or moral; or he must be as undoubtedly he is, a Spectator of every thing; for there can be no Reason or Ground to suppose the first—I say there can be no Reason to imagine he would make so glorious a Universe merely to abandon it. In this Case imagine the Deity looking on and beholding the Ways of his Creatures; some Heroes in Virtue he sees are incessantly indeavouring the Good of others, they labour thro vast difficulties, they suffer incredible Hardships and Miseries to accomplish this End, in hopes to please a Good God, and obtain his Favour, which they earnestly Pray for; what Answer can he make them within himself but this; *take the Reward Chance may give you, I do not intermeddle in these Affairs*; he sees others continually doing all manner of Evil, and bringing by their Actions Misery and Destruction among Mankind: What can he say here but this, *if Chance rewards you I shall not punish you, I am not to be concerned*. He sees the just, the innocent and the Beneficent in the Hands of the wicked and violent Oppressor; and when the good are at the Brink of Destruction they pray to him, *thou, O God, art mighty and powerful to save; help us we beseech thee*: He answers, *I cannot help you, 'tis none of my Business nor do I at all regard these things*. How is it possible to believe a wise and an infinitely Good Being can be delighted in this Circumstance; and be utterly unconcern'd what becomes of the Beings and Things he has created; for thus, we must believe him idle and unactive, and that his glorious Attributes of Power, Wisdom and Goodness are no more to be made use of.

In the Third Place. If you say he has decreed some things and left others to the Events of Nature and Free Agency, Which he never alters or interrupts; Still you unGod him, if I may be allow'd the Expression; he has nothing to do; he can cause us neither Good nor harm; he is no more to be regarded than a lifeless Image, than Dagon, or Baal, or Bell and the Dragon; and as in both the other Suppositions foregoing, that Being which from its Power is most able to Act, from its Wisdom knows best how to act, and from its Goodness would always certainly act best, is in this Opinion supposed to become the most unactive of all Beings and remain everlastingly Idle; an Absurdity, which when considered or but barely seen, cannot be swallowed without doing the greatest Violence to common Reason, and all the Faculties of the Understanding.

We are then necessarily driven into the fourth Supposition, That the Deity sometimes interferes by his particular Providence, and sets aside the Events which would otherwise have been produc'd in the Course of Nature, or by the Free Agency of Men; and this is perfectly agreeable with what we can know of his Attributes and Perfections: But as some may doubt whether 'tis possible there should be such a Thing as free Agency in Creatures; I shall just offer one Short Argument on that Account and proceed to shew how the duties of Religion necessarily follow the Belief of a Providence. You acknowledge that God is infinitely Powerful, Wise and Good, and also a free Agent; and you will not deny that he has communicated to us part of his Wisdom, Power and Goodness; i.e. he has made us in some Degree Wise, potent and good; and is it then impossible for him to communicate any Part of his Freedom, and make us also in some Degree Free? Is not even his *infinite* Power sufficient for this? I should be glad to hear what Reason any Man can give for thinking in that Manner; 'tis sufficient for me to shew tis not impossible, and no Man I think can shew 'tis improbable, but much more might be offer'd to demonstrate clearly that Men are in some Degree free Agents, and accountable for their Actions; however, this I may possibly reserve for another Discourse hereafter if I find Occasion.

Lastly If God does not sometimes interfere by his Providence tis either because he cannot, or because he will not; which of these Positions will you choose? There is a righteous Nation grievously oppress'd by a cruel Tyrant, they earnestly intreat God to deliver them; If you say he cannot, you deny his infinite Power, which at first acknowledg'd; if you say he will not, you must directly deny his infinite Goodness. You are then of necessity oblig'd to allow, that 'tis highly reasonable to believe a Providence because tis highly absurd to believe otherwise.

Now if tis unreasonable to suppose it out of the Power of the Deity to help and favour us particularly or that we are out of his Hearing or Notice or that Good Actions do not procure more of his Favour than ill Ones. Then I conclude, that believing a Providence we have the Foundation of all true Religion; for we should love and revere that Deity for his Goodness and thank him for his Benefits; we should adore him for his Wisdom, fear him for his Power, and pray to him for his Favour and Protection; and this Religion will be a Powerful Regulator of our Actions, give us Peace and Tranquility within our own Minds, and render us Benevolent, Useful and Beneficial to others.

Self-Denial Not the Essence of Virtue (1735)

This short piece of Franklin's appeared anonymously in his Pennsylvania Gazette. *That the "correspondent" is actually Franklin himself is indicated by a passage in his* Autobiography *in which he confesses that from time to time the* Gazette *ran "little Pieces of my own which had been first compos'd for Reading in our Junto." One of these journalistic squibs was "a Discourse on Self denial, showing that Virtue was not secure, till its Practice became a Habitude, and was free from the Opposition of contrary Inclination."*

Self-Denial Not the Essence of Virtue *is vintage Franklin. In it we see him*

80   *once again hammering away at what he takes to be irrational Christian dogma—in this case, the ethical excellence of asceticism—and offering as a normative substitute a quite Aristotelian analysis of virtue as rational habituation to good actions. What is of moral significance for Franklin is pragmatic consequence, not the purity (or lack thereof) of intention. The assumption that ethical actions are utility-laden and promotive of the commonweal is characteristic of deism.*

Franklin's publication of this piece on self-denial was probably intended as much to raise hackles as to instruct and edify. Whether it succeeded in the latter goal is unknown, but it certainly accomplished the former, prompting an indignant response in the 4 March issue of the American Weekly Mercury. *We also know that Franklin took to heart his definition of virtue as habituation to good deeds. His self-imposed "program for arriving at moral perfection," described in the* Autobiography, *had its origins in precisely this analysis (see selections from the* Autobiography, *below).*

To the Printer of the *Gazette.*

   That SELF-DENIAL *is not the* ESSENCE OF VIRTUE.

It is commonly asserted, that without *Self-Denial* there is no Virtue, and that the greater the *Self-Denial* the greater the Virtue.

If it were said, that he who cannot deny himself in any Thing he inclines to, tho' he knows it will be to his Hurt, has not the Virtue of *Resolution* or *Fortitude*, it would be intelligible enough; but as it stands it seems obscure or erroneous.

Let us consider some of the Virtues singly.

If a Man has no inclination to *wrong* People in his Dealings, if he feels no Temptation to it, and therefore never does it; can it be said that he is not a just Man? If he is a just Man, has he not the Virtue of Justice?

If to a certain Man, idle Diversions have nothing in them that is tempting, and therefore he never relaxes his Application to Business for their Sake; is he not an Industrious Man? Or has he not the Virtue of Industry?

I might in like manner instance in all the rest of the Virtues: But to make the Thing short, As it is certain, that the more we strive against the Temptation to any Vice, and practise the contrary Virtue, the weaker will that Temptation be, and the stronger will be that Habit; 'till at length the Temptation has no Force, or entirely vanishes: Does it follow from thence, that in our Endeavours to overcome Vice, we grow continually less and less Virtuous; till at length we have no Virtue at all?

If Self-Denial be the Essence of Virtue, then it follows, that the Man who is naturally temperate, just, &c. is not virtuous; but that in order to be virtuous, he must, in spite of his natural Inclinations, wrong his Neighbours, and eat and drink, &c. to excess.

But perhaps it may be said, that by the Word *Virtue* in the above Assertion, is meant, *Merit*; and so it should stand thus; Without Self-Denial there is no Merit; and the greater the Self-Denial the greater the Merit.

The Self-denial here meant, must be when our Inclinations are towards Vice, or else it would still be Nonsense.

By Merit is understood, Desert; and when we say a Man merits, we mean that he deserves Praise or Reward.

We do not pretend to merit any thing of God, for he is above our Services; and the Benefits he confers on us, are the Effects of his Goodness and Bounty.

All our Merit then is with regard to one another, and from one to another.

Taking then the Assertion as it last stands,

If a Man does me a Service from a natural benevolent Inclination, does he deserve less of me than another who does me the like Kindness against his Inclination?

If I have two Journeymen, one naturally industrious, the other idle, but both perform a Days Work equally good, ought I to give the latter the most Wages?

Indeed, lazy Workmen are commonly observ'd to be more extravagant in their Demands than the Industrious; for if they have not more for their Work, they cannot live so well: But tho' it be true to a Proverb, *That Lazy Folks take the most Pains*, does it follow that they deserve the most Money?

If you were to employ Servants in Affairs of Trust, would you not bid more for one you knew was naturally honest, than for one naturally roguish, but who had lately acted honestly? For Currents whose natural Channel is damm'd up, (till the new Course is by Time worn sufficiently deep and become natural,) are apt to break their Banks. If one Servant is more valuable than another, has he not more Merit than the other? And yet this is not on Account of Superior Self-denial.

Is a Patriot not praise-worthy, if Publick Spirit is natural to him?

Is a Pacing-Horse less valuable for being a natural Pacer?

Nor in my Opinion has any Man less Merit for having in general natural virtuous Inclinations.

The Truth is, that Temperance, Justice, Charity, &c. are Virtues, whether practis'd with or against our Inclinations; and the Man who practises them, merits our Love and Esteem: And Self-denial is neither good nor bad, but as 'tis apply'd: He that denies a Vicious Inclination is Virtuous in proportion to his Resolution, but the most perfect Virtue is above all Temptation, such as the Virtue of the Saints in Heaven: And he who does a foolish, indecent or wicked Thing, merely because 'tis contrary to his Inclination, (like some mad Enthu-

82   siasts I have read of, who ran about naked, under the Notion of taking up the Cross) is not practising the reasonable Science of Virtue, but is lunatick.

Dialogue between Two Presbyterians (1735)

Franklin ran this composition in his Pennsylvania Gazette *on 10 April 1735, signing it simply "A.B.C.D." There was good reason for the anonymity. This is one of Franklin's strongest published denunciations of Calvinist doctrine and sectarian parochialism. Although militant deists such as Paine and Palmer later penned criticisms of orthodoxy that make the* Dialogue *seem mild in comparison, its publication was a bold move for the moderate Franklin. (At the risk of sounding uncharitable, it was also a cunning business maneuver for a newspaperman to sell more papers by fanning an already hot issue.)*

There is no doubt, however, that Franklin was angry. The incident that sparked the piece was the persecution (as Franklin saw it) of the Reverend Samuel Hemphill (referred to as "Mr. H." in the Dialogue*). Hemphill was an Irish-born Presbyterian clergyman who emigrated to Pennsylvania in 1734—partly, it seems, because charges of unorthodoxy had gotten him into trouble in Ireland. But his past followed him to the New World. Two early sermons in New Castle prompted an official inquiry into his doctrinal purity. Acquitted by the presbytery, Hemphill left New Castle and moved to Philadelphia, where he became assistant minister to the congregation Franklin earlier had left in disgust. While serving in this capacity, so Franklin tells us, Hemphill regularly preached sermons that had "little of the dogmatical kind, but inculcated strongly the Practice of Virtue, or what in the religious Stile are called Good Works." The officiating minister, one Jebediah Andrews, as well as some members of the congregation, found these sermons theologically unacceptable. On 7 April 1735, Hemphill once again was charged with unorthodoxy, and a synodical commission was called to investigate.*

Franklin was outraged by what he took to be the small-minded sectarianism of the Presbyterian establishment and joined the controversy by defending Hemphill in the Dialogue. *But the work is much more than merely a brief for Hemphill. It is significant as a deistic indictment of one of the central tenets of Calvinism—justification by faith.*

In the Dialogue, *Franklin criticizes the precept that faith (as opposed to good works) is the only road to salvation by turning the Christian establishment's primary weapon—scriptural authority—against it. He argues that a careful study of the Gospels reveals that the main thrust of Jesus' teaching is moral in tenor, that Jesus emphatically tells his followers that good works and not faith in his divinity are the key to the Kingdom of Heaven, and that virtue is "a doctrine exactly agreeable to Christianity." Franklin rhetorically concedes that faith is a necessary condition for virtuous behavior, but he defines "faith" as trust in the purity of Jesus' moral teaching and example, not in his godhead.*

Moreover, Franklin castigates the Calvinist establishment for its assumption that its basic doctrines are infallible. Protestantism, he argues, correctly criticizes the Roman church for its endorsement of papal inerrancy. How then, he asks, "can we modestly claim Infallibility *for our selves or our Synods in our way of Interpreting?" Franklin's point is that humans are by nature fallible in their reasoning and that consequently a rigid fidelity to written-in-stone doctrine is always suspect. As he characteristically observes, "Peace, Unity and Virtue in any Church are more to be regarded than Orthodoxy." These two themes—the importance of virtue and the soundness of keeping an open mind about religious matters—reappear time and again throughout Franklin's writings.*

Franklin's defense of Hemphill was unsuccessful—it may, in fact, have exacerbated Hemphill's already precarious situation. At any rate, Hemphill was unanimously censored by the members of the Commission of the Synod on 27 April 1735. Moreover, the commission suspended him from the ministry for doctrines "Unsound and Dangerous, contrary to the sacred Scriptures and our excellent Confession and Catechisms." Franklin followed up in the 17 July issue of the Gazette *with a harsh criticism of the commission's decision. Again, however, his efforts were to no avail. The verdict against Hemphill remained, and the unhappy minister, as Franklin recalls in his* Autobiography, *"left us in search elsewhere of better fortune."*

. . . *S.* Good Morrow! I am glad to find you well and abroad; for not having seen you at Meeting lately, I concluded you were indispos'd.

T. Tis true I have not been much at Meeting lately, but that was not occasion'd by any Indisposition. In short, I stay at home, or else go to Church, because I do not like Mr. H. Your new-fangled Preacher.

S. I am sorry we should differ in Opinion upon any Account; but let us reason the Point calmly; what Offense does Mr. H. give you?

T. Tis his Preaching disturbs me: He talks of nothing but the Duties of Morality: I do not love to hear so much of Morality: I am sure it will carry no Man to Heaven, and I do not think it fit to be preached in a Christian Congregation.

S. I suppose you think no Doctrine fit to be preached in a Christian congregation, but such as Christ and his Apostles used to preach.

T. To be sure I think so.

S. I do not conceive then how you can dislike the Preaching of Morality, when you consider, that Morality made the principal Part of their Preaching as well as of Mr. H's. What is Christ's Sermon on the Mount but an excellent moral Discourse, towards the end of which, (as foreseeing that People might in time come to depend more upon their *Faith* in him, than upon *Good Works,* for their Salvation) he tells the Hearers plainly, that their saying to him, *Lord,*

84 *Lord,* (that is, professing themselves his Disciples or *Christians*) should give them no Title to Salvation, but their *Doing* the Will of his Father; and that tho' they have prophesied in his Name, yet he will declare to them, as Neglecters of Morality, that he never knew them.

T. But what do you understand by that Expression of Christ's, *Doing the Will of my Father?*

S. I understand it to be the Will of God, that we should live virtuous, upright, and good-doing Lives; as the Prophet understood it, when he said, *What doth the Lord require of thee, O Man, but to do justly, love Mercy, and walk humbly with the Lord thy God.*

T. But is not Faith recommended in the New Testament as well as Morality?

S. Tis true, it is. Faith is recommended as a Means of producing Morality: Our Saviour was a Teacher of Morality or Virtue, and they that were deficient and desired to be taught, ought first to *believe* in him as an able and faithful Teacher. Thus Faith would be a Means of producing Morality, and Morality of Salvation. But that from such Faith alone Salvation may be expected, appears to me to be neither a Christian Doctrine nor a reasonable one. And I should as soon expect, that my bare Believing Mr. Grew* to be an excellent Teacher of the Mathematicks, would make me a Mathematician, as that Believing in Christ would of it self make a Man a Christian.

T. Perhaps you may think, that tho' Faith alone cannot save a Man, Morality or Virtue alone, may.

S. Morality or Virtue is the End, Faith only a Means to obtain that end: And if the End be obtained, it is no matter by what Means. What think you of these Sayings of Christ, when he was reproached for conversing chiefly with gross Sinners, *The whole,* says he, *need not a Physician, but they that are sick;* and, *I come not to call the Righteous, but Sinners, to Repentance:* Does not this imply, that there were good Men, who, without Faith in him, were in a State of Salvation? And moreover, did he not say of Nathanael, while he was yet an Unbeliever in him, and thought no Good could possibly come out of Nazareth, *Behold an Israelite indeed, in whom there is no Guile!* that is, *behold a virtuous upright Man.* Faith in Christ, however, may be and is of great Use to produce a good Life, but that it can conduce nothing towards Salvation where it does not conduce to Virtue, is, I suppose, plain from the Instance of the Devils, who are far from being Infidels, *they believe,* says the Scipture, *and tremble.* There were some indeed, even in the Apostles' Days, that set a great Value upon Faith, distinct from Good Works, they merely idolized it, and

---

*Ed.: The reference is to Theophilus Grew, a popular tutor of mathematics in the Philadelphia area. Grew was appointed professor of mathematics in the Academy and College of Philadelphia in 1751, a position he held until his death eight years later.

thought that a Man ever so righteous could not be saved without it: But one of the Apostles, to show his Dislike of such Notions, tells them, that not only those heinous Sins of Theft, Murder, and Blasphemy, but even *Idleness*, or the Neglect of a Man's Business, was more pernicious than mere harmless Infidelity, *He that neglects to provide for them of his own House*, says he, *is WORSE than an Infidel*. St. James, in his second Chapter, is very zealous against these Cryers-up of Faith, and maintains that Faith without Virtue is useless, *Wilt thou know, O vain Man*, says he, *that Faith without Works is dead*; and, *shew me your Faith without your Works, and I will shew you mine by my Works*. Our Saviour, when describing the Last Judgment, and declaring what shall give Admission into Bliss, or exclude from it, says nothing of *Faith* but what he says against it, that is, that those who cry *Lord, Lord*, and profess to have *believed* in his Name, have no Favour to expect on that Account; but declares that 'tis the Practice, or the omitting the Practice of the Duties of Morality, *Feeding the Hungry, cloathing the Naked, visiting the Sick*, &c. in short, 'tis the Doing or not Doing all the Good that lies in our Power, that will render us the Heirs of Happiness or Misery.

T. But if Faith is of great Use to produce a good Life, why does not Mr. H. preach up Faith as well as Morality?

S. Perhaps it may [be] this, that as the good Physician suits his Physick to the Disease he finds in the Patient, so Mr. H. may possibly think, that though Faith in Christ be properly first preach'd to Heathens and such as are ignorant of the Gospel, yet since he knows that we have been baptized in the Name of Christ, and educated in his Religion, and call'd after his Name, it may not be so immediately necessary to preach *Faith* to us who abound in it, as *Morality* in which we are evidently deficient: For our late Want of Charity to each other, our Heart-burnings and Bickerings are notorious. St. James says, *Where Envying and Strife is, there is Confusion and every evil Work*: and where Confusion and every evil Work is, *Morality* and Good-will to Men, can, I think, be no unsuitable Doctrine. But surely *Morality* can do us no harm. Upon a Supposition that we all have Faith in Christ already, as I think we have, where can be the Damage of being exhorted to Good Works? Is Virtue Heresy; and Universal Benevolence False Doctrine, that any of us should keep away from Meeting because it is preached there?

T. Well, I do not like it, and I hope we shall not long be troubled with it. A Commission of the Synod will sit in a short Time, and try this Sort of Preaching.

S. I am glad to hear that the Synod are to take it into Consideration. There are Men of unquestionable Good Sense as well as Piety among them, and I doubt not but they will, by their Decision, deliver our Profession from the satirical Reflection, which a few uneasy People of our Congregation have of late given Occasion for, to wit, That the Presbyterians are going to persecute, silence and condemn a good Preacher, for exhorting them to be honest and charitable to one another and the rest of Mankind.

T. If Mr. H. is a Presbyterian Teacher, he ought to preach as Presbyterians used to preach; or else he may justly be condemn'd and silenc'd by our Church Authority. We ought to abide by the Westminster Confession of Faith; and he that does not, ought not to preach in our Meetings.

S. The Apostasy of the Church from the primitive Simplicity of the Gospel, came on by Degrees; and do you think that the Reformation was of a sudden perfect, and that the first Reformers knew at once all that was right or wrong in Religion? Did not Luther at first preach only against selling of Pardons, allowing all the other Practices of the Romish Church for good? He afterwards went further, and Calvin, some think, yet further. The Church of England made a Stop, and fix'd her Faith and Doctrine by 39 Articles; with which the Presbyterians not satisfied, went yet farther; but being too self-confident to think, that as their Fathers were mistaken in some Things, they also might be in some others; and fancying themselves infallible in *their* Interpretations, they also ty'd themselves down by the Westminster Confession. But has not a Synod that meets in King George the Second's Reign, as much Right to interpret Scripture, as one that met in Oliver's Time? And if any Doctrine then maintain'd is, or shall hereafter be found not altogether orthodox, why must we be for ever confin'd to that, or to any, Confession?

T. But if the Majority of the Synod be against any Innovation, they may justly hinder the Innovator from Preaching.

S. That is as much as to say, if the Majority of the Preachers be in the wrong, they may justly hinder any Man from setting the People right; for a *Majority* may be in the wrong as well as the *Minority*, and frequently are. In the beginning of the Reformation, the *Majority* was vastly against the Reformers, and continues so to this Day; and, if, according to your Opinion, they had a Right to silence the *Minority*, I am sure the *Minority* ought to have been silent. But tell me, if the Presbyterians in this Country, being charitably inclin'd, should send a Missionary into Turkey, to propagate the Gospel, would it not be unreasonable in the Turks to prohibit his Preaching?

T. It would, to be sure, because he comes to them for their good.

S. And if the Turks, believing us in the wrong, as we think them, should out of the same charitable Disposition, send a Missionary to preach Mahometanism to us, ought we not in the same manner to give him free Liberty of preaching his Doctrine?

T. It may be so; but what would you infer from that?

S. I would only infer, that if it would be thought reasonable to suffer a Turk to preach among us a Doctrine diametrically opposite to Christianity, it cannot be reasonable to silence one of our own Preachers, for preaching a Doctrine exactly agreeable to Christianity, only because he does not perhaps zealously propagate all the Doctrines of an old Confession. And upon the whole, though the *Majority* of the Synod should not in all respects approve of Mr. H's Doctrine, I do not however think they will find it proper to condemn him. We have justly deny'd the Infallibility of the Pope and his Councils and Synods in their Interpretations of Scripture, and can we modestly claim *Infallibility* for our selves or our Synods in our way of Interpreting? Peace, Unity and Virtue in any Church are more to be regarded than Orthodoxy. In the present weak State of human Nature, surrounded as we are on all sides with Ignorance and Error, it little becomes poor fallible Man to be positive and dogmatical in his Opinions. No Point of Faith is so plain, as that *Morality* is our Duty, for all Sides agree in that. A virtuous Heretick shall be saved before a wicked Christian: for there is no such Thing as voluntary Error. Therefore, since 'tis an Uncertainty till we get to Heaven what true Orthodoxy in all points is, and since our Congregation is rather too small to be divided, I hope this Misunderstanding will soon be got over, and that we shall as heretofore unite again in mutual *Christian Charity.*

T. I wish we may. I'll consider of what you've said, and wish you well.

S. Farewell.

To Josiah and Abiah Franklin (13 April 1738)

This letter, written by Franklin to his parents, is probably in response to rumors of his religious unorthodoxy. Compare this version with the one immediately following it—a draft of a letter addressed by Franklin to his father only, which appears to have never been sent.

Honour'd Father and Mother

I have your Favour of the 21st of March in which you both seem concern'd lest I have imbib'd some erroneous Opinions. Doubtless I have my Share, and when the natural Weakness and Imperfection of Human Understanding is considered, with the unavoidable Influences of Education, Custom, Books and Company, upon our Ways of thinking, I imagine a Man must have a good deal of Vanity who believes, and a good deal of Boldness who affirms, that all the Doctrines he holds, are true; and all he rejects, are false. And perhaps the same may be justly said of every Sect, Church and Society of men when they assume to themselves that Infallibility which they deny to the Popes and Councils. I think Opinions should be judg'd of by their Influences and Effects; and if a Man holds none that tend to make him less Virtuous or more vicious, it may be concluded he holds none that are dangerous; which I hope is the Case with me. I am sorry you should have any Uneasiness on my Account, and if it were a thing possible for one to alter his Opinions in order to please others, I know none whom I ought more willingly to oblige in that respect than your selves:

88   But since it is no more in a Man's Power *to think* than *to look* like another, methinks all that should be expected from me is to keep my Mind open to Conviction, to hear patiently and examine attentively whatever is offered me for that end; and if after all I continue in the same Errors, I believe your usual Charity will induce you rather to pity and excuse than blame me. In the mean time your Care and Concern for me is what I am very thankful for.

As to the Freemasons, unless she will believe me when I assure her that they are in general a very harmless sort of People; and have no principles or Practices that are inconsistent with Religion or good Manners, I know no Way of giving my Mother a better Opinion of them than she seems to have at present, (since it is not allow'd that Women should be admitted into that secret Society). She has, I must confess, on that Account, some reason to be displeas'd with it; but for any thing else, I must entreat her to suspend her Judgment till she is better inform'd, and in the mean time exercise her Charity.

My Mother grieves that one of her Sons is an Arian, another an Arminian. What an Arminian or an Arian is, I cannot say that I very well know; the Truth is, I make such Distinctions very little my Study; I think vital Religion has always suffer'd, when Orthodoxy is more regarded than Virtue. And the Scripture assures me, that at the last Day, we shall not be examin'd what we *thought*, but what we *did*; and our Recommendation will not be that we said *Lord, Lord*, but that we did GOOD to our Fellow Creatures. . . .

Draft of a Letter to His Father (13 April 1738[?])

I have yours of the 21st March, with another from my Mother, in which you both seem concern'd for my Orthodoxy. God only knows whether all the Doctrines I hold for true, be so or not. For my part, I must confess, I believe they are not, but I am not able to distinguish the good from the bad. And Knowing my self, as I do, to be a weak ignorant Creature, full of natural Imperfections, subject to be frequently misled by my own Reasonings, or the wrong Arguments of others, to the Influence of Education, of Custom, of Company, and the Books I read, It would be great Vanity in me to imagine that I have been so happy, as out of an infinite Number of Opinions of which a few only can be true, to select those only for my own Use. No, I am doubtless in Error as well as my Neighbours, and methinks a Man can not say, *All the Doctrines that I believe, are true; and all that I reject, are false*, without arrogantly claiming to himself that Infallibility which he denies to the Pope, with the greatest Indignation.

From such Considerations as these it follows, that I ought never to be angry with any one for differing in Judgment from me. For how know I but the Point in dispute between us, is one of those Errors that I have embrac'd as Truth. If I am in the Wrong, I should not be displeas'd that another is in the

right. If I am in the Right, 'tis my Happiness; and I should rather pity than
blame him who is unfortunately in the wrong.

The Lord's Prayer (1768[?])

Few other pieces so clearly reflect Franklin's basic conviction that religious belief should be an expression of rational inquiry conducive to utility than this sketch of a reformulated Lord's Prayer. In it, he drops what he considers to be archaic forms of address held onto merely for tradition's sake, substituting expressions he considers more representative of rational religion. As with so many of his theological musings, this selection illustrates his concern that belief in the deity be promotive of virtue.

Old Version

1. Our Father which art in Heaven,
2. Hallowed be thy Name.
3. Thy Kingdom come.
4. Thy will be done on Earth as it is in Heaven.
5. Give us this Day our daily Bread.
6. Forgive us our Debts as we forgive our Debtors.
7. And lead us not into Temptation, but deliver us from Evil.

New Version by B. F.

1. Heavenly Father,
2. May all revere thee,
3. And become thy dutiful Children and faithful Subjects.
4. May thy Laws be obeyed on Earth as perfectly as they are in Heaven.
5. Provide for us this Day as thou hast hitherto daily done.
6. Forgive us our Trespasses and enable us likewise to forgive those that offend us.
7. Keep us out of Temptation, and deliver us from Evil.

Reasons for the Change of Expression

Old Version. *Our Father which art in Heaven.*

New V.—*Heavenly Father*, is more concise, equally expressive, and better modern English.—

Old V.—*Hallowed be thy Name.* This seems to relate to an Observance among the Jews not to pronounce the proper or peculiar Name of God, they deeming it a Profanation so to do. We have in our Language no *proper Name* for God; the Word *God* being a common or general Name, expressing all chief Objects of Worship, true or false. The Word *hallowed* is almost obsolete. People now have but an imperfect Conception of the Meaning of the Petition. It is therefore proposed to change the expression into

New V.—*May all revere thee.*

Old V.—*Thy Kingdom come.* This Petition seems suited to the then Condition of the Jewish Nation. Originally their State was a Theocracy. God was their King. Dissatisfied with that kind of Government, they desired a visible earthly King in the same manner of the Nations around them. They had such Kings accordingly; but their Offerings were *due* to God on many Occasions by the Jewish Law, which when People could not pay, or had forgotten as Debtors are apt to do, it was proper to pray that those Debts might be forgiven. Our Liturgy uses neither the *Debtors* of Matthew, nor the *indebted* of Luke, but instead of them speaks of *those that trespass against us.* Perhaps the Considering it as a Christian Duty to forgive Debtors, was by the Compilers thought an inconvenient Idea in a trading Nation.—There seems however something presumptuous in this Mode of Expression, which has the Air of proposing ourselves as an Example of Goodness fit for God to imitate. *We hope you will at least be as good as we are*; you see we forgive one another, and therefore we pray that you would forgive us. Some have considered it in another sense, *Forgive us as we forgive others*; i.e. If we do not forgive others we pray that thou wouldst not forgive us. But this being a kind of conditional *Imprecation* against ourselves, seems improper in such a Prayer; and therefore it may be better to say humbly & modestly

New V.—*Forgive us our Trespasses, and enable us likewise to forgive those that offend us.* This instead of assuming that we have already in & of ourselves the Grace of Forgiveness, acknowledges our Dependance on God, the Fountain of Mercy for any Share we may have in it, praying that he would communicate of it to us.—

Old. V.—*And lead us not into Temptation.* The Jews had a Notion, that God sometimes tempted, or directed or permitted the Tempting of People. Thus it was said he tempted Pharaoh; directed Satan to tempt Job; and a false Prophet to tempt Ahab, &c. Under this Persuasion it was natural for them to pray that he would not put them to such severe Trials. We now suppose that Temptation, so far as it is supernatural, comes from the Devil only, and this Petition continued conveys a Suspicion which in our present Conception seems unworthy of God, therefore might be altered to

New V.—*Keep us out of Temptation.* Happiness was not increas'd by the Change, and they had reason to wish and pray for a Return of the Theocracy, or Government of God. Christians in these Times have other Ideas when they speak of the Kingdom of God, such as are perhaps more adequately express'd by

New V.—*And become thy Dutiful Children & faithful Subjects.*

Old V.—*Thy Will be done on Earth as it is in Heaven.*

New V.—*May thy Laws be obeyed on Earth as perfectly as they are in Heaven.*

Old V.—*Give us this Day our daily Bread.* Give us what is *ours*, seems to put us in a Claim of Right, and to contain too little of the grateful Acknowledgment and Sense of Dependance that becomes Creatures who live on the daily Bounty of their Creator. Therefore it is changed to

New V.—*Provide for us this Day, as thou hast hitherto daily done.*

Old V.—*Forgive us our Debts as we forgive our Debtors.* Matthew.

Forgive us our Sins, for we also forgive every one that is indebted to us. Luke.

Selections from Franklin's
Autobiography (1771, 1784, 1788)

Few memoirs have achieved the lasting appeal of Franklin's Autobiography. *His recollections provide an urbane glimpse into a remarkable personality—although it is an incomplete glimpse, since the* Autobiography *only covers the first five decades of Franklin's long life. More significantly, his reminiscences shed light upon the character and temperament of an entire era. The* Autobiography *is an exercise in social, intellectual, and political history. It is also a document that attests to Franklin's lifelong fidelity to sectarian tolerance, virtuous behavior, and deistic religious sensibilities.*

The following excerpts from the Autobiography *discuss Franklin's early retreat from the dogmatic materialism defended in his* Dissertation; *his conviction that rational religion, unadorned with supernaturalist tenets, is most worthy of both the deity and reflective humans; his disgust with doctrinal bigotry; his famous "program of moral perfection," by which he sought to test his Aristotelian belief that virtue is a matter of habit; his memories and appraisal of the Reverend George Whitefield, one of the central figures in the Great Awakening revivalist movement, which swept through the colonies between 1739 and 1742; and his insistence that no particular religious sect has a monopoly on the divine but rather that all, to one degree or another, contain elements of truth.*

Franklin wrote his memoirs on three separate occasions. Selection (1) here is taken from the portion he wrote in 1771; selection (2) from that of 1784; and the final three selections from the manuscript of 1788.

(1)

My parents had early given me religious impressions, and brought me through my childhood piously in the Dissenting way. But I was scarce fifteen, when, after doubting by turns of several points, as I found them disputed in the different books I read, I began to doubt of Revelation itself. Some books against Deism fell into my hands; they were said to be the substance of sermons preached at Boyle's Lectures. It happened that they wrought an effect on me

92

quite contrary to what was intended by them; for the arguments of the Deists, which were quoted to be refuted, appeared to me much stronger than the refutations; in short, I soon became a thorough Deist. . . . [But] I began to suspect that this doctrine, though it might be true, was not very useful. My London pamphlet, [Franklin's 1725 *Dissertation on Liberty and Necessity, Pleasure and Pain*] which . . . from the attributes of God, his infinite wisdom, goodness and power, concluded that nothing could possibly be wrong in the world, and that vice and virtue were empty distinctions, no such things existing, appeared now not so clever a performance as I once thought it; and I doubted whether some error had not insinuated itself unperceived into my argument, so as to infect all that followed, as is common in metaphysical reasoning.

I grew convinced that *truth, sincerity* and *integrity* in dealings between man and man were of the utmost importance to the felicity of life; and I formed written resolutions, which still remain in my journal book, to practice them ever while I lived. Revelation had indeed no weight with me, as such; but I entertained an opinion that, though certain actions might not be bad *because* they were forbidden by it, or good *because* it commanded them, yet probably these actions might be forbidden *because* they were bad for us, or commanded *because* they were beneficial to us, in their own natures, all the circumstances of things considered. And this persuasion, with the kind hand of Providence, or some guardian angel, or accidental favorable circumstances and situations, or all together, preserved me, through this dangerous time of youth, and the hazardous situations I was sometimes in among strangers, remote from the eye and advice of my father, without any willful gross immorality or injustice, that might have been expected from my want of religion. I say willful, because the instances I have mentioned had something of *necessity* in them, from my youth, inexperience, and the knavery of others. I had therefore a tolerable character to begin the world with; I valued it properly, and determined to preserve it. . . .

(2)

I had been religiously educated as a Presbyterian; and though some of the dogmas of that persuasion, such as *the eternal decrees of God, election, reprobation, etc.*, appeared to me unintelligible, others doubtful, and I early absented myself from the public assemblies of the sect, Sunday being my studying day, I never was without some religious principles. I never doubted, for instance, the existence of the Deity; that he made the world, and governed it by his Providence; that the most acceptable service of God was the doing good to man; that our souls are immortal; and that all crime will be punished, and virtue rewarded, either here or hereafter. These I esteemed the essentials of every religion; and, being found in all the religions we had in our country, I respected them all, though with different degrees of respect, as I found them more or less mixed with other articles, which, without any tendency to inspire, promote, or confirm morality, served principally to divide us, and make us unfriendly to one another. This respect to all, with an opinion that the worst had some good effects, induced me to avoid all discourse that might tend to lessen the good opinion another might have of his own religion; and as our province increased in people, and new places of worship were continually wanted, and generally erected by voluntary contribution, my mite for such purpose, whatever might be the sect, was never refused.

Though I seldom attended any public worship, I had still an opinion of propriety, and of its utility when rightly conducted, and I regularly paid my annual subscription for the support of the only Presbyterian minister* or meeting we had in Philadelphia. He used to visit me sometimes as a friend, and admonish me to attend his administrations, and I was now and then prevailed on to do so, once for five Sundays successively. Had he been in my opinion a good preacher, perhaps I might have continued, notwithstanding the occasion I had for the Sunday's leisure in my course of study; but his discourses were chiefly either polemic arguments, or explications of the peculiar doctrines of our sect, and were all to me very dry, uninteresting, and unedifying, since not a single moral principle was inculcated or enforced, their aim seeming to be rather to make us Presbyterians than good citizens.

At length he took for his text that verse of the fourth chapter of Philippians, *Finally, brethren, whatsoever things are true, honest, just, pure, lovely, or of good report, if there be any virtue, or any praise, think on these things.* And I imagined, in a sermon on such a text, we could not miss of having some morality. But he confined himself to five points only, as meant by the apostle, viz.: 1. Keeping holy the Sabbath day. 2. Being diligent in reading the holy Scriptures. 3. Attending duly the public worship. 4. Partaking of the Sacrament. 5. Paying a due respect to God's ministers. These might be all good things; but, as they were not the kind of good things that I expected from that text, I despaired of ever meeting with them from any other, was disgusted, and attended his preaching no more. I had some years before composed a little Liturgy, or form of prayer, for my own private use, entitled, *Articles of Belief and Acts of Religion.* I returned to the use of this, and went no more to the public assemblies. My conduct might be blameable, but I leave it, without attempting further to excuse it; my present purpose being to relate facts, and not to make apologies for them.

It was about this time I conceived the bold and arduous project of arriving at moral perfection. I wished to live without committing any fault at any time;

---

*Ed.: The Presbyterian minister referred to is Jebediah Andrews, who was also involved in the Hemphill affair; see introduction to *Dialogue between Two Presbyterians.*

I would conquer all that either natural inclination, custom, or company might lead me into. As I knew, or thought I knew, what was right and wrong, I did not see why I might not always do the one and avoid the other. But I soon found I had undertaken a task of more difficulty than I had imagined. While my care was employed in guarding against one fault, I was often surprised by another; habit took the advantage of inattention; inclination was sometimes too strong for reason. I concluded, at length, that the mere speculative conviction that it was our interest to be completely virtuous, was not sufficient to prevent our slipping; and that the contrary habits must be broken, and good ones acquired and established, before we can have any dependence on a steady, uniform rectitude of conduct. For this purpose I therefore contrived the following method.

In the various enumerations of the moral virtues I had met with in my reading, I found the catalogue more or less numerous, as different writers included more or fewer ideas under the same name. Temperance, for example, was by some confined to eating and drinking, while by others it was extended to mean the moderating every other pleasure, appetite, inclination, or passion, bodily or mental, even to our avarice and ambition. I proposed to myself, for the sake of clearness, to use rather more names, with fewer ideas annexed to each, then a few names with more ideas; and I included under thirteen names of virtues all that at that time occurred to me as necessary or desirable, and annexed to each a short precept, which fully expressed the extent I gave to its meaning.

These names of virtues, with their precepts, were:

1. TEMPERANCE.—Eat not to dullness; drink not to elevation.

2. SILENCE.—Speak not but what may benefit others or yourself; avoid trifling conversation.

3. ORDER.—Let all your things have their places; let each part of your business have its time.

4. RESOLUTION.—Resolve to perform what you ought; perform without fail what you resolve.

5. FRUGALITY.—Make no expense but to do good to others or yourself; i.e., waste nothing.

6. INDUSTRY.—Lose no time; be always employed in something useful; cut off all unnecessary actions.

7. SINCERITY.—Use no hurtful deceit; think innocently and justly, and, if you speak, speak accordingly.

8. JUSTICE.—Wrong none by doing injuries, or omitting the benefits that are your duty.

9. MODERATION.—Avoid extremes; forbear resenting injuries so much as you think they deserve.

10. CLEANLINESS.—Tolerate no uncleanliness in body, clothes, or habitation.

11. TRANQUILITY.—Be not disturbed at trifles, or at accidents common or unavoidable.

12. CHASTITY.—Rarely use venery but for health or offspring, never to dullness, weakness, or the injury of your own or another's peace or reputation.

13. HUMILITY.—Imitate Jesus and Socrates.

My intention being to acquire the *habitude* of all these virtues, I judged it would be well not to distract my attention by attempting the whole at once, but to fix it on one of them at a time; and, when I should be master of that, then to proceed to another, and so on, till I should have gone through the thirteen; and, as the previous acquisition of some might facilitate the acquisition of certain others, I arranged them with that view, as they stand above. Temperance first, as it tends to procure that coolness and clearness of head, which is so necessary where constant vigilance was to be kept up, and guard maintained against the unremitting attraction of ancient habits, and the force of perpetual temptations. This being acquired and established, Silence would be more easy; and my desire being to gain knowledge at the same time that I improved in virtue, and considering that in conversation it was obtained rather by the use of the ears than of the tongue, and therefore wishing to break a habit I was getting into of prattling, punning, and joking, which only made me acceptable to trifling company, I gave *Silence* the second place. This and the next, *Order*, I expected would allow me more time for attending to my project and my studies. *Resolution*, once become habitual, would keep me firm in my endeavors to obtain all the subsequent virtues. *Frugality* and Industry freeing me from my remaining debt, and producing affluence and independence, would make more easy the practice of Sincerity and Justice, etc., etc. . . .

It will be remarked that, though my scheme was not wholly without religion, there was in it no mark of any of the distinguishing tenets of any particular sect. I had purposely avoided them; for, being fully persuaded of the utility and excellency of my method, and that it might be serviceable to people in all religions, and intending some time or other to publish it, I would not have any thing in it that should prejudice any one, of any sect, against it. I purposed writing a little comment on each virtue, in which I would have shown the advantages of possessing it, and the mischiefs attending its opposite vice; and I should have called my book THE ART OF VIRTUE, because it would have shown the means and manner of obtaining virtue, which would have distinguished it from the mere exhortation to be good, that does not instruct and indicate the means, but is like the apostle's man of verbal charity, who only without showing to the naked and hungry how or where they might get clothes or victuals, exhorted them to be fed and clothed.—James ii, 15, 16.

But it so happened that my intention of writing and publishing this comment was never fulfilled. I did, indeed, from time to time, put down short hints of the sentiments, reasonings, etc., to be made use of in it, some of which I have still by me; but the necessary close attention to private business in the earlier part of my life, and my public business since, have occasioned my postponing it; for, it being connected in my mind with *a great and extensive project*, that required the whole man to execute, and which an unforeseen succession of employs prevented my attending to, it has hitherto remained unfinished.

In this piece it was my design to explain and enforce this doctrine, that vicious actions are not hurtful because they are forbidden, but forbidden because they are hurtful, the nature of man alone considered; that it was therefore, every one's interest to be virtuous who wished to be happy even in this world; and I should, from this circumstance (there being always in the world a number of rich merchants, nobility, states, and princes, who have need of honest instruments for the management of their affairs, and such being so rare), have endeavored to convince young persons that no qualities were so likely to make a poor man's fortune as those of probity and integrity. . . .

(3)

I put down, from time to time, on pieces of paper, such thoughts as occurred to me. . . . Most of these are lost; but I find one purporting to be the substance of an intended creed, containing, as I thought, the essentials of every known religion, and being free of every thing that might shock the professors of any religion. It is expressed in these words, viz.:

"That there is one God, who made all things.

"That he governs the world by his providence.

"That he ought to be worshiped by adoration, prayer, and thanksgiving.

"But that the most acceptable service to God is doing good to man.

"That the soul is immortal.

"And that God will certainly reward virtue and punish vice, either here or hereafter."

(4)

In 1739 arrived among us from Ireland the Reverend Mr. Whitefield, who had made himself remarkable there as an itinerant preacher. He was at first permitted to preach in some of our churches; but the clergy, taking a dislike to him, soon refused him their pulpits, and he was obliged to preach in the fields. The multitudes of all sects and denominations that attended his sermons were enormous, and it was a matter of speculation to me, who was one of the number, to observe the extraordinary influence of his oratory on his hearers, and how much they admired and respected him, notwithstanding his common abuse of them, by assuring them they were naturally *half beasts and half devils*. It was wonderful to see the change soon made in the manners of our inhabitants. From being thoughtless or indifferent about religion, it seemed as if all the world were growing religious, so that one could not walk through the town in an evening without hearing psalms sung in different families of every street.

And it being found inconvenient to assemble in the open air, subject to its inclemencies, the building of a house to meet in was no sooner proposed, and persons appointed to receive contributions, but sufficient sums were soon received to procure the ground and erect the building, which was one hundred feet long and seventy broad, about the size of Westminster Hall; and the work was carried on with such spirit as to be finished in a much shorter time than could have been expected. Both house and ground were vested in trustees, expressly for the use of any preacher of any religious persuasion who might desire to say something to the people at Philadelphia; the design in building not being to accommodate any particular sect, but the inhabitants in general; so that even if the Mufti of Constantinople were to send a missionary to preach Mohammedanism to us, he would find a pulpit at his service.

Mr. Whitefield, on leaving us, went preaching all the way through the colonies to Georgia. The settlement of that province had lately been begun, but, instead of being made with hardy, industrious husbandmen, accustomed to labor, the only people fit for such an enterprise, it was with families of broken shop-keepers and other insolvent debtors, many of indolent and idle habits, taken out of the jails, who, being set down in the woods, unqualified for clearing land, and unable to endure the hardships of a new settlement, perished in numbers, leaving many helpless children unprovided for. The sight of their miserable situation inspired the benevolent heart of Mr. Whitefield with the idea of building an Orphan House there, in which they might be supported and educated. Returning northward, he preached up this charity, and made large collections, for his eloquence had a wonderful power over the hearts and purses of his hearers, of which I myself was an instance.

I did not disapprove of the design, but, as Georgia was then destitute of materials and workmen, and it was proposed to send them from Philadelphia at a great expense, I thought it would have been better to have built the house there, and brought the children to it. This I advised; but he was resolute in his first project, rejected my counsel, and I therefore refused to contribute. I happened soon after to attend one of his sermons, in the course of which I perceived he intended to finish with a collection, and I silently resolved he should get nothing from me. I had in my pocket a handful of copper money, three or four silver dollars, and five pistoles in gold. As he proceeded I began to soften, and concluded to give the coppers. Another stroke of his oratory made me ashamed of that, and determined me to give the silver; and he finished so admirably, that I emptied my pocket wholly into the collector's dish, gold and all. At this sermon there was also one of our club, who being of my sentiments respecting the building in Georgia, and suspecting a collection might be intended, had, by precaution, emptied his pockets before he came from home. Towards the conclusion of the discourse, however, he felt a strong desire to give, and applied to a neighbor, who stood near him, to borrow some money for the purpose. The application was unfortunately made to perhaps the only man in the company who had the firmness not to be affected by the preacher. His answer was, *At any other time, Friend Hopkinson, I would lend to thee freely; but not now, for thee seems to be out of thy right senses. . . .*

The following instance will show something of the terms on which we stood. Upon one of his [Whitefield's] arrivals from England at Boston, he wrote to me that he should come soon to Philadelphia, but knew not where he could lodge when there, as he understood his old friend, and host, Mr. Benezet [probably Anthony Benezet, a Quaker educator and reformer], was removed to Germantown. My answer was, "You know my house; if you can make shift with its scanty accommodations, you will be most heartily welcome." He replied, that if I made that kind offer for Christ's sake, I should not miss of a reward. And I returned, *"Don't let me be mistaken; it was not for Christ's sake, but for your sake."* One of our common acquaintance jocosely remarked, that, knowing it to be the custom of the saints, when they received any favour, to shift the burden of the obligation from off their own shoulders, and place it in heaven, I had contrived to fix it on earth. . . .

(5)

[The] embarrassments that the Quakers suffered from having established and published it as one of their principles that no kind of war was lawful, and which being once published, they could not afterwards, however they might change their minds, easily get rid of, reminds me of what I think a more prudent conduct in another sect among us, that of the Dunkers. I was acquainted with one of its founders, Michael Welfare, soon after it appeared. He complained to me that they were grievously calumniated by the zealots of other persuasions, and charged with abominable principles and practices to which they were utter strangers. I told him this had always been the case with new sects and that to put a stop to such abuse, I imagined it might be well to publish the articles of their belief and the rules of their discipline. He said that it had been proposed among them, but not agreed to for this reason: "When we were first drawn together as a society," says he, "it had pleased God to enlighten our minds so far as to see that some doctrines which we once esteemed truths were errors, and that others which we had esteemed errors were real truths. From time to time he has been pleased to afford us further light, and our principles have been improving and our errors diminishing. Now we are not sure that we are arrived at the end of this progression, and at the perfection of spiritual or theological knowledge; and we fear that if we should once print our confession of faith, we should feel ourselves as if bound and confined by it, and perhaps be unwilling to receive further improvement, and our successors still more so, as conceiving what their elders and founders had done to be something sacred, never to be departed from." This modesty in a sect is perhaps a singular instance in the history of mankind, every other sect supposing itself in possession of all truth, and that those who differ are so far in the wrong—like a man travelling in foggy weather: Those at some distance before him on the road he sees wrapped up in the fog, as well as those behind him, and also the people in the fields on each side; but near him all appears clear, tho' in truth he is as much in the fog as any of them. To avoid this kind of embarrassment, the Quakers have of late years been gradually declining the public service in the Assembly and in the magistracy, choosing rather to quit their power than their principle.

The Levée (1779[?])

On its surface, this short piece conveys a political rather than a religious message. Probably written in 1779, it is a rather transparent allegorical condemnation of the monarchy of George III. Just as the biblical Job was unjustly brought low by a divine monarch influenced by the rumor-mongering of a courtier (Satan), so the colonies have been unfairly treated by an earthly monarch's misguided harkening to his "malicious courtiers." The political lesson is obvious: "Trust not a single person with the government of your state." Absolute power is capable of corrupting even a celestial ruler.

But the very fact that Franklin couches his allegory in biblical terms reflects his deistic dissatisfaction with Christian dogma and scriptural authority. In Franklin's interpretation of the Book of Job, Satan is not the only villain. God also emerges with dirty hands, acting as he does, on Satan's prompting, in a manner that Franklin obviously sees as condemnable. One of the motifs in American deism, defended by moderates and militants alike, was the claim that it was unworthy of the deity to perform actions that would be unethical if done by mortals. Scriptural passages (such as those about Job's trials) that suggested God occasionally acts arbitrarily or unjustly supported the deistic contention that the Christian notion of God was incorrect and even blasphemous. In writing The Levée, then, Franklin may have had more in mind than simply blasting political monarchy. He may also have been subtly taking a stab at a concept of God he considered to be irrational and unconducive to moral rectitude.

In the first chapter of Job we have an account of a transaction said to have arisen in the court, or at the *levée*, of the best of all possible princes, or of governments by a single person, viz. that of God himself.

At this *levée*, in which the sons of God were assembled, Satan also appeared.

It is probable the writer of that ancient book took his idea of this *levée* from those of the eastern monarchs of the age he lived in.

It is to this day usual at the *levées* of princes, to have persons assembled who are enemies to each other, who seek to obtain favor by whispering calumny and detraction, and thereby ruining those that distinguish themselves by their virtue and merit. And kings frequently ask a familiar question or two, of every one in the circle, merely to show their benignity. These circumstances are particularly exemplified in this relation.

If a modern king, for instance, finds a person in the circle who has not lately been there, he naturally asks him how he has passed his time since he last had the pleasure of seeing him? the gentleman perhaps replies that he has been in the country to view his estates, and visit some friends. Thus Satan being asked whence he cometh? answers, "From going to and fro in the earth, and walking up and down in it." And being further asked, whether he had considered the uprightness and fidelity of the prince's servant Job, he immediately displays all the malignance of the designing courtier, by answering with another question: "Doth Job serve God for naught? Hast thou not given him immense wealth, and protected him in the possession of it? Deprive him of that, and he will curse thee to thy face." In modern phrase, Take away his places and his pensions, and your Majesty will soon find him in the opposition.

This whisper against Job had its effect. He was delivered into the power of his adversary, who deprived him of his fortune, destroyed his family, and completely ruined him.

The book of Job is called by divines a sacred poem, and, with the rest of the Holy Scriptures, is understood to be written for our instruction.

What then is the instruction to be gathered from this supposed transaction?

Trust not a single person with the government of your state. For if the Deity himself, being the monarch may for a time give way to calumny, and suffer it to operate the destruction of the best of subjects; what mischief may you not expect from such power in a mere man, though the best of men, from whom the truth is often industriously hidden, and to whom falsehood is often presented in its place, by artful, interested, and malicious courtiers?

And be cautious in trusting him even with limited powers, lest sooner or later he sap and destroy those limits, and render himself absolute.

For by the disposal of places, he attaches to himself all the placeholders, with their numerous connexions, and also all the expecters and hopers of places, which will form a strong party in promoting his views. By various political engagements for the interest of neighbouring states or princes, he procures their aid in establishing his own personal power. So that, through the hopes of emolument in one part of his subjects, and the fear of his resentment in the other, all opposition falls before him.

To Joseph Priestley (8 February 1780)

American deism was a child of the Enlightenment and, like its progenitor, was an ardent believer in the inevitable progress of science and the ultimate perfection of humans and societies. Reason, as expressed through the natural sciences, would eradicate the vestiges of ecclesial superstition, fear, and bigotry, thereby liberating humanity from the traditional impediments to progress. Moral as well as technical improvement, the conquest of passions as well as nature, were certainties.

Franklin was probably more enamored of the promise of the physical sciences than any other American deist (with the possible exception of Jefferson), and in this letter to Joseph Priestley (1733–1804), the chemist and Unitarian, he asserts his faith in the inevitable victory of Reason. His reflections not only illustrate his deistic confidence in the ability of reason and science to improve the human condition but also strikingly anticipate twentieth-century scientific achievements.

Dear Sir,

Your kind Letter of September 27 came to hand but very lately, the Bearer having stayed long in Holland. I always rejoice to hear of your being still employ'd in experimental Researches into Nature, and of the Success you meet with. The rapid Progress *true* Science now makes, occasions my regretting sometimes that I was born so soon. It is impossible to imagine the Height to which may be carried, in a thousand years, the Power of Man over Matter. We may perhaps learn to deprive large Masses of their Gravity, and give them absolute Levity, for the sake of easy Transport. Agriculture may diminish its Labour and double its Produce; all Diseases may by sure means be prevented or cured, not excepting even that of Old Age, and our Lives lengthened at pleasure even beyond the antediluvian Standard. O that moral Science were in as fair a way of Improvement, that Men would cease to be Wolves to one another, and that human Beings would at length learn what they now improperly call Humanity! . . .

To ——————— (?) (3 July 1786[?])

Franklin the deist was not cut from the same cloth as Paine, Palmer, or even Jefferson. Except for one or two exceptions (such as his Dialogue between Two Presbyterians*), he studiously avoided publishing potentially offensive statements of his religious sentiment.*

There are probably several reasons for his discretion. First, he seemed temperamentally unsuited for theological shouting matches; as he tells us in his Autobiography, *he considered one of his life's errata to have been his youthful indulgence in "disputatious" arguments over religious matters. Second, he appears to have taken seriously his own ethical defenses of religious toleration and was willing to coexist peacefully with Christian sectarians so long as they reciprocated his live-and-let-live attitude. Third, as he makes clear in the* Autobiography *as well as his 1738 letter to his parents, he thought it reasonable to suspect that some of his religious views were incorrect and that the only appropriate reaction to this likelihood was a refusal to pontificate about them. Finally, it would have been characteristic of Franklin, who was a preeminently practical man, to wish to avoid the social opprobrium that often befell more vocal deists of his day. Franklin, in short, was a moderate deist, in doctrine as well as attitude.*

But this letter to an unknown correspondent—possibly Tom Paine—suggests yet another explanation for Franklin's moderation: his suspicion that orthodox Christianity, even if fundamentally incorrect about the nature of the deity, might promote morality in its adherents. Franklin was preoccupied his entire life with ethics and early on had become convinced that virtue was dependent on an individual's habituation to good acts, regardless of the intentions that motivate them. Christianity, as he says in this letter, might be the catalyst for such habit formation: The "Motives of Religion" might restrain otherwise rudderless persons in the practice of virtue "till it becomes habitual, which is the great Point for its Security." *To destroy that bearing is to risk opening the floodgates to moral anarchy.*

To the later militant deists, such prudential caution would smack of frightened hypocrisy. But to the moderate Franklin, no doubt further mellowed by age, the willingness to sacrifice public morality for the sake of deism was socially unsound as well as ethically reprehensible.

Dear Sir,

I have read your Manuscript with some Attention. By the Argument it contains against the Doctrines of a particular Providence, tho' you allow a general providence, you strike at the Foundation of all Religion. For without the Belief of a Providence, that takes Cognizance of, guards, and guides, and may favour particular Persons, there is no Motive to Worship a Deity, to fear its Displeasure, or to pray for its Protection. I will not enter into any Discussion of your Principles, tho' you seem to desire it. At present I shall only give you my Opinion, that, though your Reasonings are subtile, and may prevail with some Readers, you will not succeed so as to change the general Sentiments of Mankind on that Subject, and the Consequence of printing this Piece will be, a great deal of Odium drawn upon yourself, Mischief to you, and no Benefit to others. He that spits against the Wind, spits in his own Face.

But, were you to succeed, do you imagine any Good would be done by it? You yourself may find it easy to live a virtuous Life, without the Assistance afforded by Religion; you having a clear perception of the Advantages of Virtue, and the Disadvantages of Vice, and possessing a Strength of Resolution sufficient to enable you to resist common Temptations. But think how great a Proportion of Mankind consists of weak and ignorant Men and Women, and of inexperienc'd, and inconsiderate Youth of both Sexes, who have need of the Motives of Religion to restrain them in the Practice of it till it becomes *habitual*, which is the great Point for its Security. And perhaps you are indebted to her originally, that is, to your Religious Education, for the Habits of Virtue upon which you now justly value yourself. You might easily display your excellent Talents of reasoning upon a less hazardous subject, and thereby obtain a Rank with our most distinguish'd Authors. For among us it is not necessary, as among the Hottentots, that a Youth, to be receiv'd into the Company of men, should prove his Manhood by beating his Mother.

I would advise you, therefore, not to attempt unchaining the Tyger, but to burn this Piece before it is seen by any other Person; whereby you will save yourself a great deal of Mortification from the Enemies it may raise against you, and perhaps a good deal of Regret and Repentance. If men are so wicked as we now see them *with religion*, what would they be *if without it*. I intend this Letter itself as a *Proof* of my Friendship, and therefore add no *Professions* to it. . . .

Motion for Prayers in the Convention
(28 June 1787)

In 1787 Franklin, rich in years and honor, was once again called on to exercise virtue in the public interest: He was elected a Pennsylvania delegate to the Constitutional Convention. After a month of heated debate that sometimes degenerated into full-scale bickering, Franklin had had enough. He appealed to the delegates' consciences by moving that the sessions be opened with prayer.

Franklin's motion (which was almost unanimously rejected) is itself rather unremarkable. But when placed in context, it affirms that the old man still subscribed to the views on divine providence he had defended some fifty-five years earlier (as in On the Providence of God in the Government of the World*). It also underscores his steadfast deistic faith in the benevolence of the deity, the necessity of government by human reason, and tolerance of all religious sects (as witnessed by its final suggestion that clergy of all persuasions be invited to lead the convention in prayer).*

Mr. President,

The small Progress we have made, after 4 or 5 Weeks' close Attendance and continual Reasonings with each other, our different Sentiments on almost every Question, several of the last producing as many *Noes* as *Ayes*, is, methinks, a melancholy Proof of the Imperfection of the Human Understanding. We indeed seem to *feel* our own want of political Wisdom, since we have been running all about in Search of it. We have gone back to ancient History for Models of Government, and examin'd the different Forms of those Republics, which, having been originally form'd with the Seeds of their own Dissolution, now no longer exist; and we have view'd modern States all round Europe, but find none of their Constitutions suitable to our Circumstances.

In this Situation of this Assembly, groping, as it were, in the dark to find Political Truth, and scarce able to distinguish it when presented to us, how has it happened, Sir, that we have not hitherto once thought of humbly applying to the Father of Lights to illuminate our Understandings? In the Beginning of the Contest with Great Britain, when we were sensible of Danger, we had daily Prayers in this Room for the Divine Protection. Our Prayers, Sir, were heard;— and they were graciously answered. All of us, who were engag'd in the Struggle, must have observed frequent Instances of a superintending Providence in our Favour. To that kind Providence we owe this happy Opportunity of Consulting in Peace on the Means of establishing our future national Felicity. And have we now forgotten that powerful Friend? or do we imagine we no longer need its assistance? I have lived, Sir, a long time; and the longer I live, the more convincing proofs I see of this Truth, *that* GOD *governs in the Affairs of Men.* And if a Sparrow cannot fall to the Ground without His Notice, is it probable that an Empire can rise without His Aid? We have been assured, Sir, in the Sacred Writings, that "except the Lord build the House, they labour in vain that build it." I firmly believe this; and I also believe, that, without his concurring Aid, we shall succeed in this political Building no better than the Builders of Babel; we shall be divided by our little, partial, local Interests, our Projects will be confounded, and we ourselves shall become a Reproach and a Bye-word down to future Ages. And, what is worse, Mankind may hereafter, from this unfortunate Instance, despair of establishing Government by human Wisdom, and leave it to Chance, War, and Conquest.

I therefore beg leave to move,

That henceforth Prayers, imploring the Assistance of Heaven and its Blessing on our Deliberations, be held in this Assembly every morning before we proceed to Business; and that one or more of the Clergy of this city be requested to officiate in that Service.

To Ezra Stiles (9 March 1790)

The following letter to Ezra Stiles, president of Yale College, was written five weeks before Franklin's death. Although an orthodox Calvinist in his later years, Stiles had gone through a long period of religious confusion, turning first to deism and then to Arminianism before his midlife "rebirth." His own history of doubt lends a certain poignancy to his request for an account of Franklin's religious sentiments.

In his reply to Stiles, Franklin echoes the basic deistic catechism he had endorsed in his earlier credos of 1728, 1731, and 1784. The general themes of benevolent providence, virtue, and religious tolerance, central to Franklin's lifelong religious perspective, are reaffirmed, as is his dislike of theological speculation (or "metaphysical reasoning," as he would have said). Finally, and most interestingly, Franklin's reply contains one of his few public confessions of doubt about the divinity of Jesus—although, characteristically, he adds that if such a belief is promotive of public virtue, it serves a good purpose.

Reverend and Dear Sir,

. . . You desire to know something of my Religion. It is the first time I have been questioned upon it. But I cannot take your Curiosity amiss, and shall endeavour in a few Words to gratify it. Here is my Creed. I believe in one God, Creator of the Universe. That he governs it by his Providence. That he ought to be worshipped. That the most acceptable Service we render to him is doing good to his other Children. That the soul of Man is immortal, and will be treated with Justice in another Life respecting its Conduct in this. These I take to be the fundamental Principles of all sound Religion, and I regard them as you do in whatever Sect I meet with them.

As to Jesus of Nazareth, my Opinion of whom you particularly desire, I think the System of Morals and his Religion, as he left them to us, the best the World ever saw or is likely to see; but I apprehend it has received various corrupting Changes, and I have, with most of the present Dissenters in England, some Doubts as to his Divinity; tho' it is a question I do not dogmatize upon, having never studied it, and think it needless to busy myself with it now, when I expect soon an Opportunity of knowing the Truth with less Trouble. I see no harm, however, in its being believed, if that Belief has the good Consequence, as probably it has, of making his Doctrines more respected and better observed; especially as I do not perceive, that the Supreme takes it amiss, by distinguishing the Unbelievers in his Government of the World with any peculiar Marks of his Displeasure.

I shall only add, respecting myself, that, having experienced the Goodness of that Being in conducting me prosperously thro' a long life, I have no doubt of its Continuance in the next, though without the smallest Conceit of meriting such Goodness. . . .

Thomas Jefferson

Reason and Free Inquiry Are the Only Effectual Agents against Errors

Most of the American deists were regularly vilified from the pulpit and in the popular press as godless apostates. All of them, with the possible exception of Franklin, were favorite and predictable targets of both personal attacks and public censure. But it is arguable that Thomas Jefferson (1743–1826) suffered the most from the calumny his deism prompted. He was an intensely—almost obsessively—private man who rarely revealed himself in either public or personal communications, yet his political career and national prominence spotlighted the unorthodoxy of his religious convictions. His political enemies gleefully invoked this nonconformity to call his administrative ability into question. Similarly, his Christian opponents self-righteously used it to attack his personal integrity. During his tenure as president, almost a hundred pamphlets and scores of newspaper articles denounced him as a "French infidel and atheist." The clergy preached fire-and-brimstone sermons warning that his leadership would destroy established religion and public morality, so frightening the members of their congregations that many of them actually hid their Bibles when Jefferson was elected president. Alexander Hamilton, Jefferson's political archrival, contemptuously (and publicly) dismissed him as an "atheist and fanatic." And as late as 1830 the Philadelphia Public Library refused to catalogue his collected works on the grounds that he had died an "infidel." In short, Jefferson's high profile as a national figure made his religious heterodoxy easy prey for any group disgruntled with his politics, personality, or philosophy. It is little wonder that toward the end of his life, disgusted with public acrimony and besieged by religious bigotry, he plaintively said, "I am of a sect by myself, as far as I know."

A voracious reader his entire life, Jefferson early on imbibed the heady brew of the Enlightenment's New Learning. While a student at the College of William and Mary, he fell under the influence of William Small, who occupied the chair of mathematics and natural science. Prompted by Small, whom Jefferson always remembered with affectionate respect, he devoured British and French philosophy, soon switching allegiance from the Anglican tradition into which he had been born to Enlightenment rationalism. He was particularly impressed by Locke's argument that tolerance in matters of conscience and a political respect for the natural rights of equality and liberty were the twin foundations of a just and felicitous society. Jefferson's absorption of Locke obviously echoed later in his drafting of the Declaration of Independence, as well as in his republican orientation while serving as secretary of state, vice president, and eventually president. But his indebtedness to the principles of rational liberalism is also apparent in his *Notes on Virginia* (1785) and the justly acclaimed "Act for Establishing Religious Freedom" (1786).

Jefferson was too zealous a reader to be a systematic scribbler. As a result, most of his corpus consists of correspondence, the sheer volume of which is staggering even by the eighteenth century's epistle-loving standards. The reader of Jefferson's letters, particularly the ones devoted to discussions of his deism, is immediately struck by three things: the breadth of his learning, his talent (like Paine's) for coining pithy phrases that eloquently express volumes, and his unswerving fidelity to the standards of reason and tolerance. Contrary to the accusations of his critics, Jefferson was no atheist. But he had little patience for religious sentiment that slipped into "enthusiasm" by neglecting the boundaries of rational reflection and empirical investigation. For Jefferson, theological speculation enjoyed no privileged position. It was subject to the same standards of "reason and free inquiry . . . the only effectual agents against error" as all knowledge claims.

The selections here from Jefferson include excerpts from his *Notes on Virginia*, the "Act for Establishing Religious Freedom" in its entirety, and epistolary reflections on religion spanning the years 1787 to 1825. They deal primarily with the three issues that most exercised Jefferson the deist: religious and political liberty, textual and theological criticism, and morality.

Jefferson's conviction that matters of religious conscience are outside the reach of either public or legal sanction is most strongly expressed in Query XVII of his *Notes on Virginia*. There Jefferson laments that religious intolerance, one of the original reasons for the colonial exodus to America, had entrenched itself in Virginia. True, the May 1776 national declaration of rights had "declared it to be a truth, and a natural right, that the exercise of religion should be free" and had reversed the existing statutory provisions regulating many religious obligations. But the common law tradition still endorsed by Virginia continued to allow the persecution of heresy, thereby in Jefferson's mind inconsistently perpetuating "that religious slavery under which a people have been willing to remain, who [otherwise] have lavished their lives and fortunes for the establishment of their civil freedom."

In opposing common law's interdiction of heterodoxy, Jefferson argues that "the rights of conscience" cannot be submitted to the law, that "we are answerable for them [only] to our God." The law's purview extends solely to those actions that inflict harm on others. "But," concludes Jefferson, "it does me no injury for my neighbour to say there are twenty gods, or no God. It neither picks my pocket nor breaks my leg." Consequently, private religious conviction is beyond the pale of civil jurisdiction.

Moreover, the subordination of matters of conscience to legal or public standards encourages a uniformity of action and thought that enervates both the individual and society and encourages oppression: "Subject opinion to coercion: whom will you make your inquisitors? Fallible men; men governed by bad passions, by private as well as public reasons. And why subject it to coercion? To produce uniformity. But is uniformity of opinion desirable? No more than of face and stature." Religion in the truest sense of the word—a reflective, ethical, and free self-determination in matters of conscience—will flourish if left to individual discretion. Legal coercion of opinion only serves "to make one half the world fools, and the other half hypocrites." Jefferson's eloquent defense of religious liberty achieved its purpose. One year after the publication of *Notes on Virginia*, he drafted and successfully pushed through the Virginia assembly his "Act for Establishing Religious Freedom." It redressed the injustices he had described in his book and remained one of his proudest accomplishments.

Jefferson felt so strongly about the necessity for universal tolerance in religious conviction because he believed that reason was the final arbiter in theological dispute and that its powers to discriminate between truth and error could flourish only in a nonoppressive environment. Like the other American deists, Jefferson was persuaded that sectarian doctrines based on supernaturalistic claims of revelation were fundamentally suspect. In his estimation, reason can infer God's existence through observation of and reflection on the natural world: "I hold (without appeal to revelation) that when we take a view of the Universe, in its parts general or particular, it is impossible for the human mind not to perceive and feel a conviction of design, consummate skill, and indefinite power in every atom of its composition," all of which points to a divine First Cause (letter to John Adams, 11 April 1823). Moreover, the same data necessarily leads to the conviction that the First Cause is also good and perfect (letter to Ezra Stiles Ely, 25 June 1819). But beyond these two inferences reason cannot go. Consequently, there is no justification for accepting the dogmas of Christian faith. In fact, there are good grounds for rejecting them, since they violate the standards of observable natural uniformity and logical possibility. Even if they cannot be conclusively repudiated as false, they *can* be dismissed as nonsensical. "Ideas," argues Jefferson, "must be distinct before reason can act on them" (letter to F. A. Van der Kemp, 30 July 1816). But theological claims about the incarnation, resurrection, revelation, the Trinity, and miracles are indistinct if not downright murky.

Jefferson's rigorously empiricist criteria for the determination of truth and meaning prompted pioneering work on his part in the textual criticism of Christian doctrine. Although it has been overlooked by commentators on his religious perspective, Jefferson's hermeneutical analysis of Scripture anticipated the modern "demythologization" movement of Rudolph Bultmann by some two hundred years.

Jefferson was convinced that Scripture—particularly the New Testament—was a confused hybrid of rational ethical and religious sentiments and sheer nonsense. The former, he felt, accurately reflects the actual beliefs of the man—not god—Jesus. Like so many (but not all) of his fellow deists, Jefferson saw Jesus as an early proponent of rational religion whose teachings are reducible to three propositions: that there is one perfect God, that a future state of reward and punishment exists, and that "to love God with all thy heart, and thy neighbour as thyself, is the sum of religion" (letter to Benjamin Waterhouse, 26 June 1822). As deists in the first decade of the nineteenth century would later put it, the heart of Jesus' *real* message is "theophilanthropy": the love of God and man. These three tenets Jefferson wholeheartedly endorses. It is the "Platonic" absurdities with which later Christian theologians had embellished Scripture that Jefferson deplores. As he wrote to Joseph Priestley on 9 April 1803, "To the corruption of Christianity I am indeed opposed; but not to the genuine precepts of Jesus himself."

How, then, to distinguish between the original doctrine and its subsequent adulteration? Through historical exegesis of the text, answers Jefferson, in which the fantastical accounts and logical impossibilities are mercilessly excised from the rationally plausible. As early as 1787, in a letter to his nephew Peter Carr, Jefferson described his method of textual criticism:

> Fix reason firmly in her seat, and call to her tribunal every fact, every opinion. . . . Read the bible then, as you would read Livy or Tacitus. The facts which are within the ordinary course of nature you will believe on the authority of the writer, as you do those of the same kind in Livy or Tacitus. The testimony of the writer weighs in their favor in one scale, and their not being against the laws of nature does not weigh against them. But those facts in the bible which contradict the laws of nature, must be examined with more care. . . . Here you must recur to the pretension of the writer. . . . Examine upon what evidence his pretensions are founded, and whether that evidence is so strong as that its falsehood would be more improbable than a change of the laws of nature in the case he relates.

Adherence to this rule of thumb, according to Jefferson, would enable the careful reader to discriminate between scriptural truth and falsity. Just as the rational person rejects stories in Livy or Tacitus about showers of blood or talking statues because they violate the lessons of experience, so he or she should dismiss scriptural accounts of miracles for the same reason. Similarly, just

110   as those anecdotes by secular historians that are rationally plausible and do not contradict contemporary science are reliable, so too are their analogues in sacred historical accounts. Jefferson's approach to the demystification of Christian Scripture, then, is in keeping with his fundamental conviction that "reason and free inquiry are the only effectual agents against error."

Seeking to bring about a "euthanasia for Platonic Christianity," Jefferson spent several years purging Scripture of its nondeistic elements. He rewrote the Gospels, by disregarding their allusions to supernaturalist doctrine, snipping out what he accepted as expressions of Jesus' original precepts, and pasting those (in English, French, Latin, and Greek) into a copybook. Moreover, he wrote several drafts of a "Synopsis" or "Summary" of the true Christian religion, complete with his reasons for rejecting orthodox adulterations of it (see the letters to Joseph Priestley, 9 April 1803; Benjamin Rush, 21 April 1803; John Adams, 12 October 1813). Jefferson intended his synopsis to be an outline of a more comprehensive study, but, as with so many other projected works, he never undertook its composition.

In addition to his emphasis on freedom of conscience and scriptural demythologization, Jefferson the deist was also preoccupied with questions of morality and the basis of ethics. True to his essentially naturalistic orientation, Jefferson argued that moral awareness, like all knowledge, ultimately rests on experience. The knowledge of moral truth stems from an innate moral faculty, or what he sometimes referred to as "conscience" or "instinct." But the prescriptions of this faculty are not reflections of mere social convention, much less subjective caprice. Instead, they mirror the objective natural laws of individual felicity and social utility. "Nature hath implanted in our breasts . . . a moral instinct" that defines our duty (letter to Thomas Law, 13 June 1814). When reason heeds that instinct, humans act in such a way as to promote their own and others' welfare. True, certain individuals perform hurtful and therefore wicked actions. But this is no more evidence against the existence of an innate moral faculty than blindness is disproof of the human faculty of vision. Education, the tolerant interplay of ideas, and equal opportunity are necessary conditions for the activation of the moral faculty. Hence, that society is best that promotes environmental conditions conducive to the conscious emergence of the natural light of morality. It is against this background that Jefferson's comments on the distinction between natural and artificial aristocracy should be read (letter to John Adams, 28 October 1813). True or natural aristocrats are those who rationally heed the moral light, act accordingly, and justly earn the acclaim and admiration of their fellows. Artificial or pseudo-aristocrats, on the other hand, are those who, through mere accidents of birth such as physical strength or social position, assume without deserving prestige and influence.

Although not a systematic philosopher, Jefferson, along with Elihu Palmer, was the most sophisticated American proponent of the deistic worldview. One can argue with some of his conclusions—particularly his sometimes ambiguous descriptions of the moral faculty—but it is difficult to doubt either his integrity or the sincerity of his convictions. He once wrote that humans "are answerable not for the rightness but the uprightness" of their beliefs. Judged by his own standard, Jefferson passes the test.

On Freedom of Conscience
(From *Notes on Virginia*, 1785)

The first settlers in this country were emigrants from England, of the English Church, just at a point of time when it was flushed with complete victory over the religious of all other persuasions. Possessed, as they became, of the powers of making, administering, and executing the laws, they showed equal intolerance in this country with their Presbyterian brethren, who had emigrated to the northern government. The poor Quakers were flying from persecution in England. They cast their eyes on these new countries as asylums of civil and religious freedom; but they found them free only for the reigning sect. Several acts of the Virginia assembly of 1659, 1662, and 1693, had made it penal in parents to refuse to have their children baptized; had prohibited the unlawful assembling of Quakers; had made it penal for any master of a vessel to bring a Quaker into the State; had ordered those already here, and such as should come thereafter, to be imprisoned till they should abjure the country; provided a milder punishment for their first and second return, but death for their third; had inhibited all persons from suffering their meetings in or near their houses, entertaining them individually, or disposing of books which supported their tenets. If no execution took place here, as did in New England, it was not owing to the moderation of the church, or spirit of the legislature, as may be inferred from the law itself; but to historical circumstances which have not been handed down to us. The Anglicans retained full possession of the country about a century. Other opinions began then to creep in, and the great care of the government to support their own church, having begotten an equal degree of indolence in its clergy, two-thirds of the people had become dissenters at the commencement of the present revolution. The laws, indeed, were still oppressive on them, but the spirit of the one party had subsided into moderation, and of the other had risen to a degree of determination which commanded respect.

The present state of our laws on the subject of religion is this. The convention of May 1776, in their declaration of rights, declared it to be a truth, and a natural right, that the exercise of religion should be free; but when they proceeded to form on that declaration the ordinance of government, instead of taking up every principle declared in the bill of rights, and guarding it by legislative sanction, they passed over that which asserted our religious rights, leaving them as they found them. The same convention, however, when they met as a member of the general assembly in October, 1776, repealed all *acts of*

Parliament which had rendered criminal the maintaining any opinions in matters of religion, the forbearing to repair to church, and the exercising any mode of worship; and suspended the laws giving salaries to the clergy, which suspension was made perpetual in October, 1779. Statutory oppressions in religion being thus wiped away, we remain at present under those only imposed by the common law, or by our own acts of assembly. At the common law, *heresy* was a capital offence, punishable by burning. Its definition was left to the ecclesiastical judges, before whom the conviction was, till the statute of the 1 El. c. 1 circumscribed it, by declaring, that nothing should be deemed heresy, but what had been so determined by authority of the canonical scriptures, or by one of the four first general councils, or by other council, having for the grounds of their declaration the express and plain words of the scriptures. Heresy, thus circumscribed, being an offence against the common law, our act of assembly of October 1777, c. 17, gives cognizance of it to the general court, by declaring that the jurisdiction of that court shall be general in all matters at the common law. The execution is by the writ *De haeretico comburendo*. By our own act of assembly of 1705, c. 30, if a person brought up in the Christian religion denies the being of a God, or the Trinity, or asserts there are more gods than one, or denies the Christian religion to be true, or the scriptures to be of divine authority, he is punishable on the first offence by incapacity to hold any office or employment ecclesiastical, civil, or military; on the second by disability to sue, to take any gift or legacy, to be guardian, executor, or administrator, and by three years' imprisonment without bail. A father's right to the custody of his own children being founded in law on his right of guardianship, this being taken away, they may of course be severed from him, and put by the authority of a court into more orthodox hands. This is a summary view of that religious slavery under which a people have been willing to remain, who have lavished their lives and fortunes for the establishment of their civil freedom. The error seems not sufficiently eradicated, that the operations of the mind, as well as the acts of the body, are subject to the coercion of the laws. But our rulers can have no authority over such natural rights, only as we have submitted to them. The rights of conscience we never submitted, we could not submit. We are answerable for them to our God. The legitimate powers of government extend to such acts only as are injurious to others. But it does me no injury for my neighbour to say there are twenty gods, or no God. It neither picks my pocket nor breaks my leg. If it be said, his testimony in a court of justice cannot be relied on, reject it then, and be the stigma on him. Constraint may make him worse by making him a hypocrite, but it will never make him a truer man. It may fix him obstinately in his errors, but will not cure them. Reason and free inquiry are the only effectual agents against error. Give a loose to them, they will support the true religion by bringing every false one to their tribunal, to the test of their investigation. They are the natural enemies of error, and of error only. Had not the Roman government permitted free inquiry, Christianity could never have been introduced. Had not free inquiry been indulged at the era of the reformation, the corruptions of Christianity could not have been purged away. If it be restrained now, the present corruptions will be protected, and new ones encouraged. Was the government to prescribe to us our medicine and diet, our bodies would be in such keeping as our souls are now. Thus in France the emetic was once forbidden as a medicine, and the potato as an article of food. Government is just as infallible, too, when it fixes systems in physics. Galileo was sent to the Inquisition for affirming that the earth was a sphere; the government had declared it to be as flat as a trencher, and Galileo was obliged to abjure his error. This error, however, at length prevailed, the earth became a globe, and Descartes declared it was whirled round its axis by a vortex. The government in which he lived was wise enough to see that this was no question of civil jurisdiction, or we should all have been involved by authority in vortices. In fact, the vortices have been exploded, and the Newtonian principle of gravitation is now more firmly established, on the basis of reason, than it would be were the government to step in, and to make it an article of necessary faith. Reason and experiment have been indulged, and error has fled before them. It is error alone which needs the support of government. Truth can stand by itself. Subject opinion to coercion: whom will you make your inquisitors? Fallible men; men governed by bad passions, by private as well as public reasons. And why subject it to coercion? To produce uniformity. But is uniformity of opinion desirable? No more than of face and stature. Introduce the bed of Procrustes then, and as there is danger that the large men may beat the small, make us all of a size, by lopping the former and stretching the latter. Difference of opinion is advantageous in religion. The several sects perform the office of a *censor morum* over each other. Is uniformity attainable? Millions of innocent men, women, and children, since the introduction of Christianity, have been burnt, tortured, fined, imprisoned; yet we have not advanced one inch towards uniformity. What has been the effect of coercion? To make one half the world fools, and the other half hypocrites. To support roguery and error all over the earth. Let us reflect that it is inhabited by a thousand millions of people. That these profess probably a thousand different systems of religion. That ours is but one of that thousand. That if there be but one right, and ours that one, we should wish to see the nine hundred and ninety-nine wandering sects gathered into the fold of truth. But against such a majority we cannot effect this by force. Reason and persuasion are the only practicable instruments. To make way for these, free inquiry must be indulged; and how can we wish others to indulge it while we refuse it ourselves. But every State, says an inquisitor, has established some religion. No two, say I, have established the same. Is this a proof of the infallibility of establishments? Our sister States of Pennsylvania and New York, however, have long subsisted without any establishment at all. The experiment was new and doubtful when they made it. It has answered beyond conception. They flourish infinitely. Religion is well supported; of various kinds, indeed, but all good enough; all sufficient to preserve peace and order; or if a sect arises, whose tenets would subvert morals, good sense has fair play, and reasons and laughs it our of doors, without suffering the State to be troubled with it. They do not hang more malefactors than we do. They are not more disturbed with religious dissensions. On the contrary, their harmony is unparalleled, and can be ascribed to nothing but their unbounded tolerance, because there is no other circumstance in which they differ from every nation on earth. They have made the happy discovery, that the way to silence religious disputes, is to take no notice of them. Let us too give this experiment fair play, and get rid, while we may, of those tyrannical laws. It is true, we are as yet secured against them by the spirit of the times. I doubt whether the people of this country would suffer an execution for heresy, or a three years' imprisonment for not comprehending the mysteries of the Trinity. But is the spirit of the people an infallible, a permanent reliance? Is it government? Is this the kind of protection we receive in return for the rights we give up? Besides, the spirit of the times may alter, will alter. Our rulers will become corrupt, our people careless. A single zealot may commence persecutor, and better men be his victims. It can never be too often repeated, that the time for fixing every essential right on a legal basis is while our rulers are honest, and ourselves united. From the conclusion of this war we shall be going down hill. It will not then be necessary to resort every moment to the people for support. They will be forgotten, therefore, and their rights disregarded. They will forget themselves, but in the sole faculty of making money, and will never think of uniting to effect a due respect for their rights. The shackles, therefore, which shall not be knocked off at the conclusion of this war, will remain on us long, will be made heavier and heavier, till our rights shall revive or expire in a convulsion.

An Act for Establishing Religious Freedom, Passed in the Assembly of Virginia in the Beginning of the Year 1786

Well aware that Almighty God hath created the mind free; that all attempts to influence it by temporal punishments or burdens, or by civil incapacitations, tend only to beget habits of hypocrisy and meanness, and are a departure from the plan of the Holy Author of our religion, who being Lord both of body and mind, yet chose not to propagate it by coercions on either, as was in his Almighty power to do; that the impious presumption of legislators and rulers, civil as well as ecclesiastical, who, being themselves but fallible and uninspired men have assumed dominion over the faith of others, setting up their own opinions and modes of thinking as the only true and infallible, and as such endeavoring to impose them on others, hath established and maintained false religions over the greatest part of the world, and through all time; that to compel a man to furnish contributions of money for the propagation of opinions which he disbelieves, is sinful and tyrannical; that even the forcing him to support this or that teacher of his own religious persuasion, is depriving him of the comfortable liberty of giving his contributions to the particular pastor whose morals he would make his pattern and whose powers he feels most persuasive to righteousness, and is withdrawing from the ministry those temporal rewards, which proceeding from an approbation of their personal conduct, are an additional incitement to earnest and unremitting labors for the instruction of mankind; that our civil rights have no dependence on our religious opinions, more than our opinions in physics or geometry; that, therefore, the proscribing any citizen as unworthy the public confidence by laying upon him an incapacity of being called to the offices of trust and emolument, unless he profess or renounce this or that religious opinion, is depriving him injuriously of those privileges and advantages to which in common with his fellow citizens he has a natural right; that it tends also to corrupt the principles of that very religion it is meant to encourage, by bribing, with a monopoly of worldly honors and emoluments, those who will externally profess and conform to it; that though indeed these are criminal who do not withstand such temptation, yet neither are those innocent who lay the bait in their way; that to suffer the civil magistrate to intrude his powers into the field of opinion and to restrain the profession or propagation of principles, on the supposition of their ill tendency, is a dangerous fallacy, which at once destroys all religious liberty, because he being of course judge of that tendency, will make his opinions the rule of judgment, and approve or condemn the sentiments of others only as they shall square with or differ from his own; that it is time enough for the rightful purposes of civil government, for its officers to interfere when principles break out into overt acts against peace and good order; and finally, that truth is great and will prevail if left to herself, that she is the proper and sufficient antagonist to error, and has nothing to fear from the conflict, unless by human interposition disarmed of her natural weapons, free argument and debate, errors ceasing to be dangerous when it is permitted freely to contradict them.

Be it therefore enacted by the General Assembly, That no man shall be compelled to frequent or support any religious worship, place or ministry whatsoever, nor shall be enforced, restrained, molested, or burthened in his body or goods, nor shall otherwise suffer on account of his religious opinions or belief; but that all men shall be free to profess, and by argument to maintain, their opinions in matters of religion, and that the same shall in nowise diminish, enlarge, or affect their civil capacities.

And though we well know this Assembly, elected by the people for the ordinary purposes of legislation only, have no power to restrain the acts of succeeding assemblies, constituted with the powers equal to our own, and that therefore to declare this act irrevocable, would be of no effect in law, yet we are free to declare, and do declare, that the rights hereby asserted are of the natural rights of mankind, and that if any act shall be hereafter passed to repeal the present or to narrow its operation, such act will be an infringement of natural right.

To Peter Carr (10 August 1787)

Jefferson was minister to France when he penned this letter of advice to his orphaned nephew Peter Carr. It is, as Jefferson says, "a sketch of the sciences to which I would wish you to apply." Included in its various injunctions are Jefferson's ruminations on ethics and religion.

Dear Peter

. . . He who made us would have been a pitiful bungler if he had made the rules of our moral conduct a matter of science. For one man of science, there are thousands who are not. What would have become of them? Man was destined for society. His morality therefore was to be formed to this object. He was endowed with a sense of right and wrong merely relative to this. This sense is as much a part of his nature as the sense of hearing, seeing, feeling; it is the true foundation of morality, and not the το καλον ["the beautiful"] truth, &c., as fanciful writers have imagined. The moral sense, or conscience, is as much a part of man as his leg or arm. It is given to all human beings in a stronger or weaker degree, as force of members is given them in a greater or less degree. It may be strengthened by exercise, as may any particular limb of the body. This sense is submitted indeed in some degree to the guidance of reason; but it is a small stock which is required for this: even a less one than what we call Common sense. State a moral case to a ploughman and a professor. The former will decide it as well, and often better than the latter, because he has not been led astray by artificial rules. In this branch therefore read good books because they will encourage as well as direct your feelings. . . . Above all things lose no occasion of exercising your dispositions to be grateful, to be generous, to be charitable, to be humane, to be true, just, firm, orderly, courageous &c. Consider every act of this kind as an exercise which will strengthen your moral faculties, and increase your worth.

4. Religion. Your reason is now mature enough to examine this object. In the first place divest yourself of all bias in favour of novelty and singularity of opinion. Indulge them in any other subject rather than that of religion. It is too important, and the consequences of error may be too serious. On the other hand shake off all the fears and servile prejudices under which weak minds are servilely crouched. Fix reason firmly in her seat, and call to her tribunal every fact, every opinion. Question with boldness even the existence of a god; be-

cause, if there be one, he must more approve of the homage of reason, than that of blindfolded fear. You will naturally examine first the religion of your own country. Read the bible then, as you would read Livy or Tacitus. The facts which are within the ordinary course of nature you will believe on the authority of the writer, as you do those of the same kind in Livy and Tacitus. The testimony of the writer weighs in their favor in one scale, and their not being against the laws of nature does not weigh against them. But those facts in the bible which contradict the laws of nature, must be examined with more care, and under a variety of faces. Here you must recur to the pretensions of the writer to inspiration from god. Examine upon what evidence his pretensions are founded, and whether that evidence is so strong as that its falsehood would be more improbable than a change of the laws of nature in the case he relates. For example in the book of Joshua we are told the sun stood still several hours. Were we to read that fact in Livy or Tacitus we should class it with their showers of blood, speaking of statues, beasts &c., but it is said that the writer of that book was inspired. Examine therefore candidly what evidence there is of his having been inspired. The pretension is entitled to your inquiry, because millions believe it. On the other hand you are Astronomer enough to know how contrary it is to the law of nature that a body revolving on its axis, as the earth does, should have stopped, should not by that sudden stoppage have prostrated animals, trees, buildings, and should after a certain time have resumed its revolution, and that without a second general prostration. Is this arrest of the earth's motion, or the evidence which affirms it, most within the law of probabilities? You will next read the new testament. It is the history of a personage called Jesus. Keep in your eye the opposite pretensions. 1. Of those who say he was begotten by god, born of a virgin, suspended and reversed the laws of nature at will, and ascended bodily into heaven; and 2. of those who say he was a man, of illegitimate birth, of a benevolent heart, enthusiastic mind, who set out without pretensions to divinity, ended in believing them, and was punished capitally for sedition by being gibbeted according to the Roman law which punished the first commission of that offence by whipping, and the second by exile or death *in furea*. . . . Do not be frightened from this inquiry by any fear of its consequences. If it ends in a belief that there is no god, you will find incitements to virtue in the comfort and pleasantness you feel in its exercise, and the love of others which it will procure you. If you find reason to believe there is a god, a consciousness that you are acting under his eye, and that he approves you, will be a vast additional incitement. If that there be a future state, the hope of a happy existence in that increases the appetite to deserve it; if that Jesus was also a god, you will be comforted by a belief of his aid and love. In fine, I repeat that you must lay aside all prejudice on both sides, and neither believe nor reject any thing because any other persons, or description of persons have rejected or believed it. Your own reason is the only oracle

118 given you by heaven, and you are answerable not for the rightness but uprightness of the decision. . . .

To the Rev. Isaac Story (5 December 1801)
Jefferson responds to a nine-page manuscript entitled "The Metempsychosis-doc-trine, in a limited sense, defended," written by Story.

Sir
    Your favor of Oct. 27 was received some time since, and read with pleasure.
It is not for me to pronounce on the hypothesis you present of a transmigration
of souls from one body to another in certain cases. The laws of nature have
withheld from us the means of physical knowledge of the country of spirits and
revelation has, for reasons unknown to us, chosen to leave us in the dark as we
were. When I was young I was fond of the speculations which seemed to
promise some insight into that hidden country, but observing at length that
they left me in the same ignorance in which they had found me, I have for very
many years ceased to read or to think concerning them, and have reposed my
head on that pillow of ignorance which a benevolent creator has made so soft
for us knowing how much we should be forced to use it. I have thought it
better by nourishing the good passions, and controlling the bad, to merit an
inheritance in a state of being of which I can know so little, and to trust for the
future to him who has been so good for the past. I perceive too that these
speculations have with you been only the amusement of leisure hours; while
your labours have been devoted to the education of your children, making
them good members of society, to the instructing men in their duties, and
performing the other offices of a large parish. . . .

To Joseph Priestley (9 April 1803)
Jefferson offers an early description of his planned but never written study of the Christian religion. For his synopsis of the proposed treatise, see the 1803 letter to Rush, next.

Dear Sir
    While on a short visit lately to Monticello, I received from you a copy of
your comparative view of Socrates and Jesus, and I avail myself of the first
moment of leisure after my return to acknowledge the pleasure I had in the
perusal of it, and the desire it excited to see you take up the subject on a more
extensive scale. In consequence of some conversation with Dr. Rush in the
years 1798–99. I had promised some day to write him a letter giving him my
view of the Christian system. I have reflected often on it since, and even

sketched the outlines in my own mind. I should first take a general view of the moral doctrines of the most remarkable of the antient philosophers, of whose ethics we have sufficient information to make an estimate: say of Pythagoras, Epicurus, Epictetus, Socrates, Cicero, Seneca, Antoninus. I should do justice to the branches of morality they have treated well, but point out the importance of those in which they are deficient. I should then take a view of the deism, and ethics of the Jews, and shew in what a degraded state they were, and the necessity they presented of a reformation. I should proceed to a view of the life, character, and doctrines of Jesus, who, sensible of the incorrectness of their ideas of the deity, and of morality, endeavored to bring them to the principles of a pure deism, and juster notions of the attributes of god, to reform their moral doctrines to the standard of reason, justice, and philanthropy, and to inculcate the belief of a future state. This view would purposely omit the question of his divinity and even of his inspiration. To do him justice it would be necessary to remark the disadvantages his doctrines have to encounter, not having been committed to writing by himself, but by the most unlettered of men, by memory, long after they had heard them from him; when much was forgotten, much misunderstood, and presented in very paradoxical shapes. Yet such are the fragments remaining as to shew a master workman, and that his system of morality was the most benevolent and sublime probably that has been ever taught; and eminently more perfect than those of any of the antient philosophers. His character and doctrines have received still greater injury from those who pretend to be his special disciples, and who have disfigured and sophisticated his actions and precepts, from views of personal interest, so as to induce the unthinking part of mankind to throw off the whole system in disgust, and to pass sentence as an imposter on the most innocent, the most benevolent the most eloquent and sublime character that ever has been exhibited to man.—This is the outline; but I have not the time, and still less the information which the subject needs. It will therefore rest with me in contemplation only. You are the person who of all others would do it best, and most promptly. You have all the materials at hand, and you put together with ease. I wish you could be induced to extend your late work to the whole subject. . . .

To Benjamin Rush (21 April 1803)

Dear Sir

In some of the delightful conversations with you, in the evenings of 1798–99, which served as an Anodyne to the afflictions of the crisis through which the country was then labouring, the Christian religion was sometimes our topic: and I then promised you that, one day or other, I would give you my views of it. They are the result of a life of enquiry and reflection, and very different from that Anti-Christian system, imputed to me by those who know

120 nothing of my opinions. To the corruptions of Christianity, I am indeed opposed; but not to the genuine precepts of Jesus himself. I am a Christian, in the only sense in which he wished any one to be; sincerely attached to his doctrines, in preference to all others; ascribing to himself every human excellence, and believing he never claimed any other. At the short intervals, since these conversations, when I could justifiably abstract my mind from public affairs, this subject has been under my contemplation. But the more I considered it, the more it expanded beyond the measure of either my time or information. In the moment of my late departure from Monticello, I received from Doctr. Priestley his little treatise of "Socrates and Jesus compared." This being a section of the general view I had taken of the field, it became a subject of reflection, while on the road, and unoccupied otherwise. The result was, to arrange in my mind a Syllabus, or Outline, of such an Estimate of the comparative merits of Christianity, as I wished to see executed, by some one of more leisure and information for the task than myself. This I now send you, as the only discharge of my promise I can probably ever execute. And, in confiding it to you, I know it will not be exposed to the malignant perversions of those who make every word from me a text for new misrepresentations and calumnies. I am moreover averse to the communication of my religious tenets to the public; because it would countenance the presumption of those who have endeavored to draw them before that tribunal, and to seduce public opinion to erect itself into that Inquisition over the rights of conscience, which the laws have so justly proscribed. It behooves every man, who values liberty of conscience for himself, to resist invasions of it in the case of others; or their case may, by change of circumstances, become his own. It behooves him too, in his own case, to give no example of concession, betraying the common right of independent opinion, by answering questions of faith, which the laws have left between god and himself. Accept my affectionate salutations.

Syllabus of an Estimate of the Merit of the Doctrines
of Jesus, compared with those of others.

In a comparative view of the Ethics of the enlightened nations of antiquity, of the Jews, and of Jesus, no notice should be taken of the corruptions of reason, among the antients, to wit, the idolatry and superstition of the vulgar, Nor of the corruptions of Christianity by the learned among its professors.

Let a just view be taken of the moral principles inculcated by the most esteemed of the sects of antt. philosophy, or of their individuals; particularly Pythagoras, Socrates, Epicurus, Cicero, Epictetus, Seneca, Antoninus.
I. Philosophers.

1. Their precepts related chiefly to ourselves, and the government of those passions which, unrestrained, would disturb our tranquility of mind. In this branch of Philosophy they were really great.

2. In developing our duties to others, they were short and defective. They embraced indeed the circles of kindred and friends: and inculcated patriotism, or the love of our country in the aggregate, as a primary obligation: towards our neighbors and countrymen, they taught justice, but scarcely viewed them as within the circle of benevolence. Still less have they inculcated peace, charity, and love to our fellow men, or embraced with benevolence, the whole family of mankind.

II. Jews.

1. Their system was Deism, that is, the belief in one only god. But their ideas of him, and of his attributes, were degrading and injurious.

2. Their Ethics were not only imperfect, but often irreconcilable with the sound dictates of reason and morality, as they respect intercourse with those around us: and repulsive, and anti-social, as respecting other nations. They needed reformation therefore in an eminent degree.

III. Jesus.

In this state of things among the Jews, Jesus appeared. His parentage was obscure, his condition poor, his education null, his natural endowments great, his life correct and innocent; he was meek, benevolent, patient, firm, disinterested, and of the sublimist eloquence.

The disadvantages under which his doctrines appear are remarkable.

1. Like Socrates and Epictetus, he wrote nothing himself.

2. But he had not, like them, a Xenophon or an Arrian to write for him. . . . On the contrary, all the learned of his country, entrenched in its power and riches, were opposed to him lest his labours should undermine their advantages: and the committing to writing his life and doctrines, fell on unlettered and ignorant men: who wrote too from memory, and not till long after the transactions had passed.

3. According to the ordinary fate of those who attempt to enlighten and reform mankind, he fell an early victim to the jealousy and combination of the altar and the throne; at about 33 years of age, his reason having not yet attained the maximum of its energy, nor the course of his preaching, which was but of about 3 years at most, presented occasions for developing a compleat system of morals.

4. Hence the doctrines which he really delivered were defective as a whole, And fragments only of what he did deliver have come to us, mutilated, mistated, and often unintelligible.

5. They have been still more disfigured by the corruptions of schismatising followers, who have found an interest in sophisticating and perverting the simple doctrines he taught, by engrafting on them the mysticisms of a Graecian Sophist, frittering them into subtleties, and obscuring them with jargon, until they have caused good men to reject the whole in disgust, and to view Jesus himself as an impostor.

122   Nothwithstanding these disadvantages, a system of morals is presented to
us, which, if filled up in the true style and spirit of the rich fragments he left us,
would be the most perfect and sublime that has ever been taught by man.

The question of his being a member of the god-head, or in direct communication with it, claimed for him by some of his followers, and denied by others,
is foreign to the present view, which is merely an estimate of the intrinsic merits
of his doctrines.

1. He corrected the Deism of the Jews, confirming them in their belief of
one only god, and giving them juster notions of his attributes and government.

2. His moral doctrines relating to kindred and friends were more pure and
perfect, than those of the most correct of the philosophers, and greatly more
so than those of the Jews. And they went far beyond both in inculcating universal philanthropy, not only to kindred and friends, to neighbors and countrymen, but to all mankind, gathering all into one family, under the bonds of love,
charity, peace, common wants, and common aids. A development of this head
will evince the peculiar superiority of the system of Jesus over all others.

3. The precepts of Philosophy, and of the Hebrew code, laid hold of actions
only. He pushed his scrutinies into the heart of man; erected his tribunal in the
region of his thoughts, and purified the waters at the fountain head.

4. He taught, emphatically, the doctrine of a future state; which was either
doubted or disbelieved by the Jews: and wielded it with efficacy, as an important incentive, supplementary to the other motives to moral conduct.

To John Adams (12 October 1813)

*Jefferson reflects on the "corruption" of Christianity and refers to his edited "Phi-
losophy of Jesus of Nazareth," a compilation of New Testament synoptic texts
stripped of their supernaturalist doctrine.*

Dear Sir

. . . To compare the morals of the old, with those of the new testament,
would require an attentive study of the former, a search thro' all its books for
its precepts, and through all its history for its practices, and the principles they
prove. As commentaries too on these, the philosophy of the Hebrews must be
enquired into, their Mishna, their Gemara, Cabbala, Jezirah, Sohar, Cosri, and
their Talmud must be examined and understood, in order to do them full
justice. Brucker, it would seem, has gone deeply into these Repositories of their
ethics, and Enfield, his epitomiser, concludes in these words. "Ethics were so
little understood among the Jews, that, in their whole compilation called the
Talmud, there is only one treatise on moral subjects. Their books of Morals
chiefly consisted in a minute enumeration of duties. From the law of Moses
were deduced 613 precepts, which were divided into two classes, affirmative

and negative, 248 in the former, and 365 in the latter. It may serve to give the reader some idea of the low state of moral philosophy among the Jews in the Middle age, to add, that of the 248 affirmative precepts, only 3 were considered as obligatory upon women; and that, in order to obtain salvation, it was judged sufficient to fulfill any one single law in the hour of death; the observance of the rest being deemed necessary, only to increase the felicity of the future life. What a wretched depravity of sentiment and manners must have prevailed before such corrupt maxims could have obtained credit! It is impossible to collect from these writings a consistent series of moral Doctrine." Enfield, B. 4 chap. 3. It was the reformation of this "wretched depravity" of morals which Jesus undertook. In extracting the pure principles which he taught, we should have to strip off the artificial vestments in which they have been muffled by priests, who have travestied them into various forms, as instruments of riches and power to themselves. We must dismiss the Platonists and Plotinists, the Stagyrites and Gamalielites, the Eclectics the Gnostics and Scholastics, their essences and emanations, their Logos and Demi-urgos, Aeons and Daemons male and female, with a long train Etc. Etc. Etc. or, shall I say at once, of Nonsense. We must reduce our volume to the simple evangelists, select, even from them, the very words only of Jesus, paring off the Amphibologisms into which they have been led by forgetting often, or not understanding, what had fallen from him, by giving their own misconceptions as his dicta, and expressing unintelligbly for others what they had not understood themselves. There will be found remaining the most sublime and benevolent code of morals which has ever been offered to man. I have performed this operation for my own use, by cutting verse by verse out of the printed book, and arranging the matter which is evidently his, and which is as easily distinguishable as diamonds in a dunghill. The result is an octavo of 46 pages of pure and unsophisticated doctrines, such as were professed and acted on by the *unlettered* apostles, the Apostolic fathers, and the Christians of the 1st century. Their Platonising successors indeed, in after times, in order to legitimate the corruptions which they had incorporated into the doctrines of Jesus, found it necessary to disavow the primitive Christians, who had taken their principles from the mouth of Jesus himself, of his Apostles, and the Fathers contemporary with them. They excommunicated their followers as heretics, branding them with the opprobrious name of Ebionites or Beggars.

For a comparison of the Graecian philosophy with that of Jesus, materials might be largely drawn from the same source. Enfield gives a history, and detailed account of the opinions and principles of the different sects. These relate to the gods, their natures, grades, places and powers; the demi-gods and daemons, and their agency with man; the Universe, its structure, extent, production and duration; the origin of things from the elements of fire, water, air, and earth; the human soul, its essence and derivation; the summum bonum

124 and finis bonorum; with a thousand idle dreams and fancies on these and other subjects the knowledge of which is withheld from man, leaving but a short chapter for his moral duties, and the principal section of that given to what he owes himself, to precepts for rendering him impassible, and unassailable by the evils of life, and for preserving his mind in a state of constant serenity.

Such a canvas is too broad for the age of seventy, and especially of one whose chief occupations have been in the practical business of life. We must leave therefore to others, younger and more learned than we are, to prepare this euthanasia for Platonic Christianity, and its restoration to the primitive simplicity of its founder. I think you give a just outline of the theism of the three religions when you say that the principle of the Hebrew was the fear, of the Gentile the honor, and of the Christian the love of God.

An expression in your letter of Sep. 14 that "the human understanding is a revelation from its maker" gives the best solution, that I believe can be given, of the question, What did Socrates mean by his Daemon? He was too wise to believe, and too honest to pretend that he had real and familiar converse with a superior and invisible being. He probably considered the suggestions of his conscience, or reason, as revelations, or inspirations from the Supreme mind, bestowed, on important occasions, by a special superintending providence. . .

To John Adams (28 October 1813)
Jefferson expresses his views about the "natural aristocracy" promoted by freedom of conscience and opportunity, as well as the "progressive" nature of "Science."

Dear Sir

. . . Experience proves that the moral and physical qualities of man, whether good or evil, are transmissible in a certain degree from father to son. But I suspect that the equal rights of men will rise up against this privileged Solomon, and oblige us to continue acquiescence under the Ἀμαυρωσις γενεος ἀστων [degeneration of the race of men] which Theognis complains of, and to content ourselves with the accidental aristoi produced by the fortuitous concourse of breeders. For I agree with you that there is a natural aristocracy among men. The grounds of this are virtue and talents. Formerly bodily powers gave place among the aristoi. But since the invention of gunpowder has armed the weak as well as the strong with missile death, bodily strength, like beauty, good humor, politeness and other accomplishments, has become but an auxiliary ground of distinction. There is also an artificial aristocracy founded on wealth and birth, without either virtue or talents; for with these it would belong to the first class. The natural aristocracy I consider as the most precious gift of nature for the instruction, the trusts, and government of society. And indeed it would have been inconsistent in creation to have formed man for the social state, and not to have provided virtue and wisdom enough to manage the concerns of the society. May we not even say that that form of government is the best which provides the most effectually for a pure selection of these natural aristoi into the offices of government? The artificial aristocracy is a mischievous ingredient in government, and provision should be made to prevent its ascendancy. On the question, What is the best provision, you and I differ; but we differ as rational friends, using the free exercise of our own reason, and mutually indulging its errors. *You* think it best to put the Pseudo-aristoi into a separate chamber of legislation where they may be hindered from doing mischief by their coordinate branches, and where also they may be a protection to wealth against the Agrarian and plundering enterprises of the Majority of the people. I think that to give them power in order to prevent them from doing mischief, is arming them for it, and increasing instead of remedying the evil. For if the coordinate branches can arrest their action, so may they that of the coordinates. Mischief may be done negatively as well as positively. Of this a cabal in the Senate of the U.S. has furnished many proofs. Nor do I believe them necessary to protect the wealthy; because enough of these will find their way into every branch of the legislature to protect themselves. From 15 to 20 legislatures of our own, in action for 30 years past, have proved that no fears of an equalisation of property are to be apprehended from them.

I think the best remedy is exactly that provided by all our constitutions, to leave to the citizens the free election and separation of the aristoi from the pseudo-aristoi, of the wheat from the chaff. In general they will elect the real good and wise. In some instances, wealth may corrupt, and birth blind them; but not in sufficient degree to endanger society. . . .

At the first session of our legislature after the Declaration of Independence, we passed a law abolishing entails. And this was followed by one abolishing the privilege of Primogeniture, and dividing the lands of intestates equally among all their children, or other representatives. These laws, drawn by myself, laid the axe to the root of Pseudo-aristocracy. And had another which I prepared been adopted by the legislature, our work would have been compleat. It was a Bill for the more general diffusion of learning. This proposed to divide every county into wards of 5 or 6 miles square, like your townships; to establish in each ward a free school for reading, writing and common arithmetic; to provide for the annual selection of the best subjects from these schools who might receive at the public expence a higher degree of education at a district school; and from these district schools to select a certain number of the most promising

126 subjects to be compleated at an University, where all the useful sciences should be taught. Worth and genius would thus have been sought out from every condition of life, and compleatly prepared by education for defeating the competition of wealth and birth for public trusts. . . .

With respect to Aristocracy, we should further consider that, before the establishment of the American states, nothing was known to History but the Man of the old world, crowded within limits either small or overcharged, and steeped in the vices which that situation generates. A government adapted to such men would be one thing; but a very different one, that for the Man of these states. Here every one may have land to labor for himself if he chooses; or, preferring the exercise of any other industry, may exact for it such compensation as not only to afford a comfortable subsistence, but wherewith to provide for a cessation from labor in old age. Every one, by his property, or by his satisfactory situation, is interested in the support of law and order. And such men may safely and advantageously reserve to themselves a wholesome control over the public affairs and a degree of freedom, which in the hands of the Canaille of the cities of Europe, would be instantly perverted to the demolition and destruction of every thing public and private. The history of the last 25 years of France, and of the last 40 years in America, nay of its last 200 years, proves the truth of both parts of this observation.

But even in Europe a change has sensibly taken place in the mind of Man. Science had liberated the ideas of those who read and reflect, and the American example had kindled feelings of right in the people. An insurrection has consequently begun, of science, talents and courage against rank and birth, which have fallen into contempt. It has failed in its first effort, because the mobs of the cities, the instrument used for its accomplishment, debased by ignorance, poverty and vice, could not be restrained to rational action. But the world will recover from the panic of this first catastrophe. Science is progressive, and talents and enterprise on the alert. Resort may be had to the people of the country, a more governable power from their principles and subordination; and rank, and birth, and tinsel-aristocracy will finally shrink into insignificance, even there. This however we have no right to meddle with. It suffices for us, if the moral and physical condition of our own citizens qualifies them to select the able and good for the direction of their government, with a recurrence of elections at such short periods as will enable them to displace an unfaithful servant before the mischief he meditates may be irremediable. . . .

To Thomas Law (13 June 1814)

Jefferson replies to Law's Second Thoughts on Instinctive Impulses *(Philadelphia, 1813), which defended an ethical system purporting to be a "regular science, founded on primordial, universal, invariable principles."*

Dear Sir

The copy of your Second thoughts on Instinctive impulses with the letter accompanying it, was received just as I was setting out on a journey to this place [Poplar Forest], two or three days distant from Monticello. I brought it with me, and read it with great satisfaction; and with the more, as it contained exactly my own creed on the foundation of morality in man. It is really curious that, on a question so fundamental, such a variety of opinions should have prevailed among men; and those too of the most exemplary virtue and first order of understanding. It shews how necessary was the care of the Creator in making the moral principle so much a part of our constitution as that no errors of reasoning or of speculation might lead us astray from its observance in practice. Of all the theories on this question, the most whimsical seems to have been that of Wollaston, who considers *truth* as the foundation of morality. The thief who steals your guinea does wrong only inasmuch as he acts a lie, in using your guinea as if it were his own. Truth is certainly a branch of morality, and a very important one to society. But, presented as its foundation, it is as if a tree, taken up by the roots, had its stem reversed in the air, and one of its branches planted in the ground.—Some have made the *love of god* the foundation of morality. This too is but a branch of our moral duties, which are generally divided into duties to god, and duties to man. If we did a good act merely from the love of god and a belief that it is pleasing to him, whence arises the morality of the Atheist? It is idle to say as some do, that no such being exists. We have the same evidence of the fact as of most of those we act on, to wit, their own affirmations, and their reasonings in support of them. I have observed indeed generally that, while in protestant countries the defections from the Platonic Christianity of the priests is to Deism, in Catholic countries they are to Atheism. Diderot, D'Alembert, D'Holbach, Condorcet, are known to have been among the most virtuous of men. Their virtue then must have had some other foundation than the love of god.

The το καλον of others is founded in a different faculty, that of taste, which is not even a branch of morality. We have indeed an innate sense of what we call beautiful: but that is exercised chiefly on subjects addressed to the fancy, whether thro' the eye, in visible forms, as landscape, animal figure, dress, drapery, architecture, the composition of colours &c. or to the imagination directly, as imagery, style, or measure in prose or poetry, or whatever else constitutes the domain of criticism, or taste, a faculty entirely distinct from the moral one. Self-interest, or rather Self love, or *Egoism*, has been more plausibly substituted as the basis of morality. But I consider our relations with others as constituting the boundaries of morality. With ourselves we stand on the ground of identity, not of relation; which last, requiring two subjects, excludes self-love confined to a single one. To ourselves, in strict language, we can owe no duties, obligation requiring also two parties. Self-love therefore is no part of morality. Indeed it is exactly its counterpart. It is the sole antagonist of virtue, leading us constantly by our propensities to self-gratification in violation of our moral duties to others. Accordingly it is against this enemy that are erected the batteries of moralists and religionists, as the only obstacle to the practice of morality. Take from man his selfish propensities, and he can have nothing to seduce him from the practice of virtue. Or subdue those propensities by education, instruction, or restraint, and virtue remains without a competitor. Egoism, in a broader sense, has been thus presented as the source of moral action. It has been said that we feed the hungry, clothe the naked, bind up the wounds of the man beaten by thieves, pour oil and wine into them, set him on our own beast, and bring him to the inn, because we receive ourselves pleasure from these acts. So Helvetius, one of the best men on earth, and the most ingenious advocate of this principle, after defining "interest" to mean, not merely that which is pecuniary, but whatever may procure us pleasure or withdraw us from pain (de l'Esprit, 2.1) says (ib. 2.2) "the humane man is he to whom the sight of misfortune is insupportable and who, to rescue himself from this spectacle, is forced to succour the unfortunate object." This indeed is true. But it is one step short of the ultimate question. These good acts give us pleasure: but how happens it that they give us pleasure? Because nature hath implanted in our breasts a love of others, a sense of duty to them, a moral instinct in short, which prompts us irresistibly to feel and to succour their distresses; and protests against the language of Helvetius (ib. 2.5) "what other motive than self interest could determine a man to generous actions? It is as impossible for him to love what is good for the sake of good, as to love evil for the sake of evil." The creator would indeed have been a bungling artist, had he intended man for a social animal, without planting in him social dispositions. It is true they are not planted in every man; because there is no rule without exceptions; but it is false reasoning which converts exceptions into the general rule. Some men are born without the organs of sight, or of hearing, or without hands. Yet it would be wrong to say that man is born without these faculties; and sight, hearing and hands may with truth enter into the general definition of Man.

The want or imperfection of the moral sense in some men, like the want or imperfection of the senses of sight and hearing in others, is no proof that it is a general characteristic of the species. When it is wanting we endeavor to supply the defect by education, by appeals to reason and calculation, by presenting to the being so unhappily conformed other motives to do good, and to eschew evil; such as the love, or the hatred or rejection of those among whom he lives and whose society is necessary to his happiness, and even existence; demonstrations by sound calculation that honesty promotes interest in the long run; the rewards and penalties established by the laws; and ultimately the prospects of a future state of retribution for the evil as well as the good done while here.

These are the correctives which are supplied by education, and which exercise the functions of the moralist, the preacher and legislator: and they lead into a course of correct action all those whose depravity is not too profound to be eradicated. Some have argued against the existence of a moral sense, by saying that if nature had given us such a sense, impelling us to virtuous actions, and warning us against those which are vicious, then nature would also have designated, by some particular earmarks, the two sets of actions which are, in themselves, the one virtuous, and the other vicious: whereas we find in fact, that the same actions are deemed virtuous in one country, and vicious in another. The answer is that nature has constituted *utility* to man the standard and test of virtue. Men living in different countries, under different circumstances, different habits, and regimens, may have different utilities. The same act therefore may be useful, and consequently virtuous, in one country, which is injurious and vicious in another differently circumstanced. I sincerely then believe with you in the general existence of a moral instinct. I think it the brightest gem with which the human character is studded; and the want of it as more degrading than the most hideous of the bodily deformities. I am happy in reviewing the roll of associates in this principle which you present in your 2d letter, some of which I had not before met with. To these might be added Lord Kaims, one of the ablest of our advocates, who goes so far as to say, in his Principles of Natural Religion, that a man owes no duty to which he is not urged by some impulsive feeling. This is correct if referred to the standard of general feeling in the given case, and not to the feeling of a single individual. Perhaps I may misquote him, it being fifty years since I read his book. . . .

To Charles Thomson (9 January 1816)

Jefferson acknowledges receipt of Thomson's A Synopsis of the Four Evangelists; or, A Regular History of the Conception, Birth, Doctrine, Miracles, Death, Resurrection, and Ascension of Jesus, in the Words of the Evangelists *(Philadelphia, 1815).*

My Dear and Antient Friend
    . . . I too have made a wee little book, from the same materials, which I call the Philosophy of Jesus. It is a paradigma of his doctrines, made by cutting the texts out of the book, and arranging them on the pages of a blank book, in a certain order of time or subject. A more beautiful or precious morsel of ethics I have never seen. It is a document in proof that *I* am a *real Christian*, that is to say, a disciple of the doctrines of Jesus, very different from the Platonists, who call *me* infidel, and *themselves* Christians and preachers of the gospel, while they draw all their characteristic dogmas from what its Author never said nor saw. They have compounded from the heathen mysteries a system beyond the

130   comprehension of man, of which the great reformer of the vicious ethics and deism of the Jews, were he to return on earth, would not recognise one feature. . . .

To Francis Adrian Van der Kemp (30 July 1816)

Van der Kemp was a New York Unitarian to whom Jefferson had earlier sent a copy of his syllabus on Christian doctrine.

Dear Sir

Your favor of July 14 is received, and I am entirely satisfied with the disposition you made of the Syllabus, keeping my name unconnected with it, as I am sure you have done. I should really be gratified to see a full and fair examination of the ground it takes. I believe it to be the only ground on which reason and truth can take their stand, and that only against which we are told that the gates of hell shall not finally prevail. Yet I have little expectation that the affirmative can be freely maintained in England. We know it could not here. For altho' we have freedom of religious opinion by law, we are yet under the inquisition of public opinion: and in England it would have both law and public opinion to encounter. The love of peace, and a want of either time or taste for these disquisitions, induce silence on my part as to the contents of this paper, and all explanations and discussions which might arise out of it; and this must be my apology for observing the same silence on the questions of your letter. I leave the thing to the evidence of the books on which it claims to be founded, and with which I am persuaded you are more familiar than myself.—Altho' I rarely waste time in reading on theological subjects, as mangled by our Pseudo-Christians, yet I can readily suppose Basanistos may be amusing. Ridicule is the only weapon which can be used against unintelligible propositions. Ideas must be distinct before reason can act upon them; and no man ever had a distinct idea of the trinity. It is the mere Abracadabra of the mountebanks calling themselves the priests of Jesus. If it could be understood it would not answer their purpose. Their security is in their faculty of shedding darkness, like the scuttle fish, thro' the element in which they move, and making it impenetrable to the eye of a pursuing enemy. And there they will skulk, until some rational creed can occupy the void which the obliteration of their duperies would leave in the minds of our honest and unsuspecting brethren. Whenever this shall take place, I believe that Christianism may be universal and eternal. I salute you with great esteem and respect.

To Margaret Bayard Smith (6 August 1816)

Smith had inquired if a recent rumor was true—that Jefferson had professed belief in Christianity.

I have received, dear Madam, your very friendly letter of July 21 and Assure you that I feel with deep sensibility its kind expressions towards my self, and the more as from a person than whom no others could be more in sympathy with my own affections. I often call to mind the occasions of knowing your worth, which the societies of Washington furnished; and none more than those derived from your much valued visit to Monticello. I recognise the same motives of goodness in the solicitude you express on the rumor supposed to proceed from a letter of mine to Charles Thomson on the subject of the Christian religion. It is true that, in writing to the translator of the Bible and Testament, that subject was mentioned: but equally so that no adherence to any particular mode of Christianity was there expressed; nor any change of opinions suggested. A change from what? The priests indeed have heretofore thought proper to ascribe to me religious, or rather antireligious sentiments, of their own fabric, but such as soothed their resentments against the Act of Virginia for establishing religious freedom. They wished him to be thought Atheist, Deist, or Devil, who could advocate freedom from their religious dictations. But I have ever thought religion a concern purely between our god and our consciences, for which we were accountable to him, and not to the priests. I never told my own religion, nor scrutinised that of another. I never attempted to make a convert, nor wished to change another's creed. I have ever judged of the religion of others by their lives: and by this test, my dear Madam, I have been satisfied yours must be an excellent one, to have produced a life of such exemplary virtue and correctness. For it is in our lives, and not from our words, that our religion must be read. By the same test the world must judge me. But this does not satisfy the priesthood. They must have a positive, a declared assent to all their interested absurdities. My opinion is that there would never have been an infidel, if there had never been a priest. The artificial structures they have built on the purest of all moral systems, for the purpose of deriving from it pence and power, revolts those who think for themselves, and who read in that system only what is really there. These therefore they brand with such nicknames as their enmity chooses gratuitously to impute. I have left the world, in silence, to judge of causes from their effects: and I am consoled in this course, my dear friend, when I perceive the candor with which I am judged by your justice and discernment; and that, notwithstanding the slanders of the Saints, my fellow-citizens have thought me worthy of trusts. The imputations of irreligion having spent their force, they think an imputation of change might now be turned to account as a bolster for their duperies. I shall leave them, as heretofore to grope on in the dark. . . .

To Ezra Stiles Ely (25 June 1819)
Jefferson comments on Ely's Conversation on the Science of the Human Mind *(Philadelphia, 1819).*

132   Your favor Sir, of the 14th has been duly received, and with it the book you were so kind as to forward to me. For this mark of attention be pleased to accept my thanks. The science of the human mind is curious, but it is one on which I have not indulged myself in much speculation. The times in which I have lived, and the scenes in which I have been engaged, have required me to keep the mind too much in action to have leisure to study minutely its laws of action. I am therefore little qualified to give an opinion on the comparative worth of books on that subject, and little disposed to do it on any book. Yours has brought the science within a small compass and that is a merit of the 1st order; and especially with one to whom the drudgery of letter writing often denies the leisure of reading a single page in a week. On looking over the summary of the contents of your book, it does not seem likely to bring into collision any of those sectarian differences which you suppose may exist between us. In that branch of religion which regards the moralities of life, and the duties of a social being, which teaches us to love our neighbors as ourselves, and to do good to all men, I am sure that you and I do not differ. We probably differ on that which relates to the dogmas of theology, the foundation of all sectarianism, and on which no two sects dream alike; for if they did they would then be of the same. You say you are a Calvinist. I am not. I am of a sect by myself, as far as I know. I am not a Jew: and therefore do not adopt their theology, which supposes the god of infinite justice to punish the sins of the fathers upon their children, unto the 3d and 4th generation: and the benevolent and sublime reformer of that religion has told us only that god is good and perfect, but has not defined him. I am therefore of his theology, believing that we have neither words nor ideas adequate to that definition. And if could all, after his example, leave the subject as undefinable, we should all be of one sect, doers of good and eschewers of evil. No doctrines of his lead to schism. It is the speculations of crazy theologists which have made a Babel of a religion the most moral and sublime ever preached to man, and calculated to heal, and not to create differences. These religious animosities I impute to those who call themselves his ministers, and who engraft their casuistries on the stock of his simple precepts. I am sometimes more angry with them than is authorised by the blessed charities which he preached. . . .

To William Short (4 August 1820)

Dear Sir

    I owe a letter for your favor of June 29 which was received in due time, and there being no subject of the day of particular interest I will make this a supplement to mine of Apr. 13. My aim in that was to justify the character of Jesus against the fictions of his pseudo-followers which have exposed him to the inference of being an imposter. For if we could believe that he really countenanced the follies, the falsehoods and the Charlatanisms which his biographers father on him, and admit the misconstructions, interpolations and theorisations of the fathers of the early, and fanatics of the latter ages, the conclusion would be irresistible by every sound mind, that he was an imposter. I give no credit to their falsifications of his actions and doctrines; and, to rescue his character, the postulate in my letter asked only what is granted in reading every other historian. When Livy or Siculus, for example, tell us things which coincide with our experience of the order of nature, we credit them on their word, and place their narrations among the records of credible history. But when they tell us of calves speaking, of statues sweating blood, and other things against the course of nature, we reject these as fables, not belonging to history. In like manner, when an historian, speaking of a character well known and established on satisfactory testimony imputes to it things incompatible with that character, we reject them without hesitation, and assent to that only for which we have better evidence. Had Plutarch informed us that Caeser and Cicero passed their whole lives in religious exercises, and abstinence from the affairs of the world, we should reject what was so inconsistent with their established characters, still crediting what he relates in conformity with our ideas of them. So again, the superlative wisdom of Socrates is testified by all antiquity, and placed on ground not to be questioned. When therefore Plato puts into his mouth such fancies, such paralogisms and sophisms as a schoolboy would be ashamed of, we conclude they were the whimsies of Plato's own foggy brain, and acquit Socrates of puerilities so unlike his character. (Speaking of Plato I will add that no writer antient or modern has bewildered the world with more ignes fatui than this renowned philosopher, in Ethics, in Politics and Physics. In the latter, to specify a single example, compare his views of the animal economy, in his Timaeus, with those of Mrs. Bryan in her Conversations on chemistry, and weigh the science of the canonised philosopher against the good sense of the unassuming lady. But Plato's visions have furnished a basis for endless systems of mystical theology, and he is therefore all but adopted as a Christian saint.—It is surely time for men to think for themselves, and to throw off the authority of names so artificially magnified. But to return from this parenthesis, I say that) this free exercise of reason is all I ask for the vindication of the character of Jesus. We find in the writings of his biographers matter of two distinct descriptions. First a ground work of vulgar ignorance, of things impossible, of superstitions, fanaticisms, and fabrications. Intermixed with these again are sublime ideas of the supreme being, aphorisms and precepts of the purest morality and benevolence, sanctioned by a life of humility, innocence, and simplicity of manners, neglect of riches, absence of worldly ambition and honors, with an eloquence and persuasiveness which have not been surpassed. These could not be inventions of the grovelling authors who relate them. They are far beyond the powers of their feeble minds. They shew that there was a character, the subject of their history, whose splendid conceptions were above all suspicion of being interpolations from their hands. Can we be at a loss in separating such materials, and ascribing each to its genuine author? The difference is obvious to the eye and to the understanding, and we may read, as we run, to each his part; and I will venture to affirm that he who, as I have done, will undertake to winnow this grain from its chaff, will find it not to require a moment's consideration. The parts fell asunder of themselves as would those of an image of metal and clay.

There are, I acknowledge, passages not free from objection, which we may with probability ascribe to Jesus himself; but claiming indulgence from the circumstances under which he acted. His object was the reformation of some articles in the religion of the Jews, as taught by Moses. That Seer had presented, for the object of their worship, a being of terrific character, cruel, vindictive, capricious and unjust. Jesus, taking for his type the best qualities of the human head and heart, wisdom, justice, goodness, and adding to them power, ascribed all of these but in infinite perfection, to the supreme being, and formed him really worthy of their adoration. Moses had either not believed in a future state of existence, or had not thought it essential to be explicitly taught to his people. Jesus inculcated that doctrine with emphasis and precision. Moses had bound the Jews to many idle ceremonies, mummeries and observances of no effect towards producing the social utilities which constitute the essence of virtue. Jesus exposed their futility and insignificance. The one instilled into his people the most anti-social spirit towards other nations; the other preached philanthropy and universal charity and benevolence.—The office of reformer of the superstitions of a nation is ever dangerous. Jesus had to walk on the perilous confines of reason and religion: and a step to right or left might place him within the grip of the priests of the superstition, a bloodthirsty race, as cruel and remorseless as the being whom they represented as the family god of Abraham, of Isaac and of Jacob, and the local god of Israel. They were constantly laying snares too to entangle him in the web of the law. He was justifiable therefore in avoiding these by evasions, by sophisms, by misconstructions and misapplications of scraps of the prophets, and in defending himself with these their own weapons as sufficient, ad hominems, at least. That Jesus did not mean to impose himself on mankind as the son of god physically speaking I have been convinced by the writings of men more learned than myself in that lore. But that he might conscientiously believe himself inspired from above, is very possible. The whole religion of the Jews, inculcated on him from his infancy, was founded in the belief of divine inspiration. The fumes of the most disordered imaginations were recorded in their religious code, as special communications of the deity; and as it could not but happen that, in the course of ages, events would now and then turn up to which some of these vague rhapsodies might be accommodated by the aid of allegories, figures, types, and other tricks upon words, they have not only preserved their credit with the Jews of all subsequent times, but are the foundation of much of the religions of those who have schismatised from them. Elevated by the enthusiasm of a warm and pure heart, conscious of the high strains of an eloquence which had not been taught him, he might readily mistake the coruscations of his own fine genius for inspirations of an higher order. This belief carried therefore no more personal imputation, than the belief of Socrates that himself was under the care and admonitions of a guardian daemon. And how many of our wisest men still believe in the reality of these inspirations, while perfectly sane on all other subjects. Excusing therefore, on these considerations, those passages in the gospels which seem to bear marks of weakness in Jesus, ascribing to him what alone is consistent with the great and pure character of which the same writings furnish proofs, and to their proper authors their own trivialities and imbecilities, I think myself authorised to conclude the purity and distinction of his character in opposition to the impostures which those authors would fix upon him: and that the postulate of my former letter is no more than is granted in all other historical works. . . .

To Jared Sparks (4 November 1820)
Jefferson acknowledges Sparks's Letters on the Ministry, Ritual, and Doctrines of the Protestant Episcopal Church *(Baltimore, 1820).*

Sir

Your favor of Sep. 18 is just received, with the book accompanying it. Its delay was owing to that of the box of books from Mr. Guegan, in which it was packed. Being just setting out on a journey I have time only to look over the summary of contents. In this I see nothing in which I am likely to differ materially from you. I hold the precepts of Jesus, as delivered by himself, to be the most pure, benevolent, and sublime which have ever been preached to man. I adhere to the principles of the first age; and consider all subsequent innovations as corruptions of his religion, having no foundation in what came from him. The metaphysical insanities of Athanasius, of Loyola, and of Calvin, are to my understanding, mere relapses into polytheism, differing from paganism only by being more unintelligible. The religion of Jesus is founded on the Unity of God, and this principle chiefly, gave it triumph over the rabble of heathen gods then acknowledged. Thinking men of all nations rallied readily to the doctrine of one only god, and embraced it with the pure morals which Jesus inculcated. If the freedom of religion, guaranteed to us by law *in theory,* can ever rise *in practice* under the overbearing inquisition of public opinion, truth will prevail over fanaticism, and the genuine doctrines of Jesus, so long perverted by his

136 pseudo-priests, will again be restored to their original purity. This reformation will advance with the other improvements of the human mind but too late for me to witness it. . . .

To Benjamin Waterhouse (26 June 1822)

Dear Sir

. . . The doctrines of Jesus are simple, and tend all to the happiness of man.

1. that there is one God, and he all-perfect:

2. that there is a future state of rewards and punishment:

3. that to love God with all thy heart, and they neighbor as thyself, is the sum of religion.

These are the great points on which he endeavored to reform the religion of the Jews. But compare with these the demoralising dogmas of Calvin.

1. that there are three Gods:

2. that good works, or the love of our neighbor are nothing:

3. that Faith is every thing: and the more incomprehensible the proposition, the more merit in its faith:

4. that Reason in religion is of unlawful use:

5. that God, from the beginning, elected certain individuals to be saved, and certain others to be damned; and that no crimes of the former can damn them, no virtues of the latter save.

Now which of these is the true and charitable Christian? he who believes and acts on the simple doctrines of Jesus? or the impious dogmatists of Athanasius and Calvin? Verily, I say that these are the false shepherds, foretold as to enter, not by the door into the sheep-fold, but to climb up some other way. They are mere Usurpers of the Christian name, teaching a Counter-religion, made up of the deliria of crazy imaginations, as foreign from Christianity as is that of Mahomet. Their blasphemies have driven thinking men into infidelity, who have too hastily rejected the supposed Author himself, with the horrors so falsely imputed to him. Had the doctrines of Jesus been preached always as purely as they came from his lips, the whole civilised world would now have been Christian. I rejoice that in this blessed country of free enquiry and belief, which has surrendered its creed and conscience to neither kings nor priests, the genuine doctrine of one only God is reviving, and I trust that there is not a *young man* now living in the US. who will not die an Unitarian.

But much I fear that when this great truth shall be re-established, its Votaries will fall into the fatal error of fabricating formulas of creed, and Confessions of faith, the engines which so soon destroyed the religion of Jesus, and made of Christendom a mere Aceldama: that they will give up morals for mysteries, and Jesus for Plato. How much wiser are the Quakers, who, agreeing in the fundamental doctrine of the gospel, schismatize about no mysteries, and keeping within the pale of Common sense, suffer no speculative differences of opinion, any more than of feature, to impair the love of their brethren. Be this the wisdom of Unitarians; this the holy mantle which shall cover within its charitable circumference all who believe in one God, and who love their neighbor.—I conclude my sermon with sincere assurances of my friendly esteem and respect.

To John Adams (11 April 1823)

Dear Sir

The wishes expressed, in your last favor, that I may continue in life and health until I become a Calvinist, at least in his exclamation of "*mon Dieu*! jusque à quand!" [Lord, how long!] would make me immortal. I can never join Calvin in addressing *his god*. He was indeed an Atheist, which I can never be; or rather his religion was Daemonism. If ever man worshipped a false god, he did. The being described in his 5 points is not the God whom you and I acknowledge and adore, the Creator and benevolent governor of the world; but a daemon of malignant spirit. It would be more pardonable to believe in no god at all, than to blaspheme him by the atrocious attributes of Calvin. Indeed I think that every Christian sect gives a great handle to Atheism by their general dogma that, without a revelation, there would not be sufficient proof of the being of a god. Now one sixth of mankind only are supposed to be Christians: the other five sixths then, who do not believe in the Jewish and Christian revelation, are without a knowledge of the existence of a god! This gives completely a gain de cause to the disciples of Ocellus, Timaeus, Spinoza, Diderot and D'Holbach. The argument which they rest on as triumphant and unanswerable is that, in every hypothesis of Cosmogony you must admit an eternal pre-existence of something; and according to the rule of sound philosophy, you are never to employ two principles to solve a difficulty when one will suffice. They say then that it is more simple to believe at once in the eternal pre-existence of the world, as it is now going on, and may for ever go on by the principle of reproduction which we see and witness, than to believe in the eternal pre-existence of an ulterior cause, or Creator of the world, a being whom we see not, and know not, of whose form substance and mode or place of existence, or of action no sense informs us, no power of the mind enables us to delineate or comprehend. On the contrary I hold (without appeal to revelation) that when we take a view of the Universe, in its parts general or particular, it is impossible for the human mind not to perceive and feel a conviction of design, consummate skill, and indefinite power in every atom of its composition. The movements of the heavenly bodies, so exactly held in their course by the balance of centrifugal and centripetal forces, the structure of our earth itself, with its distribution of lands, waters and atmosphere, animal and vegetable bodies, examined in all their minutest particles, insects mere atoms of life, yet as perfectly organised as man or mammoth, the mineral substances,

138   their generation and uses, it is impossible, I say, for the human mind not to believe that there is, in all this, design, cause and effect, up to an ultimate cause, a fabricator of all things from matter and motion, their preserver and regulator while permitted to exist in their present forms, and their regenerator into new and other forms. We see, too, evident proofs of the necessity of a superintending power to maintain the Universe in its course and order. Stars, well known, have disappeared, new ones have come into view, comets, in their incalculable courses, may run foul of suns and planets and require renovation under other laws; certain races of animals are become extinct; and, were there no restoring power, all existences might extinguish successively, one by one, until all should be reduced to a shapeless chaos. So irresistible are these evidences of an intelligent and powerful Agent that, of the infinite numbers of men who have existed thro' all time, they have believed, in the proportion of a million at least to Unit, in the hypothesis of an eternal pre-existence of a creator, rather than in that of a self-existent Universe. Surely this unanimous sentiment renders this more probable than that of the few in the other hypothesis. Some early Christians indeed have believed in the coeternal pre-existence of both the Creator and the world, without changing their relation of cause and effect. That this was the opinion of St. Thomas, we are informed by Cardinal Toleto, in these words "Deus ab aeterno fuit jam omnipotens, sicut cum produxit mundum. Ab aeterno potuit producere mundum.—Si sol ab aeterno esset, lumen ab aeterno esset; et si pes, similiter vestigium. At lumen et vestigium effectus sunt efficientis solis et pedis; potuit ergo cum causâ aeterno effectus coaeterna esse. Cujus sententiae est S. Thomas Theologorum primus" [God has been omnipotent forever, just as when he made the world. He has had the power to make the world forever. If the sun were in existence forever, light would have been in existence forever; and if a foot, then likewise a footprint. But light and footprint are the effects of an efficient sun and foot; therefore the effect has had the power to be co-eternal with the eternal cause. Of this opinion is St. Thomas, the first of the theologians].

Of the nature of this being we know nothing. Jesus tells us that "God is a spirit." 4 John 24, but without defining what a spirit is 'πνευμα ὁ Θεοζ' [God is spirit]. Down to the 3d century we know that it was still deemed material; but of a lighter subtler matter than our gross bodies. So says Origen. "Deus igitur, cui anima similis est, juxta Originem, reapte corporalis est; sed graviorum tantum ratione corporum incorporeus" [God, therefore, to whom the soul is similar, in consequences of its origin, is in reality corporeal; but He is incorporeal in comparison with so much heavier bodies]. These are the words of Huet in his commentary on Origen. Origen himself says "appellatio ἀσωματον apud nostros scriptores est inusitata et incognita" [The word 'unembodied,' among our writers, is not used or known]. So also Tertullian "quis autem negabit Deum esse Corpus, etsi deuş spiritus? Spiritum etiam corporis sui generis, in suâ effigie." ["Yet who will deny that God is body, although God is spirit? Indeed He is spirit of His own type of body, in His own image."] Tertullian. These two fathers were of the 3d century. Calvin's character of this supreme being seems chiefly copied from that of the Jews. But the reformation of these blasphemous attributes, and substitution of those more worthy, pure and sublime, seems to have been the chief object of Jesus in his discourses to the Jews: and his doctrine of the Cosmogony of the world is very clearly laid down in the 3 first verses of the 1st chapter of John, in these words,.

ἐν αρχη ἦν ὁ λόγος καὶ ὁ λόγος ἦν πρὸς τὸν Θεόν, καὶ ἦν ὁ λόγος. Οὗτος ἦν ἐν ἀρχη πρὸς τὸν Θεὸν. Πάντα δι' αντοῦ ἐγένετο. Καὶ κωρὶς αὐτοῦ ἐγένετο οὐδὲ ἕν, ὃ γέγονεν.

Which truly translated means "in the beginning God existed, and reason (or mind) was with God, and that mind was God. This was in the beginning with God. All things were created by it, and without it was made not one thing which was made." Yet this text, so plainly declaring the doctrine of Jesus that the world was created by the supreme, intelligent being, has been perverted by modern Christians to build up a second person of their tritheism by a mistranslation of the word λογος. One of its legitimate meanings indeed is "a word." But, in that sense, it makes an unmeaning jargon: while the other meaning "reason," equally legitimate, explains rationally the eternal pre-exist-ence of God, and his creation of the world. Knowing how incomprehensible it was that "a word," the mere action or articulation of the voice and organs of speech could create a world, they undertake to make of this articulation a second pre-existing being, and ascribe to him, and not to God, the creation of the universe. The Atheist here plumes himself on the uselessness of such a God, and the simpler hypothesis of a self-existent universe. The truth is that the greatest enemies to the doctrines of Jesus are those calling themselves the expositors of them, who have perverted them for the structure of a system of fancy absolutely incomprehensible, and without any foundation in his genuine words. And the day will come when the mystical generation of Jesus, by the supreme being as his father in the womb of a virgin will be classed with the fable of the generation of Minerva in the brain of Jupiter. But we may hope that the dawn of reason and freedom of thought in these United States will do away all this artificial scaffolding, and restore to us the primitive and genuine doctrines of this the most venerated reformer of human errors.

So much for your quotation of Calvin's "mon dieu! jusque à quand" in which, when addressed to the God of Jesus, and our God, I join you cordially, and await his time and will with more readiness than reluctance. May we meet there again, in Congress, with our antient Colleagues, and receive with them the seal of approbation "Well done, good and faithful servants."

140   To Alexander Smyth (17 January 1825)
Smyth had sent Jefferson his Explanation of the Apocalypse, or Revelation of St. John *(Washington, D.C., 1825)*.

Dear Sir

I have duly received 4 proof sheets of your explanation of the Apocalypse, with your letters of Dec. 29 and Jan. 8 in the last of which you request that, so soon as I shall be of opinion that the explanation you have given is correct, I would express it in a letter to you. From this you must be so good as to excuse me, because I make it an invariable rule to decline ever giving opinions on new publications in any case whatever. No man on earth has less taste or talent for criticism than myself, and least and last of all should I undertake to criticise works on the Apocalypse. It is between 50 and 60 years since I read it, and I then considered it as merely the ravings of a Maniac, no more worthy, nor capable of explanation than the incoherences of our own nightly dreams. I was therefore well pleased to see, in your first proof-sheet, that it was said to be not the production of St. John, but of Cerinthus, a century after the death of that Apostle. Yet the change of the Author's name does not lessen the extravagances of the composition, and come they from whomsoever they may, I cannot so far respect them as to consider them as an allegorical narrative of events, past or subsequent. There is not coherence enough in them to countenance any suite of rational ideas. You will judge therefore from this how impossible I think it that either your explanation, or that of any man in the heavens above, or on the earth beneath, can be a correct one. What has no meaning admits no explanation. And pardon me if I say, with the candor of friendship, that I think your time too valuable, and your understanding of too high an order, to be wasted on these paralogisms. You will perceive, I hope, also that I do not consider them as revelations of the supreme being, whom I would not so far blaspheme as to impute to him a pretension of revelation, couched at the same time in terms which, he would know, were never to be understood by those to whom they were addressed. In the candor of these observations, I hope you will see proofs of the confidence, esteem and respect which I truly entertain for you.

Ethan Allen

Nature Is God's Revelation

Ethan Allen (1737–89) is primarily remembered today as the romantically flamboyant leader of the "Green Mountain Boys." But during his lifetime he was also notorious for his authorship of what is America's first systematic treatise on deism: *Reason the Only Oracle of Man* (or, in some editions, *Oracles of Reason*). This work, first published in 1784, quickly earned Allen the dubious reputation, as Yale's Ezra Stiles put it, of a "profane & impious Deist." Allen himself pretended not to be so sure. As he says in the preface to his book, "I am generally denominated a Deist, the reality of which I never disputed, being conscious I am no Christian, except mere infant baptism makes me one; and as to being a Deist, I know not strictly speaking, whether I am one or not, for I have never read their writings." There is little reason, however, to take this disclaimer at face value. Allen's rejection of Christianity is clearly based on deistic principles. Moreover, many of his central arguments in support of rational religion are reminiscent of those employed by such British deists as Toland and Charles Blount (1654–93), who in the final year of his life published an anti-Christian tract entitled *Oracles of Reason*.

The future "profane & impious Deist" was born 10 January 1737 in Litchfield, Connecticut, but spent his formative years on the southwestern frontier, to which his family had moved shortly after his birth. Although echoes of the Great Awakening's religious fundamentalism must have reached those settlements during his childhood, Allen appears not to have been overly influenced by them. By the time his father died in 1755, he seems to have already lost whatever fidelity to orthodoxy he might at one time have possessed.

His father's death left Allen the sole support of his mother and seven siblings, thus ending his chances for a college education. But after working a couple of years on the family farm, he enlisted in the army and served in the French and Indian War. He afterward relocated to Vermont, where by 1769 he had become "colonel commandant" of the Green Mountain Boys, a local militia called up in response to a boundary dispute between New York, New Hampshire, and Vermont. His leadership of the militia was so successful that by 1771 the governor of New York had offered a twenty-pound reward for his capture; in 1774 it was increased to a full hundred. Past sins appear to have been forgiven if not entirely forgotten with the outbreak of war between the colonies and England, and Allen was quickly catapulted to the status of a hero after his capture of Fort Ticonderoga in 1775. Six months later he was a prisoner of war in Canada, captured during a rather foolhardy assault on Montreal, and sat out much of the remaining hostilities in a cell. After the war, he devoted himself to local Vermont politics and farmirfg until his death from apoplexy, reportedly after a night of heavy drinking, in 1789.

Allen was the author of several pamphlets and numerous articles, but the only one of his works to stand the test of time is his *Reason the Only Oracle of Man*. Ironically, however, it is also the most poorly written one. It is too long, redundant, and sometimes impenetrably convoluted. Allen himself seems to have been aware of its cumbersome style, as indicated in the following confession with which he prefaced the treatise:

> In my youth I was much disposed to contemplation, and at my com-
> mencement in manhood, I committed to manuscript such sentiments
> or arguments as appeared most consonant to reason, lest through the
> debility of memory my improvement should have been less gradual:
> This method of scribbling I practised for many years, from which I
> experienced great advantages in the progression of learning and knowl-
> edge, the more so as I was deficient in education, and had to acquire the
> knowledge of grammar and language, as well as the art of reasoning,
> principally from a studious application to it, which after all I am sensible,
> lays me under disadvantages, particularly in matters of composition.

Although Allen was straightforward about his lack of expertise in composition (a confession of no great sacrifice, since its truth was apparent in the book), he may have been less candid about a much more significant issue: the true authorship of *Reason the Only Oracle*. There is some debate about whether he or a friend, Thomas Young, actually wrote it. Young was a free-thinking physician whom Allen had known in his youth, and it seems evident that Young, a relatively well-educated man, introduced Allen to the British deistic tradition. *Reason the Only Oracle* was published after Young's death, and his widow maintained that Allen had plagiarized from her husband's manuscripts. Allen's defenders responded that at worst the manuscript had been coauthored by the two men with the understanding that the one who outlived the other would publish it. Allen himself chose to remain silent and carried the truth about the treatise's authorship to his grave.

Regardless of who wrote the book, however, it became the young Republic's first sustained defense of deism. Moreover, it exerted an immense influence on American free thought—despite the fact that the Bennington, Vermont, printer who typeset the manuscript refused to release it for two years and that when he did a possibly arsonous fire in his warehouse destroyed all but thirty copies. But the few issues that survived circulated widely and were soon pirated at an alarming rate. In fact, the book was reprinted (in conservative Boston, no less) as late as 1854. It seems certain, then, that for every Ezra Stiles who dismissed the book as a pack of "scurrillous Reflexions," for every Timothy Dwight who insisted that its author "In Satan's cause . . . bustled, bruised and swore," there were hundreds of people in the Early Republic who read, pondered, and applauded Allen's homespun defense of rational religion.

The selections here from Allen's *Reason the Only Oracle* revolve, in typical deistic fashion, around the ideas of God, reason, and morality.

In writing about the deity, Allen argues that its existence is demonstrated a posteriori. Experience teaches that all events are causally dependent on preceding ones, so it follows that the "vast system of causes and effects are [likewise] necessarily connected." This points to a First Cause of the entire set of perceptible events. The First Cause maintains providential regularity in reality—indeed, Allen goes so far as to identify the natural harmony with God. Of course, the perceived dependency of individual events does not entail an analogous causal dependency of reality in general, but this is a logical point that escaped Allen as well as many other American deists. For him and them, the causal argument remained a sufficient demonstration of divine existence. In Allen's words, "The display of God's providence is that by which the evidence of his being is evinced to us."

But the rational investigation of nature does not merely establish God's existence. It also provides insight into divine and human nature. Experience shows that physical reality exhibits constancy, uniformity, regularity; it is, in short, rational. If God is the First Cause of reality, God must possess the attributes characteristic of it, since the effect of a cause always reveals the cause's essence. Consequently, God is likewise rational, constant, and perfectly wise and benevolent. Similarly, since humans themselves are effects of divine causation, they must also reflect, albeit imperfectly, its nature. The human species, then, possesses reason, eternal although finite, which enables it to read and understand the laws of nature that constitute God's revelation of himself.

Like so many of the later American deists, Allen goes to great pains to defend human reason against orthodox Christianity's charge of depravity and insufficiency as an epistemological criterion. For Allen, since natural law is "co-extensive and co-existent with reason, and binding on all intelligent beings in the universe," there is a direct symmetry between the mental faculty of reason and the rational nature of the universe. Hence, when humans think and act rationally, they comprehend reality and at the same time reflect divine wisdom and goodness. It follows for Allen, then, that the moral and physical sciences are promoted by the exercise of reason and corrupted by a denial of it. True, the book of nature can be misread if humans allow their prejudices and unexamined opinions to sully their judgments. But nature, not supernaturalistic doctrine, nonetheless remains the sole reliable guide for the promotion of science, morality, and happiness.

In keeping with his Enlightenment-based panrationalism, Allen denounces scriptural revelation as "beyond human understanding" and thus as an illegitimate form of knowledge; the doctrine of the Trinity as a logical absurdity, since its postulation of three separate but undivided substances in the deity violates the law of identity; and miraculous interventions, because they "imply mutability in the wisdom of God" and offer no cogent explanation for the phenomena they claim to describe. Moreover, in a reformulation that set the stage for later deistic apologies, he denies that faith is mystical or that the person of faith is ethically superior to others. In a very empiricist move indeed, Allen redefines faith as "the last result of the understanding, or the same which we call the conclusion, it is the consequence of a greater or less deduction of reasoning from certain premises previously laid down." As such, faith in the correct sense of the word denotes the last claim in a chain of inferential reasoning. It is only the proponents of revealed religion who accept a corrupted version of faith as a mysterious and logically gratuitous illumination. Since, however, the word properly refers to logical deduction, and since humans are incapable of assenting to propositions "contrary to their [rational] judgments," there is no special merit in acquiescing to faith-based propositions. Such assent is only to be expected of rational individuals.

Just as reason is the sole arbiter in the investigation of natural philosophy and theological speculation, so it is also the necessary condition for ethical behavior and human happiness. Morality, says Allen, "does not derive its nature from [holy] books, but from the fitness of things." It is "acquired from reason and experience." The latter tells us which actions are conducive and which detrimental to our well-being; the former enables us to prescribe ethical codes and principles reflecting that knowledge. An ethical system grounded in religion, on the other hand, "subjects mankind to sacerdotal empire; which is erected on . . . imbecility." Allen concedes that traditional religious creeds have sometimes defended admirable ethical principles, but such instances represent a rational reaction to the light of nature rather than a mysteriously revealed inspiration. Since genuine religious sensibility is in essence the knowledge of virtue and the desire to pursue it and avoid wickedness, religion should be based on rational contemplation of physical and human nature, not on "arbitrary ceremonies, or mere positive institutions, abstractly considered from the moral rectitude of things." Although Allen failed to elaborate on the precise principles that support ethical behavior—a task left to the more able Elihu Palmer—his naturalistic orientation was to resound in later deistic theories of morality.

A good portion of Allen's treatise is concerned with arguments denying the divinity of Jesus. He attacks this central Christian doctrine from two fronts. First, and less convincingly, he insists that Jesus' own words as recorded in Scripture reveal that he never claimed to be divine. Second, and more substantially, Allen argues that insofar as God by definition is essentially one and possesses unlimited attributes such as infinitude, eternality, and omnipotence, it is logically impossible that "God should become a man . . . and that man should become a God." There is an "infinite disproportion" between two such entities that precludes the possibility—much less likelihood—of that contradictory union. Such a being would have to simultaneously exhibit limited and unlimited attributes—a situation repugnant to reason.

Allen is not content simply to gainsay the divinity of Jesus. He also assails the God of Scripture as being an arbitrary and immoral deity who violates every norm of distributive justice known to humans. The Christian God, for example, unwarrantedly sentences humans to eternal punishment for what must necessarily be finite crimes. In addition, he countenances and performs actions in both the Old and New Testaments that transgress the moral "fitness of things." Such an incongruity is not possible for the Grand Architect, because "the same reasons cannot fail to hold good in the divine mind as in that of the human, for the rules of justice are essentially the same whether applied to the one or to the other, having their uniformity in the eternal truth and reason of things."

In the final analysis, cumbersome and long-winded as it is, Allen's *Reason the Only Oracle of Man* is an able synthesis of the central tenets of Enlightenment deism. He was probably the least acute of all the American deists, yet the issues he raised and the arguments he presented served as prototypes for later and more sophisticated defenses of rational religion.

Reason the Only Oracle of Man, or a Compenduous System of Natural Religion

I.1. The Duty of Reforming Mankind from Superstition and Error and the Good Consequences of It.*

The desire of knowledge has engaged the attention of the wise and curious among mankind in all ages, which has been productive of extending the arts and sciences far and wide in the several quarters of the globe, and excited the contemplative to explore nature's laws in a gradual series of improvement, 'till philosophy, astronomy, geography and history, with many other branches of science, have arrived to a great degree of perfection.

It is nevertheless to be regretted, that the bulk of mankind, even in those

---

*Ed.: The numbers indicate locations in Allen's original text—here, for example, chapter I, section 1.

146 nations which are most celebrated for learning and wisdom, are still carried down the torrent of superstition, and entertain very unworthy apprehensions of the BEING, PERFECTIONS, CREATION and PROVIDENCE of GOD, and their duty to him, which lays an indispensable obligation on the philosophic friends of human nature, unanimously to exert themselves in every lawful, wise and prudent method, to endeavour to reclaim mankind from their ignorance and delusion, by enlightening their minds in those great and sublime truths concerning God and his providence, and their obligations to moral rectitude, which in this world, and that which is to come, cannot fail greatly to affect their happiness and well being.

Though "*None by searching can find out God, or the Almighty to perfection*"; YET I am persuaded, that if mankind would dare to exercise their reason as freely on those divine topics, as they do in the common concerns of life, they would, in a great measure rid themselves of their blindness and superstition, gain more exalted ideas of God and their obligations to him and one another, and be proportionably delighted and blessed with the views of his moral government, make better members of society, and acquire many powerful incentives to the practice of morality, which is the last and greatest perfection that human nature is capable of.

I.2. Of the Being of a God

The Laws of Nature having subjected mankind to a state of absolute dependence on something out of, and manifestly beyond themselves, or the compound exertion of their natural powers, gave them the first conception of a superior principle existing; otherwise they could have had no possible conception of a superintending power. But this sense of dependency, which results from experience and reasoning on the facts, which every day cannot fail to produce, has uniformly established the knowledge of our dependence to every of the species who are rational, which necessarily involves or contains in it the idea of a ruling power, or that there is a GOD, which ideas are synonymous.

This is the first glimpse of a Deity, and powerfully attracts the rational mind to make farther discoveries, which, through the weakness of human reasonings opens a door for errors and mistakes respecting the divine essense, though there is no possibility of our being deceived in our first conceptions of a superintending power. Of which more will be observed in its order.

The globe with its productions, the planets in their motions, and the starry heavens in their magnitudes, surprise our senses, and confound our reason, in their munificent lessons of instruction concerning GOD, by means whereof we are apt to be more or less lost in our ideas of the object of divine adoration, though at the same time every one is truly sensible that their being and preservation is from GOD. We are too apt to confound our ideas of GOD with his works, and take the latter for the former. Thus barbarous and unlearned nations have imagined, that inasmuch as the sun in its influence is beneficial to them in bringing forward the spring of the year, causing the production of vegetation, and food for their subsistence, that therefore it is their GOD: while others have located other parts of creation, and ascribe to them the prerogatives of God; and mere creatures and images have been substituted to be Gods by the wickedness or weakness of man, or both together. It seems that mankind in most ages and parts of the world have been fond of corporeal Deities with whom their outward senses might be gratified, or as fantastically diverted from the just apprehension of the true God, by a supposed supernatural intercourse with invisible and mere spiritual beings, to whom they ascribe divinity, so that through one means or other, the character of the true God has been much neglected, to the great detriment of truth, justice, and morality in the world; nor is it possible, that mankind can be uniform in their religious opinions, or worship God according to knowledge, except they can form a consistent arrangement of ideas of the Divine character. This therefore shall be the great object of the following pages, to which all others are only subordinate; for the superstructure of our religion will be proportionate to the notions we entertain of the divinity whom we adore. A sensibility of mere dependence includes an idea of something, on which we depend (call it by what name we will) which has a real existence, in as much as a dependency on nonentity is inadmissible, for that the absence or non-existence of all being could not have caused an existence to be. But should we attempt to trace the succession of the causes of our dependence, they would exceed our comprehension though every of them, which we could understand, would be so many evidences (of the displays) of a God. Although a sense of dependency discloses to our minds the certainty of a Supreme Being, yet it does not point out to us the object, nature or perfections of that being; this belongs to the province of reason, and in our course of ratiocination on the succession of causes and events. Although we extend our ideas retrospectively ever so far upon the succession, yet no cause in the extended order of succession, which depends upon another prior to itself, can be in the independent cause of all things: nor is it possible to trace the order of the succession of causes back to that self-existent cause, inasmuch as it is eternal and infinite, and therefore cannot be traced out by succession, which operates according to the order of time, consequently can bear no more proportion to the eternity of God, than time itself may be supposed to do, which has no proportion at all; as the succeeding arguments respecting the eternity and infinity of God will evince. But notwithstanding the series of the succession of causes cannot be followed in a retrospective succession up the self-existent or eternal cause, it is nevertheless a perpetual and conclusive evidence of a God. For a succession of causes, considered collectively, can be nothing more than effects of the independent cause, and as much dependent on it, as those dependent causes are upon one another; so that we may with

148 certainty conclude that the system of nature, which we call by the name of natural causes, is as much dependent on a self-existent cause, as an individual of the species in the order of generation is dependent on its progenitors for existence. Such part of the series of nature's operations, which we understand, has a regular and necessary connection with, and dependence on its parts, which we denominate by the names of cause and effect. From hence we are authorised from reason to conclude, that the vast system of causes and effects are thus necessarily connected, (speaking of the natural world only) and the whole regularly and necessarily dependent on a self-existent cause; so that we are obliged to admit an independent cause, and ascribe self-existence to it, otherwise it could not be independent, and consequently not a God. But the eternity or manner of the existence of a self-existent and independent being is to all finite capacities utterly incomprehensible; yet this is so far from an objection against the reality of such a being, that it is essentially necessary to support the evidence of it; for if we could comprehend that being, whom we call God, he would not be God, but must have been finite, and that in the same degree as those may be supposed to be, who could comprehend him; therefore so certain as God is, we cannot comprehend his essence, eternity or manner of existence. This should always be premised, when we assay to reason on the being, perfection, eternity and infinity of God, or of his creation and providence. As far as we understand nature, we are become acquainted with the character of God; for the knowledge of nature is the revelation of God. If we form in our imagination a compenduous idea of the harmony of the universe, it is the same as calling God by the name of harmony, for there could be no harmony without regulation, and no regulation without a regulator, which is expressive of the idea of a God. Nor could it be possible, that there could be order or disorder, except we admit of such a thing as creation, and creation contains in it the idea of a creator, which is another appellation for the Divine Being, distinguishing God from his creation. Furthermore there could be no proportion, figure or motion without wisdom and power; wisdom to plan, and power to execute, and these are perfections, when applied to the works of nature, which signify the agency or superintendency of God. If we consider nature to be matter, figure and motion, we include the idea of God in that of motion; for motion implies a mover, as much as creation does a creator. If from the composition, texture, and tendency of the universe in general, we form a complex idea of general good resulting therefrom to mankind, we implicitly admit a God by the name of good, including the idea of his providence to man. And from hence arises our obligation to love and adore God, because he provides for, and is beneficent to us: abstract the idea of goodness from the character of God, and it would cancel all our obligations to him, and excite us to hate and detest him as a tyrant; hence it is, that ignorant people are superstitiously misled into a conceit that they hate God, when at the same time it is only the idol of their own imagination, which they truly ought to hate and be ashamed of; but were such persons to connect the ideas of power, wisdom, goodness and all possible perfection in the character of God, their hatred toward him would be turned into love and adoration.

For mankind to hate truth as it may bring their evil deeds to light and punishment, is very easy and common; but to hate truth as truth, or God as God, which is the same as to hate goodness for its own sake, unconnected with any other consequences, is impossible even to a (premised) diabolical nature itself. If we advert to the series of the causes of our being and preservation in the world, we shall commence a retrospective examination from son to father, grand-father and great-grandson, and so on to the supreme and self-existent father of all: and as to the means of our preservation or succeeding causes of it, we may begin with parental kindness in nourishing, succouring and providing for us in our helpless age, always remembering it to have originated from our eternal father, who implanted that powerful and sympathetic paternal affection in them.

By extending our ideas in a larger circle, we shall perceive our dependence on the earth and waters of the globe, which we inhabit, and from which we are bountifully fed and gorgeously arrayed, and nextly extend our ideas to the sun, whose fiery mass darts its brilliant rays of light to our terraqueous ball with amazing velocity, and whose region of inexhaustible fire supplies it with fervent heat, which causes vegetation and gilds the various seasons of the year with ten thousand charms: this is not the achievement of man, but the workmanship and providence of God. But how the sun is supplied with materials thus to perpetuate its kind influences, we know not. But will any one deny the reality of those beneficial influences, because we do not understand the manner of the perpetuality of that fiery world, or how it became such a body of fire; or will any one deny the reality of nutrition by food, because we do not understand the secret operation of the digesting powers of animal nature, or the minute particulars of its cherishing influence, none will be so stupid as to do it. Equally absurd would it be for us to deny the providence of God, by "whom we live, move, and have our being," because we cannot comprehend it.

We know that earth, water, fire and air in their various compositions subserve us, and we also know that these elements are devoid of reflection, reason or design; from whence we may easily infer, that a wise, understanding, and designing being has ordained them to be thus subservient. Could blind chance constitute order and decorum, and consequently a providence? That wisdom, order, and design should be the production of non-entity, or of chaos, confusion and old night, is too absurd to deserve a serious confutation, for it supposeth that there may be effects without a cause, viz: produced by non-entity, or that chaos and confusion could produce the effects of power, wisdom and goodness; such absurdities as these we must assent to, or subscribe to the

150   doctrine of a self-existent and providential being. Chaos itself would necessarily include the idea of a creator, inasmuch as it supposes a positive existence, though it precludes the idea of a Providence, which cannot exist without order, tendency and design.

But Chaos could no more exist independent of a Creator than the present aptly disposed system of nature. For there could be no fortuitous jumble, or chaos of original atoms, independent of or previous to creation, as nonentity could not produce the materials. *Nothing from nothing and there remains nothing, but something from nothing is contradictory and impossible.* The evidence of the being and providence of a God, is so full and compleat, that we cannot miss of discerning it, if we but open our eyes and reflect on the visible creation. The display of God's providence is that by which the evidence of his being is evinced to us, for though mere Chaos would evince the certainty of a Creator, yet that abstracted method of argument could not have been conceived of, or known by us, was it not for the exercise of God's Providence, (by whom we have our being;) though that argument in itself would have been true whether it had been used by us or not: for the reason of propositions and just inferences in themselves, are in truth the same, independent of our conceptions of them, abstractedly considered from our existence.

The benefit accruing to us from reasoning and argument, as it respects our knowledge and practice, is to explore the truth of things, as they are in their own nature, this is our wisdom. All other conceptions of things are false and imaginary. We cannot exercise a thought on any thing whatever, that has a positive existence, but if we trace it thoroughly it will center in an independent cause, and be evidential of a God. Thus it is from the works of nature that we explore its great author; but all inquisitive minds are lost in their searches and researches into the immensity of the divine fullness, from whence our beings and all our blessings flow.

III.1. *The Doctrine of the Infinite*
Evil of Sin Considered

That God is infinitely good in the eternal displays of his providence has been argued in the seventh section of the second chapter, from which we infer, that there cannot be an infinite evil in the universe, inasmuch as it would be incompatible with infinite good; yet there are many who imbibe the doctrine of the infinite evil of sin, and the maxim on which they predicate their arguments in its support, are, that the greatness of sin, or adequateness of its punishment, is not to be measured, or its viciousness ascertained by the capacity and circumstances of the offender, but by the capacity and dignity of the being against whom the offence is committed; and as every transgression is against the authority and law of God, it is therefore against God; and as God is infinite, therefore sin is an infinite evil; and from hence infer the infinite and vindictive wrath of God against sinners, and of his justice in dooming them, as some say, to infinite, and as others say, to eternal misery; the one without degree or measure, and the other without end of duration.

Admitting this maxim for truth, that the transgressions or sins of mankind are to be estimated, as to their heinousness, by the dignity and infinity of the divine nature, then it will follow, that all sins would be equal; which would confound all our notions of the degrees or aggravations of sin; so that the sin would be the same to kill my neighbour as it would be to kill his horse: For the divine nature, by this maxim, being the rule by which man's sin is to be estimated, and always the same, there could therefore be no degrees in sin or guilt, any more than there are degrees of perfection in God, whom we all admit to be infinite, and who for that reason only cannot admit of any degrees of enlargement. Therefore as certain as there are degrees in sin, the infinity of the divine nature cannot be the standard whereby it is to be ascertained; which single consideration is a sufficient confutation of the doctrine of the infinite evil of sin, as predicated on that maxim; inasmuch as none are so stupid as not to discern that there are degrees and aggravations in sin.

I recollect a discourse of a learned Ecclesiastic, who was labouring in support of this doctrine, his first proposition was: "*That moral rectitude was infinitely pleasing to God.*" From which he deduced this inference, viz; "*That a contrariety to moral rectitude was consequently infinitely displeasing to God and infinitely evil.*" That the absolute moral rectitude of the divine nature is infinitely well pleasing to God, will not be disputed; for this is none other but perfect and infinite rectitude; but there cannot in nature be an infinite contrariety thereto, or any being infinitely evil, or infinite in any respect whatever; except we admit a self-existent and infinite diabolical nature, which is too absurd to deserve argumentative confutation. Therefore, as all possible moral evil must result from the agency of finite beings, consisting in their sinful deviations from the rules of eternal unerring order and reason, which is moral rectitude in the abstract; we infer, that, provided *all finite beings in the universe*, had not done any thing else but sin and rebel against God, reason and moral rectitude in general; all possible moral evil would fall as much short of being infinite, as all finite capacities, complexly considered, would fail of being infinite; which would bear no proportion at all. For tho' *finite minds*, as has been before argued, bear a *resemblance to God*, yet they bear *no proportion* to his *infinity*; and therefore there is not and cannot be any being, beings, or agency of being or beings, complexly considered or otherwise, which are infinite in capacity, or which are infinitely evil and detestable in the sight of God, in that unlimited sense; for the *actions* or *agency* of *limited beings* are also *limited*, which is the same as *finite*: so that both the virtues and vices of man are finite; they are not virtuous or vicious but in degree; therefore moral evil is finite and bounded.

Though there is one and but one infinite good, which is God, and there can

152   be no dispute, but that God judges, and approves or disapproves of all things and beings, and agencies of beings, as in truth they are, or in other words judges of every thing as being what it is; but to judge a *finite evil* to be *infinite*, would be *infinitely erroneous* and disproportionable: for so certain as there is a distinction between *infinity* and *finitude*, so certain finite *sinful agency* cannot be *infinitely evil*: or in other words *finite offences* cannot be *infinite*. Nor is it possible that the greatest of sinners should in justice deserve infinite punishment, or their nature sustain it; *finite beings* may as well be supposed to be capable of *infinite happiness* as of *infinite misery*, but the rank which they hold in the universe exempts them from either: it nevertheless admits them to a state of agency, probation or trial, consequently to interchangeable progressions in moral good and evil, and of course to alternate happiness or misery. We will dismiss the doctrine of the *infinite evil of sin* with this observation, that as no *mere creature* can suffer an *infinitude* of misery or of punishment, it is therefore incompatible with the wisdom of God, so far to capacitate creatures to sin, as in his constitution of things to foreclose himself from *adequately* punishing them for it.

III.2. *The Moral Government of* God
Incompatible with Eternal Punishment

Having considered the doctrine of the infinite evil of sin, we proceed to the consideration of that of eternal damnation. Though it is in the nature of things impossible, that an infinite weight of punishment should be inflicted on the wicked, nevertheless, admitting a never ending punishment on them to be just and consistent with the moral government of God, it would be in itself possible. Therefore in order to determine the question concerning eternal punishment, (which cannot be eternal with respect to the preceding eternity, though it may be possible with respect to that which succeeds the aera of the existence of the wicked,) we must advert to the providence of God, as it respects the moral world particularly. That God in his creation and providence ultimately designed the good of being in general, has been clearly evinced in the preceding pages; nor can this doctrine of the divine munificence be objected to, except it is disputed whether God be a good and gracious being or not, which to do would be highly criminal: for a good being would have good purposes the ultimate end of its conduct, though it be supposed to be a mere creature, but perfectly so as applicable to the economy of God, who must be supposed to have had the good and happiness of his creation, the ultimate end and design of his providence.

    The wisest and best of men may not succeed in their benevolent purposes to serve mankind, for want of wisdom, opportunity or power; but this is no ways applicable to God, who can and will effect the ultimate purposes of his providence. Such expressions as these may be thought to militate against the

agency of man; but it ought to be considered, that though God has implanted 153
a principle of liberty in our minds, it is in some respects limited; he has not put
it in our power eternally to ruin ourselves, for our agency is as eternal as our
existence; so that the agency of this life cannot constitute an eternal happiness
or misery for us in this world or worlds to come, but our agency in its particular
periods is temporary, and so are its rewards and punishments. For as our minds
cannot comprehend eternity, so neither can the consequences of our agency,
which is happiness or misery[,] extend to it; for we are limited beings and act
in certain circumstances in all and every respect, except as to existence without
end; and this it is which renders our agency eternal as it respects the succeeding
eternity: God's government of the natural and moral worlds is the same as his
providence, so that when we speak of the moral government of God, we mean
that display of his providence which respects moral beings: The former is governed by fate, but the latter by rewards and punishment.

It is from the knowledge of right and wrong, good and evil that we are
capable of moral government; and it is from the deficiency of this principle of
knowledge, in the natural world, that it is subjected to mechanical laws, so that
the natural world includes every part of the creation, which is below the dignity
of a rational nature, which cannot be subject to mechanical operations, but is
in the order of things more exalted than gross creation, consisting of elements
or matter variously compounded, tempered and modified, with its cohesion,
attraction and all other of its qualities, properties, proportions, motions and
harmony of the whole. And as the natural world is made subservient to the
moral, the government of it may therefore be truly and properly said to belong
to the providence of God, which it otherwise could not, inasmuch as rational
beings are benefited thereby; but the government of mere material, inanimate
and unintelligent beings, abstractly considered from moral beings, could not
have been an object of divine providence, nor would such a supposed government constitute a providence; inasmuch as it would be void of sensibility, happiness and goodness. This being premised, we proceed more particularly to the
consideration of the moral government of God, in the exercise whereof it is not
to be supposed, that he would counteract his eternal plan of doing good to,
and happifying being in general; and inasmuch as eternal punishment is incompatible with this great and fundamental principle of wisdom and goodness, we
may for certain conclude, that such a punishment will never have the divine
approbation, or be inflicted on any intelligent being or beings in the infinitude
of the government of God. For an endless punishment defeats the very end of
its institution, which in all wise and good governments is as well to reclaim
offenders, as to be examples to others; but a government, which does not
admit of reformation and repentance, must unavoidably involve its subjects in
misery; for the weakness of creatures will always be a source of error and inconstancy, and a wise governor, as we must admit God to be, would suit his

government to the capacity and all other circumstances of the governed; and instead of inflicting eternal damnation on his offending children, would rather interchangeably extend his beneficence with his vindictive punishments, so as to alienate them from sin and wickedness, and incline them to morality; convincing them from experimental suffering, that sin and vanity are their greatest enemies, and that in GOD and *moral rectitude* their *dependence* and *true happiness* consists, and by reclaiming them from *wickedness and error*, to the *truth*, and to *the love and practice of virtue*, give them occasion to *glorify* GOD *for the wisdom and goodness of his government*, and to be ultimately happy under it. But we are told that the eternal damnation of a part of mankind greatly augments the happiness of the elect, who are represented as being vastly the less numerous, (a diabolical temper of mind in the elect:) Besides, how narrow and contracted must such notions of infinite justice and goodness be? Who would imagine that the Deity conducts his providence similar to the detestable despots of this world. O *horrible* most *horrible impeachment* of DIVINE GOODNESS! rather let us exaltedly suppose that God eternally had the ultimate best good of being, generally and individually in his view, with the reward of the virtuous and the punishment of the vicious, and that no other punishment will ever be inflicted, merely *by the divine administration*, but what will *finally* terminate in the BEST GOOD of the PUNISHED, and thereby subserve the great and important ends of the divine government, and be productive of *the restoration and felicity of all finite rational nature.*

Mankind in general seems to be evidently impressed with a sense and strong expectation of judgment to come, after animal life is ended; wherein the disorders, injustice and wickedness, which have been acted by rational agents, shall be fully and righteously adjusted, and the delinquents punished; and that such, who obey the laws of reason, or moral rectitude, may be rewarded according to their works: this apprehension is so general with all denominations and secretaries of men, that it is rather the intuition of nature than mere tradition. It is nevertheless to be considered, that this notion of accountability, and judgment to come, has not gone so far as to determine, whether the incorrigible sinner, from the close of human life, shall be everlastingly debarred from reformation and repentance, and precluded from the favour of God or not; but having taught a just and righteous judgment, left it as the prerogative of God to proportion the rewards of the virtuous and the punishments of the wicked, with their respective durations, which we find by reasoning cannot be eternal, and consequently must be temporary; but in what degrees, manner or proportions of intenseness, or of duration, we cannot comprehend, but must wait the decision of the righteous judge, whose omniscience takes cognizance of the thoughts, designs and actions of his creatures; and whose impartial justice will hold the balance and extend interchangeable happiness or misery to them, according to their respective merits or demerits, or the virtues or vices of their minds, in certain temporary periods coextensive with our immortality: and though the judgments of God may be vastly more severe and terrible to incorrigible sinners beyond the grave, than such as can be inflicted, or conceived of in this life, yet we may by reasoning from the wisdom and goodness of God and the nature and capacity of the human mind determine, that its happiness or misery cannot be perpetual and eternal.

The most weighty arguments deducible from the divine nature have been already offered, *to wit*, the ultimate end of God, in creation and providence, to do the greatest possible good and benignity to being in general, and consequently, that the great end and design of punishment, in the divine government, must be to reclaim, restore, and bring revolters from moral rectitude back to embrace it, and to be ultimately happy; as also, that an eternal punishment, would defeat the very end and design of punishment itself; and that no good consequences to the punished could arise out of a never ending destruction; but that a total, everlasting, and irreparable evil would take place on such part of the moral creation, as may be thus sentenced to eternal and remediless perdition; which would argue imperfection either in the creation, or moral government of God, or in both.

Furthermore, provided there was, in the nature of things, a liability of eternal destruction to any one intelligent being, there must consequently have been the same liability in all, or the justice and goodness of God would not be equal or uniform. But if there could have been, in the nature and fitness of things, a possibility of perpetually and eternally happifying the moral world, without agency, probation or trial, there can be no dispute, but that the God of nature would have adopted such a measure, and have made it needless and impossible for us to have speculated on the causes of our misery: and inasmuch as such a plan has not taken place, we may infer, that it was not possible, in the reason and fitness of things, that it should; and as imperfection opened the door to error and wickedness, or to a deviation from moral rectitude; which has actually taken place in the system of rational beings, and punishment also as a necessary consequence of it, it therefore follows, that if eternal punishment was possible, to any one of the rational creation, it must hold equally so to the whole, or the divine system of fitness would be unequal. From which we infer, that though God in his creation and providence, designed the ultimate best good and felicity of the moral world, he had nevertheless so far departed from his eternal plan, or intention, that it was liable to be frustrated, and that universal misery and eternal damnation was possible to overspread the whole; all this necessarily follows on the position, that any rational natures are liable to eternal destruction; and therefore the doctrine of the possibility, or liability, of eternal punishment, is inadmissible.

Furthermore, accountability, probation or trial, are in nature inseparably connected with the existence of moral beings, and must eternally remain so to be, for weakness and imperfection is that which subjects all finite rational beings to trial and is the only ground of the possibility of it. All intelligent agents therefore, except the most high God, are probationers. A state of improvement is necessarily connected with that of trial and proficiency. What reason can be given to make it appear, that the immortal souls of mankind, in their succeeding state of existence, may not err, and more or less deviate from the rules of eternal unerring order and reason; they must be admitted to be capable of moral action, for it is essential to their existence; and though the next state of being may be ever so much dissimilar from this, in the mode or manner of it, yet we shall be but creatures in that state, and why not liable to error, transgression and blame, and also to punishment for the same; for as finiteness or imperfection are the grounds of the liability of our present offences, that liability will eternally continue, and that in proportion to our future imperfection. Could God have established any creature, or race of creatures, in a confirmed and perpetual happiness, by a sovereign act of omnipotence, consistent with his moral perfections, and the nature of intelligent agents themselves, we should have experienced such a confirmation in this life. But a confirmed and perpetual state of blessedness, will agree to no character short of God's: this is therefore his prerogative, and it is the absolute perfection of his nature, which confirms him in that state. But as to finite cogitative beings, they cannot in the nature of things, be any more confirmed in happiness, than they can in moral rectitude, which is the ground and source of it; nor is it possible for an imperfect nature to attain to perfection, though they may be eternally improving; nor can they be perpetually morally good, for perpetual uniformity is perfection itself; but they are always liable to change, to error and sin, and consequently to misery, which is inseparably connected with it, as the only certain means of repentance, reformation and restoration.

Moral good is the only source from whence a rational mind can be supplied with a happiness agreeable to the dignity of its nature. It would be impossible for omnipotence itself to make a vicious mind taste the ecstatic felicity of a moral happiness, so long as it may be supposed to be vicious, inasmuch as morality, in the nature of the thing itself, is prerequisite to such a happiness, without the possession and actual enjoyment of which the mind cannot be mentally happy, or enjoy itself agreeable to its discerning, conscious and sentimental nature; but must disapprove of the erroneous departure (or its vicious pursuits) from the amiable rules of moral fitness, and feel proportionably guilty and miserable. Nor could pardon or atonement alter the condition of a vicious mind, for miserable it must be, as long as it remains vicious, whether God be supposed to forgive the wickedness of it or not; for it is the conscious exercise of moral goodness only, which is capable of happifying the rational mind; therefore such reflections, pursuits and habits, which are comprised in our agency, as will in their own nature admit of a rational happiness, make us happy;

and such agency of man as is inadequate and improper to constitute such happiness, and which naturally tends to misery will involve us therein; and miserable we must be, until the bias and disposition of the mind is turned from moral evil to moral good, which is the same as repentance and restoration. This is the eternal law of nature, respecting the agency and the happiness or misery of imperfect rational nature, throughout its never ending agency and trial; and consequently, our eternity, will be as much diversified with happiness and misery, as our agency may be supposed to alternately partake of moral good and evil. So certain as we retain our rational nature, in our succeeding state of existence, we shall be capable of moral actions, which admit of proficiency, agency and trial; and not only so, but subjects us to agency and accountability, as much as in this life, or in any condition of finite reason whatever; and every improvement of a rational mind, alters the consciousness of it, and consequently the happiness or the misery of it. Absolute power may inflict physical evils, but is utterly incapable of inflicting those of a moral nature; nor can mere positive injunction by law affect the consciences of rational beings, who must be either happy or miserable on the basis of their own agency, and consciousness of merit or demerit.

It has been owing to improvement that we have progressively advanced from the knowledge and capacity of childhood to that of manhood, and to our improvement, which is the same as agency, in moral good and evil, that has alternately made us happy or unhappy in a mental sense; from hence we infer, that if rational nature, in the world to come, is essentially analogous to what it is in this life, agency and probation will be continued with the immortality of the soul, be the manner of its existence, or of its communicating or receiving ideas as it will.

Furthermore, the doctrine of a future improvement, or agency, may be argued from the death of infants and children. None will pretend that they have an opportunity of proficiency in this life, therefore we infer, that if such a state be requisite to fit and improve their feeble minds for the enjoyment of a rational happiness, agency must be continued to the future state; and admitting that they are immortal, and that agency is precluded from the world to come, they would remain children in knowledge eternally; nor could any departed soul, on such a position, expand its rational functions beyond its size of understanding at the time of departing this life which would make immortality to man a cypher, except as to the perpetuation of their powers of cogitation in a limited circumference; the reflection whereof would be more or less rude and incoherent; which at best would be but a small fund for an eternal contemplation.

But if it be admitted, that the souls of mankind, of every age and denomination, will in their futurity be progressive in knowledge, (which must be the case with cogitative beings) then it necessarily follows, that agency and trial

158   proceed hand in hand with it. Therefore it is impossible, that there should be a particular day of judgment, in which mankind, or any, or either of them, shall receive their eternal sentence of happiness or misery; for such a sentence is inconsistent with any further trial or agency, and therefore is inadmissible.

Furthermore, proficiency or agency, is inconsistent with a confirmed state of happiness or of misery; for in the same proportion as our ideas, pursuits, intentions and habits vary, so does our happiness or misery.

Finite minds cannot be confirmedly happy or miserable, any more than they can be absolutely identical which is the prerogative of the divine mind: finite intelligences gain ideas by a succession of thinking, and are happy or miserable in proportion as the succession of ideas will admit; and every succession in the multiplicity of thinking, is incompatible with a proper identity of mind, (except as to the principle of thinking itself) was it to be perfectly identical, it could not admit of a succession of ideas, which is the same as addition, nor of a diminution of them, but would be confined to one perception only, and in this case, the happiness or misery, resulting from it, would be as identical as the perception itself may be supposed to be, and incapable of enlargement or diminution; which might be denominated a confirmed state. But a confirmed state is utterly incompatible with a state of improvement, and is applicable to the divine perfection only. Inasmuch as succession of thinking cannot be ascribed to God, he is therefore identically the same, but progressive agents, are always capable of additional knowledge, which lays them under additional obligations to moral government, and thus duty is always co-extensive with the improvement of rational agents; and inasmuch as agency, proficiency and accountability, are in nature co-existent, or concomitant with intelligent finite beings, we infer, that the doctrine of eternal damnation is without foundation, for that it would, if true, put a final end to any further agency, trial or accountability, therefore, so certain as our agency is eternal our condemnation cannot be so.

V.1. Speculations on the Doctrine of the
Depravity of Human Reason

In the course of our speculations on divine providence we proceed next to the consideration of the doctrine of the depravity of human reason; a doctrine derogatory to the nature of man, and the rank and character of being which he holds in the universe, and which, if admitted to be true overturns knowledge and science and renders learning, instruction and books useless and impertinent; inasmuch as reason, depraved or spoiled, would cease to be reason; as much as the mind of a raving madman would of course cease to be rational: admitting the depravity of reason, the consequence would unavoidably follow, that as far as it may be supposed to have taken place in the minds of mankind, they could be no judges of it, in consequence of their supposed depravity; for without the exercise of reason, we could not understand what reason is, which would be necessary for us previously to understand, in order to understand what it is not; or to distinguish it from that which is its reverse. But for us to have the knowledge of what reason is, and the ability to distinguish it from that which is depraved, or is irrational, is incompatible with the doctrine of the depravity of our reason. Inasmuch as to understand what reason is, and to distinguish it from that which is marred or spoiled, is the same to all intents and purposes, as to have, exercise and enjoy, the principle of reason itself, which precludes its supposed depravity: so that it is impossible for us to understand what reason is, and at the same time determine that our reason is depraved; for this would be the same as when we know that we are in possession and exercise of reason, to determine that we are not in possession or exercise of it.

It may be, that some, who embrace the doctrine of the depravity of human reason, will not admit, that it is wholly and totally depraved, but that it is in a great measure marred or spoiled. But the foregoing arguments are equally applicable to a supposed depravity in part, as in the whole. For in order to judge whether reason be depraved in part, or not, it would be requisite to have an understanding, of what reason may be supposed to have been, previous to its premised depravity; and to have such a knowledge of it, would be the same as to exercise and enjoy it in its lustre and purity; which would preclude the notion of a depravity in part, as well as in the whole; for it would be utterly impossible for us to judge of reason undepraved and depraved, but by comparing them together. But for depraved reason to make such a comparison, is contradictory and impossible; so that, if our reason had been depraved, we could not have had any conception of it any more than a beast. Men of small faculties in reasoning cannot comprehend the extensive reasonings of their superiors, how then can a supposed depraved reason, comprehend that reason which is uncorrupted and pure? To suppose that it could, is the same as to suppose that depraved and undepraved reason is alike, and if so there needs no further dispute about it.

There is a manifest contradiction in applying the term *depraved*, to that of reason, the ideas contained in their respective definitions will not admit of their association together, as the terms convey heterogeneous ideas; for reason spoiled, marred, or robbed of its perfection, ceaseth to be rational, and should not be called reason; inasmuch as it is premised to be depraved, or degenerated from a rational nature; and in consequence of the deprivation of its nature, should also be deprived of its name, and called subterfuge, or some such like name, which might better define its real character.

Those who invalidate reason, ought seriously to consider, *"Whether they argue against reason with or without reason; if with reason, then they establish the principle, that they are labouring to dethrone:"* but if they argue without reason, (which, in order to be consistent with themselves, they must do) they are out of the reach of rational conviction, nor do they deserve a rational argument.

We are told that the knowledge of the depravity of reason, was first communicated to mankind by the immediate inspiration of God. But inasmuch as reason is supposed to be depraved, what principle could there be in the human irrational soul, which could receive or understand the inspiration, or on which it could operate, so as to represent, to those whom it may be supposed were inspired, the knowledge of the depravity of (their own and mankind's) reason (in general:) For a rational inspiration must consist of rational ideas; which presupposes, that the minds of those who were inspired, were rational, previous to such their inspiration; which would be a downright contradiction to the inspiration itself; the import of which was to teach the knowledge of the depravity of human research, which without reason could not be understood, and with reason it would be understood, that the inspiration was false.

Will any advocates for the depravity of reason suppose, that inspiration ingrafts or superadds the essence of reason itself, to the human mind? Admitting it to be so, yet such inspired persons could not understand any thing of reason, before the reception of such supposed inspiration; nor would such a premised inspiration, prove to its possessors, or receivers, that their reason had ever been depraved. All that such premised inspired persons could understand, or be conscious of, respecting reason, would be after the inspiration may be supposed to have taken effect, and made them rational beings, and then instead of being taught by inspiration, that their reason had been previously depraved, they could have had no manner of consciousness of the existence or exercise of it, 'till the imparting the principle of it by the supposed energy of inspiration; nor could such supposed inspired persons communicate the knowledge of such a premised revelation to others of the species, who for want of a rational nature, could not be supposed, *on this position*, to be able to receive the impressions of reason.

That there are degrees in the knowledge of rational beings, and also in their capacities to acquire it, cannot be disputed, as it is so very obvious among mankind. But in all the retrospect gradations from the exalted reasonings of a Locke or a Newton, down to the lowest exercise of it among the species, still it is reason, and not depraved; for a less degree of reason by no means implies a depravity of it, nor does the impairing of reason argue its depravity, for what remains of reason, or rather of the exercise of it, is reason still. But there is not, and cannot be such a thing, as depraved reason, for that which is rational is so, and for that reason cannot be depraved, whatever its degree of exercise may be supposed to be.

A blow on the head, or fracture of the perecranium, as also palsies and many other casualties that await our sensorium; retard, and in some cases wholly prevent the exercise of reason, for a longer, or shorter period; and sometimes through the stage of human life; but in such instances as these, reason is not depraved, but ceases in a greater or less degree, or perhaps wholly ceases its rational exertions or operations; by reason of the breaches, or disorders of the organs of sense, but in such instances, wherein the organs become rectified, and the senses recover their usefulness, the exercise of reason returns; free from any blemish or depravity. For the cessation of the exercise of reason, by no means depraves it.

There is in God's infinite plenitude of creation and providence, such an infinite display of reason, that the most exalted finite rational beings, fall infinitely short of the comprehension thereof. For though the most inconsiderable rational beings, who can discern any truth at all, bear a resemblance or likeness to God, as well as every rational nature of whatever degree in the scale of being, yet neither the greatest or least of them can bear any manner of proportion to God; inasmuch as no possible degree of reason or knowledge, can bear any proportion to that reason and knowledge, which is eternal and infinite, as has been before argued. And though human reason cannot understand every thing, yet in such things, which it does understand, its knowledge which is acquired by reasoning, is as true and certain, as the divine knowledge may be supposed to be: for to more than understand a thing, speaking of that particular, is impossible even to omniscience itself. For knowledge is but knowledge, and that only whether it is in the divine mind, or ours, or in any other intelligences; therefore knowledge is not imperfect; for a knowledge of any thing is the same as to have right ideas of it, or ideas according to truth, and as all knowledge of things in general must be predicated on truth, it will agree in the divine or human mind.

From what has been argued on this subject, in this and the preceding chapters, it appears, that reason is not, and cannot be depraved, but that it bears a likeness to divine reason, is of the same kind, and in its own nature as uniform as truth, which is the test of it; though in the divine essence, it is eternal and infinite, but in man it is eternal only, as it respects their immortality, and finite, as it respects capaciousness. Such people as can be prevailed upon to believe, that their reason is depraved, may easily be led by the nose, and duped into superstition at the pleasure of those, in whom they confide, and there remain from generation to generation: for when they throw by the law of reason, *the only one* which God gave them to direct them in their speculations and duty, they are exposed to ignorant or insidious teachers, and also to their own irregular passions, and to the folly and enthusiasm of those about them, which nothing but reason can prevent or restrain: Nor is it a rational supposition that the commonality of mankind would ever have mistrusted, that their reason was depraved, had they not been told so, and it is whispered about, that the first insinuation of it was from the Priests; (though the Arminian Clergymen in the circle of my acquaintance have exploded the doctrine.) Should we admit the depravity of reason, it would equally affect the priesthood, or any other teachers of that doctrine, with the rest of mankind; but for depraved creatures to receive and give credit to a depraved doctrine, started and taught by depraved creatures, is the greatest weakness and folly imaginable, and comes nearer a proof of the doctrine of a total depravity, than any arguments which have ever been advanced in support of it.

V.2. Containing a Disquisition of the Law of Nature,
as it Respects the Moral System, Interspersed
with Observations on Subsequent Religions

That mankind are by nature endowed with sensation and reflection, from which results the powers of reason and understanding, will not be disputed. The senses are well calculated to make discoveries of external objects, and to communicate those notices, or simple images of things to the mind, with all the magnificent simplicity of nature, which opens an extensive field of contemplation to the understanding, enabling the mind to examine into the natural causes and consequences of things, and to investigate the knowledge of moral good and evil, from which, together with the power of agency, results the human conscience. This is the original of moral obligations and accountability, which is called natural religion; for without the understanding of truth from falsehood, and right from wrong, which is the same as justice from injustice, and a liberty of agency, which is the same as a power of proficiency in either moral good or evil; mankind would not be rational or accountable creatures. Undoubtedly it was the ultimate design of our creator, in giving us being, and furnishing us with those noble compositions of mental powers and sensitive aptitudes, that we should, in, by, and with that nature, serve and honor him: and with those united capacities search out and understand our duty to him, and to one another, with the ability of practising the same, as far as may be necessary for us, in this life. To object against the sufficiency of natural religion, to effect the ultimate best good of mankind, would be derogating from the wisdom, justice and goodness of God, who in the course of his providence to us has adopted it: besides, if natural religion may be supposed to be deficient, what security can we have that any subsequent revealed religion should not be so also? For why might not a second religion from God, be as insufficient or defective as a first religion from him may be supposed to be? From hence we infer, that if natural religion is insufficient to dictate mankind in the way of their duty, and make them ultimately happy, there is an end to religion in general. But as certain as God is perfect, in wisdom and goodness, natural religion is sufficient and complete; and having had the divine approbation, and naturally resulting from a rational nature, is as universally promulgated to mankind as reason itself. But to the disadvantage of the claim of all subsequent religions, *called revelations, whether denominated inspired, external, supernatural, or what not,* they came too late into the world to be essential to the well being of mankind, or to point out to them the only way to heaven and everlasting blessedness: Inasmuch as far the greatest part of mankind, who have ever lived in this world, had departed this life previous to the aeras and promulgations of such revelations. Besides, those subsequent revelations to the law of nature, began the same as human traditions have ever done, in very small circumferences, in the respective parts of the world where they have been inculcated, and made their progress as time, chance and opportunity presented. Does this look like the contrivance of heaven and the only way of salvation? or is it not more like this world and the device of man? Undoubtedly the great parent of mankind laid a just and sufficient foundation of salvation for every of them, for otherwise such of them, who may be supposed not to be thus provided for, would not have whereof to glorify God for their being, but on the contrary would have just matter of complaint against his providence or moral government, for involuntarily necessitating them into a wretched and miserable existence, and that without end or remedy; which would be ascribing to God a more extensive injustice than is possible to be charged on the most barbarous despots that ever were among mankind.

But to return to our speculations upon the law of nature. That this divine law surpasses all positive institutions, that have been ushered into the world since its creation, as much as the wisdom and goodness of God exceeds that of man, is beautifully illustrated in the following quotation; "But it may be said, what is virtue? it is the faithful discharge of those obligations which reason dictates. And what is wisdom itself? but a portion of intelligence" with which the creator has furnished us, in order to direct us in our duty. It may be further asked, what is this duty? whence does it result? and by what law is it prescribed? I answer, that the law which prescribed it is the immutable will of God; to which right reason obliges us to conform ourselves, and in this conformity virtue consists. No law which has commenced since the creation, or which may ever cease to be in force, can constitute virtue; for before the existence of such a law, mankind could not be bound to observe it, but they were certainly under an obligation to be virtuous from the beginning. Princes may make laws and repeal them, but they can neither make nor destroy virtue, and how indeed should they be able to do what is impossible to the Deity himself: virtue being as immutable in its nature as the divine will, which is the ground of it.* A Prince may command his subjects to pay certain taxes or subsidies, may forbid them

---

*Virtue, did not derive its nature merely from the omnipotent will of God, but also from the eternal truth and moral fitness of things; which was the eternal reason, why they were eternally approved by God, and immutably established by him, to be what they are; and so far as our duty is connected with those eternal measures of moral fitness, or we are able to act upon them, we give such actions, or habits, the name of virtue or morality. But when we in writing or conversation say, that virtue is grounded on the divine will, we should at the same time include in the complex idea of it, that the divine will, which constituted virtue, was eternally and infinitely reasonable.

to export certain commodities, or to introduce those of a foreign country. The faithful observance of these laws makes obedient subjects, but does not make virtuous men: and would any one seriously think himself possessed of a virtue the more for not having dealt in painted calicoe; or if the prince should by his authority abrogate these laws, would any one say he had abrogated virtue. It is thus with all positive laws: they all had a beginning, are all liable to exceptions, and may be dispensed with, and even abolished. That law alone, which is ingraven on our hearts by the hand of the creator, is unchangeable and of universal and eternal obligation. That law, says Cicero, is not a human invention, nor an arbitrary political institution, it is in its nature eternal and of universal obligation. The violence Tarquin offered to Lucretia, was breach of that eternal law, and though the Romans at that time might have no written law which condemned such kind of crimes, his offence was not the less heinous; for this law of reason did not then begin, when it was first committed to writing: its original is as antient as the divine mind. For the true, primitive and supreme law, is no other than the unerring reason of the great Jupiter. And in another place he says; this law is founded in nature, it is universal, immutable and eternal, it is subject to no change from any difference of place, or time, it extends invariably to all ages and nations, like the sovereign dominion of that being, who is the author of it.

The promulgation of this supreme law to creatures, is co-extensive and co-existent with reason, and binding on all intelligent beings in the universe; and is that eternal rule of fitness, as applicable to God, by which the creator of all things conducts his infinitude of providence, and by which he governs the moral system of being, according to the absolute perfection of his nature. From hence we infer, that admitting those subsequent revelations, which have more or less obtained credit in the world, as the inspired laws of God, to be consonant to the laws of nature, yet they could be considered as none other but mere transcripts therefrom, promulgated to certain favorite nations, when at the same time all mankind was favoured with the original. The moral precepts contained in Moses's decalogue to the people of Israel, were previously known to every nation under heaven, and in all probability by them as much practised as by the tribes of Israel. Their keeping the seventh day of the week as a sabbath, was an arbitrary imposition of Moses (as many other of his edicts were) and not included in the law of nature. But as to such laws of his, or those of any other legislator, which are morally fit, agree with, and are a part of the natural law, as for instance; "Thou shalt not covet," or "Kill." These positive injunctions cannot add any thing to the law of nature, inasmuch as it contains an entire and perfect system of morality; nor can any positive injunctions or commands enforce the authority of it, or confer any additional moral obligation on those to whom they are given to obey; the previous obligation of natural religion, having either been as binding as reason can possibly conceive of, or the order and constitution of the moral rectitude of things, as resulting from God, can make it to be.

To illustrate the argument of the obligatory nature of the natural law, let us revise the commandments of the decalogue, by premising that Moses had said thou shalt covet, thou shalt steal and murder; would any one conclude, that the injunctions would have been obligatory, surely they would not, for a positive command to violate the law of nature could not be binding on any rational being, how then came the injunctions of Moses, or any others, to be binding in such cases, in which they coincide with the law of nature? We answer, merely in consequence of the obligatory sanctions of the natural law, which does not at all depend on the authority of Moses or of any other Legislator, short of him who is eternal and infinite: nor is it possible that the Jews, who adhere to the law of Moses, should be under greater obligation to the moral law, than the Japanese; or the Christians than the Chinese; for the same God extends the same moral government over universal rational nature, independent of Popes, Priests and Levites. But with respect to all mere positive institutions, injunctions, rites and ceremonies, that do not come within the jurisdiction of the law of nature, they are political matters, and may be expected, perpetuated, dispensed with, abolished, reenacted, compounded or diversified, as conveniency, power, opportunity, inclination, or interest, or all together may dictate; inasmuch as they are not founded on any stable or universal principle of reason, but change with the customs, fashions, traditions and revolutions of the world; having no centre of attraction, but interest, power and advantages of a temporary nature.

When we reflect on the state and circumstances of mankind in this world, their various languages and interchangeable methods of communicating intelligence to each other, (which are subject to perpetual alterations and refinements) the insuperable difficulties in translating antient writings, with any considerable degree of perfection; as also our being exposed to the villainous practices of impostors, with a variety of other deceptions, blunders and inaccuracies, which unavoidably attend written and diverse or variously translated revelations; we cannot too much admire the wisdom and goodness of God in imparting his law to us in the constitution of our rational nature, to point out our duty in all circumstances and vicissitudes of human life; which a written revelation would not be able to do, admitting, that it had sustained no serious alterations from its first composure, which we will premise to have been perfect: for human affairs are so constantly changing and varying, that the same action, or conduct, would, under different circumstances, be alternately good and evil; and to have our duty in every of the multiplicity of incidental circumstances and changes of life, pointed out to us by a written revelation, would compose a Bible of a monstrous size. Furthermore, as every individual of the human race is attended with more or less diversity of circumstances of action

166   in life, therefore in order for us to be taught our duty by a written revelation, it would be requisite, that each individual of mankind should have their particular, and diverse revelation; in which their particular duty might be known in all cases: so that we should suspend our actions, until we may be supposed to have turned to the particular paragraph of our respective revelations, and consulted them, in order to conduct our agency thereby (in which case printing would be in great demand.) Still there would be a difficulty in understanding an external printed revelation, or which paragraph of the bulky volume would be applicable to the various parts of the conduct of human agency; so that we should be obliged finally to make use of (depraved) reason, to understand it, or, in other words, should be obliged to make use of the deistical Bible to explain and understand our own, which brings us back again to the religion of nature or reason. Was it not that we were rational creatures, it would have been as ridiculous to have pretended to have given us a Bible, for our instruction in matters of religion or morality, as it would to a stable of horses. And on the other hand, admitting that we naturally understand moral good and evil, it renders such a book no ways essential to us, though if it be admitted to be argumentative and instructive, it might, like other sensible writings, subserve mankind; but if it is supposed to be in part defective in reason, and interspersed with superstition, it would, under the sanction of divine authority, be vastly more prejudicial to mankind, than as though it was stamped merely by the authority of man; for an error in that which is received as infallible, can never be confuted or rectified; inasmuch as it usurps the authority of human reason. Furthermore, admitting that the copies of written revelation, which are now extant in the world, perfectly accord with their several original manuscripts (which is impossible to be true) yet they could not be equally instructive to mankind with the productions of a variety of modern authors, who have written since their epocha, inasmuch as the world has ever since been improving in learning and science; and as those written revelations must necessarily have been (as to their subject matter and all and every other particular) accommodated to the state, circumstances and degrees of learning and knowledge, of those, to whom the revelations were first supposed to have been communicated, and also to those to whom it was afterwards taught, and it would reduce it below the understanding of this age. For it appears from the scripture accounts, that shepherds, fishermen, and the illiterate of those early ages of the world, were principally made use of as the promulgators thereof to the rest of mankind, and that "Not many wise or noble," were "Called," or embraced their revelations in the early times, "But the weak things of this world" were "Chosen," for which reason they were called "Babes:" Though after such religion became popular, princes and politicians of several parts of the world promoted it as an instrument of state-policy. Be this as it will, the first promulgators of written revelations could not reveal to the world more than they knew themselves; nor could they be made to know any more than their capacity (under their then circumstances) was capable of receiving: any external written revelation is therefore utterly incompatible with a progressive or increasing state of knowledge. We will premise, that the world's dissolution will be postponed one hundred thousand million of years from this epocha, or that it will eternally remain, what an idle conceit would it be for us to suppose, that the succeeding generations of mankind, in their religious knowledge, will be chained down to the theology of those positive written revelations, which were introduced into the world, in its early, illiterate, and superstitious age; this would be utterly subversive of a state of proficiency, much the same as for a man to consult his nonage for rules of knowledge, and instruction to govern his manhood.

Was the creator and Governor of the universe to erect a particular academy of arts and sciences in this world, under his immediate inspection, with tutors rightly organized, and intellectually qualified to carry on the business of teaching, it might like other colleges (and possibly in a superior manner,) instruct its scholars. But that God should have given a revelation of his will to mankind, as, his law, and to be continued to the latest posterity as such, which is premised to be above the capacity of their understanding; is contradictory and in its own nature impossible. Nor could a revelation to mankind, which comes within the circle of their knowledge, be edifying or instructive to them, for it is a contradiction to call that which is above my comprehension, or that which I already, (from natural sagacity) understand, a revelation to me: to tell me, or inspire me, with the knowledge of that which I knew before, would reveal nothing to me and to reveal that to me which is supernatural or above my comprehension, is contradictory and impossible. But the truth of the matter is, that mankind are restricted by the law of nature to acquire knowledge or science progressively, as before argued. From which we infer the impropriety, and consequently the impossibility, of God's having ever given us any manuscript copy of his eternal law: for that to reveal it as first would bring it on a level with the infancy of knowledge then in the world, or (fishermen, shepherds, and illiterate people could not have understood it) which would have brought it so low, that it could not be instructive or beneficial to after generations in their progressive advances in science and wisdom.

VII.5. Miracles Could Not Be Instructive to Mankind

Should we admit the intervention of Miracles, yet they could not enlarge our ideas of the power of God. For that to unmake nature universally, and to impress it with new and opposite laws from those of its eternal establishment, could require no greater exertion of power, than that which is Omnipotent, and which must have been exerted in the eternal creation, regulation and support of the universe. But any supposed miraculous alteration of nature, must imply mutability in the wisdom of God; and therefore is inadmissible. Should God miraculously raise a dead person to life again, would the restoring life argue a greater exertion of power in God than in first giving existence to that life? surely it could not: From all which we infer, that miracles cannot enlarge our ideas of the power of God. We proceed next to enquire, what advantages could accrue to mankind by them in the way of teaching and instruction? For this must be the great end proposed by them. That they cannot teach us any thing relative to the omnipotence of God, has been evinced; but that they militate against his wisdom: and furthermore, that they cannot prove the divine authority of written revelation, or the mission of its respective teachers to any country, people or nation, any farther or longer than the miraculous works are actually continued, has been sufficiently argued in the preceding section. It remains farther to be considered, that they are incapable of instructing us in the subject-matter, doctrine, proposition or inference of any premised written revelation; or of giving us any insight into the precepts or injunctions thereof, or to communicate any sort of intelligence or knowledge respecting its contents. The premised, sudden and miraculous alterations of the common course of nature might astonish us; but such alterations or changes, do not evince that they have any thing to do with us, or we with them in the way of teaching and instruction; for truth and falsehood, right and wrong, justice and injustice, virtue and vice, or moral good and evil are in their distinct natures diametrically opposite to each other, and necessarily and eternally will remain so to be, and that, independent of miracles or revealed religion. It is by reason we investigate the knowledge of moral good and evil, it is that which lays us under a moral obligation, and it is not a miracle or revelation that can alter the moral rectitude of things, or prove that to be truth, which in its nature is not so. Therefore admitting ever so many miracles, and revelations, we should still have to recur to reason and argument, the old and only way of exploring truth and distinguishing it from falsehood, or understanding true religion from imposture or error. For though miracles might evince the divine mission of the clergy, and the divinity of the christian revelation, to us, were they in fact wrought in this enlightened age for that purpose, yet they are not calculated to expound or explain it, but would perplex and confound us, in our logical and doctrinal speculations, nature and reason being opposed to them as before argued. Such supposed miraculous changes in nature, would to us be mysterious, and altogether unintelligible, and consequently could not come within our deliberation on the right understanding, or comments on a supposed written revelation; the understanding of which, after all the bustle about miracles, must be investigated by reason: and revelation itself be either approved or disapproved by it. From the foregoing reasonings we infer, that miracles cannot be edifying or instructive to us; and though they are strenuously urged as a proof of the divine legation of the first promulgators of revelation, and their successors; nevertheless, where the premised miracles became extinct, their divine authority and the evidence of the infallibility of revelation, became extinct also.

IX.1. *Of the Nature of* Faith *and Wherein It Consists*

Faith in Jesus Christ and in his Gospel throughout the New-Testament, is represented to be an essential condition of the eternal salvation of mankind. *"Knowing that a man is not justified by the works of the law, but by the faith of Jesus Christ, even we have believed in Jesus Christ, that we might be justified by the faith of Christ, and not by the works of the law, for by the works of the law shall no flesh be justified."* Again, *"If thou shalt confess the Lord Jesus Christ, and believe in thine heart that God hath raised him from the dead, thou mayest be saved." And again, "He that believeth and is baptised shall be saved, but he that believeth not shall be damned."* Faith is the last result of the understanding, or the same which we call the conclusion, it is the consequence of a greater or less deduction of reasoning from certain premises previously laid down; it is the same as believing or judging of any matter of fact, or assenting to or dissenting from the truth of any doctrine, system or position; so that to form a judgment, or come to a determination in one's own mind, or to believe, or to have faith, is in reality the same thing, and is synonymously applied both in writing and speaking; for example, *"Abraham believed in God."* Again, *"for he,"* speaking of Abraham, *"judged him faithful who had promised"* and again, *"his faith was counted unto him for righteousness."* It is not only in scripture that we meet with examples of the three words, to wit, belief, judgment and faith, to stand for the marks of our ideas for the same thing, but also all intelligible writers and speakers, apply these phrases synonymously, and it would be good grammar and sense for us to say that we have faith in a universal providence, or that we believe in a universal providence, or that we judge that there is a universal providence. These three different phrases, in communicating our ideas of providence, do every of them exhibit the same idea, to all persons of common understanding, who are acquainted with the English Language. In fine every one's experience may convince them, that they cannot assent to, or dissent from the truth of any matter of fact, doctrine or proposition whatever, contrary to their judgment; for the act of the mind in assenting to, or dissenting from any position, or in having faith or belief in favor of, or against any doctrine, system or proposition, could not amount to any thing more or less, than the act of the judgment, or last dictate of the understanding, whether the understanding be supposed to be rightly informed or not; so that our faith in all cases is as liable to err, as our reason is to misjudge of the truth; and our minds act faith in disbelieving any doctrine or system of religion to be true, as much as in believing it to be so. From hence it appears, that the mind cannot act faith in opposition to its judgment, but that it is the resolution of the understanding itself committed to memory or writing, and can never be considered distinct from it. And inasmuch as faith necessarily results from reasoning, forcing itself upon our minds by the evidence of truth, or the mistaken apprehension of it, without any act of choice of ours, there cannot be any thing, which pertains to, or partakes of the nature of moral good or evil in it. For us to believe such doctrines or systems of religion, as appear to be credibly recommended to our reason, can no more partake of the nature of goodness or morality, than our natural eyes may be supposed to partake of it in their perception of colours; for the faith of the mind, and the sight of the eye are both of them necessary consequences, the one results from the reasonings of the mind, and the other from the perception of the eye. To suppose a rational mind without the exercise of faith, would be as absurd as to suppose a proper and compleat eye without sight, or the perception of the common objects of that sense. The short of the matter is this, that without reason we could not have faith, and without the eye or eyes we could not see. But once admitting that we are rational, faith follows of course, naturally resulting from the dictates of reason.

Furthermore, it is observable, that in all cases wherein reason makes an erroneous conclusion, faith is likewise erroneous, and that in the same proportion as the conclusion may be supposed to be faulty and irregular: for it is the established order of human nature, that faith should always conform to the decrees of the judgment, whether it be right or wrong, or partly both. From hence it follows, that errors in faith, and consequently in practice, are more or less unavoidable. We are therefore obliged to substitute sincerity in the room of knowledge, in all cases wherein knowledge is not attainable, for we cannot look into the eternal order of unerring reason and perfect rectitude, so as in all cases to regulate our minds and consciences from thence. We must therefore adopt the principle of sincerity, since it is always supposed to aim at perfection, and to come as near it as the informities of our nature will admit, (for otherwise it could not be sincerity) which is the highest pretension to goodness, that we can lawfully aspire to. There are therefore good or bad designs and intentions, which crown all our actions, and denominate them to be either good or bad, virtuous or vicious. Those who are vicious and abandoned to wickedness, may, and often do, possess more knowledge, and consequently a more extensive faith than those who are ignorant and virtuous: their sin does not consist in the want of understanding or faith, but in their omission of cultivating in their own minds the love and practice of virtue, or in not bringing their designs, intentions, dispositions and habits to a conformity thereto. A good conscience, predicated on knowledge as far as that is attainable, and on sincerity for the rest of our conduct, always was and will be essential to a rational happiness, which results from a consciousness of moral rectitude, and thus it is that mankind, by seeking after the truth, and conforming (as far as human frailty will permit) to moral rectitude, may attain to the enjoyment of a good conscience, although in doctrinal or speculative points of religion, or in creeds, they may be supposed to be ever so erroneous.

X.3. *The Imperfection of Knowledge in the Person of Jesus Christ, Incompatible with His Divinity, with Observations on the Hypostatical Union of the Divine and Human Nature*

That Jesus Christ was not God is evident from his own words, where, speaking of the day of judgment, he says, "*Of that day and hour knoweth no man, no not the angels which are in Heaven, neither the Son, but the Father.*" This is giving up all pretension to divinity, and acknowledging in the most explicit manner, that he did not know all things, but compares his understanding to that of man and of angels; "*of that day and hour knoweth no man, no not the angels which are in heaven, neither the son.*" Thus he ranks himself with finite beings, and with them acknowledges, that he did not know the day and hour of judgment, and at the same time ascribes a superiority of knowledge to the father, for that he knew the day and hour of judgment.

That he was a mere creature is further evident from his prayer to the father, saying, "*Father, if it be possible, let this cup pass from me, nevertheless, not my will but thine be done.*" These expressions speak forth the most humble submission to his father's will, authority and government, and however becoming so submissive a disposition to the divine government would be, in a creature, it is utterly inconsistent and unworthy of a God, or of the person of Jesus Christ, admitting him to have been a divine person, or of the essence of God.

What notions can we entertain that the divine essence should be divided, and one part assume an authority over the other; or that the other should wield obedience; this is a contradiction, inasmuch as essence cannot be divided, but is the same, without distinction, either in its nature, authority or government.

To suppose one part of the divine nature to exercise authority over another, is the same as to suppose, that part of the essence of God was weak and imperfect, and not capable of holding a share in the divine government, which would reduce it to the state and condition of a creature, and divest it of its divinity. Nor would the consequences of such a supposed imperfection in the essence of God end here, but would necessarily involve the divine nature, in weakness, misery and imperfection; and extinguish every idea of the existence of a God: This is the necessary consequence of deifying Christ. But if Jesus Christ was not of the essence of God, he must have been a mere creature: as there cannot be any being but who is either finite or infinite, as has been before argued.

But we are told of a hypostatical union of the divine and human nature. But wherein does it consist? Does it unite the two natures so as to include the human nature in the essence of God? If it does not it does not deify the person of Christ; for the essence of God is that which makes him to be what he is; but if the hypostatical union includes human nature in the divine, then there would be an addition of the human nature to the essence of God, in which case the divine nature would be no longer perfectly simple, but compounded, and would be diverse from what it may be supposed to have been the eternity preceding such premised union; in which connection the divine nature must have changed from its eternal identity. He could not be the same God he was previous to his union with humanity; for if the union of natures is supposed to have made no alteration in the divine essence, it is a contradiction to call it a union; for the hypostatical union must be supposed to be something or nothing, if it be nothing, then there is no such union, but if it is any thing real, it necessarily produces mutability in the divine nature. Now, if the divine nature was eternally perfect and compleat, it could not receive the addition of the nature of man, but if it was not perfect in the eternity preceding the premised hypostatical union, it could not have been perfected by the addition of another imperfection.

The doctrine of the *incarnation* itself, and the *virgin mother*, does not merit a serious confutation and therefore is passed in silence, except the mere mention of it.

XII.6. *The Person of* Jesus Christ, *Considered in a Variety of Different Characters, Each of Which Are Incompatible with a Participation of the Divine Nature. That a* Redemption, *Wrought Out by Inflicting the Demerits of* Sin *upon the* Innocent, *Would Be* Unjust, *and That It Could Contain No* Mercy *or* Goodness *to the Universality of Being, Considered Inclusively*

It is impossible that God should suffer or change, or the person of Jesus Christ, as far as he may be supposed to be of the essence of God; for the absolute perfection of the divine nature exempts it from suffering, weakness, or any manner of imperfection. Therefore Jesus Christ, in the nature in which he is premised to have suffered, could not be God.

But on the position that Christ was a mere creature, as the *Arians* believe, though ever so exalted, all the obedience or righteousness he could have acquired or attained to, would have been necessary for the discharge of his own duty as an accountable creature. Admitting that he had imputed it to others, he must have been miserable himself for the deficiency thereof, except his righteousness had been acquired by works of supererogation, or except he is supposed to be capable of a moral happiness without righteousness or goodness, and if he may be supposed to have been capable of such a happiness without those moral qualifications requisite thereto, why might not mankind in general have been capable of it upon the same footing of deficiency, without his imputed righteousness? however it is no way probable admitting it to be possible, that any exalted, wise and understanding being would part with the essentials of his own happiness; *viz.* his morality to others; and for them, and in their stead, actually suffer a great and dreadful weight of misery, and thus at an equal expence of his own happiness and goodness, redeem a race of sinful and guilty creatures; for there could not on this thesis, be any advantage to the system of finite beings, considered collectively, or any mercy or goodness displayed to being in general. What mercy would there be in reprieving or restoring a race of condemned creatures from misery, by inflicting an equal condemnation or punishment on a premised innocent and exalted finite being, which should have been inflicted on the guilty? Humanity obliges us to be kind and benevolent, but never obliges us to suffer for criminals (nor could such a suffering excuse them from their just demerits) but justice and self-preservation forbids it; for all finite beings are under greater obligations to themselves than to any other creature or race of creatures whatever; so that there could be no justice or goodness in one being's suffering for another, nor is it at all compatible with reason to suppose, that God was the contriver of such a propitiation.

The practice of imputing one person's crime to another, in capital offences among men, so that the innocent should suffer for the guilty, has never yet been introduced into any court of judicature in the world, or so much as practised in any civilised country; And the manifest reason in this, as in all other cases of imputation, is the same, viz. it confounds personal merit and demerit.

The murderer ought to die for the demerit of his crime, but if the court exclude the idea of personal demerit (guilt being always the inherent property of the guilty and of them only) they might as well sentence one person to death for the murder of another: for justice would be wholly blind was it not predicated on the idea of the fact of a personal demerit, on the identical person who was guilty of the murder: nor is it possible to reward merit abstractly considered from its personal agents. These are facts that universally hold good in human governments. The same reasons cannot fail to hold good in the divine mind as in that of the human, for the rules of justice are essentially the same whether applied to the one or to the other, having their uniformity in the eternal truth and reason of things.

But it is frequently objected, that inasmuch as one person can pay, satisfy and discharge a cash debt for another, redeem him from prison and set him at liberty, therefore Jesus Christ might become responsible for the sins of mankind, or of the elect, and by suffering their punishment atone for them, and free them from their condemnation. But it should be considered, that comparisons darken or reflect light upon an argument according as they are either pertinent or impertinent thereto; we will therefore examine the comparison, and see if it will with propriety apply to the atonement.

Upon the Christian scheme, Christ the son was God, and equal with God the father, or with God the Holy Ghost, and therefore original sin must be considered to be an offence equally against each of the persons of the premised Trinity, and being of a criminal nature could not be discharged or satisfied by cash or produce, as debts of a civil contract are, but by suffering; and it has already been proved to be inconsistent with the divine or human government, to inflict the punishment of the guilty upon the innocent, though one man may discharge another's debt in cases where lands, chattels or cash are adequate to it; but what capital offender was ever discharged by such commodities?

Still there remains a difficulty on the part of Christianity, in accounting for one of the persons in the premised trinity's satisfying a debt due to the impartial justice of the unity of the three persons. For God the son to suffer the condemnation of guilt in behalf of man, would not only be unjust in itself, but incompatible with his divinity, and the retribution of the justice of the premised trinity of persons in the godhead (of whom God the son must be admitted to be one) toward mankind; for this would be the same as to suppose God to be judge, criminal and executioner, which is inadmissible.

But should we admit for argument's sake, that God suffered for original sin, yet taking into one complex idea the whole mental system of being, universally, both finite and infinite, there could have been no display of grace, mercy, or goodness to being in general, in such a supposed redemption of mankind; inasmuch as the same quantity or degree of evil is supposed to have taken place upon being, universally considered, as would have taken place, had finite individuals, or the race of Adam, suffered according to their respective demerits.

Should we admit that there is a trinity of persons in the divine essence, yet the one could not suffer without the other, for essence cannot be divided in suffering, any more than in enjoyment. The essence of God is that which includes the divine nature, and the same identical nature must necessarily partake of the same glory, honor, power, wisdom, goodness and absolute uncreated and unlimited perfection, and is equally exempted from weakness and suffering. Therefore, as certain as Christ suffered he was not God, but whether he is supposed to be God or man, or both, he could not in justice have suffered for original sin, which must have been the demerit of its perpetrators as before argued.

Supposing Christ to have been both God and man, he must have existed in two different essences, *viz.* the essence of God and the essence of man. And if he existed in two distinct and separate essences, there could be no union between the divine and human natures. But if there is any such thing as an hypostatical union between the divine and human natures, it must unite both natures in one essence, which is impossible: for the divine nature being infinite, could admit of no addition or enlargement, and consequently cannot allow of a union with any nature whatever. Was such an union possible in itself, yet, for a superior nature to unite with an inferior one in the same essence, would be degrading to the former, as it would put both natures on a level by constituting an identity of nature: the consequences whereof would either deify man, or divest God of his divinity, and reduce him to the rank and condition of a creature; inasmuch as the united essence must be denominated either divine or human.

That God should become a man, is impossible, and that man should become a God, is equally impossible and absurd. But if the divine nature retains its absolute perfection, and the nature of man its infirmity, then a premised hypostatical union between them would imply a union of weakness and imperfection to the nature and essence of God; for so certain as human nature is imperfect and united with the divine, so certain perfection must be supposed to unite with imperfection, but it is contradictory and unworthy of the divine nature to form such a hypostatical junction. Furthermore to suppose that two essences are contained in one, is as great a contradiction, as to suppose, that two units are one, and one unit is two: for if two essences have a positive existence, they must exist in two distinct and separate natures, for that, which constitutes but one nature, is and necessarily must be contained in but one essence, so *vice versa*, that which constitutes two essences, at the same time gives existence to two natures, for a nature cannot exist without an essence, nor an essence without a nature; for essence is identity itself. But that there should be two identities in the same nature or essence, is impossible and contradictory, therefore Jesus Christ could not be both God and man, for this plain reason, that if he was one of them, he could not be the other; for God and man are not and cannot be one and the same, for that there is an infinite disproportion between them; for which reason they cannot be hypostatically united in one nature or essence. The divine mind comprehends all possible knowledge, with one entire and infinite reflection without a succession of thinking. Nor is it compatible with the omnipresence of God to ascribe motion to him, for it would imply absence in him from place, and be a downright contradiction to his being every where present; therefore that mind, which intuitively understands all things, and is every where present, is exalted above our narrow conceptions or traditions of uniting with the animal or cogitative nature of man, any more than with the universe in general. Our intelligence would contribute nothing to his mind, and the body of man would be but a circumscribed and inconsistent vehicle to enwrap, or inclose that mind, which is eternal and infinite. A man is finite and cannot be in but one place at the same time, his motion from one place to another as regularly and necessarily excludes him from one place, as it introduces him into another; he thinks by succession and by parts, and is liable to errors and mistakes in theory and practice; and ignorance, vanity and infirmity are more or less the lot of humanity. How arrogant is it then in man to pretend a union with the divine nature, who is infinitely above our praises or adoration? But we are told, that the hypostatical union is a mysterious one. Nevertheless it is a union or not a union, if it is a union of the divine and human natures, they must be comprised in one and the selfsame essence, or otherwise it is such a mysterious union, that it is not a union, which is no mystery at all, but a barefaced absurdity. For that which we can comprehend to be unreasonable and contradictory, is by no means mysterious. That only is mysterious, which we cannot understand to be reasonable or unreasonable, true or false, right or wrong, which is not the case respecting the hypostatical union: for admitting it to be true, the human mind must reflect, reason and judge of things in and with the divine mind. But as the divine mind does not think or reflect by succession, and the human mind cannot exert its thinking faculty any otherwise than by succession, it could not think or reflect in or with the divine mind at all; for the divine omniscience, comprehending all things, would also comprehend the thoughts and reasonings of the human mind, whether they are supposed to be right or wrong. But the finite mind would be lost and swallowed up in the divine, without adding any thing to it, except it be imperfection. Nor is it possible in itself, that an intelligent finite being, who thinks by succession, should be united in one essence with that mind, which is infinite, and does not think by succession: For infinity of intelligence cannot admit of addition, nor could the infinite and finite mind think together in one and the same mind, as the manner of their perceptions, as well as the extent of them, would be infinitely different, and consequently there could be no union between them. But the human mind, by a progressive and finite mode of reflection, would act and judge of things, not only distinctly from, but opposite to the eternal mind, which naturally obstructs or precludes the union. Besides, if the human mind acts separately and individually from the divine mind, it acts in the same manner as our minds do, and like them would be liable not only to imperfection, but to sin and misery; a union too wretched to be ascribed to the divine nature. But admitting the union between the infinite and finite minds, they would be but one mind, and conscious of the same.consciousness, for otherwise they could not be the same, or pertain to the same essence. But that a finite mind could be conscious of an infinite or all comprehending consciousness, or compose any part of it, is absurd; as a consciousness is not compounded of parts, as parts cannot comprise infinity. And as to moral and physical evil, the infinite mind is at as great a remove therefrom as from finiteness itself, and consequently could not jointly suffer with the person of a supposed mediator.

But it may be objected that Jesus Christ was not possessed of a human mind, and that the hypostatical union consisted in the uniting of the divinity with the animal part of the nature of man only. But such a union would of consequence subject the divine nature to a state of suffering, and obnoxiously expose it to physical evils. To suppose that it did not, is the same as to suppose, that there was no such union, for if it be really a union, it must be attended with the necessary consequences of a union of the divine nature with the animal part of the nature of man, or otherwise it is a contradiction to call it a union. But if the divine nature did not suffer in the person of Christ, and he was by nature

void of a human mind, then it follows, that it was the mere animal body of
Christ that suffered for original sin, in which, intelligent nature, either divine
or human, did not bear a part. But if it be supposed, that the hypostatical union
united the divine nature with that of the human, consisting of cogitation and
sensation, then the previous arguments stand fairly opposed to the doctrine of
the hypostatical union, which is submitted to the reader.

XIV.2. Morality Derived from Natural Fitness, and Not from Tradition

Such parts or passages of the scriptures as inculcate morality, have a tendency
to subserve mankind, the same as all other public investigations or teachings of
it, may be supposed to have; but are neither better or worse for having a place
in the volume of those writings denominated canonical; for morality does not
derive its nature from books, but from the fitness of things; and though it may
be more or less, interspersed through the pages of the Alkoran, its purity and
rectitude would remain the same; for that it is founded in eternal right; and
whatever writings, books or oral speculations, best illustrate or teach this moral
science, should have the preference. The knowledge of this as well as all other
sciences, is acquired from reason and experience, and (as it is progressively
obtained) may with propriety be called, the revelation of God, which he has
revealed to us in the constitution of our rational natures: and as it is congenial
with reason and truth cannot (like other revelations) partake of imposture. This
is natural religion, and could be derived from none other but God. I have
endeavoured, in this treatise, to prune this religion from those excrescences,
with which Craft on the one hand, and Ignorance on the other, have loaded
it; and to hold it up to view in its native simplicity, free from alloy; and have
throughout the contents of the volume, addressed the reason of mankind, and
not their passions, traditions or prejudices; for which cause, it is no wise probable that it will meet with any considerable approbation.

Most of the human race, by one means or other are prepossessed with
principles opposed to the religion of reason. In these parts of America, they are
most generally taught, that they are born into the world in a state of enmity to
God and moral good, and are under his wrath and curse, that the way to
Heaven and future blessedness is out of their power to pursue, and that it is
incumbered with mysteries which none but the Priests can unfold, that we
must "*be born again*," have a special kind of faith, and be regenerated; or in
fine, that human nature, which they call "the old man," must be destroyed,
perverted, or changed by them, and by them new modeled, before it can be
admitted into the Heavenly kingdom. Such a plan of superstition, as far as it
obtains credit in the world, subjects mankind to sacerdotal empire; which is
erected on the imbecility of human nature. Such of mankind, as break the
fetters of their education, remove such other obstacles as are in their way, and

have the confidence publicly to talk rational, exalt reason to its just supremacy, and vindicate truth and the ways of God's providence to men; are sure to be stamped with the epithet of irreligious, infidel, profane, and the like. But it is often observed of such a man, that *he is morally honest,* and as often replied, *what of that? Morality will carry no man to heaven.* So that all the satisfaction the honest man can have while the superstitious are squibbing hell fire at him, is to retort back upon them that they are priest ridden.

Most people place religion in arbitrary ceremonies, or mere positive institutions, abstractly considered from the moral rectitude of things, and in which religion does not and cannot consist, and thus delude themselves with an empty notion of religion, which, in reality is made up of tradition and superstition, and in which moral obligation is not concerned; not considering that a conformity to moral rectitude, which is morality in the abstract, is the sum of all religion, that ever was or can be in the universe; as there can be no religion in that in which there is no moral obligation; except we make religion to be void of reason, and if so, all argument about it is at an end.

The manner of the existence, and intercourse of human souls, after the dissolution of their bodies by death, being inconceivable to us in this life, and all manner of intelligence between us and departed souls impracticable, the priests have it in their power to amuse us, with a great variety of visionary apprehensions of things in the world to come, which, while in this life, we cannot contradict from experience, the test of great part of our certainty (especially to those of ordinary understandings) and having introduced mysteries into their religion, make it as incomprehensible to us, (in this natural state) as the manner of our future existence; and from scripture authority, having invalidated reason as being carnal and depraved, they proceed further to teach us from the same authority, that "*the natural man knoweth not the things of the spirit, for they are foolishness unto him, neither can he know them for they are spiritually discerned.*" A spiritualizing teacher is nearly as well acquainted with the kingdom of Heaven, as a man can be with his home lot. He knows the road to heaven and eternal blessedness, to which happy regions, with the greatest assurance, he presumes to pilot his dear disciples, and unfold to them the mysteries of the canonical writings, and of the world to come; they catch the enthusiasm and see with the same sort of spiritual eyes, with which they can pierce religion through and through, and understand the spiritual meaning of the scriptures, which before had been "a dead letter" to them, particularly the revelations of St. John the Divine, and the allusion of the horns therein mentioned. The most obscure and unintelligible passages of the Bible, come within the compass of their spiritual discerning, as apparently as figures do to a mathematician: Then they can sing songs out of the Canticles, saying, "I am my beloved's and my beloved is mine;" and being at a loose from the government of reason, please themselves with any fanaticisms they like best, as that of their being "*snatched as brands out of the burning, to enjoy the special and eternal favour of God, not from any worthiness or merit in them, but merely from the sovereign will and pleasure of God, while millions of millions, as good by nature and practice as they, were left to welter eternally, under the scalding drops of divine vengeance;*" not considering, that if it was consistent with the perfections of God to save them, his salvation could not fail to have been uniformly extended to all others, whose circumstances may be supposed to be similar to, or more deserving than theirs, for equal justice cannot fail to apply in all cases in which equal justice demands it. But these deluded people resolve the divine government altogether into sovereignty; "*even so Father, for so it seemed good in thy sight.*" And as they exclude reason and justice from their imaginary notions of religion, they also exclude it from the providence or moral government of God. Nothing is more common, in the part of the country where I was educated, than to hear those infatuated people, in their public and private addresses, acknowledge to their creator, from the desk and elsewhere, "*hadst thou, O Lord, laid judgment to the line and righteousness to the plummet, we had been in the grave with the dead and in hell with the damned, long before this time.*" Such expressions from the creature to the creator are profane, and utterly incompatible with the divine character. Undoubtedly, (all things complexly considered) the providence of God to man is just, inasmuch as it has the divine approbation.

The superstitious thus let up a spiritual discerning, independent of, and in opposition to reason, and their mere imaginations pass with each other, and with themselves, for infallible truth. Hence it is, that they despise the progressive and wearisome reasonings of philosophers (which must be admitted to be a painful method of arriving at truth) but as it is the only way in which we can acquire it, I have pursued the old natural road of ratiocination, concluding, that as this spiritual discerning is altogether inadequate to the management of any of the concerns of life, or of contributing any assistance or knowledge towards the perfecting of the arts and sciences, it is equally unintelligible and insignificant in matters of religion: and therefore conclude, that if the human race in general, could be prevailed upon to exercise common sense in religious concerns, those spiritual fictions would cease, and be succeeded by reason and truth.

XIV.3. Of the Importance of the Exercise of Reason, and Practice of Morality, in Order to the Happiness of Mankind

The period of life is very uncertain, and at the longest is but short: a few years bring us from infancy to manhood, a few more to a dissolution; pain, sickness and death are the necessary consequences of animal life. Through life we struggle with physical evils, which eventually are certain to destroy our earthly composition; and well would it be for us did evils end here; but alas! moral evil has been more or less predominant in our agency, and though natural evil is unavoidable, yet moral evil may be prevented or remedied by the exercise of virtue. Morality is therefore of more importance to us than any or all other attainments; as it is a habit of mind, which, from a retrospective consciousness of our agency in this life, we should carry with us into our succeeding state of existence, as an acquired appendage of our rational nature, and as the necessary means of our mental happiness. Virtue and vice are the only things in this world, which, with our souls, are capable of surviving death; the former is the rational and only procuring cause of all intellectual happiness, and the latter of conscious guilt and misery; and therefore, our indispensable duty and ultimate interest is, to love, cultivate and improve the one, as the means of our greatest good, and to hate and abstain from the other, as productive of our greatest evil. And in order thereto, we should so far divest ourselves of the incumbrances of this world, (which are too apt to engross our attention) as to enquire a consistent system of the knowledge of religious duty, and make it our constant endeavour in life to act conformably to it. The knowledge of the being, perfections, creation and providence of GOD, and of the immortality of our souls, is the foundation of religion. . . . And as the Pagan, Jewish, Christian and Mahometan countries of the world have been overwhelmed with a multiplicity of revelations diverse from each other, and which, by their respective promulgators, are said to have been immediately communicated to them by the intervening agency of angels (as in the instance of the invisible Gabriel to Mahomet) and as those revelations have been received and credited, by far the greater part of the inhabitants of the several countries of the world (on whom they have been obtruded) as supernaturally revealed by God or Angels, and which, in doctrine and discipline, are in most respects repugnant to each other, it fully evinces their imposture, and authorizes us, without a lengthy course of arguing, to determine with certainty, that not more than one if any of them, had their original from God; as they clash with each other; which is ground of high probability against the authenticity of each of them.

A revelation, that may be supposed to be really of the institution of God, must also be supposed to be perfectly consistent or uniform, and to be able to stand the test of truth; therefore such pretended revelations, as are tendered to us as the contrivance of heaven, which do not bear that test, we may be morally certain, was either originally a deception, or has since, by adulteration become spurious. Furthermore, should we admit, that among the numerous revelations on which the respective priests have given the stamp of divinity, some one of them was in reality of divine authority, yet we could no otherwise, as rational beings, distinguish it from others, but by reason.

Reason therefore must be the standard, by which we determine the respective claims of revelation; for otherwise we may as well subscribe to the divinity of the one as of the other, or to the whole of them, or to none at all. So likewise on this thesis, if reason rejects the whole of those revelations, we ought to return to the religion of nature and reason.

Undoubtedly it is our duty, and for our best good, that we occupy and improve the faculties, with which our Creator has endowed us, but so far as prejudice, or prepossession of opinion prevails over our minds, in the same proportion, reason is excluded from our theory or practice. Therefore if we would acquire useful knowledge, we must first divest ourselves of those impediments; and sincerely endeavour to search out the truth; and draw our conclusions from reason and just argument, which will never conform to our inclination, interest or fancy; but we must conform to that if we would judge rightly. As certain as we determine contrary to reason, we make a wrong conclusion; therefore, our wisdom is, to conform to the nature and reason of things, as well in religious matters, as in other sciences. Preposterously absurd would it be, to negative the exercise of reason in religious concerns, and yet, be actuated by it in all other and less occurrences of life. All our knowledge of things is derived from God, in and by the order of nature, out of which we cannot perceive, reflect or understand any thing whatsoever; our external senses are natural and so are our souls; by the instrumentality of the former we perceive the objects of sense, and with the latter we reflect on them. And those objects are also natural; so that ourselves, and all things about us, and our knowledge collected therefrom, is natural, and not supernatural. . . .

We may and often do, connect or arrange our ideas together, in a wrong or improper manner, for the want of skill or judgment, or through mistake or the want of application, or through the influence of prejudice; but in all such cases, the error does not originate from the ideas themselves, but from the composer; for a system, or an arrangement of ideas justly composed; always contain the truth; but an unjust composition never fails to contain error and falsehood. Therefore an unjust connection of ideas is not derived from nature, but from the imperfect composition of man. Misconnection of ideas is the same as misjudging, and has no positive existence, being merely a creature of the imagination; but nature and truth are real and uniform; and the rational mind by reasoning, discerns the uniformity, and is thereby enabled to make a just composition of ideas, which will stand the test of truth. But the fantastical illuminations of the credulous and superstitious part of mankind, proceed from weakness, and as far as they take place in the world, subvert the religion of REASON and TRUTH.

Constantin François Chasseboeuf, Comte de Volney

Let Man Study Nature's Laws!

The Comte de Volney (1757–1820) was American neither by birth nor adoption; indeed, he resided in the United States only three short years. But he is included here because no other continental contemporary of the American deists exerted a greater influence on them. His major work, *Ruins; or, Meditations on the Revolutions of Empires* (1791), was required reading for deists on this side of the Atlantic. Its deistic rejection of revealed religion, and its defense of naturalistic religion and morality, impressed Freneau, Paine, Palmer, and other American advocates of deism. Thomas Jefferson was so struck by the book that he began a translation, which was eventually completed by Joel Barlow, another admirer of Volney. As late as the mid-nineteenth century, the *Ruins* was still being castigated by orthodox theologians who claimed that it had served "to unchristianize" thousands of American readers. It is, of course, true that other French freethinkers were studied and endorsed by American deists: Voltaire, d'Holbach, and Claude Helvétius spring readily to mind. But Volney was clearly the favorite and molded the temperament of American deism to a far greater degree than did his better-remembered fellow savants.

Volney was born in Craon, France, the son of a well-to-do member of the landed gentry. In his youth he roamed extensively throughout the Middle East, studying its customs, languages, and religions, and subsequently published two popular accounts of his travels (*Voyage en Égypte et en Syrie*, 1787; and *Considérations sur la guerre des Turcs et de la Russie*, 1788). *Ruins* appeared three years later and was clearly influenced by his exposure to non-European cultures. Imprisoned during the French Terror, he later regained favor and was sent to the United States in 1795 as an agent of the French government. While in America, he became a close associate of Jefferson's, who subsequently suffered no little political embarrassment when Volney was accused of planning the French reoccupation of Louisiana and sent packing back to Europe in 1798. But Volney seems to have possessed a remarkable talent for surviving political intrigues and crises, and his failure as an agent provocateur did not overly damage his career. Although no admirer of Napoleon, he served under him and was rewarded with the title of comte. After the Restoration, he equally well served the House of Bourbon, which gratefully elevated him to the peerage. Despite his flexibility in cooperating with a variety of political regimes, Volney remained a moderate liberal, faithful to Enlightenment ideals, to the end of his life. At his death in 1820, he was one of France's most respected intellectuals.

The *Ruins* is a curious work. Its praise of reason and natural religion places it squarely in the Enlightenment tradition, but its fanciful style and mode of presentation are startlingly romantic in flavor. The book is best described as a study in what would today be designated as comparative religion. Volney guides the reader, with the aid of a mythical "legislator" or "Genius," through a survey of the various creeds and doctrines of the world's religions. The book's central thesis is that all sectarian religions are expressions of geographical locale, environment, and tradition and as such are contingent on not only historical contexts but temporal ones as well. In arguing along these lines, Volney concludes that no particular creed—including Christianity—has a monopoly on universal and immutable religious truth. Instead, each is relative to its own time and place, even if all do share a common and hence trustworthy core of belief. The purpose of *Ruins* is to point out precisely what that core is and to establish around it a religion worthy of human rationality and divine dignity. What Montesquieu's *Spirit of the Laws* did for theories of human nature, then, Volney's *Ruins* did for religious belief. It is not surprising that the book was detested by orthodox Christians and applauded by heterodox deists.

The selections here from Volney's *Ruins* open on a fanciful assembly of representatives from each of the world's revealed religions. The gathering is presided over by the mysterious "legislator," who seems to be a personification of the spirit of Reason. Each sect is invited to explain why it is superior to all others. The ultimate purpose of the debate is to ascertain why there exists conflict and disagreements between adherents of different religions and whether or not they can be reconciled. As the legislator tells the assembly, "Truth is one, your persuasions are various; many of you therefore are in error."

In the debate that follows, each of the devotees offers a brief for the universal truth of one tradition. All, for example, insist that the foundations of their faiths rest on unquestionable divine revelation, as recorded in their various sacred scriptures. But the legislator reminds them that their respective revelations contradict one another and that there are no living witnesses to attest to the truth of the original putative communication. Each religious spokesperson then insists that the truth of his tradition is attested to by the willingness of individuals to suffer martyrdom in its defense. The legislator's response is quite Lockean in tenor: Sincerity and fervor of belief do not guarantee the truth of that which is believed. The clergy parry by pointing to accounts of miracles demonstrating divine favor. The legislator replies that since each tradition appeals to a different set of conflicting miraculous interventions, it is impossible to decide which to trust. A similar criticism is made when the sectarians turn to their separate doctrinal beliefs. The conclusion is that the contradictions between the varieties of revealed religion cannot be resolved so long as the devotees of those traditions "prejudicially" insist that their path is the only correct one. Sectarian opinions are accidents of birth, reflections of historical context erroneously transmitted from one generation to the next as absolute truth. "How is it," asks the legislator, "that such a hazard should be a ground of conviction, an argument of truth?"

How is the puzzle of religious contradiction to be solved? By accepting, answers the legislator, only those beliefs that are "capable of verification" through either experience or reason, and by suspending judgment—and especially conviction—about the rest. Dispute arises between sectarians about tenets they can in no way verify but cling to out of fear and attachment to tradition. As such, affectations, prejudices, and vanity blind them to the contingency of their doctrinal beliefs and foment mutual charges of heresy and savage persecution. There is, however, a way out of the impasse: the recognition that nature provides a more reliable guide to both the divine and morality than supernaturalist (and nonverifiable) mysteries. As Volney puts it, "The only means of establishing harmony is to return to nature, and take for a guide and regulator the order of things which she has founded." In order to steer the various sectarians out of their morass of superstition and prejudice, the legislator then drills them in a catechism of natural religion—"The Law of Nature."

The law of nature, the legislator tells the assembly, "is the constant and regular order of facts, by which God governs the universe; an order which his wisdom presents to the senses and to the reason of men, as an equal and common rule for their actions, to guide them, without distinction of country or of sect, towards perfection and happiness." A close study, then, of natural philosophy reveals the nonhistorical universal principles that serve as the foundation for the different varieties of justified belief—theological, scientific, ethical, political. It improves the felicity of individuals and the utility of society and does not sully the worship of God, as do supernaturalist doctrines, "with the foul ingredients of all the weaknesses and passions entailed on humanity."

Especially interesting within the context of American deism is the naturalistic ethics Volney derives from his law of nature. It clearly influenced Elihu Palmer's later systematic analysis of moral principle; along with Palmer's, Volney's is the only serious attempt to elaborate a uniquely deistic ethic. According to Volney, the law of nature points to one human imperative: self-preservation. To act in conformity to the natural order of things is to ensure survival; to rebel against it leads to disaster. Sensation, or the capacity for pleasure and pain, serves as the physical barometer for determining whether one's actions are compatible with the natural order. Violations of that order bring pain to oneself and others and are accordingly evil. But conformity to it enhances pleasure for all and is thereby virtuous. Vice and virtue, then, originate with human behavior and need not be reduced to supernatural explanations. Humans thus are absolute masters of their fates, artisans of their own destinies. A judiciously rational compliance with nature furthers human progress and happiness. But a prejudicial retreat from reason into superstition and bigotry will ultimately collapse the fruits of human labor into pitiful and ghostly ruins.

Ruins; or, Meditations on the Revolutions of Empires

Problem of Religious Contradiction

The various groups having taken their places, an unbounded silence succeeded to the murmurs of the multitude, and the legislator said: "Chiefs and doctors of mankind! you remark how the nations, living apart, have hitherto followed different paths, each believing its own to be that of truth. If however, truth is one, and opinions are various, it is evident that some are in error. If then such vast numbers of us are in the wrong, who shall dare to say, I am in the right? Begin therefore by being indulgent in your dissensions. Let us all seek truth as if no one possessed it. The opinions which to this day have governed the world, originating from chance, propagated in obscurity, admitted without discussion, accredited by a love of novelty and imitation, have usurped their empire in a clandestine manner. It is time, if they are well founded, to give a solemn stamp to their certainty, and legitimate their existence. Let us summon them this day to a general scrutiny, let each propound his creed, let the whole assembly be the judge, and let that alone be acknowledged true which is so for the whole human race."

Then, by order of position, the first standard on the left was allowed to speak: "You are not permitted to doubt," said their chiefs, "that our doctrine is the only true and infallible one. First it is revealed by God himself—"

"So is ours," cried all the other standards, "and you are not permitted to doubt it."

"But at least," said the legislator, "you must propose it; for we cannot believe what we do not know."

"Our doctrine is proved," replied the first standard, "by numerous facts; by a multitude of miracles, by resurrections of the dead, by rivers dried up, by mountains removed, etc."

"And we also," cried all the others, "we have numberless miracles:" and each began to recount the most incredible things.

"Their miracles," said the first standard, "are imaginary; or the fictions of the evil spirit, who has deluded them."

"They are yours," said the others, "that are imaginary;" and each group, speaking of itself, cried out: "None but ours are true; all the others are false."

The legislator asked: "Have you living witnesses?"

"No," replied they all: "the facts are ancient, the witnesses are dead, but their writings remain."

"Be it so," replied the legislator; "but if they contradict each other, who shall reconcile them?"

"Just judge!" cried one of the standards, "the proof that our witnesses have seen the truth is that they died to confirm it, and our faith is sealed with the blood of martyrs."

"And ours too," said the other standards: "we have thousands of martyrs who died in the most excruciating torments, without every denying the truth." Then the Christians of every sect, the Mussulmen, the Indians, the Japaneses, recited endless legends of confessors, martyrs, penitents, etc.

And one of these parties having denied the martyrology of the others: "Well," said they, "we will then die ourselves to prove the truth of our belief."

And instantly a crowd of men of every religion and every sect, presented themselves to suffer the torments of death. Many even began to tear their arms, and to beat their heads and breasts, without discovering any symptom of pain.

But the legislator preventing them: "O men!" said he, "hear my words with patience: if you die to prove that two and two make four, will your death render this truth more evident?"

"No," answered all.

"And if you die to prove that they make five, will that make them five? Again they all answered, "No."

"What then is your persuasion to prove, if it changes not the existence of things? Truth is one, your persuasions are various; many of you therefore are in error. Now, if man, as is evident, can persuade himself of error, what does his persuasion prove?

"If error has its martyrs, what is the criterion of truth?

"If the evil spirit works miracles, what is the distinctive character of God?

"Besides, why resort forever to incomplete and insufficient miracles? Instead of changing the course of nature, why not rather change opinions? Why murder and terrify men, instead of instructing and correcting them?

"O credulous, but opinionated mortals! none of us know what was done yesterday, what is even doing today under our eyes, and we swear to what was done two thousand years ago!

"Oh, the weakness, and yet the pride of men! the laws of nature are immutable and profound, our minds are full of illusion and frivolity, and yet we would comprehend everything, determine everything! Verily, it is easier for the whole human race to be in an error, than to change the nature of an atom."

"Well then," said one of the doctors, "let us lay aside the evidence of fact, since it is uncertain; let us come to argument, the proofs inherent in the doctrine."

Then came forward, with a look of confidence, an Imam of the law of Mahomet; and, having advanced into the circle, turned towards Mecca and recited with great fervor his confession of faith: "Praised be God," said he, with a solemn and imposing voice! "The light shineth with full evidence, and truth has no need of examination:" then showing the Coran: "Here," said he, "is the light of truth in its proper essence. There is no doubt in this book; it conducts with safety him who walks in darkness, and who receives without discussion the divine word which descended on the prophet to save the simple, and confound the wise. God has established Mahomet his minister on earth; he has given him the world, that he may subdue with the sword whoever shall refuse to receive his law: infidels dispute and will not believe; their obduracy comes from God, who has hardened their hearts to deliver them to dreadful punishments—"

At these words, a violent murmur arose on all sides, and silenced the speaker. "Who is this man," cried all the groups, "who thus gratuitously insults us? What right has he to impose his creed on us as conqueror and tyrant? Has not God endowed us, as well as him, with eyes, understanding, and reason? And have we not an equal right to use them, in choosing what to believe and what to reject? If he attacks us, shall we not defend ourselves? If he likes to believe without examination, must we therefore not examine before we believe?

"And what is this luminous doctrine that fears the light? What is this apostle of a God of clemency, who preaches nothing but murder and carnage? What is this God of justice, who punishes blindness which he himself has made? If violence and persecution are the arguments of truth, must gentleness and charity be looked on as signs of falsehood?"

A man then advancing from a neighbouring group, said to the Imam: "Admitting that Mahomet is the apostle of the best doctrine, the prophet of the true religion; have the goodness at least to tell us, in the practice of his doctrine, whether we are to follow his son-in-law Ali, or his vicars Omar and Aboubekre?"

At the sound of these names a terrible schism arose among the Mussulmen themselves: the partisans of Omar and of Ali, calling out heretics and blasphemers, loaded each other with execrations. The quarrel became so violent, that the neighbouring groups were obliged to interfere to prevent their coming to blows.

At length, tranquillity being somewhat restored, the legislator said to the Imams: "See the consequences of your principles! If you yourselves were to carry them into practice, you would destroy each other to the last man; is it not the first law of God that man should live?" Then addressing himself to the other groups: "Doubtless," said he, "this intolerant and exclusive spirit shocks every idea of justice, and overturns the whole foundation of morals and society; but before we totally reject this code of doctrine, is it not proper to hear some of its dogmas, in order not to pronounce on the forms, without having some knowledge of the substance?"

The groups having consented, the Imam began to expound how God, after having sent to the nations, lost in idolatry, twenty-four thousand prophets, had finally sent the last, the seal and perfection of all, Mahomet, on whom be the salvation of peace: how, to prevent the divine word from being any longer perverted by infidels, the supreme bounty had itself written the pages of the Coran: then explaining the particular dogmas of Islamism, the Imam unfolded how the Coran, partaking of the divine nature, was increate and eternal, like its author: how it had been sent leaf by leaf in twenty-four thousand nocturnal apparitions of the angel Gabriel: How the angel announced himself by a gentle knocking, which threw the prophet into a cold sweat; how, in the vision of one night, he had travelled over ninety heavens, riding on the animal Boraq, half a horse and half a woman: how, endowed with the gift of miracles, he walked in the sunshine without a shadow, turned dry trees to green, filled wells and cisterns with water, and split in two the body of the moon: how, by divine command, Mahomet had propagated, sword in hand, the religion the most worthy of god by its sublimity, and the best adapted for man by the simplicity of its practice, since it consisted in only eight or ten points: to profess the unity of God; to acknowledge Mahomet as his only prophet; to pray five times a day; to fast one month in the year; to go to Mecca once in our life; to pay the tenth of all we possess; to drink no wine; to eat no pork; and to make war upon the infidels; he taught that by these means every Mussulman, becoming himself an apostle and a martyr, should enjoy in this world many blessings; and at his death, his soul weighed in the balance of works, and absolved by the two black angels, should pass the infernal pit on the bridge as narrow as a hair and as sharp as the edge of a sword, and should finally be received to a region of delight, watered with rivers of milk and honey, and embalmed in all the perfumes of India and Arabia; and where the celestial houris, virgins always chaste, are eternally crowning with repeated favors the elect of God, who preserve an eternal youth.

At these words, an involuntary smile was seen on every countenance; and the various groups, reasoning on these articles of faith, exclaimed with one voice: "Is it possible that reasonable beings can admit such reveries? would not you think it a chapter from the Arabian nights?"

A Samoyed advanced into the circle: "The paradise of Mahomet," said he, "appears very desirable; but one of the means of gaining it is embarrassing: for if we must neither eat nor drink between the rising and setting sun, as he has ordered, how are we to practice that fast in my country, where the sun continues above the horizon four months without setting?"

"That is impossible," cried all the Mussulman doctors, to support the

honor of the prophet; but a hundred nations having attested the fact, the $\qquad$ *189*
infallibility of Mahomet could not but receive a severe shock.

"It is singular," said an European, "that God should be constantly revealing what takes place in heaven, without ever instructing us what is doing on the earth!"

"For my part," says an American, "I find a great difficulty in the pilgrimage; for suppose twenty-five years to a generation and only a hundred millions of males on the globe: each being obliged to go to Mecca once in his life, there must be four millions a year on the journey; and as it would be impracticable for them to return the same year, the numbers would be doubled, that is, eight millions: where would you find provisions, lodging, water, vessels for this universal procession? Here must be miracles indeed!"

"The proof," said a Catholic doctor, "that the religion of Mahomet is not revealed, is that the greater part of the ideas which serve for its basis existed a long time before, and that it is only a confused mixture of truths disfigured and taken from our holy religion and from that of the Jews; which an ambitious man has made to serve his projects of domination, and his wordly views. Peruse his book, you will see nothing there but the histories of the Bible and the Gospel, travestied into absurd fables; a tissue of vague and contradictory declamations, and ridiculous or dangerous precepts. Analyze the spirit of these precepts, and the conduct of their apostle, you will find there an artful and audacious character; which to obtain its end, works ably, it is true, on the passions of the people it had to govern. Speaking to simple and credulous men, it entertains them with miracles; they are ignorant and jealous, and it flatters their vanity by despising science; they are poor and rapacious, and it excites their cupidity by the hope of pillage; having nothing at first to give them on earth, it tells them of treasures in heaven; it teaches them to desire death as the supreme good; it threatens cowards with hell; it rewards the brave with paradise; it sustains the weak with the opinon of fatality; in short, it produces the attachment it wants by all the allurements of sense and all the power of the passions.

"How different is the character of our religion! and how completely does its empire, founded on the counteraction of our natural inclinations, and the mortification of all our passions, prove its divine origin! how forcibly does its mild and compassionate morality, its affections altogether spiritual, attest its emanation from the divinity? Many of its doctrines, it is true, soar above the reach of the understanding, and impose on reason a respectful silence; but this more fully demonstrates its revelation, since the human mind could never have imagined such mysteries." Then, holding the Bible in one hand and the four Gospels in the other, the doctor began to relate, that in the beginning, God (after having passed an eternity in inaction) took the resolution, without any known cause, of making the world out of nothing; that having created the whole universe in six days, he found himself fatigued on the seventh; that having placed the first human pair in a garden of delight, to make them completely happy, he forbade their tasting a particular fruit which he left within their reach; that these first parents, having yielded to the temptation, all their race (yet unborn) had been condemned to bear the penalty of a fault which they had not committed; that, after having left the human race to damn themselves for four or five thousand years, this God of mercy ordered a dearly beloved son, whom he had engendered without a mother, and who was as old as himself, to go and be put to death on the earth; and this, for the salvation of mankind, of whom much the greater portion, nevertheless, have ever since continued in the way of perdition; that to remedy this new difficulty, this same God, born of a virgin, having died and risen from the dead, assumes a new existence every day, and in the form of a piece of bread, multiplies himself by millions at the voice of one of the vilest of men; then passing on to the doctrine of the sacraments, he was going to treat at large of the power of absolution and reprobation, of the means of purging all sins by a little water and a few words, when, uttering the words indulgence, power of the pope, sufficient or efficacious grace, he was interrupted by a thousand cries. "It is a horrible abuse," exclaimed the Lutherans, "to pretend to remit sins for money." "The notion of the real presence," cried the Calvinists, "is contrary to the text of the gospel." "The pope has no right to decide anything of himself," cried the Jansenists; and thirty other sects, rising up and accusing each other of heresy and error, it was no longer possible to hear anything distinctly.

Silence being at last restored, the Mussulmen observed to the legislator: "since you have rejected our doctrine as containing things incredible, can you admit that of the Christians? is not theirs still more contrary to common sense and justice? a God, immaterial and infinite, to become a man? to have a son as old as himself! this god-man to become bread, to be eaten and digested! have we anything equal to that? Have the Christians an exclusive right to exact implicit faith? and will you grant them privileges of belief to our detriment?"

Some savage tribes then advanced: "What!" said they, "because a man and woman ate an apple six thousand years ago, all the human race are damned? and you call God just! What tyrant ever rendered children responsible for the faults of their fathers! What man can answer for another's actions: Is not this subversive of every idea of justice and of reason?"

Others exclaimed: "Where are the proofs, the witnesses of these pretended facts? Can we receive them without examining the evidence? The least action in a court of justice requires two witnesses; and we are ordered to believe all this on mere tradition and hearsay!"

A Jewish rabbin then addressing the assembly, said; "As to the fundamental facts we are sureties; but with regard to their form and application, the case is different, and the Christians are here condemned by their own arguments; for they cannot deny that we are the original source from which they are derived, the primitive stock on which they are grafted; and hence the reasoning is very short: either our law is from God, and then theirs is a heresy, since it differs from ours; or our law is not from God, and then theirs falls at the same time."

"But you must make this distinction," replied the Christian: "your law is from God, as typical and preparative, but not as final and absolute; you are the image of which we are the substance."

"We know," replied the rabbin, "that such are your pretensions; but they are absolutely gratuitous and false. Your system turns altogether on mystical meanings, on visionary and allegorical interpretations: with violent distortions on the letter of our books, you substitute the most chimerical ideas to the true ones, and find in them whatever pleases you, as a wild imagination will find figures in the clouds. Thus you have made a spiritual Messiah of that which, in the spirit of our prophets, is only a temporal king: you have made a redemption of the human race out of the simple reestablishment of our nation; your conception of the virgin is founded on a single phrase, which you have misunderstood. Thus you make from our scriptures whatever your fancy dictates, you even find there your trinity, though there is not the most distant allusion to it, and it is an invention of profane writers, admitted into your system with a host of other opinions of every religion and of every sect, during the anarchy of the three first centuries of your era."

At these words, the Christian doctors crying sacrilege and blasphemy, sprang forward in a transport of fury to fall upon the Jew. And a troop of monks in motley dresses of black and white, advanced with a standard, on which were painted pincers, gridirons, lighted fagots and the words justice, charity, mercy: "We must," said they, "make an example of these impious wretches, and burn them for the glory of God." They began even to prepare the pile, when a Mussulman answered in a strain of irony: "This then is your religion of peace, that meek and beneficent system which you so much extol! This is that evangelical charity which combats infidelity with persuasive mildness, and repays injuries with patience! Ye hypocrites! it is thus that you deceive mankind; thus that you propagate your accursed errors! When you were weak, you preached liberty, toleration, peace; when you are strong, you practise persecution and violence." —And he was going to begin the history of the wars and slaughters of Christianity, when the legislator demanding silence, suspended this scene of discord.

The monks, affecting a tone of meekness and humility, exclaimed, "It is not ourselves that we avenge, it is the cause of God, it is his glory that we defend."

"And what right have you, more than we," said the Imams, "to constitute yourselves the representatives of God? Have you privileges that we have not? Are you not men like us?"

"To defend God," said another group, "to pretend to avenge him, is to insult his wisdom and his power. Does he not know better than men what befits his dignity?"

"Yes," replied the monks, "but his ways are secret."

. . . Then the legislator having commanded silence and recalled the dispute to its true object, said, "Chiefs and instructors of the people, you came together in search of truth; at first, every one of you, thinking he possessed it, demanded of the others an implicit faith; but receiving the contrariety of your opinions, you found it necessary to submit them to a common rule of evidence, and to bring them to one general term of comparison; and you agreed that each should exhibit the proofs of his doctrine. You began by alleging facts; but each religion and every sect, being equally furnished with miracles and martyrs, each producing an equal cloud of witnesses, and offering to support them by a voluntary death, the balance on this first point, by right of parity, remained equal.

"You then passed to the trial of reasoning; but the same arguments applying equally to contrary positions; the same assertions, equally gratuitous, being advanced and repelled with equal force, and all having an equal right to refuse assent, nothing was demonstrated. What is more, the confrontation of your systems has brought up new and extraordinary difficulties; for amidst the apparent or adventitious diversities, you have discovered a fundamental resemblance, a common groundwork; and each of you pretending to be the inventor, and first depositary, you have taxed each other with adulterations and plagiariams; and thence arises a difficult question concerning the transmission of religious ideas from people to people.

"Finally to repeat the embarrassment, when you endeavoured to explain your doctrines to each other, they appeared confused and foreign, even to their adherents; they were founded on ideas inaccessible to your senses; of consequence you had no means of judging of them, and you confessed yourselves in this respect to be only the echoes of your fathers; hence follows this other question, how came they to the knowledge of your fathers, who themselves had no other means than you to conceive them: so that, on the one hand, the succession of these ideas being unknown, and on the other, their origin and existence being a mystery, all the edifice of your religious opinions becomes a complicated problem of metaphysics and history. . . ."

Solution of the Problem of Contradictions

The legislator then resumed his discourse. "O nations!" said he, "we have heard the discussion of your opinions; and the different sentiments which divide you have given rise to many reflections, and furnished several questions which we shall propose to you to solve.

"First, considering the diversity and opposition of the creeds to which you are attached, we ask on what motives you found your persuasion; is it from a deliberate choice that you follow the standard of one prophet rather than another? Before adopting this doctrine rather than that, did you first compare? did you maturely examine them? Or have you received them only from the chance of birth, from the empire of education and habit? Are you not born Christians on the banks of the Tiber, Mussulmen on those of the Euphrates, Idolaters on the Indus, just as you are born fair in cold climates and sable under the scorching sun of Africa? And if your opinions are the effect of your fortuitous position on the earth, of consanguinity, of imitation, how is it that such a hazard should be a ground of conviction, an argument of truth?

"Secondly, when we reflect on the mutual proscriptions and arbitrary intolerance of your pretensions, we are frightened at the consequences that flow from your own principles. Nations! who reciprocally devote each other to the bolts of heavenly wrath, suppose that the universal Being whom you revere, should this moment descend from heaven on this multitude and, clothed with all his power, should sit on this throne to judge you, suppose he should say to you: 'Mortals! it is your own justice that I am going to exercise upon you. Yes, of all the religious systems that divide you, one alone shall this day be preferred; all the others, all this multitude of standards, of nations, of prophets shall be condemned to eternal destruction; this is not enough—among the particular sects of the chosen system, one only can be favored, and all the others must be condemned; neither is this enough: from this little remnant of a group, I must exclude all those who have not fulfilled the conditions enjoined by its precepts: O men! to what a small number of elect have you limited your race! to what a penury of beneficence do you reduce the immensity of my goodness! to what a solitude of admirers do you condemn my greatness and my glory?'

"But," said the legislator rising: "no matter; you have willed it so; Nations! here is an urn in which all your names are placed: one only is a prize—approach and draw this tremendous lottery—" And the nations, seized with terror, cried: "No, no; we are all brothers, all equal; we cannot condemn each other."

Then said the legislator, resuming his seat: "O men! who dispute on so many subjects, lend an attentive ear to one problem which you exhibit, and which you ought to decide yourselves." And the people giving great attention, he lifted an arm towards heaven; and pointing to the sun, said, "Nations, does that sun which enlightens you appear square or triangular?" "No," answered they with one voice, "it is round."

Then taking the golden balance that was on the altar: "This gold that you handle every day, is it heavier than the same volume of copper?" "Yes," answered all the people, "gold is heavier than copper."

Then taking the sword: "Is this iron," said the legislator, "softer than lead?" "No," said the people.

"Is sugar sweet, and gall bitter?"—"Yes."

"Do you love pleasure, and hate pain?"—"Yes."

"Thus then you are agreed in these points and many others of the same nature.

"Now, tell us, is there a cavern in the centre of the earth, or inhabitants in the moon?"

This question occasioned an universal murmur; every one answered differently, some yes, others no; one said it was probable; another said it was an idle, ridiculous question; some, that it was worth knowing; and the discord was universal.

After sometime, the legislator having obtained silence, said: "Explain to us, O nations, this problem. We have put to you several questions which you have answered with one voice, without distinction of race or of sect; white men, black men, followers of Mahomet and of Moses, worshippers of Boudda and of Jesus, all have returned the same answer. We then proposed another question, and you are all at variance! Why this unanimity in one case, and this discordance in the other?"

And the group of simple men and savages answered and said: "The reason of this is evident: in the first case we see and feel the objects; and we speak from sensation: in the second, they are beyond the reach of our senses; we speak of them only from conjecture."

"You have resolved the problem," said the legislator: "and your own consent has established this first truth:

"That whenever objects can be examined and judged of by your senses, you are agreed in opinion;

"And that you only differ when the objects are absent and beyond your reach.

"From this first truth flows another equally clear and worthy of notice. Since you agree on things which you know with certainty, it follows that you disagree only on those which you know not with certainty, and about which you are not sure; that is to say, you dispute, you quarrel, you fight for that which is uncertain, that of which you doubt. O men! is not this folly?

"Is it not then demonstrated that Truth is not the object of your contests? that it is not her cause which you defend, but that of your affections, and of your prejudices? that it is not the object, as it really is in itself, that you would verify, but the object as you would have it; that is to say, it is not the evidence of the thing that you would enforce, but your own personal opinion, your particular manner of seeing and judging. It is a power that you wish to exercise, an interest that you wish to satisfy, a prerogative that you arrogate to yourselves; it is a contest of vanity. Now, as each of you, on comparing himself to every other, finds himself his equal and his fellow, he resists by a feeling of the same right. And your disputes, your combats, your intolerance, are the effect of this right which you deny each other, and of the intimate conviction of your equality.

"Now, the only means of establishing harmony is to return to nature, and take for a guide and regulator the order of things which she has founded; and then your accord will prove this other truth:

"That real beings have in themselves an identical, constant and uniform mode of existence; and that there is in your organs a like mode of being affected by them.

"But at the same time, by reason of the mobility of these organs as subject to your will, you may conceive different affections, and find yourselves in different relations with the same objects; so that you are to them like a mirror, capable of reflecting them truly as they are, or of distorting and disfiguring them.

"Hence it follows that, whenever you perceive objects as they are, you agree among yourselves and with the objects; and the similitude between your sensations and their manner of existence, is what constitutes their truth with respect to you;

"And on the contrary, whenever you differ in your opinion, your disagreement is a proof that you do not represent them such as they are, that you change them.

"Hence also it follows, that the causes of your disagreement exist not in the objects themselves, but in your minds, in your manner of perceiving or judging.

"To establish therefore an uniformity of opinion, it is necessary first to establish the certainty, completely verified, that the portraits which the mind forms are perfectly like the originals; that it reflects the objects correctly as they exist. Now, this result cannot be obtained but in those cases where the objects can be brought to the test, and submitted to the examination of the senses. Everything which cannot be brought to this trial is for that reason alone, impossible to be determined; there exists no rule, no term of comparison, no means of certainty, respecting it.

"From this we conclude, that, to live in harmony and peace, we must agree never to decide on such subjects, and to attach to them no importance; in a word, we must trace a line of distinction between those that are capable of verification, and those that are not, and separate by an inviolable barrier, the world of fantastical beings from the world of realities; that is to say, all civil effect must be taken away from theological and religious opinions.

"This, O people! is the object proposed by a great nation freed from her fetters and her prejudices; this is the work which, under her eye, and by her orders, we had undertaken when your kings and your priests came to interrupt it. —O kings and priests! you may suspend, yet for awhile, the solemn publi-

196   cation of the laws of nature: but it is no longer in your power to annihilate or
to subvert them."

A general shout then arose from every part of the assembly; and the nations
universally, and with one voice, testified their assent to the proposals of the
legislator: "Resume," said they, "your holy and sublime labors, and bring them
to perfection! Investigate the laws which nature, for our guidance, has implanted in our breasts, and collect from them an authentic and immutable
code; nor let this code be any longer for one family only, but for us all without
exception! Be the legislator of the whole human race, as you shall be the
interpreter of nature herself; show us the line of partition between the world
of chimeras and that of realities: and teach us, after so many religions of error
and delusion, the religion of evidence and truth!"

Then the legislator, having resumed his inquiry into the physical and con-
stituent attributes of man, and examined the motives and affections which
govern him in his individual and social state, unfolded in these words the laws
on which nature herself has founded his happiness.

The Law of Nature

(I)

Q. What is the law of nature?

A. It is the constant and regular order of facts, by which God governs the
universe; an order which his wisdom presents to the senses and to the reason
of men, as an equal and common rule for their actions, to guide them, without
distinction of country or of sect, towards perfection and happiness. . . .

Q. Do such orders exist in nature?

A. Yes.

Q. What does the word nature signify?

A. The word nature bears three different senses. 1st. It signifies the universe,
the material world: in this first sense we say the beauty of nature, the richness
of nature, that is to say, the objects in the heavens and on the earth exposed
to our sight; 2dly. It signifies the power that animates, that moves the universe,
considering it as a distinct being, such as the soul is to the body: in this second
sense we say, "The intentions of nature, the incomprehensible secrets of nature." 3rdly. It signifies the partial operations of that power on each being, or
on each class of beings; and in this third sense we say, "The nature of man is
an enigma; every being acts according to its nature." Wherefore, as the actions
of each being, or of each species of beings, are subjected to constant and
general rules, which cannot be infringed without interrupting and troubling
the general or particular order, those rules of action and of motion are called
natural laws, or laws of nature.

Q. Give me examples of those laws.

A. It is a law of nature, that the sun illuminates successively the surface of the terrestrial globe;—that its presence causes both light and heat;—that heat acting upon water, produces vapors;—that those vapors rising in clouds into the regions of the air, dissolve into rain or snow, and renew incessantly the waters of fountains and of rivers.

It is a law of nature, that water flows downwards; that it endeavours to find its level; that it is heavier than air; that all bodies tend towards the earth; that flame ascends towards the heaven;—that it disorganizes vegetables and animals; that air is necessary to the life of certain animals; that, in certain circumstances, water suffocates and kills them; that certain juices of plants, certain minerals attack their organs, and destroy their life, and so on in a multitude of other instances.

Wherefore, as all those and similar facts are immutable, constant, and regular, so many real orders result from them for man to conform himself to, with the express clause of punishment attending the infraction of them, or of welfare attending their observance. So that if man pretends to see clear in darkness, if he goes in contradiction to the course of the seasons, or the action of the elements; if he pretends to remain under water without being drowned, to touch fire without burning himself, to deprive himself of air without being suffocated, to swallow poison without destroying himself, he receives from each of those infractions of the laws of nature a corporeal punishment proportionate to his fault; but if on the contrary, he observes and practises each of those laws according to the regular and exact relations they have to him, he preserves his existence, and renders it as happy as it can be: and as the only and common end of all those laws, considered relatively to mankind, is to preserve, and render them happy, it has been agreed upon to reduce the idea to one simple expression, and to call them collectively the law of nature.

(II)

Q. What are the characters of the law of nature?

A. There can be assigned ten principal ones.

Q. Which is the first?

A. To be inherent to the existence of things, and, consequently, primitive and anterior to every other law: so that all those which man has received, are only imitations of it, and their perfection is ascertained by the resemblance they bear to this primordial model.

Q. What is the second?

A. To be derived immediately from God, and presented by him to each man, whereas all other laws are presented to us by men, who may be either deceived or deceivers.

Q. Which is the third?

A. To be common to all times, and to all countries, that is to say, one and universal.

Q. Is no other law universal?

A. No: for no other is agreeable or applicable to all the people of the earth; they are all local and accidental, originating from circumstances of places and of persons; so that if such a man had not existed, or such an event happened, such a law would never have been enacted.

Q. Which is the fourth character?

A. To be uniform and invariable.

Q. Is no other law uniform and invariable?

A. No: for what is good and virtue according to one, is evil and vice according to another; and what one and the same law approves of at one time, it often condemns at another.

Q. Which is the fifth character?

A. To be evident and palpable, because it consists entirely of facts incessantly present to the senses, and to demonstration.

Q. Are not other laws evident?

A. No: for they are founded on past and doubtful facts, on equivocal and suspicious testimonies, and on proofs inaccessible to the senses.

Q. Which is the sixth character?

A. To be reasonable, because its precepts and entire doctrine are conformable to reason, and to the human understanding.

Q. Is no other law reasonable?

A. No: for all are in contradiction to the reason and the understanding of men, and tyrannically impose on him a blind and impracticable belief.

Q. Which is the seventh character?

A. To be just, because in that law, the penalties are proportionate to the infractions.

Q. Are not other laws just?

A. No: for they often exceed bounds, either in rewarding deserts, or in punishing delinquencies, and consider as meritorious or criminal, null or indifferent actions.

Q. Which is the eighth character?

A. To be pacific and tolerant, because in the law of nature, all men being brothers and equal in rights, it recommends to them only peace and toleration, even for errors.

Q. Are not other laws pacific?

A. No: for all preach dissension, discord, and war, and divide mankind by exclusive pretensions of truth and domination.

Q. Which is the ninth character?

A. To be equally beneficent to all men, in teaching them the true means of becoming better and happier.

Q. Are not other laws beneficient likewise?

A. No: for none of them teach the real means of attaining happiness; all are confined to pernicious or futile practices; and this is evident from facts, since after so many laws, so many religions, so many legislators and prophets, men are still as unhappy and as ignorant, as they were six thousand years ago.

Q. Which is the last character of the law of nature?

A. That it is alone sufficient to render men happier and better, because it comprises all that is good and useful in other laws, either civil or religious, that is to say, it constitutes essentially the moral part of them; so that if other laws were divested of it, they would be reduced to chimerical and imaginary opinions devoid of any practical utility. . . .

And such is the power of all these attributes of perfection and truth, that when in their disputes the theologians can agree upon no article of belief, they recur to the law of nature, the neglect of which, say they, forced God to send from time to time prophets to proclaim new laws; as if God enacted laws for particular circumstances, as men do, especially when the first subsists in such force, that we may assert it to have been at all times and in all countries the rule of conscience for every man of sense or understanding.

Q. If, as you say, it emanates immediately from God, does it teach his existence?

A. Yes, most positively: for, to any man whatsoever, who observes with reflection the astonishing spectacle of the universe, the more he meditates on the properties and attributes of each being, on the admirable order and harmony of their motions, the more it is demonstrated that there exists a supreme agent, an universal and identical mover, designated by the appellation of God; and so true it is that the law of nature suffices to elevate him to the knowledge of God, that all which men have pretended to know by supernatural means, has constantly turned out ridiculous and absurd, and that they have ever been obliged to recur to the immutable conceptions of natural reason.

Q. Then it is not true that the followers of the law of nature are atheists?

A. No, it is not true; on the contrary, they entertain stronger and nobler ideas of the Divinity than most other men; for they do not sully him with the foul ingredients of all the weaknesses and passions entailed on humanity.

Q. What worship do they pay him?

A. A worship wholly of action; the practice and observance of all the rules which the supreme wisdom has imposed on the motion of each being; eternal and unalterable rules, by which it maintains the order and harmony of the universe, and which, in their relations to man, constitute the law of nature.

Q. Was the law of nature known before this period?

A. It has been at all times spoken of: most legislators pretend to adopt it as the basis of their laws; but they only quote some of its precepts, and have had only vague ideas of its totality.

Q. Why?

200   A. Because, though simple in its basis, it forms in its developments and consequences, a complicated whole which requires an extensive knowledge of facts,
joined to all the sagacity of reasoning.

Q. Does not instinct alone teach the law of nature?

A. No; for by instinct is meant nothing more than that blind sentiment by
which we are actuated indiscriminately towards everything that flatters the
senses.

Q. Why then is it said that the law of nature is engraved in the hearts of all?

A. It is said for two reasons: 1st, because it has been remarked, that there are
acts and sentiments common to all men, and this proceeds from their common
organization; 2dly, because the first philosophers believed that men were born
with ideas already formed, which is now demonstrated to be erroneous.

Q. Philosophers then are fallible?

A. Yes, sometimes.

Q. Why so?

A. 1st, Because they are men; 2dly, because the ignorant call all those who
reason, right or wrong, philosophers; 3dly, because those who reason on many
subjects, and who are the first to reason on them, are liable to be deceived.

Q. If the law of nature be not written, must it not become arbitrary and ideal?

A. No; because it consists entirely in facts, the demonstration of which can be
incessantly renewed to the senses, and constitutes a science as accurate and as
precise as geometry and mathematics; and it is because the law of nature forms
an exact science, that men, born ignorant and living inattentive and heedless,
have had hitherto only a superficial knowledge of it.

(III)

Q. Explain the principles of the law of nature with relations to man.

A. They are simple; all of them are comprised in one fundamental and single
precept.

Q. What is that precept?

A. It is self-preservation.

Q. Is not happiness also a precept of the law of nature?

A. Yes: but as happiness is an accidental state, resulting only from the development of man's faculties and his social system, it is not the immediate and direct
object of nature; it is, in some measure, a superfluity annexed to the necessary
and fundamental object of preservation.

Q. How does nature order man to preserve himself?

A. By two powerful and involuntary sensations, which it has attached, as two
guides, two guardian Geniuses to all his actions: the one, a sensation of pain,
by which it admonishes him of, and deters him from, everything that tends to
destroy him; the other, a sensation of pleasure, by which it attracts and carries

him towards everything that tends to his preservation and the development of his existence.

Q. Pleasure therefore is not an evil, a sin, as casuists pretend?

A. No, only in as much as it tends to destroy life, and health, which, by the avowal of those same casuists, we derive from God himself.

Q. Is pleasure the principal object of our existence, as some philosophers have asserted?

A. No; not more than pain; pleasure is an incitement to live, as pain is a repulsion from death.

Q. How do you prove this assertion?

A. By two palpable facts; one, that pleasure when taken immoderately, leads to destruction; for instance, a man who abuses the pleasure of eating or drinking, attacks his health, and injuries his life. The other, that pain sometimes leads to self-preservation: for instance, a man who suffers a mortified member to be cut off, endures pain in order not to perish totally.

Q. But does not even this prove that our sensations can deceive us respecting the end of our preservation?

A. Yes; they can momentarily.

Q. How do our sensations deceive us?

A. In two ways; by ignorance, and by passion.

Q. When do they deceive us by ignorance?

A. When we act without knowing the action and effect of objects on our senses: for example, when a man touches nettles without knowing their stinging quality, or when he swallows opium without knowing its soporiferous effects.

Q. When do they deceive us by passion?

A. When, conscious of the pernicious action of objects, we abandon ourselves, nevertheless, to the impetuosity of our desires and appetites: for example, when a man who knows that wine intoxicates, does nevertheless drink it to excess.

Q. What is the result?

A. It results that the ignorance in which we are born, and the unbridled appetites to which we abandon ourselves, are contrary to our preservation; that consequently the instruction of our minds and the moderation of our passions are two obligations, two laws which derive immediately from the first law of preservation.

Q. But if we are born ignorant, is not ignorance a law of nature?

A. No more than to remain in the naked and feeble state of infancy. Far from being a law of nature, ignorance is an obstacle to the practice of all its laws. It is the real original sin.

Q. Why then have there been moralists who have looked upon it as a virtue and a perfection?

A. Because, from a whimsical or misanthropical disposition they have confounded the abuse of knowledge with knowledge itself: as if, because men abuse the power of speech, their tongues should be cut out: as if perfection and virtue consisted in the nullity, and not in the development and proper employ of our faculties.

Q. Instruction is therefore indispensably necessary to man's existence?

A. Yes, so indispensable, that without it he is every instant assailed and wounded by all that surrounds him; for if he does not know the effects of fire, he burns himself; those of water, he drowns himself; those of opium, he poisons himself; if, in the savage state, he does not know the wiles of animals, and the art of seizing game, he perishes through hunger; if, in the social state, he does not know the course of the seasons, he can neither cultivate the ground, nor procure nourishment; and so on, of all his actions, respecting all the wants of his preservation.

Q. But can man separately by himself acquire all this knowledge necessary to his existence, and to the development of his faculties?

A. No, not without the assistance of his fellow men, and by living in society.

Q. But is not society to man a state against nature?

A. No: it is on the contrary a necessity, a law that nature imposed on him by the very act of his organization: for 1st, nature has so constituted man, that he cannot see his species of another sex without feeling emotions and an attraction, the consequences of which induce him to live in a family, which is already a state of society; 2nd, by endowing him with sensibility, she organized him so that the sensations of others reflect within him, and excite reciprocal sentiments of pleasure and of grief, which are attractions, and indissoluble ties of society; 3rd, and finally, the state of society, founded on the wants of man, is only a further means of fulfilling the law of preservation; and to pretend that this state is out of nature, because it is more perfect, is the same as to say, that a bitter and wild fruit of the forest, is no longer the production of nature, when rendered sweet and delicious by cultivation in our gardens.

Q. Why then have philosophers called the savage state, the state of perfection?

A. Because, as I have told you, the vulgar have often given the name of philosophers to whimsical geniuses, who, from moroseness, from wounded vanity, or from a disgust to the vices of society, have conceived chimerical ideas of the savage state, in contradiction with their own system of a perfect man.

Q. What is the true meaning of the word philosopher?

A. The word philosopher signifies a lover of wisdom: wherefore, as wisdom consists in the practice of the laws of nature, the true philosopher is he who knows those laws extensively and accurately, and who conforms the whole tenor of his conduct to them.

Q. What is man in the savage state?

A. A brutal, ignorant animal, a wicked and ferocious beast, like bears and Ourang-outangs.

Q. Is he happy in that state?

A. No: for he only feels momentary sensations; and those sensations are habitually of violent wants which he cannot satisfy, since he is ignorant by nature and weak by being insulated from his species.

Q. Is he free?

A. No: he is the most abject slave that exists; for his life depends on everything that surrounds him; he is not free to eat when hungry, to rest when tired, to warm himself when cold; he is every instant in danger of perishing; wherefore nature offers but fortuitous examples of such beings; and we see that all the efforts of the human species, since its origin, solely tend to emerge from that violent state, by the pressing necessity of self-preservation.

Q. But does not this necessity of preservation engender in individuals egotism, that is to say self-love? and is not egotism contrary to the social state?

A. No: for, if by egotism you understand a propensity to hurt our neighbour, it is no longer self-love, but the hatred of others. Self-love, taken in its true sense, not only is not contrary to society, but is its firmest support by the necessity we lie under of not injuring others, lest in return they should injure us.

Thus man's preservation and the unfolding of his faculties, directed towards this end, are the true law of nature in the production of the human being: and it is from this simple and fruitful principle that are derived, are referred, and in its scale are weighed, all ideas of good and evil, of vice and virtue, of just and unjust, of truth or error, of lawful or forbidden, on which is founded the morality of individual, or of social man.

(IV)

Q. What is good, according to the law of nature?

A. It is everything that tends to preserve and perfect man.

Q. What is evil?

A. It is everything that tends to man's destruction or deterioration.

Q. What is meant by physical good and evil, and by moral good and evil?

A. By the word physical is understood, whatever acts immediately on the body. Health is a physical good; and sickness a physical evil. By moral, is meant what acts by consequences more or less remote. Calumny is a moral evil; a fair reputation is a moral good, because both one and the other occasion towards us, on the part of other men, dispositions and habitudes, which are useful or hurtful to our preservation, and which attack or favor our means of existence.

Q. Everything that tends to preserve or to produce is therefore a good?

A. Yes; and it is for that reason that certain legislators have classed amongst the

204   works agreeable to the divinity, the cultivation of a field and the fecundity of a woman.

Q. Whatever tends to give death is therefore an evil?

A. Yes: and it is for that reason some legislators have extended the idea of evil and of sin even to the murdering of animals.

Q. The murdering of a man is therefore a crime in the law of nature?

A. Yes: and the greatest that can be committed: for every other evil can be repaired, but murder alone is irreparable.

Q. What is a sin in the law of nature?

A. It is whatever tends to trouble the order established by nature, for the preservation and perfection of man and of society.

Q. Can intention be a merit or a crime?

A. No: for it is only an idea void of reality; but it is a commencement of sin and evil, by the tendency it gives towards action.

Q. What is virtue according to the law of nature?

A. It is the practice of actions useful to the individual and to society.

Q. What is meant by the word individual?

A. It means a man considered separately from every other.

Q. What is vice according to the law of nature?

A. It is the practice of actions prejudicial to the individual and to society.

Q. Have not virtue and vice an object purely spiritual and abstracted from the senses?

A. No: it is always to a physical end that they finally relate, and that end is always to destroy or preserve the body.

Q. Have vice and virtue degrees of strength and intenseness?

A. Yes: according to the importance of the faculties which they attack or which they favor; and according to the number of individuals in whom those faculties are favored or injured.

Q. Give me some examples.

A. The action of saving a man's life is more virtuous than that of saving his property; the action of saving the life of ten men, than that of saving only the life of one, and an action useful to the whole human race is more virtuous than an action that is only useful to one single nation.

Q. How does the law of nature prescribe the practice of good and virtue, and forbid that of evil and vice?

A. By the very advantages resulting from the practice of good and virtue for the preservation of our body, and by the losses which result, to our existence, from the practice of evil and vice.

Q. Its precepts are then in action?

A. Yes: they are action itself considered in its present effect and in its future consequences. . . .

Q. What is society?

A. It is every reunion of men living together under the clauses of an expressed or tacit contract, which has for its end their common preservation.

Q. Are the social virtues numerous?

A. Yes: they are in as great number as the kinds of actions useful to society; but all may be reduced to one only principle.

Q. What is that fundamental principle?

A. It is justice, which alone comprises all the virtues of society.

Q. Why do you say that justice is the fundamental and almost only virtue of society?

A. Because it alone embraces the practice of all the actions useful to it; and because all the other virtues, under the denominations of charity, humanity, probity, love of one's country, sincerity, generosity, simplicity of manners and modesty, are only varied forms and diversified applications of the axiom, Do not to another what you would not wish to be done to yourself; which is the definition of justice.

Q. How does the law of nature prescribe justice?

A. By three physical attributes inherent in the organization of man.

Q. What are those attributes?

A. They are equality, liberty, and property.

Q. How is equality a physical attribute of man?

A. Because all men having equally eyes, hands, mouths, ears, and the necessity of making use of them in order to live, have, by this reason alone, an equal right to life, and to the use of the aliments which maintain it; they are all equal before God.

Q. Do you suppose that all men hear equally, see equally, feel equally, have equal wants and passions?

A. No; for it is evident and daily demonstrated, that one is short and another long sighted; that one eats much, another little; that one has mild, another violent passions; in a word, that one is weak in body and mind, whilst another is strong in both.

Q. They are therefore really unequal.

A. Yes, in the development of their means, but not in the nature and essence of those means; they are made of the same stuff, but not in the same dimensions; nor are the weight and value equal. Our language possesses no one word capable of expressing the identity of nature, and the diversity of its form and employment. It is a proportional equality; and it is for this reason I have said, equal before God, and in the order of nature.

Q. How is liberty a physical attribute of man?

A. Because all men having senses sufficient for their preservation, no one wanting the eye of another to see, his ear to hear, his mouth to eat, his feet to walk, they are all, by this very reason, constituted naturally independent and free; no man is necessarily subjected to another, nor has he a right to domineer over him.

Q. But if a man is born strong, has he not a natural right to master the weak man?

A. No; for it is neither a necessity for him, nor a convention between them. It is an abusive extension of his strength; and here an abuse is made of the word right, which in its true meaning implies, justice or reciprocal faculty.

Q. How is property a physical attribute of man?

A. In as much as all men being constituted equal or similar to one another, and consequently independent and free, each is the absolute master, the full proprietor of his body and of the produce of his labor.

Q. How is justice derived from these three attributes?

A. In this, that men being equal and free, owing nothing to each other, have no right to require anything from one another, only in as much as they return an equal value for it; or in as much as the balance of what is given is in equilibrium with what is returned: and it is this equality, this equilibrium which is called justice, equity; that is to say that equality and justice are but one and the same word, the same law of nature, of which the social virtues are only applications and derivatives. . . .

(VI)

Q. What do you conclude from all this?

A. I conclude from it that all the social virtues are only the habitude of actions and useful to society and to the individual who practises them; That they all refer to the physical object of man's preservation; That nature having implanted in us the want of that preservation, has made a law to us of all its consequences, and a crime of everything that deviates from it; That we carry in us the seed of every virtue and of every perfection; That it only requires to be developed; That we are only happy in as much as we observe the rules established by nature for the end of our preservation; And that, all wisdom, all perfection, all law, all virtue, all philosophy, consist in the practice of these axioms founded on our own organization:

> *Preserve-thyself; Instruct-thyself; Moderate-thyself;*
> *Live for thy fellow citizens, that they may live for thee.*

Condition of Man in the Universe

After a short silence, the Genius resumed in these words:

I have told you already, O friend of truth, that man vainly ascribes his misfortunes to obscure and imaginary agents; in vain he seeks for mysterious and remote causes of his ills. . . . In the general order of the universe, his condition is doubtless subject to inconveniences, and his existence overruled by superior powers: but those powers are neither the decrees of a blind fatality, nor the caprices of whimsical and fantastic beings; like the world of which he forms a part, man is governed by natural laws, regular in their course, consistent in their effects, immutable in their essence; and those laws, the common source of good and evil, are not written among the distant stars, or hidden in mysterious codes: inherent in the nature of terrestrial beings, interwoven with their existence, they are at all times and in all places present to man, they act upon his senses, they warn his understanding, and dispense to every action its reward or punishment. Let man then study these laws! let him comprehend his own nature, and the nature of the beings that surround him, and he will know the regulators of his destiny; the causes of his evils, and the remedies he ought to apply.

When the secret power, which animates the universe, formed the globe of the earth, he implanted in the beings by whom it is inhabited, essential properties which became the law of their individual motion, the bound of their reciprocal relations, the cause of the harmony of the whole; he thereby established a regular order of causes and effects, of principles and consequences, which, under an appearance of chance, governs the universe, and maintains the equilibrium of the world: thus, he gave to fire motion and activity; to air, elasticity; weight and density to matter; he made air lighter than water, metal heavier than earth, wood less cohesive than steel; he ordered the flame to ascend, stones to fall, plants to vegetate; man, who was to be exposed to the action of so many different beings, and whose frail life was nevertheless to be preserved, was endowed with the faculty of sensation. By this faculty, all action hurtful to his existence gives him a feeling of pain and evil; and every favorable action an impression of pleasure and happiness. By these sensations, man, sometimes averted from that which wounds his senses, sometimes allured towards that which soothes them, has been obliged to cherish and preserve his own life. Thus, self-love, the desire of happiness, aversion to pain, are the essential and primary laws imposed on man by NATURE herself; the laws which the directing power, whatever it be, has established for his government, and which, like those of motion in the physical world, are the simple and fruitful principle of whatever happens in the moral world.

Such then is the condition of man: on one side exposed to the action of the elements which surround him, he is subject to many inevitable evils: and if in this decree Nature has been severe, on the other hand, just and even indulgent, she has not only tempered the evils with equivalent good, she has even enabled him to augment the good and alleviate the evil: she seems to say: "Feeble work of my hands, I owe you nothing, and I give you life; the world wherein I placed you was not made for you, yet I grant you the use of it; you will find in it a mixture of good and evil; it is for you to distinguish them, and to direct your footsteps in the paths of flowers and thorns. Be the arbiter of your own lot; I put your destiny into your hands." —Yes, man is made the artisan of his own destiny; it is he who has alternately created the successes or reverses of his fortune: and if, on a review of all the pains with which he has tormented his life, he finds reason to weep over his own weakness or imprudence, yet, considering the beginnings from which he set out, and the height attained, perhaps he has more reason to presume on his strength, and to pride himself on his genius.

Thomas Paine

My Own Mind Is My Own Church

There is scarcely a figure in American letters more vilified, idolized, and ultimately tragic than Thomas Paine (1737–1809). As long as he contented himself with polemical defenses of American independence and the right to political self-determination, he was the darling of the young Republic. But the moment he stepped over the line of orthodox respectability in religious matters, the same people who earlier had applauded him as a noble patriot excoriated him as a "lilly-livered sinical rogue," "a drunken atheist," a "detested reptile." The book that prompted these and other attacks was, of course, *The Age of Reason* (1794–95), probably the best-known treatise in the history of American deism. It is ironic, given the hostile reaction to the book's appearance, that Paine intended it as a response to the dogmatic atheism of the French Revolution. Paine, like his fellow deists on both sides of the Atlantic, was no atheist. But in the eyes of his Christian contemporaries, apostasy from scriptural faith was tantamount to godlessness.

Born in Norfolk, England, Paine was plagued with personal and professional embarrassment for the first half of his life. He tried being a corset maker, a merchant, and a customs official but failed miserably at each. One of the reasons for his lack of success was no doubt his affinity for the bottle, although it is doubtful that he was ever quite the hopeless drunkard his enemies later made him out to be. But another reason was his restlessness, partly temperamental, partly the result of his informal but at one time wide reading, which served to incapacitate him for steady and rather humdrum employment.

When he was almost forty, Paine left England and immigrated to the American colonies. There his luck swiftly and dramatically changed. His *Common Sense* (1776), the first public call for American independence, won him instant fame. His *Crisis* papers, written throughout the war, as well as *The Rights of Man* (1791–92), a defense of the French Revolution, cemented his reputation as America's leading political polemicist. Nor was his fame confined to the new Republic's shores. On the basis of his *Rights of Man*, Paine was made an honorary citizen of France and elected in 1792 to its National Convention. But his appeals for moderation during the high point of the Terror, combined with his pleas for clemency for Louis XVI, soon rankled the militant leaders of the convention, and Paine eventually found himself incarcerated in the Luxembourg prison. If we take seriously his own account of what happened, he barely escaped the usual fate of "enemies" of the Republic.

While in France, Paine wrote parts I and II of *The Age of Reason* and was one of the founders of the Society of Theophilanthropy, a Parisian deistical fraternity. He returned to the United States in 1802, to be greeted by an almost unimaginable campaign of defamation by opponents of his deistic beliefs. The last seven years of his life were spent in barely tolerable poverty and increasing bitterness. At his death in 1809, he was in the unenviable position of having lived long enough to see the American deist movement, which his *Age of Reason* had done so much to spark, in its last convulsions. Most of the influential deists—such as Elihu Palmer, Paine's close friend—had been spared that final indignity.

Paine's deistic writings qualitatively fall somewhere between the cumbersome and at times incomprehensible ruminations of Ethan Allen and the often brilliant reflections of Elihu Palmer. He was no intellectual, although he fancied himself so. Nor was his reading especially deep, which he often freely admitted. Instead, he was an amazingly effective pamphleteer, able to capture the public imagination with a finely tuned and memorable phrase. In retrospect, his role in the history of American deism is best seen as that of ideologue. He inflamed emotions and sparked debate with his incendiary locutions, but he failed to provide enough raw material in the way of solid argumentation for the fire to catch hold. That task was performed, as we will see in the next chapter, by Paine's young colleague Elihu Palmer.

The first selections from Paine are taken from *The Age of Reason* (Part I, 1794). In them, Paine divides his energy between an attack on revealed religion in general and Christianity in particular, and a defense of his deistic religion of nature.

Revelation, Paine correctly argues, is the foundation on which the three major Western religious traditions are based. This revelation, or the direct communication of God to humans, is recorded in sacred scripture, and unswerving belief in its literal truth is mandated. But according to Paine, such a mandate is unwarranted. Recorded revelation—even allowing that it actually occurred—is nothing more than hearsay, and often second- or thirdhand at that. No rational person can or ought to be expected to accept on authority what is essentially rumor, in either the secular or theological realms. Consequently, the revelatory origins of Christian dogma are evidentially suspect. After all, "a thing which everybody is required to believe, requires that the proof and evidence of it should be equal to all, and universal." But revelatory communications are by definition personal and private.

Similarly, Christianity's endorsement of miracles is a weakness rather than a strength. Miracles, asserts Paine, are such egregious violations of perceived regularity in nature that belief in them degrades the Almighty into "the character of a show-man, playing tricks to amuse and make the people stare and wonder." Moreover, acceptance of them is based on anecdotes that are centuries removed from the present day—hardly a firm evidential basis. Given, then, that stories of miracles violate everything known about the uniformity of creation, and that there is no direct or consensual experience of them, it is more rational to disbelieve than to believe in their truth. In a rather Humean-sounding passage, Paine rhetorically asks: "Is it more probable that nature should go out of her course, or that a man should tell a lie?" The answer, for Paine, is obvious.

In typical deistic style, Paine also rejects Christianity because of what he perceives as its immorality. Paine is not at his best with this line of reasoning, however; his analysis is clearly less thoughtful than, for instance, Elihu Palmer's. Paine supports his point largely by reminding his readers of the historical atrocities committed in the name of Christianity. Palmer, on the other hand, bases his indictment on a reflective examination of Christian dogma's normative implications. Nor does Paine, again unlike Palmer, attempt to spell out systematically a theory of morality superior to Christianity's. He simply stipulates, somewhat mysteriously, that "the knowledge of [morality] exists in every man's conscience" and that this knowledge includes "doing justice, loving mercy, and endeavouring to make our fellow-creatures happy."

Paine's charge that the Christian system is immoral does not extend, however, to the person of Jesus. Jesus, in Paine's estimation, advocated a morality of a "most benevolent kind." He founded no system but "called men to the practice of moral virtues, and the belief of one God." He was, in short, a good deist. But his simple religion of virtue and nature was later corrupted by the irrational metaphysics of his followers—especially, in Paine's opinion, St. Paul, "that manufacturer of quibbles."

In place of Christian theology, Paine advocates what he calls "true" theology—that is, natural philosophy, "the study of the works of God." The deity *does* reveal himself, but not through the nonsensical and immoral pages of Scripture. Instead, "the word of God is the creation we behold." This is the *true* revelation, which not only discloses God's existence but also gives rise to the physical and moral sciences.

Paine argues that an examination of the book of nature shows that creation is lawlike in its operations. This uniformity points to the existence of scientific principles that are immutable and universal and that serve as the necessary basis of all human knowledge. But the existence of such principles in turn points to the presence of a First Cause, which established them and shares their characteristics. Thus "true" theology reveals the existence of a rational deity, of an "Almighty [who] is the great mechanic of the creation, the first philosopher, and original teacher of all science." This is clearly not much of an argument. There is no obvious justification for inferring the existence of a divine First

Cause merely on the basis of perceived regularity in nature. But Paine, ever the polemicist, was not interested in encumbering the gripping eloquence of *The Age of Reason* with philosophical subtleties.

Fortunately, Paine elsewhere attempted to be more circumspect in his reflections on this point. The selection entitled "The Existence of God" is such an example. The essay was originally delivered at the first public meeting of the Parisian Society of Theophilanthropy on 16 January 1797. In it, Paine reiterates *The Age of Reason*'s conviction that the proper source of knowledge about God is nature rather than Scripture, but he also fleshes out his earlier truncated argument for the existence of the deity as First Cause. If we examine creation, he claims, we discover that matter has certain predictable properties. Many of these properties can be explained in terms of the nature of matter itself. But one attribute associated with matter points beyond it—motion. "The natural state of matter . . . is a state of rest. Motion, or change of place, is the effect of an external cause acting upon matter." Moreover, motion (or Newton's gravitation) can be either directly experienced or deduced as an attribute of all matter, both on earth and throughout the solar system. It holds reality together and allows for the lawlike interactions of its constituents. Since motion is not a property of material bodies themselves, and since it permeates all of reality and thus maintains its integrity, it must have originated with and is kept in existence by an external cause: "and that cause man calls GOD."

The final selection from Paine, "My Private Thoughts on a Future State," was written, appropriately enough, toward the end of his life. For Paine, the Christian insistence that humans can be divided into righteous and wicked (or sheep and goats) is too harsh. The race may be numerically divisible, but not morally so. A more rational—and just—alternative is to suppose that some individuals are clearly virtuous, some clearly wicked, while others—possibly the majority—are "neither good nor bad." If future existence after physical death is a possibility, Paine speculates, it follows that the first group will be rewarded, the second punished, and the third, "too insignificant for notice, will be dropped entirely." Such a conjecture, Paine concludes, is more "consistent with my idea of God's justice" than the Christian dichotomy of eternal punishment or reward. From first to last, then, Paine remained loyal to the credo expressed in the opening pages of *The Age of Reason*: "My own mind is my own church."

The Age of Reason

The Author's Profession of Faith

. . . I believe in one God, and no more; and I hope for happiness beyond this life.

I believe in the equality of man, and I believe that religious duties consist in doing justice, loving mercy, and endeavouring to make our fellow-creatures happy.

. . . I do not believe in the creed professed by the Jewish church, by the Roman church, by the Greek church, by the Turkish church, by the Protestant church, nor by any church that I know of. My own mind is my own church.

All national institutions of churches, whether Jewish, Christian, or Turkish, appear to me no other than human inventions set up to terrify and enslave mankind, and monopolize power and profit.

I do not mean by this declaration to condemn those who believe otherwise; they have the same right to their belief as I have to mine. But it is necessary to the happiness of man, that he be mentally faithful to himself. Infidelity does not consist in believing, or in disbelieving; it consists in professing to believe what he does not believe.

It is impossible to calculate the moral mischief, if I may so express it, that mental lying has produced in society. When a man has so far corrupted and prostituted the chastity of his mind, as to subscribe his professional belief to things he does not believe, he has prepared himself for the commission of every other crime. He takes up the trade of a priest for the sake of gain, and, in order to qualify himself for that trade, he begins with a perjury. Can we conceive anything more destructive to morality than this?

Of Missions and Revelations

Every national church or religion has established itself by pretending some special mission from God, communicated to certain individuals. The Jews have their Moses; the Christians their Jesus Christ, their apostles and saints; and the Turks their Mahomet; as if the way to God was not open to every man alike.

Each of those churches shows certain books, which they call *revelation*, or the Word of God. The Jews say that their Word of God was given by God to Moses face to face; the Christians say, that their Word of God came by divine inspiration; and the Turks say, that their Word of God (the Koran) was brought by an angel from heaven. Each of those churches accuses the other of unbelief; and, for my own part, I disbelieve them all.

As it is necessary to affix right ideas to words, I will, before I proceed further into the subject, offer some observations on the word *revelation*. Revelation when applied to religion, means something communicated *immediately* from God to man.

No one will deny or dispute the power of the Almighty to make such a communication if he pleases. But admitting, for the sake of a case, that something has been revealed to a certain person, and not revealed to any other person, it is revelation to that person only. When he tells it to a second person, a second to a third, a third to a fourth, and so on, it ceases to be a revelation

214

to all those persons. It is revelation to the first person only, and *hearsay* to every other, and, consequently, they are not obliged to believe it.

It is a contradiction in terms and ideas to call anything a revelation that comes to us at second hand, either verbally or in writing. Revelation is necessarily limited to the first communication. After this, it is only an account of something which that person says was a revelation made to him; and though he may find himself obliged to believe it, it cannot be incumbent on me to believe it in the same manner, for it was not a revelation made to *me*, and I have only his word for it that it was made to *him*.

When Moses told the children of Israel that he received the two tables of the commandments from the hand of God, they were not obliged to believe him, because they had no other authority for it than his telling them so; and I have no other authority for it than some historian telling me so, the commandments carrying no internal evidence of divinity with them. They contain some good moral precepts such as any man qualified to be a lawgiver or a legislator could produce himself, without having recourse to supernatural intervention. (It is, however, necessary to except the declaration which says that God *visits the sins of the fathers upon the children.* This is contrary to every principle of moral justice.)

When I am told that the Koran was written in Heaven, and brought to Mahomet by an angel, the account comes to near the same kind of hearsay evidence and second hand authority as the former. I did not see the angel myself, and therefore I have a right not to believe it.

When also I am told that a woman, called the Virgin Mary, said, or gave out, that she was with child without any cohabitation with a man, and that her betrothed husband, Joseph, said that an angel told him so, I have a right to believe them or not: such a circumstance required a much stronger evidence than their bare word for it: but we have not even this; for neither Joseph nor Mary wrote any such matter themselves. It is only reported by others that *they said so.* It is hearsay upon hearsay, and I do not choose to rest my belief upon such evidence.

It is, however, not difficult to account for the credit that was given to the story of Jesus Christ being the Son of God. He was born when the heathen mythology had still some fashion and repute in the world, and that mythology had prepared the people for the belief of such a story. Almost all the extraordinary men that lived under the heathen mythology were reputed to be the sons of some of their Gods. It was not a new thing at that time to believe a man to have been celestially begotten; the intercourse of gods with women was then a matter of familiar opinion. Their Jupiter, according to their accounts, had cohabited with hundreds; the story had therefore nothing in it either new, wonderful, or obscene; it was conformable to the opinions that then prevailed among the people called Gentiles, or mythologists, and it was those people only that believed it. The Jews, who had kept strictly to the belief of one God, and no more, and who had always rejected the heathen mythology, never credited the story.

. . . That many good men have believed this strange fable, and lived very good lives under that belief (for credulity is not a crime) is what I have no doubt of. In the first place, they were educated to believe it, and they would have believed anything else in the same manner. There are also many who have been so enthusiastically enraptured by what they conceived to be the infinite love of God to man, in making a sacrifice of himself, that the vehemence of the idea has forbidden and deterred them from examining into the absurdity and profaneness of the story. The more unnatural anything is, the more is it capable of becoming the object of dismal admiration.

. . . But if objects for gratitude and admiration are our desire, do they not present themselves every hour to our eyes? Do we not see a fair creation prepared to receive us the instant we are born—a world furnished to our hands, that cost us nothing? Is it we that light up the sun; that pour down the rain; and fill the earth with abundance? Whether we sleep or wake, the vast machinery of the universe still goes on. Are these things, and the blessings they indicate in future, nothing to us? Can our gross feelings be excited by no other subjects than tragedy and suicide? or is the gloomy pride of man become so intolerable, that nothing can flatter it but a sacrifice of the Creator?

Of Jesus Christ

Nothing that is here said can apply, even with the most distant disrespect, to the *real* character of Jesus Christ. He was a virtuous and an amiable man. The morality that he preached and practised was of the most benevolent kind; and though similar systems of morality had been preached by Confucius, and by some of the Greek philosophers, many years before, by the Quakers since, and by many good men in all ages, it has not been exceeded by any.

Jesus Christ wrote no account of himself, of his birth, parentage, or anything else. Not a line of what is called the New Testament is of his writing. The history of him is altogether the work of other people; and as to the account given of his resurrection and ascension, it was the necessary counterpart to the story of his birth. His historians, having brought him into the world in a supernatural manner, were obliged to take him out again in the same manner, or the first part of the story must have fallen to the ground.

The wretched contrivance with which this latter part is told, exceeds everything that went before it. The first part, that of the miraculous conception, was not a thing that admitted of publicity; and therefore the tellers of this part of the story had this advantage, that though they might not be credited, they could not be detected. They could not be expected to prove it, because it was not one of those things that admitted of proof, and it was impossible that the person of whom it was told could prove it himself.

But the resurrection of a dead person from the grave, and his ascension through the air, is a thing very different, as to the evidence it admits of, to the invisible conception of a child in the womb. The resurrection and ascension, supposing them to have taken place, admitted of public and ocular demonstration, like that of the ascension of a balloon, or the sun at noon day, to all Jerusalem at least. A thing which everybody is required to believe, requires that the proof and evidence of it should be equal to all, and universal; and as the public visibility of this last related act was the only evidence that could give sanction to the former part, the whole of it falls to the ground, because that evidence never was given. Instead of this, a small number of persons, not more than eight or nine, are introduced as proxies for the whole world, to say they saw it, and all the rest of the world are called upon to believe it. But it appears that Thomas did not believe the resurrection; and, as they say, would not believe without having ocular and manual demonstration himself. *So neither will I*; and the reason is equally as good for me, and for every other person, as for Thomas. . . .

Of Scripture

. . . I now go on to the book called the New Testament. The *new* Testament! that is, the *new* Will, as if there could be two wills of the Creator.

Had it been the object or the intention of Jesus Christ to establish a new religion, he would undoubtedly have written the system himself, or *procured it to be written* in his life time. But there is no publication extant authenticated with his name. All the books called the New Testament were written after his death. He was a Jew by birth and by profession; and he was the son of God in like manner that every other person is; for the Creator is the Father of All.

The first four books, called Matthew, Mark, Luke, and John, do not give a history of the life of Jesus Christ, but only detached anecdotes of him. It appears from these books, that the whole time of his being a preacher was not more than eighteen months; and it was only during this short time that those men became acquainted with him. They make mention of him at the age of twelve years, sitting, they say, among the Jewish doctors, asking and answering them questions. As this was several years before their acquaintance with him began, it is most probable they had this anecdote from his parents. From this time there is no account of him for about sixteen years. Where he lived, or how he employed himself during this interval, is not known. Most probably he was working at his father's trade, which was that of a carpenter. It does not appear that he had any school education, and the probability is, that he could not write, for his parents were extremely poor, as appears from their not being able to pay for a bed when he was born.

It is somewhat curious that the three persons whose names are the most universally recorded were of very obscure parentage. Moses was a foundling; Jesus Christ was born in a stable; and Mahomet was a mule driver. The first and the last of these men were founders of different systems of religion; but Jesus Christ founded no new system. He called men to the practice of moral virtues; and the belief of one God. The great trait in his character is philanthropy.

The manner in which he was apprehended shews that he was not much known at that time; and it shews also that the meetings he then held with his followers were in secret; and that he had given over or suspended preaching publicly. Judas could no otherways betray him than by giving information where he was, and pointing him out to the officers that went to arrest him; and the reason for employing and paying Judas to do this could arise only from the causes already mentioned, that of his not being much known, and living concealed.

The idea of his concealment, not only agrees very ill with his reputed divinity, but associates with it something of pusillanimity; and his being betrayed, or in other words, his being apprehended, on the information of one of his followers, shews that he did not intend to be apprehended, and consequently that he did not intend to be crucified.

The Christian mythologists tell us that Christ died for the sins of the world, and that he came on *purpose to die*. Would it not then have been the same if he had died of a fever or of the small pox, of old age, or of anything else?

The declaratory sentence which, they say, was passed upon Adam, in case he ate of the apple, was not, that *thou shalt surely be crucified*, but, *thou shalt surely die*. The sentence was death, and not the *manner of dying*. Crucifixion, therefore, or any other particular manner of dying, made no part of the sentence that Adam was to suffer, and consequently, even upon their own tactic, it could make no part of the sentence that Christ was to suffer in the room of Adam. A fever would have done as well as a cross, if there was any occasion for either.

This sentence of death, which, they tell us, was thus passed upon Adam, must either have meant dying naturally, that is, ceasing to live, or have meant what these mythologists call damnation; and consequently, the act of dying on the part of Jesus Christ, must, according to their system, apply as a prevention to one or other of these two *things* happening to Adam and to us.

That it does not prevent our dying is evident, because we all die; and if their accounts of longevity be true, men die faster since the crucifixion than before: and with respect to the second explanation, (including with it the *natural death* of Jesus Christ as a substitute for the *eternal death or damnation* of all mankind), it is impertinently representing the Creator as coming off, or revoking the sentence, by a pun or a quibble upon the word *death*. That manufacturer of quibbles, St. Paul, if he wrote the books that bear his name, has helped this quibble on by making another quibble upon the word *Adam*. He makes there to be two Adams; the one who sins in fact, and suffers by proxy; the other who sins by proxy, and suffers in fact. A religion thus interlarded with quibble, subterfuge, and pun, has a tendency to instruct its professors in the practice of these arts. They acquire the habit without being aware of the cause.

If Jesus Christ was the being which those mythologists tell us he was, and that he came into this world to *suffer*, which is a word they sometimes use instead of *to die*, the only real suffering he could have endured would have been *to live*. His existence here was a state of exilement or transportation from heaven, and the way back to his original country was to die. —In fine, everything in this strange system is the reverse of what it pretends to be. It is the reverse of truth, and I become so tired of examining into its inconsistencies and absurdities, that I hasten to the conclusion of it, in order to proceed to something better.

How much, or what parts of the books called the New Testament, were written by the persons whose names they bear, is what we can know nothing of, neither are we certain in what language they were originally written. The matters they now contain may be classed under two heads: anecdote, and epistolary correspondence.

The four books already mentioned, Matthew, Mark, Luke, and John, are altogether anecdotal. They relate events after they had taken place. They tell what Jesus Christ did and said, and what others did and said to him; and in several instances they relate the same event differently. Revelation is necessarily out of the question with respect to those books; not only because of the disagreement of the writers, but because revelation cannot be applied to the relating of facts by the persons who saw them done, not to the relating or recording of any discourse or conversation by those who heard it. The book called the Acts of the Apostles (an anonymous work) belongs also to the anecdotal part.

All the other parts of the New Testament, except the book of enigmas, called the Revelations, are a collection of letters under the name of epistles; and the forgery of letters has been such a common practice in the world, that the probability is at least equal, whether they are genuine or forged. . . .

Of Redemption

. . . The church has set up a system of religion very contradictory to the character of the person whose name it bears. It has set up a religion of pomp and revenue in pretended imitation of a person whose life was humility and poverty.

The invention of a purgatory, and of the releasing of souls therefrom, by

prayers, bought of the church with money; the selling of pardons, dispensations, and indulgences, are revenue laws, without bearing that name or carrying that appearance. But the case nevertheless is, that those things derive their
origin from the proxysm of the crucifixion, and the theory deduced therefrom,
which was, that one person could stand in the place of another, and could
perform meritorious services for him. The probability, therefore, is that the
whole theory or doctrine of what is called the redemption (which is said to have
been accomplished by the act of one person in the room of another) was
originally fabricated on purpose to bring forward and build all those secondary
and pecuniary redemptions upon; and that the passages in the books upon
which the idea or theory of redemption is built, have been manufactured and
fabricated for that purpose. Why are we to give this church credit, when she
tells us that those books are genuine in every part, any more than we give her
credit for everything else she has told us; or for the miracles she says she has
performed? That she *could* fabricate writings is certain, because she could write;
and the composition of the writings in question, is of that kind that anybody
might do it; and that she *did* fabricate them is not more inconsistent with
probability, than that she should tell us, as she has done, that she could and did
work miracles.

Since, then, no external evidence can, at this long distance of time, be
produced to prove whether the church fabricated the doctrine called redemption or not, (for such evidence, whether for or against, would be subject to the
same suspicion of being fabricated), the case can only be referred to the internal
evidence which the thing carries of itself; and this affords a very strong presumption of its being a fabrication. For the internal evidence is, that the theory
or doctrine of redemption has for its basis an idea of pecuniary justice, and not
that of moral justice.

If I owe a person money, and cannot pay him, and he threatens to put me
in prison, another person can take the debt upon himself, and pay it for me. But
if I have committed a crime, every circumstance of the case is changed. Moral
justice cannot take the innocent for the guilty even if the innocent would offer
itself. To suppose justice to do this, is to destroy the principle of its existence,
which is the thing itself. It is then no longer justice. It is indiscriminate revenge.

This single reflection will shew that the doctrine of redemption is founded
on a mere pecuniary idea corresponding to that of a debt which another person
might pay; and as this pecuniary idea corresponds again with the system of
second redemptions, obtained through the means of money given to the
church for pardons, the probability is that the same persons fabricated both the
one and the other of those theories; and that, in truth, there is no such thing
as redemption; that it is fabulous; and that man stands in the same relative
condition with his Maker he ever did stand, since man existed; and that it is his
greatest consolation to think so.

Let him believe this, and he will live more consistently and morally, than by any other system. It is by his being taught to contemplate himself as an out-law, as an out-cast, as a beggar, as a mumper, as one thrown as it were on a dunghill, at an immense distance from his Creator, and who must make his approaches by creeping, and cringing to intermediate beings, that he conceives either a contemptuous disregard for everything under the name of religion, or becomes indifferent, or turns what he calls devout. In the latter case, he consumes his life in grief, or the affectation of it. His prayers are reproaches. His humility is ingratitude. He calls himself a worm, and the fertile earth a dunghill; and all the blessings of life by the thankless name of vanities. He despises the choicest gift of God to man, the GIFT OF REASON; and having endeavoured to force upon himself the belief of a system against which reason revolts, he ungratefully calls it *human reason*, as if man could give reason to himself. . . .

Of Miracles

. . . Mankind have conceived to themselves certain laws, by which what they call nature is supposed to act; and that a miracle is something contrary to the operation and effect of those laws. But unless we know the whole extent of those laws, and of what are commonly called the powers of nature, we are not able to judge whether any thing that may appear to us wonderful or miraculous, be within, or be beyond, or be contrary to, her natural power of acting. . . .

Of all the modes of evidence that ever were invented to obtain belief to any system or opinion to which the name of religion has been given, that of miracle, however successful the imposition may have been, is the most inconsistent. For, in the first place, whenever recourse is had to show, for the purpose of procuring that belief (for a miracle, under any idea of the word, is a show) it implies a lameness or weakness in the doctrine that is preached. And, in the second place, it is degrading the Almighty into the character of a show-man, playing tricks to amuse and make the people stare and wonder. It is also the most equivocal sort of evidence that can be set up; for the belief is not to depend upon the thing called a miracle, but upon the credit of the reporter, who says that he saw it; and, therefore, the thing, were it true, would have no better chance of being believed than if it were a lie.

Suppose I were to say, that when I sat down to write this book, a hand presented itself in the air, took up the pen and wrote every word that is herein written; would any body believe me? Certainly they would not. Would they believe me a whit the more if the thing had been a fact? Certainly they would not. Since then a real miracle, were it to happen, would be subject to the same fate as the falsehood, the inconsistency becomes the greater of supposing the Almighty would make use of means that would not answer the purpose for which they were intended, even if they were real.

If we are to suppose a miracle to be something so entirely out of the course of what is called nature, that she must go out of that course to accomplish it, and we see an account given of such a miracle by the person who said he saw it, it raises a question in the mind very easily decided, which is, —Is it more probable that nature should go out of her course, or that a man should tell a lie? We have never seen, in our time, nature go out of her course; but we have good reason to believe that millions of lies have been told in the same time; it is, therefore, at least millions to one, that the reporter of a miracle tells a lie. . . .

In every point of view in which those things called miracles can be placed and considered, the reality of them is improbable, and their existence unnecessary. They would not, as before observed, answer any useful purpose, even if they were true; for it is more difficult to obtain belief to a miracle, than to a principle evidently moral, without any miracle. Moral principle speaks universally for itself. Miracle could be but a thing of the moment, and seen but by a few; after this it requires a transfer of faith from God to man to believe a miracle upon man's report. Instead, therefore, of admitting the recitals of miracles as evidence of any system of religion being true, they ought to be considered as symptoms of its being fabulous. It is necessary to the full and upright character of truth that it rejects the crutch; and it is consistent with the character of fable to seek the aid that truth rejects. Thus much for Mystery and Miracle. . . .

Of the Immorality of Christianity

The most detestable wickedness, the most horrid cruelties, and the greatest miseries, that have afflicted the human race, have had their origin in this thing called revelation, or revealed religion. It has been the most dishonourable belief against the character of the divinity, the most destructive to morality, and the peace and happiness of man, that ever was propagated since man began to exist. It is better, far better, that we admitted, if it were possible, a thousand devils to roam at large, and to preach publicly the doctrine of devils, if there were any such, than that we permitted one such imposter and monster as Moses, Joshua, Samuel, and the Bible prophets, to come with the pretended word of God in his mouth, and have credit among us.

Whence arose all the horrid assassinations of whole nations of men, women, and infants, with which the Bible is filled; and the bloody persecutions, and tortures unto death and religious wars, that since that time have laid Europe in blood and ashes; whence arose they, but from this impious thing called revealed religion, and this monstrous belief that God has spoken to man? The lies of the Bible have been the cause of the one, and the lies of the Testament of the other.

Some Christians pretend that Christianity was not established by the sword; but of what period of time do they speak? It was impossible that twelve men could begin with the sword: they had not the power; but no sooner were the professors of Christianity sufficiently powerful to employ the sword than they did so, and the stake and faggot too; and Mahomet could not do it sooner. By the same spirit that Peter cut off the ear of the high priest's servant (if the story be true) he would cut off his head, and the head of his master, had he been able. Besides this, Christianity grounds itself originally upon the Hebrew Bible, and the Bible was established altogether by the sword, and that in the worst use of it—not to terrify, but to extirpate. The Jews made no converts; they butchered all. The Bible is the sire of the Testament, and both are called the *word of God*. The Christians read both books; the ministers preach from both books; and this thing called Christianity is made up of both. It is then false to say that Christianity was not established by the sword.

The only sect that has not persecuted are the Quakers; and the only reason that can be given for it is, that they are rather Deists than Christians. They do not believe much about Jesus Christ, and they call the scriptures a dead letter. Had they called them by a worse name, they had been nearer the truth.

It is incumbent on every man who reverences the character of the Creator, and who wishes to lessen the catalogue of artificial miseries, and remove the cause that has sown persecutions thick among mankind, to expel all ideas of a revealed religion as a dangerous heresy, and an impious fraud. What is it that we have learned from this pretended thing called revealed religion? Nothing that is useful to man, and every thing that is dishonourable to his Maker. What is it the Bible teaches us?—rapine, cruelty, and murder. What is it the Testament teaches us?—to believe that the Almighty committed debauchery with a woman engaged to be married; and the belief of this debauchery is called faith.

As to the fragments of morality that are irregularly and thinly scattered in those books, they make no part of this pretended thing, revealed religion. They are the natural dictates of conscience, and the bonds by which society is held together, and without which it cannot exist; and are nearly the same in all religions, and in all societies. The Testament teaches nothing new upon this subject, and where it attempts to exceed, it becomes mean and ridiculous. The doctrine of not retaliating injuries is much better expressed in Proverbs, which is a collection as well from the Gentiles as the Jews, than it is in the Testament. It is there said, (XXV. 21) *"If thine enemy be hungry, give him bread to eat; and if he be thirsty, give him water to drink:"* but when it is said, as in the Testament, *"If a man smite thee on the right cheek, turn to him the other also,"* it is assassinating the dignity of forbearance, and sinking man into a spaniel.

Loving of enemies is another dogma of feigned morality, and has besides no meaning. It is incumbent on man, as a moralist, that he does not revenge an injury; and it is equally as good in a political sense, for there is no end to retaliation; each retaliates on the other, and calls it justice: but to love in proportion to the injury, if it could be done, would be to offer a premium for a crime. Besides, the word *enemies* is too vague and general to be used in a moral maxim, which ought always to be clear and defined, like a proverb. If a man be the enemy of another from mistake and prejudice, as in the case of religious opinions, and sometimes in politics, that man is different to an enemy at heart with a criminal intention; and it is incumbent upon us, and it contributes also to our own tranquillity, that we put the best construction upon a thing that it will bear. But even this erroneous motive in him makes no motive for love on the other part; and to say that we can love voluntarily, and without a motive, is morally and physically impossible.

Morality is injured by prescribing to it duties that, in the first place, are impossible to be performed, and if they could be would be productive of evil; or, as before said, be premiums for crime. The maxim *of doing as we would be done unto* does not include this strange doctrine of loving enemies; for no man expects to be loved himself for his crime or for his enmity.

Those who preach this doctrine of loving their enemies, are in general the greatest persecutors, and they act consistently by so doing; for the doctrine is hypocritical, and it is natural that hypocrisy should act the reverse of what it preaches. For my own part, I disown the doctrine, and consider it as a feigned or fabulous morality; yet the man does not exist that can say I have persecuted him, or any man, or any set of men, either in the American Revolution, or in the French Revolution; or that I have, in any case, returned evil for evil. But it is not incumbent on man to reward a bad action with a good one, or to return good for evil; and wherever it is done, it is a voluntary act, and not a duty. It is also absurd to suppose that such doctrine can make any part of a revealed religion. We imitate the moral character of the Creator by forbearing with each other, for he forbears with all; but this doctrine would imply that he loved man, not in proportion as he was good, but as he was bad.

If we consider the nature of our condition here, we must see there is no occasion for such a thing as *revealed religion*. What is it we want to know? Does not the creation, the universe we behold, preach to us the existence of an Almighty power, that governs and regulates the whole? And is not the evidence that this creation holds out to our senses infinitely stronger than any thing we can read in a book, that any imposter might make and call the word of God? As for morality, the knowledge of it exists in every man's conscience.

Of Christian Theology and True Theology

As to the Christian system of faith, it appears to me as a species of atheism; a sort of religious denial of God. It professes to believe in a man rather than in God. It is a compound made up chiefly of man-ism with but little deism, and is as near to atheism as twilight is to darkness. It introduces between man and his Maker an opaque body, which it calls a redeemer, as the moon introduces her opaque self between the earth and the sun, and it produces by this means a religious or an irreligious eclipse of light. It has put the whole orbit of reason into shade.

The effect of this obscurity has been that of turning everything upside down, and representing it in reverse; and among the revolutions it has thus magically produced, it has made a revolution in Theology.

That which is now called natural philosophy, embracing the whole circle of science, of which astronomy occupies the chief place, is the study of the works of God, and of the power and wisdom of God in his works, and is the true theology.

As to the theology that is now studied in its place, it is the study of human opinions and of human fancies *concerning* God. It is not the study of God himself in the works that he has made, but in the works or writings that man has made; and it is not among the least of the mischiefs that the Christian system has done to the world, that it has abandoned the original and beautiful system of theology, like a beautiful innocent, to distress and reproach, to make room for the hag of superstition. . . .

It is a fraud of the Christian system to call the sciences *human inventions*; it is only the application of them that is human. Every science has for its basis a system of principles as fixed and unalterable as those by which the universe is regulated and governed. Man cannot make principles, he can only discover them.

For example: Every person who looks at an almanack sees an account when an eclipse will take place, and he sees also that it never fails to take place according to the account there given. This shews that man is acquainted with the laws by which the heavenly bodies move. But it would be something worse than ignorance, were any church on earth to say that those laws are an human invention.

It would also be ignorance, or something worse, to say that the scientific principles, by the aid of which man is enabled to calculate and foreknow when an eclipse will take place, are an human invention. Man cannot invent any thing that is eternal and immutable; and the scientific principles he employs for this purpose must be, and are, of necessity, as eternal and immutable as the laws by which the heavenly bodies move, or they could not be used as they are to ascertain the time when, and the manner how, an eclipse will take place.

The scientific principles that man employs to obtain the foreknowledge of an eclipse, or of any thing else relating to the motion of the heavenly bodies, are contained chiefly in that part of science that is called trigonometry, or the properties of a triangle, which, when applied to the study of the heavenly bodies, is called astronomy; when applied to direct the course of a ship on the ocean, it is called navigation; when applied to the construction of figures drawn by a rule and compass, it is called geometry; when applied to the construction of plans of edifices, it is called architecture; when applied to the measurement of any portion of the surface of the earth, it is called land-surveying. In fine, it is the soul of science. It is an eternal truth: it contains the *mathematical demonstration* of which man speaks, and the extent of its uses are unknown.

It may be said, that man can make or draw a triangle, and therefore a triangle is an human invention.

But the triangle, when drawn, is no other than the image of the principle: it is a delineation to the eye, and from thence to the mind, of a principle that would otherwise be imperceptible. The triangle does not make the principle, any more than a candle taken into a room that was dark, makes the chairs and tables that before were invisible. All the properties of a triangle exist independently of the figure, and existed before any triangle was drawn or thought of by man. Man had no more to do in the formation of those properties or principles, than he had to do in making the laws by which the heavenly bodies move; and therefore the one must have the same divine origin as the other.

In the same manner as, it may be said, that man can make a triangle, so also, may it be said, he can make the mechanical instrument called a lever. But the principle by which the lever acts, is a thing distinct from the instrument, and would exist if the instrument did not; it attaches itself to the instrument after it is made; the instrument, therefore, can act no otherwise than it does act; neither can all the efforts of human invention make it act otherwise. That which, in all such cases, man calls the *effect*, is no other than the principle itself rendered perceptible to the senses.

Since, then, man cannot make principles, from whence did he gain a knowledge of them, so as to be able to apply them, not only to things on earth, but to ascertain the motion of bodies so immensely distant from him as all the heavenly bodies are? From whence, I ask, *could* he gain that knowledge, but from the study of the true theology?

It is the structure of the universe that has taught this knowledge to man. That structure is an ever-existing exhibition of every principle upon which every part of mathematical science is founded. The offspring of this science is mechanics; for mechanics is no other than the principles of science applied practically. The man who proportions the several parts of a mill uses the same scientific principles as if had the power of constructing an universe, but as he cannot give to matter that invisible agency by which all the component parts of the immense machine of the universe have influence upon each other, and act in motional unison together, without any apparent contact, and to which man has given the name of attraction, gravitation, and repulsion, he supplies the place of that agency by the humble imitation of teeth and cogs. All the parts of man's microcosm must visibly touch. But could he gain a knowledge of that agency, so as to be able to apply it in practice, we might then say that another *canonical book* of the word of God had been discovered. . . .

226   It is from the study of the true theology that all our knowledge of science is derived; and it is from that knowledge that all the arts have originated.

The Almighty lecturer, by displaying the principles of science in the structure of the universe, has invited man to study and to imitation. It is as if he had said to the inhabitants of this globe that we call ours, "I have made an earth for man to dwell upon, and I have rendered the starry heavens visible, to teach him science and the arts. He can now provide for his own comfort, AND LEARN FROM MY MUNIFICENCE TO ALL, TO BE KIND TO EACH OTHER."

Of what use is it, unless it be to teach man something, that his eye is endowed with the power of beholding, to an incomprehensible distance, an immensity of worlds revolving in the ocean of space? Or of what use is it that this immensity of worlds is visible to man? What has man to do with the Pleiades, with Orion, with Sirius, with the star he calls the north star, with the moving orbs he has named Saturn, Jupiter, Mars, Venus, and Mercury, if no uses are to follow from their being visible? A less power of vision would have been sufficient for man, if the immensity he now possesses were given only to waste itself, as it were, on an immense desert of space glittering with shows.

It is only by contemplating what he calls the starry heavens, as the book and school of science, that he discovers any use in their being visible to him, or any advantage resulting from his immensity of vision. But when he contemplates the subject in this light, he sees an additional motive for saying, that *nothing was made in vain*; for in vain would be this power of vision if it taught man nothing.

Of True Revelation; and of God

But some perhaps will say—Are we to have no word of God—no revelation? I answer yes. There is a Word of God; there is a revelation.

THE WORD OF GOD IS THE CREATION WE BEHOLD: And it is in *this word*, which no human invention can counterfeit or alter, that God speaketh universally to man. . . .

It is always necessary that the means that are to accomplish any end be equal to the accomplishment of that end, or the end cannot be accomplished. It is in this that the difference between finite and infinite power and wisdom discovers itself. Man frequently fails in accomplishing his end, from a natural inability of the power to the purpose; and frequently from the want of wisdom to apply power properly. But it is impossible for infinite power and wisdom to fail as man faileth. The means it useth are always equal to the end: but human language, more especially as there is not an universal language, is incapable of being used as an universal means of unchangeable and uniform information; and therefore it is not the means that God useth in manifesting himself universally to man.

It is only in the CREATION that all our ideas and conceptions of a *word of God* can unite. The Creation speaketh an universal language, independently of human speech or human language, multiplied and various as they be. It is an ever existing original, which every man can read. It cannot be forged; it cannot be counterfeited; it cannot be lost; it cannot be altered; it cannot be suppressed. It does not depend upon the will of man whether it shall be published or not; it publishes itself from one end of the earth to the other. It preaches to all nations and to all worlds; and this *word of God* reveals to man all that is necessary for man to know of God.

Do we want to contemplate his power? We see it in the immensity of the creation. Do we want to contemplate his wisdom? We see it in the unchangeable order by which the incomprehensible Whole is governed. Do we want to contemplate his munificence? We see it in the abundance with which he fills the earth. Do we want to contemplate his mercy? We see it in his not withholding that abundance even from the unthankful. In fine, do we want to know what God is? Search not the book called the scripture, which any human hand might make, but the scripture called the Creation.

The only idea man can affix to the name of God, is that of a *first cause*, the cause of all things. And, incomprehensibly difficult as it is for a man to conceive what a first cause is, he arrives at the belief of it, from the tenfold greater difficulty of disbelieving it. It is difficult beyond description to conceive that space can have no end; but it is more difficult to conceive an end. It is difficult beyond the power of man to conceive an eternal duration of what we call time; but it is more impossible to conceive a time when there shall be no time.

In like manner of reasoning, everything we behold carries in itself the internal evidence that it did not make itself. Every man is an evidence to himself, that he did not make himself; neither could his father make himself, nor his grandfather, nor any of his race; neither could any tree, plant, or animal make itself; and it is the conviction arising from this evidence, that carries us on, as it were, by necessity, to the belief of a first cause eternally existing, of a nature totally different to any material existence we know of, and by the power of which all things exist; and this first cause, man calls God.

It is only by the exercise of reason, that man can discover God. Take away that reason, and he would be incapable of understanding anything; and in this case it would be just as consistent to read even the book called the Bible to a horse as to a man. How then is it that those people pretend to reject reason?

Almost the only parts in the book called the Bible, that convey to us any idea of God, are some chapters in Job, and the 19th Psalm; I recollect no other. Those parts are true *deistical* compositions; for they treat of the *Deity* through his works. They take the book of Creation as the word of God; they refer to no other book; and all the inferences they make are drawn from that volume.

228   I insert in this place the 19th Psalm, as paraphrased into English verse by Addison. I recollect not the prose, and where I write this I have not the opportunity of seeing it:

> The spacious firmament on high,
> With all the blue ethereal sky,
> And spangled heavens, a shining frame,
> Their great original proclaim.
> The unwearied sun, from day to day,
> Does his Creator's power display,
> And publishes to every land
> The work of an Almighty hand.
> Soon as the evening shades prevail,
> The moon takes up the wondrous tale,
> And nightly to the list'ning earth
> Repeats the story of her birth;
> Whilst all the stars that round her burn,
> And all the planets, in their turn,
> Confirm the tidings as they roll,
> And spread the truth from pole to pole.
> What though in solemn silence all
> Move round this dark terrestrial ball;
> What though no real voice, nor sound,
> Amidst their radiant orbs be found,
> In reason's ear they all rejoice,
> And utter forth a glorious voice,
> Forever singing as they shine,
> THE HAND THAT MADE US IS DIVINE.

What more does man want to know, than that the hand or power that made these things is divine, is omnipotent? Let him believe this, with the force it is impossible to repel if he permits his reason to act, and his rule of moral life will follow of course.

The allusions in Job have all of them the same tendency with this Psalm; that of deducing or proving a truth that would be otherwise unknown, from truths already known.

I recollect not enough of the passages in Job to insert them correctly; but there is one that occurs to me that is applicable to the subject I am speaking upon. "Canst thou by searching find out God; canst thou find out the Almighty to perfection?"

I know not how the printers have pointed this passage, for I keep no Bible; but it contains two distinct questions that admit of distinct answers. First,

Canst thou by *searching* find out God? Yes. Because, in the first place, I know I did not make myself, and yet I have existence; and by *searching* into the nature of other things, I find that no other thing could make itself; and yet millions of other things exist; therefore it is, that I know, by positive conclusion resulting from this search, that there is a power superior to all those things, and that power is God.

Secondly, Canst thou find out the Almighty to *perfection?* No. Not only because the power and wisdom He has manifested in the structure of the Creation that I behold is to me incomprehensible; but because even this manifestation, great as it is, is probably but a small display of that immensity of power and wisdom, by which millions of other worlds, to me invisible by their distance, were created and continue to exist. . . .

Conclusion

Here we are. The existence of an Almighty power is sufficiently demonstrated to us, though we cannot conceive, as it is impossible we should, the nature and manner of its existence. We cannot conceive how we came here ourselves, and yet we know for a fact that we are here. We must know also, that the power that called us into being, can if he please, and when he pleases, call us to account for the manner in which we have lived here; and therefore, without seeking any other motive for the belief, it is rational to believe that he will, for we know beforehand that he can. The probability or even possibility of the thing is all that we ought to know; for if we knew it as a fact, we should be the mere slaves of terror; our belief would have no merit, and our best actions no virtue.

Deism then teaches us, without the possibility of being deceived, all that is necessary or proper to be known. The creation is the Bible of the deist. He there reads, in the hand-writing of the Creator himself, the certainty of his existence, and the immutability of his power; and all other Bibles and Testaments are to him forgeries. The probability that we may be called to account hereafter, will, to reflecting minds, have the influence of belief; for it is not our belief or disbelief that can make or unmake the fact. As this is the state we are in, and which it is proper we should be in, as free agents, it is the fool only, and not the philosopher, nor even the prudent man, that will live as if there were no God.

But the belief of a God is so weakened by being mixed with the strange fable of the Christian creed, and with the wild adventures related in the Bible, and the obscurity and obscene nonsense of the Testament, that the mind of man is bewildered as in a fog. Viewing all these things in a confused mass, he confounds fact with fable; and as he cannot believe all, he feels a disposition to reject all. But the belief of a God is a belief distinct from all other things, and ought not to be confounded with any. The notion of a Trinity of Gods has enfeebled the belief of *one* God. A multiplication of beliefs acts as a division of belief; and in proportion as anything is divided, it is weakened.

Religion, by such means, becomes a thing of form instead of fact; of notion instead of principle: morality is banished to make room for an imaginary thing called faith, and this faith has its origin in a supposed debauchery; a man is preached instead of a God; an execution is an object for gratitude; the preachers daub themselves with the blood, like a troop of assassins, and pretend to admire the brilliancy it gives them; they preach a humdrum sermon on the merits of the execution; then praise Jesus Christ for being executed, and condemn the Jews for doing it.

A man, by hearing all this nonsense lumped and preached together, confounds the God of the Creation with the imagined God of the Christians, and lives as if there were none.

Of all the systems of religion that ever were invented, there is none more derogatory to the Almighty, more unedifying to man, more repugnant to reason, and more contradictory in itself, than this thing called Christianity. Too absurd for belief, too impossible to convince, and too inconsistent for practice, it renders the heart torpid, or produces only atheists and fanatics. As an engine of power, it serves the purpose of despotism; and as a means of wealth, the avarice of priests; but so far as respects the good of man in general, it leads to nothing here or hereafter.

The only religion that has not been invented, and that has in it every evidence of divine originality, is pure and simple deism. It must have been the first and will probably be the last that man believes. But pure and simple deism does not answer the purpose of despotic governments. They cannot lay hold of religion as an engine but by mixing it with human inventions, and making their own authority a part; neither does it answer the avarice of priests, but by incorporating themselves and their functions with it, and becoming, like the government, a party in the system. It is this that forms the otherwise mysterious connection of church and state; the church human, and the state tyrannic.

Were a man impressed as fully and strongly as he ought to be with the belief of a God, his moral life would be regulated by the force of belief; he would stand in awe of God, and of himself, and would not do the thing that could not be concealed from either. To give this belief the full opportunity of force, it is necessary that it acts alone. This is deism.

But when, according to the Christian Trinitarian scheme, one part of God is represented by a dying man, and another part, called the Holy Ghost, by a flying pigeon, it is impossible that belief can attach itself to such wild conceits.

It has been the scheme of the Christian church, and of all the other invented systems of religion, to hold man in ignorance of the Creator, as it is of government to hold him in ignorance of his rights. The systems of the one are as false as those of the other, and are calculated for mutual support. The study of theology as it stands in Christian churches, is the study of nothing; it is founded on nothing; it rests on no principles; it proceeds by no authorities; it has no data; it can demonstrate nothing; and admits of no conclusion. Not any thing can be studied as a science without our being in possession of the principles upon which it is founded; and as this is not the case with Christian theology, it is therefore the study of nothing.

Instead then of studying theology, as is now done, out of the Bible and Testament, the meanings of which books are always controverted, and the authenticity of which is disproved, it is necessary that we refer to the Bible of the creation. The principles we discover there are eternal, and of divine origin: they are the foundation of all the science that exists in the world, and must be the foundation of theology.

We can know God only through his works. We cannot have a conception of any one attribute, but by following some principle that leads to it. We have only a confused idea of his power, if we have not the means of comprehending something of its immensity. We can have no idea of his wisdom, but by knowing the order and manner in which it acts. The principles of science lead to this knowledge; for the Creator of man is the Creator of science, and it is through that medium that man can see God, as it were, face to face.

Could a man be placed in a situation, and endowed with power of vision to behold at one view, and to contemplate deliberately, the structure of the universe, to mark the movements of the several planets, the cause of their varying appearances, the unerring order in which they revolve, even to the remotest comet, their connection and dependence on each other, and to know the system of laws established by the Creator, that governs and regulates the whole; he would then conceive, far beyond what any church theology can teach him, the power, the wisdom, the vastness, the munificence of the Creator. He would then see that all the knowledge man has of science, and that all the mechanical arts by which he renders his situation comfortable here, are derived from that source: his mind, exalted by the scene, and convinced by the fact, would increase in gratitude as it increased in knowledge: his religion or his worship would become united with his improvement as a man: any employment he followed that had connection with the principles of the creation,—as everything of agriculture, of science, and of the mechanical arts, has,—would teach him more of God, and of the gratitude he owes to him, than any theological Christian sermon he now hears. Great objects inspire great thoughts; great munificence excites great gratitude; but the grovelling tales and doctrines of the Bible and the Testament are fit only to excite contempt.

Though man cannot arrive, at least in this life, at the actual scene I have described, he can demonstrate it, because he has knowledge of the principles upon which the creation is constructed. We know that the greatest works can be represented in model, and that the universe can be represented by the same means. The same principles by which we measure an inch or an acre of ground will measure to millions in extent. A circle of an inch diameter has the same geometrical properties as a circle that would circumscribe the universe. The same properties of a triangle that will demonstrate upon paper the course of a ship, will do it on the ocean; and, when applied to what are called the heavenly bodies, will ascertain to a minute the time of an eclipse, though those bodies are millions of miles distant from us. This knowledge is of divine origin; and it is from the Bible of the creation that man has learned it, and not from the stupid Bible of the church, that teaches man nothing.

All the knowledge man has of science and of machinery, by the aid of which his existence is rendered comfortable upon earth, and without which he would be scarcely distinguishable in appearance and condition from a common animal, comes from the great machine and structure of the universe. The constant and unwearied observations of our ancestors upon the movements and revolutions of the heavenly bodies, in what are supposed to have been the early ages of the world, have brought this knowledge upon earth. It is not Moses and the prophets, nor Jesus Christ, nor his apostles, that have done it. The Almighty is the great mechanic of the creation, the first philosopher, and original teacher of all science. Let us then learn to reverence our master, and not forget the labours of our ancestors. . . .

The Existence of God

Religion has two principal enemies, fanaticism and infidelity, or that which is called atheism. The first requires to be combated by reason and morality, the other by natural philosophy.

The existence of a God is the first dogma of the Theophilanthropists. It is upon this subject that I solicit your attention; for though it has been often treated of, and that most sublimely, the subject is inexhaustible; and there will always remain something to be said that has not been before advanced. I go therefore to open the subject, and to crave your attention to the end.

The universe is the bible of a true Theophilanthropist. It is there that he reads of God. It is there that the proofs of His existence are to be sought and to be found. As to written or printed books, by whatever name they are called, they are the works of man's hands, and carry no evidence in themselves that god is the Author of any of them. It must be in something that man could not make that we must seek evidence for our belief, and that something is the universe, the true Bible—the inimitable work of god.

Contemplating the universe, the whole system of Creation, in this point of light, we shall discover, that all that which is called natural philosophy is properly a divine study. It is the study of God through His works. It is the best study, by which we can arrive at a knowledge of His existence, and the only one by which we can gain a glimpse of His perfection.

Do we want to contemplate His power? We see it in the immensity of the creation. Do we want to contemplate His wisdom? We see it in the unchangeable order by which the incomprehensible WHOLE is governed. Do we want to contemplate His munificence? We see it in the abundance with which he fills the earth. Do we want to contemplate His mercy? We see it in His not withholding that abundance even from the unthankful. In fine, do we want to know what GOD is? Search not written or printed books, but the Scripture called the *creation.*

It has been the error of the schools to teach astronomy and all the other sciences and subjects of natural philosophy as accomplishments only; whereas they should be taught theologically, or with reference to the *Being* who is the Author of them: for all the principles of science are of divine origin. Man cannot make, or invent, or contrive principles; he can only discover them, and he ought to look through the discovery to the Author.

When we examine an extraordinary piece of machinery, an astonishing pile of architecture, a well executed statue, or a highly finished painting where life and action are imitated, and habit only prevents our mistaking a surface of light and shade for cubical solidity, our ideas are naturally led to think of the extensive genius and talents of the artist.

When we study the elements of geometry, we think of Euclid. When we speak of gravitation, we think of Newton. How then is it that when we study the works of God in the creation we stop short, and do not think of GOD? It is from the error of the schools in having taught those subjects as accomplishments only, and thereby separated the study of them from the *Being* who is the Author of them.

The schools have made the study of theology to consist in the study of opinions in written or printed books; whereas theology should be studied in the works or books of the Creation. The study of theology in books of opinions has often produced fanaticism, rancor and cruelty of temper; and from hence have proceeded the numerous persecutions, the fanatical quarrels, the religious burnings and massacres, that have desolated Europe.

But the study of theology in the works of the creation produces a direct contrary effect. The mind becomes at once enlightened and serene, a copy of the scene it beholds: information and adoration go hand in hand; and all the social faculties become enlarged.

The evil that has resulted from the error of the schools in teaching natural philosophy as an accomplishment only has been that of generating in the pupils a species of atheism. Instead of looking through the works of creation to the Creator himself, they stop short and employ the knowledge they acquire to create doubts of His existence. They labor with studied ingenuity to ascribe everything they behold to innate properties of matter, and jump over all the rest by saying that matter is eternal.

Let us examine this subject; it is worth examining; for if we examine it through all its cases, the result will be that the existence of a SUPERIOR CAUSE, or that which man calls GOD, will be discoverable by philosophical principles.

In the first place, admitting matter to have properties, as we see it has, the question still remains, how came matter by those properties? To this they will answer that matter possessed those properties eternally. This is not solution, but assertion; and to deny it is equally as impossible of proof as to assert it. It is then necessary to go further; and therefore I say—if there exist a circumstance that is *not* a property of matter, and without which the universe, or to speak in a limited degree, the solar system composed of planets and a sun, could not exist a moment, all the arguments of atheism, drawn from properties of matter, and applied to account for the universe, will be overthrown, and the existence of a superior cause, or that which man calls God, becomes discoverable, as is before said, by natural philosophy.

I go now to show that such a circumstance exists, and what it is.

The universe is composed of matter, and, as a system, is sustained by motion. Motion is *not a property* of matter, and without this motion, the solar system could not exist. Were motion a property of matter, that undiscovered and undiscoverable thing called perpetual motion would establish itself. It is because motion is not a property of matter, that perpetual motion is an impossibility in the hand of every being but that of the Creator of motion. When the pretenders to atheism can produce perpetual motion, and not till then, they may expect to be credited.

The natural state of matter, as to place, is a state of rest. Motion, or change of place, is the effect of an external cause acting upon matter. As to that faculty of matter that is called gravitation, it is the influence which two or more bodies have reciprocally on each other to unite and be at rest. Everything which has hitherto been discovered, with respect to the motion of the planets in the system, relates only to the laws by which motion acts, and not to the cause of motion. Gravitation, so far from being the cause of motion to the planets that compose the solar system, would be the destruction of the solar system were revolutionary motion to cease; for as the action of spinning upholds a top, the revolutionary motion upholds the planets in their orbits, and prevents them from gravitating and forming one mass with the sun. In one sense of the word, philosophy knows, and atheism says, that matter is in perpetual motion. But the motion here meant refers to the *state* of matter, and that only on the surface of the earth. It is either decomposition, which is continually destroying the form of bodies of matter, or recomposition, which renews that matter in the same or another form, as the decomposition of animal or vegetable substances enters into the composition of other bodies. But the motion that upholds the solar system is of an entire different kind, and is not a property of matter. It operates also to an entire different effect. It operates to *perpetual* *preservation*, and to prevent *any change* in the state of the system.

Giving then to matter all the properties which philosophy knows it has, or all that atheism ascribes to it, and can prove, and even supposing matter to be eternal, it will not account for the system of the universe, or of the solar system, because it will not account for motion, and it is motion that preserves it. When, therefore, we discover a circumstance of such immense importance that without it the universe could not exist, and for which neither matter, nor any nor all the properties can account, we are by necessity forced into the rational conformable belief of the existence of a cause superior to matter, and that cause man calls GOD.

As to that which is called nature, it is no other than the laws by which motion and action of every kind, with respect to unintelligible matter, are regulated. And when we speak of looking through nature up to nature's God, we speak philosophically the same rational language as when we speak of looking through human laws up to the Power that ordained them.

God is the power of the first cause, nature is the law, and matter is the subject acted upon.

But infidelity, by ascribing every phenomenon to properties of matter, conceives a system for which it cannot account, and yet it pretends to demonstration. It reasons from what it sees on the surface of the earth, but it does not carry itself on the solar system existing by motion. It sees upon the surface a perpetual decomposition and recomposition of matter. It sees that an oak produces an acorn, an acorn an oak, a bird an egg, an egg a bird, and so on. In things of this kind it sees something which it calls a natural cause, but none of the causes it sees is the cause of that motion which preserves the solar system.

Let us contemplate this wonderful and stupendous system consisting of matter, and existing by motion. It is not matter in a state of rest, nor in a state of decomposition or recomposition. It is matter systematized in perpetual orbicular or circular motion. As a system that motion is the life of it: as animation is life to an animal body, deprive the system of motion and, as a system, it must expire. Who then breathed into the system the life of motion? What power impelled the planets to move, since motion is not a property of the matter of which they are composed? If we contemplate the immense velocity of this motion, our wonder becomes increased, and our adoration enlarges itself in the same proportion. To instance only one of the planets, that of the earth we inhabit, its distance from the sun, the center of the orbits of all the planets, is, according to observations of the transit of the planet Venus, about one hundred million miles; consequently, the diameter of the orbit, or circle in which the earth moves round the sun, is double that distance; and the measure of the circumference of the orbit, taken as three times its diameter, is six hundred million miles. The earth performs this voyage in three hundred and sixty-five days and some hours, and consequently moves at the rate of more than one million six hundred thousand miles every twenty-four hours.

Where will infidelity, where will atheism, find cause for this astonishing velocity of motion, never ceasing, never varying, and which is the preservation of the earth in its orbit? It is not by reasoning from an acorn to an oak, from an egg to a bird, or from any change in the state of matter on the surface of the earth, that this can be accounted for. Its cause is not to be found in matter, nor in anything we call nature. The atheist who affects to reason, and the fanatic who rejects reason, plunge themselves alike into inextricable difficulties. The one perverts the sublime and enlightening study of natural philosophy into a deformity of absurdities by not reasoning to the end. The other loses himself in the obscurity of metaphysical theories, and dishonors the Creator by treating the study of His works with contempt. The one is a half-rational of whom there is some hope, the other a visionary to whom we must be charitable.

When at first thought we think of a Creator, our ideas appear to us undefined and confused; but if we reason philosophically, those ideas can be easily arranged and simplified. *It is a Being whose power is equal to His will.*

Observe the nature of the will of man. It is of an infinite quality. We cannot conceive the possibility of limits to the will. Observe, on the other hand, how exceedingly limited is his power of acting compared with the nature of his will. Suppose the power equal to the will, and man would be a God. He would will a creation, and could make it. In this progressive reasoning, we see in the nature of the will of man half of that which we conceive in thinking of God; add the other half, and we have the whole idea of a Being who could make the universe, and sustain it by perpetual motion; because He could create that motion.

We know nothing of the capacity of the will of animals, but we know a great deal of the difference of their powers. For example, how numerous are the degrees, and how immense is the difference of power, from a mite to a man. Since then everything we see below us shows a progression of power, where is the difficulty in supposing that there is, at the *summit of all things*, a Being in whom an infinity of power unites with the infinity of the will? When this simple idea presents itself to our mind, we have the idea of a perfect Being that man calls God.

It is comfortable to live under the belief of the existence of an infinite protecting power; and it is an addition to that comfort to know that such a belief is not a mere conceit of the imagination, as many of the theories that are called religious are; nor a belief founded only on tradition or received opinion; but is a belief deducible by the action of reason upon the things that compose the system of the universe; a belief arising out of visible facts. So demonstrable is the truth of this belief that if no such belief had existed, the persons who now controvert it would have been the persons who would have produced and propagated it; because by beginning to reason they would have been led to reason progressively to the end, and thereby have discovered that matter and the properties it has will not account for the system of the universe, and that there must necessarily be a superior cause.

It was the excess to which imaginary systems of religion had been carried, and the intolerance, persecutions, burnings and massacres they occasioned, that first induced certain persons to propagate infidelity; thinking, that upon the whole it was better not to believe at all than to believe a multitude of things and complicated creeds that occasioned so much mischief in the world. But those days are past, persecution has ceased, and the antidote then set up against it has no longer even the shadow of apology. We profess, and we proclaim in peace, the pure, unmixed, comfortable and rational belief of a God as manifested to us in the universe. We do this without any apprehension of that belief being made a cause of persecution as other beliefs have been, or of suffering persecution ourselves. To God, and not to man, are all men to account for their belief.

It has been well observed, at the first institution of this Society, that the dogmas it professes to believe are from the commencement of the world; that they are not novelties, but are confessedly the basis of all systems of religion, however numerous and contradictory they may be. All men in the outset of the religion they profess are Theophilanthropists. It is impossible to form any system of religion without building upon those principles, and therefore they are not sectarian principles, unless we suppose a sect composed of all the world.

I have said in the course of this discourse that the study of natural philosophy is a divine study, because it is the study of the works of God in the creation. If we consider theology upon this ground, what an extensive field of improvement in things both divine and human opens itself before us! All the principles of science are of divine origin. It was not man that invented the principles on which astronomy, and every branch of mathematics, are founded and studied. It was not man that gave properties to the circle and the triangle. Those principles are eternal and immutable. We see in them the unchangeable nature of the Divinity. We see in them immortality, an immortality existing after the material figures that express those properties are dissolved in dust.

The Society is at present in its infancy, and its means are small; but I wish to hold in view the subject I allude to, and instead of teaching the philosophical branches of learning as ornamental accomplishments only, as they have hitherto been taught, to teach them in a manner that shall combine theological knowledge with scientific instruction. To do this to the best advantage some instruments will be necessary, for the purpose of explanation, of which the Society is not yet possessed. But as the views of this Society extend to public good as well as to that of the individual, and as its principles can have no enemies, means may be devised to procure them.

If we unite to the present instruction a series of lectures on the ground I have mentioned, we shall, in the first place, render theology the most delightful and entertaining of all studies. In the next place we shall give scientific instruction to those who could not otherwise obtain it. The mechanic of every profession will there be taught the mathematical principles necessary to render him a proficient in his art; the cultivator will there see developed the principles of vegetation; while, at the same time, they will be led to see the hand of God in all these things.

My Private Thoughts on a Future State

I have said in the first part of *The Age of Reason*, that "*I hope for happiness after this life.*" This hope is comfortable to me, and I presume not to go beyond the comfortable idea of hope, with respect to a future state.

I consider myself in the hands of my Creator, and that He will dispose of me after this life consistently with His justice and goodness. I leave all these matters to Him, as my Creator and friend, and I hold it to be presumption in man to make an article of faith as to what the Creator will do with us hereafter. I do not believe because a man and a woman make a child that it imposes on the Creator the unavoidable obligation of keeping the being so made in eternal existence hereafter. It is in His power to do so, or not to do so, and it is not in our power to decide which He will do.

The book called the New Testament, which I hold to be fabulous and have shown to be false, gives an account in Matthew XXV of what is there called the last day, or the day of judgment.

The whole world, according to that account, is divided into two parts, the righteous and the unrighteous, figuratively called the sheep and the goats. They are then to receive their sentence. To the one, figuratively called the sheep, it says, "*Come ye blessed of my Father, inherit the kingdom prepared for you from the foundation of the world.*" To the other, figuratively called the goats, it says, "*Depart from me, ye cursed, into everlasting fire, prepared for the devil and his angels.*"

Now the case is, the world cannot be thus divided: the moral world, like the physical world, is composed of numerous degrees of character, running imperceptibly one into the other, in such a manner that no fixed point of division can be found in either. That point is nowhere, or is everywhere.

The whole world might be divided into two parts numerically, but not as to moral character; and therefore the metaphor of dividing them, as sheep and goats can be divided, whose difference is marked by their external figure, is absurd. All sheep are still sheep; all goats are still goats; it is their physical nature to be so. But one part of the world are not all good alike, nor the other part all wicked alike. There are some exceedingly good; others exceedingly wicked.

There is another description of men who cannot be ranked with either the one or the other—they belong neither to the sheep nor the goats; and there is still another description of them who are so very insignificant, both in character and conduct, as not to be worth the trouble of damning or saving, or of raising from the dead.

My own opinion is, that those whose lives have been spent in doing good, and endeavoring to make their fellow-mortals happy, for this is the only way in which we can serve God, *will be happy hereafter*; and that the very wicked will meet with some punishment. But those who are neither good nor bad, or are too insignificant for notice, will be dropped entirely.

That is my opinion. It is consistent with my idea of God's justice, and with the reason that God has given me, and I gratefully know that He has given me a large share of that divine gift.

Elihu Palmer

Reason, the Glory of Our Nature

Although nearly forgotten today, Elihu Palmer (1764–1806) is unquestionably the chief of American deists. Almost single-handedly, Palmer metamorphosed Enlightenment deism into a popular movement that rocked the Early Republic's religious and moral sensibilities in the opening years of the nineteenth century. He imbued it with a strident militancy it hitherto had lacked by extending its standard criticisms of ecclesial hegemony to denunciations of political and social oppression, arguing that the "double despotism" of church and state were twin obstacles to the improvement of the race. He insisted that a rational investigation of the laws of nature disclosed the basis of ethical principles as well as religious ones and that both condemned the subjugation of women, the enslavement of peoples of color, and the coercion of conscience. Using the lecture circuit and the printed word, he spread his message with an eloquence and intellectual sophistication that forced even his most intractable opponents to take him seriously. He was, in short, not only the leading deist and social activist of his day but was one of the Early Republic's finest thinkers. After him, neither popular religion nor theological discourse in the United States would be quite the same.

The son of a Connecticut farmer, Palmer was educated at Dartmouth College and ordained in the Presbyterian tradition. After losing at least two pulpits because of his increasingly liberal interpretations of Christian doctrine, he relocated to Philadelphia in 1791 and joined the newly founded Universal Society, an organization espousing a rather confused mixture of liberal Christianity and deism. Palmer's association with the society was brief. After attempting under its auspices to deliver a discourse against the divinity of Jesus, he was run out of town by an outraged mob. He retreated with his wife and children to western Pennsylvania, where he read law with a brother and was admitted to the bar.

In the spring of 1793 Palmer forsook the wilderness and returned to Philadelphia to establish himself in law. Although there is no record, it is unlikely that the city's inhabitants had forgotten or forgiven his earlier apostasy enough for him to have picked up much business as an attorney. To make matters worse, Palmer refused to retreat from his radical religious views. During a Fourth of July oration at Federal Point, he took the opportunity to repeatedly denounce "priestcraft" as an enemy to "reason and liberty," which only reinforced orthodox Philadelphia's dismissal of him as a godless and dangerous infidel.

But a worse fate than the calumny of his fellow citizens soon befell Palmer. One month after his Federal Point oration, the great yellow fever epidemic of 1793 swept through the city. Both Palmer and his wife fell ill. She died, while Palmer was left permanently and totally blind. Many Philadelphians sanctimoniously saw Palmer's affliction as divine retribution. Benjamin Rush less piously suggested that Palmer lost his sight because he had refused to be bled during his illness. In any case, blindness spelled an end to his legal career, and Palmer knew it. Upon his recovery, he embarked on his final calling: He became a freelance deistical preacher.

In the thirteen years remaining to him, Palmer tirelessly stumped the eastern seaboard, spreading the deistic message. After spending some time in Georgia immediately after his recovery, he made his way north, where he helped found the Deistical Society of New York in late 1795 and drafted the organization's statement of principles. New York City henceforth became his base of operations. From there, he helped organize deistical societies in other states, dictated scores of journal articles and pamphlets, and periodically traveled to Baltimore, Newburgh, Philadelphia, and other cities to deliver his increasingly popular lectures against the "double despotism" of religious bigotry and political oppression. He helped found and later assumed editorship of *The Temple of Reason*, the first major deistic newspaper in the Early Republic. When *The Temple* ceased publication in 1803, he replaced it with the *Prospect*, a weekly that ran for two years and was almost solely written by Palmer himself. At his death in 1806 (which occurred, characteristically, while he was on a lecture tour), Palmer was the best known—and hated—deist of his time.

Despite both his blindness and his crushing schedule, Palmer somehow found the time and energy to compose one of the Early Republic's philosophical classics: *Principles of Nature; or, A Development of the Moral Causes of Happiness and Misery among the Human Species* (1801). The book is a distillation and refinement of the hundreds of speeches, tracts, and newspaper articles Palmer had produced in earlier years. Its primary purpose was to argue for a naturalistic ethics based on the notions of "reciprocal justice" and "universal benevolence," but it was much more than just a treatise on ethics. It was also a textbook of militant deism, providing a complete critique of Christianity's supernaturalistic assumptions as well as a thorough explanation of deism's naturalistic ones. The book was an immediate success, notwithstanding its occasional stylistic clumsiness (partly attributable, no doubt, to the fact that it had been dictated), and ran through three editions in Palmer's lifetime. Its chief merit was that it defended deism in an accessible yet rigorous manner. It avoided conceptual intricacies and technical jargon, which might baffle popular audiences, without eschewing logical argumentation and demonstration. It

242   was the only Early Republic treatise on deism that was more philosophical than polemical. It was also the first philosophical work of the new nation to enjoy such widespread popularity.

In the selections here from *Principles of Nature*, the standard by which Palmer both criticizes Christianity and advocates deism and naturalistic ethics is reason—"righteous and immortal reason," "the glory of our nature." For Palmer as for most Enlightenment thinkers, the definitive characteristic of the human species is its ability to dispassionately collect and appraise empirical evidence and then logically infer generalizations from it. If used correctly, this rational faculty is capable of exploring the natural realm, promoting social utility, enhancing individual felicity, and ensuring progress. If retarded through bigotry, superstition, or ignorance, it mutates to the point where it can be invoked as a justification for spiritual and political oppression. Palmer's entire career as a deist was devoted to encouraging his listeners to employ their reason freely and courageously and to distrust authority, whether theological or political. His *Principles* is just such a judicious exercise, as it demonstrates what he takes to be the absurdities of revealed religion, and then elucidates the normative and conceptual superiority of the religion of nature.

Palmer's case against Christianity attacks on two fronts. First, he dismisses it on logical grounds. The doctrine of eternal damnation is absurd, because it treats what by definition must be finite acts on the part of humans as if they were infinitely deserving of punishment. The doctrine of miracles violates the uniformity, consistency, and perfection of nature, thereby establishing religion "upon the ruin of the consistent harmony of the divine perfection; upon the ruin of all principle and all confidence." It is an "affront to the character" of the deity because it implies that God plays a catch-up game with creation, seeking to redress past errors or oversights through miraculous intervention. But such an assumption does violence to the divine attributes of wisdom, power, and goodness. Finally, Palmer rejects the doctrine of scriptural revelation as likewise inchoate. Following Paine's lead in *The Age of Reason*, Palmer argues that revelation can only be direct communication from God to a specific individual. As such, even though the revealed message or commandment may be binding to its immediate recipient, it can scarcely be so to others to whom the recipient relays it. At that point, it is mere hearsay and properly subject to the same doubts that any rational person has about all secondhand information.

Next, Palmer rejects Christianity because of what he sees as the immorality of its tenets. For Palmer, "all morality that is genuine, is drawn from the nature and condition of rational beings." Reason tells us, for example, that the virtuous person is one who acts consistently, who takes responsibility for his or her actions, and who refuses to punish innocents. But Christian dogma violates each of these premises. Scripture defends an ethical double standard, in which

God performs with impunity actions that would be condemned if performed by a human. The doctrine of original sin suggests that vices and virtues are transferable from one person to another, thereby eroding personal responsibility. Moreover, the doctrines of grace and rejuvenation imply that human virtue is insufficient for either individual felicity or morality, thus depriving humans of liberty as well as dignity. The atonement makes a virtue out of savagely punishing a blameless person—a futile attempt to eradicate evil with evil that violates common intuitions about distributive justice. In short, given the irrational basis of its moral prescriptions, Christianity twists the God of nature into an "arbitrary and malevolent tyrant," unworthy of either veneration or respect. Although certain isolated moral maxims in Christianity are admittedly praiseworthy, Palmer denies they are uniquely Christian in origin since they were defended earlier by pagan philosophers. It is not enough for a religious system to contain a few noble principles. It must provide a "*system* of genuine morality," based on reason, benevolence, and consistency. This Christianity utterly fails to do.

Palmer's alternative to Christianity, as expressed here in the selections "The Religion of Nature" and "Principles of the Deistical Society of the State of New York," is typically deistic. God is described as the First Cause, immutable and good, who sets in motion equally immutable laws of nature. But in his reflections on the basis of moral principle in *Principles of Nature*, Palmer breaks new ground, for no other deist in the American tradition so systematically applied the Enlightenment's naturalistic orientation to ethical theory.

For Palmer, "moral principles," or the foundations of ethics, must be based on "the physical constitution of human nature." Evil and virtue are the products of human actions, not the mysterious interventions of a god or a devil. In fact, Palmer goes so far as to say that morality does not depend on the existence of the deity. Instead, it is "founded in the nature of man" and "rests upon the relations and the properties of human life." In accepting this naturalistic premise as his starting point, Palmer obviously parts company with the traditional Christian ethical theory of divine command, which argues that an action is only virtuous or wicked insofar as it is commanded or forbidden by God.

But what are the relations and properties of human life from which ethical principles can be inferred? Sensation, answers Palmer, the physical capacity of experiencing pain and pleasure. It is obvious that the former is destructive of human well-being, while the latter is promotive of it. Reason dictates that the sensible person, then, will act in such a way as to maximize his or her chances for pleasure and minimize the possibility of pain. But the rational person also recognizes that his or her actions toward others are reciprocated in kind. Consequently, prudential self-interest demands that the individual behave toward others in such a way as to encourage reactions on their parts beneficial to his or her well-being. Otherwise, human existence is reduced to a condition of pain and vicious competition very much reminiscent of Thomas Hobbes's state of nature.

This analysis of the physical basis of well-being gives rise to Palmer's two primary ethical principles: "universal benevolence" and "reciprocal justice." The first argues that the actions of sensitive, communal creatures always result in "perpetual reprisals." Consequently, self-interest dictates that the most reasonable mode of behavior is one of benevolence to all of sentient creation. The second argues that since all sentient creatures are equally capable of experiencing deleterious pain or promotive pleasure, each has an equal right to avoid the one and nurture the other. This suggests that all humans have an obligation to treat others as they themselves would rationally desire to be treated.

Clearly Palmer's naturalistic ethics has affinities with other ethical models of his day. The similarity to Hobbes has already been noted, and there are also parallels with the moral theories of James Stewart (1749–1822) and Volney. But, as mentioned previously, Palmer's naturalistic ethical theory, despite its partially derivative character, is the only attempt by an American deist to extend Enlightenment naturalism to its logical normative conclusion. Given deism's emphasis on the primacy of virtue, this is no small accomplishment.

Principles of Nature; or, A Development of the Moral Causes of Happiness and Misery among the Human Species

Critique of Christianity

Ignorance and Christianity

Believers in the Christian system of religion, are seldom aware of the difficulties into which their theological theories have plunged them. They are in habits of bestowing on this religion the most unqualified applause, and in most cases, no doubt, the most sincere approbation; but the errors and absurdities, the immorality and the incorrectness of principle, have never made any serious impression upon their minds. The dreadful idea of opposing that which has been called divine, strikes with terror the uninstructed mind, and ignorance feeds the ecclesiastical deception. Ignorance is an excellent friend to an ancient system of error, to the church and the different projects by which mankind have been enslaved. If you can once persuade a man, that he is totally ignorant of the subject on which you are about to discourse, you can make him believe any thing. Impositions of this kind are furnished by every days experience; and the victim of such imposition, is commonly the first to applaud the instrument of his ruin.

Nothing can be more true, nothing more certain, or important, than that man owes to himself due respect, that his intellect is an object of veneration, and its result interwoven with the best interest of human society. The distorted exhibitions of imaginary beings contained in all ancient theology, ought to excite within us a strong desire to discover truth, and reclaim the dignity which nature gave to man. Fanaticism, when armed with the artillery of Heaven, ought not to be permitted to shake the throne or empire of reason; the base is immortal, and the superstructure will be augmented in beauty and excellence, in proportion to the progress of knowledge and the destruction of religious bigotry. It is remarkable that, with many honest minds, the consciousness of intellectual independence has never been realized, and fear has prevented the activity of thought and the development of truth.

Sacred Scripture and Revelation

The Christian religion is compound and combination of all the theological writings of the followers of Moses and Jesus. We have no evidence that either of these men wrote any part, either of the Old or New Testament. From Genesis to the Apocalypse of St. John, a vast variety of fact, fable, principle, wickedness, and error is exhibited to view. The book, though bound together, appears to be in many respects discordant; the historical part has no accurate connection; the moral part is distorted, deficient, or wicked; the doctrinal parts are either unintelligible, or contrary to moral and philosophical truth. These positions shall be proved in the course of the examination of these sacred writings; it is sufficient for the present that the consideration which relates to the origin and nature of such productions, should form the basis of our inquiry. It is because man has forgotten the dignity of his nature; it is because he does not realize the force of his faculties, that he consents to yield to the impositions of superstition. What is a book, whether it be denominated sacred or not, unless the human mind is capable of discovering the evidence by which the truth of such book can be substantiated? The Bible, which means nothing more than a book; the scriptures of the Old and New Testaments, which mean nothing more than the heterogeneous writings contained in the former, and the incoherent and unintelligible will of various beings contained in the latter; what are all these to the correct decisions of human intellect, unless the matter therein contained can be collated with the immortal principles of truth in the system of nature. . . .

If the sentiments and the doctrines be consistent with the nature of things, [one] may, on this account, pronounce them true; but they are true because they are consistent, and not because they have been revealed. . . . But . . . this book is said to be given by divine inspiration; but is it possible that inspiration can be either transferred, translated, altered, or revised? Certainly the very nature of the thing forbids it. If the scriptures be given by divine inspiration, their contents must be communicated to certain individuals by supernatural power. These individuals had no such power to transfer to other individuals with the same force of authority, the celestial information which they had received. If it were binding on the first persons who received it, it could not be equally so upon the second, for the nature and force of the communication were essentially destroyed. The first power that communicated was divine, the second was human; the first was incapable of error, the second deceptive and fallacious. If it were therefore to be admitted that any human beings were ever inspired, it would not follow that the result of that inspiration could be communicated with certitude or divine authority to any other minds. The idea of transferring celestial information received by supernatural means, is absurd and impossible; it is as impossible as that man could become a God, and exercise the attributes of the Divinity. The idea of translating a supernatural system of religion, is equally incorrect. The readers of such a system, even in the original languages, could not know that the things therein contained were inspired by God himself, if those few be accepted who were supposed to be the recipients of such sacred instruction; much less could the reader in subsequent ages be assured of the truth or validity of such translated doctrines. To render this system correct, and keep up the chain of divine connection, it is not only necessary that the first prophets and apostles should have been inspired, but that all the translators, transcribers, printers, and printers' boys, should have been inspired also. In deficiency of such arrangement, the Christian believer at the present day, must be uncertain whether he believes in holy writ, or the imaginary conceptions and wild reveries of the human understanding. If inspiration be a thing founded in truth, there can be no occasion to alter or revise it. It is defect alone that creates the necessity of alteration and revision. If, therefore, the Bible was right at first, every alteration is a deviation from that rectitude; and consequently, in proportion as the scriptures have been altered and revised in modern times, the Christian believer has been led astray; he has not believed in the real and true word of God. If the scriptures were wrong at first, the faith of the primitive Christian, was nothing more than a delusive error; in either of these cases we are thrown into a dilemma, from which, clerical ingenuity alone will be able to extricate us. . . .

Original Sin, Atonement and Faith

We shall now proceed to an examination of the doctrines of the Christian religion, and compare them with the principles of a genuine and natural morality, the nature and character of man, and the perfections of the intelligent Creator of the universe. If the founder of this religion was destitute of authority in his mission, the doctrines which are applicable to him will fall of course; but so strong are the prejudices of mankind in favour of these doctrines, that it becomes necessary to expose the immorality of them before we can expect that they will be relinquished. The most important doctrines of this supposed celestial scheme, are those of original sin, atonement, faith. . . . This strange and unnatural system, called the Christian religion, commences the development of its dogmas, by the destruction of every principle of distributive justice. It makes the intelligent beings who are now in existence accountable for the errors and vices of a man who lived six thousand years ago; a man who, its advocates say, God created upright, free from every kind of impurity, and placed in a state of uniform happiness, with a strong natural propensity to the practice of every virtue, and an equally strong aversion to every vicious and immoral principle; created in the image of God himself, and possessing an unqualified attachment to celestial purity and goodness. This man, nevertheless, transgressed the divine law, and this solitary violation becomes temporarily and eternally fatal to the human race. Moral impurity assumes a new shape, and becomes transferable through successive generations. Though none of this man's descendants could possibly be partakers of this original criminality, they are, nevertheless, implicated in the consequences and effects of his primary apostasy. *They sinned with him, and fell with him, in his first transgression.* This is the language of pious and learned divines, and of the rectitude of the principle, we are not permitted to doubt, under pain of eternal damnation. But truth compels us to assert, that this doctrine, called original sin, is, in the first place, totally impossible, and in the second place, that it is as immoral and unjust, as the Creator is righteous and benevolent. The virtues and the vices of intelligent beings are not of a transferable but of a personal nature. In a moral point of view, the amiable or useful qualities of one man cannot become those of another, neither can the vices of one be justifiably punished in the person of another. Every man is accountable for himself; and when he can take no cognizance of the intentions or actions of any other man, how can he be justly responsible for their injurious effects, or applauded for any benefits resulting from them? If Adam or any other man, who lived several thousand years ago, was guilty of any immoral conduct, what has that to do with the moral condition of the present generation? Is a man to become criminal before he has existed? or, is he to be criminated afterwards, by the immoral conduct of those who lived long before him? Has not every man errors enough of his own to answer for, without being implicated in the injurious consequences resulting from the bad conduct of his neighbour? Shall there be no line of moral precision, by which human beings can be tried, condemned, or acquitted? It seems by the general tenor of this doctrine, that every rule of moral precision is here totally disregarded, and setting aside the want of justice, the whole business wears a farcical and ludicrous appearance. This original evil so destructive to the human race, commences by the eating of what is called the forbidden fruit. Whether this fruit was an apple, a peach, or an orange, is not material for us to know; if it was either the one or the other of these, and the truth was good, there could be no harm in eating it, and if bad, let him take the consequence whose ignorance or temerity induced the action. But whether good or bad, whether eaten or not eaten, is nothing for us, and we are neither worse nor better for reading this foolish story. The moral impurity of the heart can bear no possible relation to the criminality of Adam, or any other man of that day or generation. Let Adam, therefore, and his partner Eve, together with the Devil and his snakes, attend to their own concerns, and if they have fallen into difficulties by their own follies and vices, let them extricate themselves as well as they are able. For myself, I have so much regard for all of them, that I hope they will not be damned forever. For notwithstanding much noise and clamour has been raised, I think that neither party was so bad as the pious ambassadors of Heaven have represented them. The story is almost too foolish to deserve a serious examination. Let intelligent man study his own nature, and the passions of his heart, let him observe his relative condition and the springs of his action, and he will soon discern the causes of his calamity. He will find that disorganization or physical death is an unavoidable appendage of animal life. That the very construction of his nature insures the certainty of a subsequent derangement, and that the primary qualities of all sensitive beings gradually lead to dissolution. No organic perfectibility of animal existence has been discovered yet, which is capable of excluding the anticipation of decay through the progressive operations of physical causes upon the constitution; and perfect moral rectitude, though it were capable of extending the period, could not give ultimate durability to beings organized like ourselves; nevertheless, we are told that death spiritual, temporal, and eternal, are the consequences of his primitive apostasy. By spiritual death, is meant moral turpitude of heart and character; but this in many beings, obtains but partially, and is always the effect of personal infraction of moral principle, bearing no possible relation to Adam. By temporal death, is meant that death which experience teaches us to be the fate of every creature in the present world, and this death, though an essential ingredient in the constitution of nature, is foolishly and unphilosophically attributed to the sin of Adam. If Adam, previous to his supposed apostasy, had been thrown into a fire, or immersed in water, would not one of these elements have disorganized him, or the other have drowned him? or would he have returned from these trials with all the beauties of youth and vivacity in his appearance? If it be contended that he would, a constitution must then be attributed to him of which the human mind can form no conception. If it be admitted that he must have perished, temporal death can then no longer be attributed to the commission of moral evil, and it must be acknowledged as an essential property of our primary and physical organization; and that death is as natural as life in the order of the world. By eternal death, is meant a state of endless punishment; and so powerful is the influence of this sin of Adam, upon the human race, that they all become liable to eternal torments on this account. One would have supposed that after having brought temporal death into the world, by this transgression, and after having corrupted every moral principle of the human heart, the contrivers of the scheme might have been contented, without annexing to this crime, any other fatal consequences; but fanaticism and superstition delight in murder, misery, and eternal fire; and to this flaming lake I wish them a speedy passage, never more to rise to insult the dignity, or destroy the happiness of the human race. To punish the temporary and finite crimes of a finite life with eternal fire, would be to relinquish every principle of distributive justice, and to act like an arbitrary and malevolent tyrant. All the sins that ever have been committed do not deserve this unlimited severity of punishment; and to attribute to one solitary infraction of a moral law, these terrible consequences, is to lose sight of infinite benevolence and eternal justice. It is to represent the God of Nature as cruel and vindictive, and even less merciful than the majority of his creatures; it destroys all degrees in moral turpitude, and inflicts on a petty offender, a punishment not merited by the greatest criminal. It is therefore evident that this original sin has not produced, and that it could not produce, any of the consequences which have been attributed to it, for death is one of the physical properties of our nature. Vice is the result of individual and personal infractions of moral law, and an eternal hell is a bugbear of superstition, which has never answered, and never can answer any valuable purpose even in preventing crimes.

Another important doctrine of the Christian religion, is the atonement supposed to have been made by the death and sufferings of the pretended Saviour of the world; and this is grounded upon principles as regardless of justice as the doctrine of original sin. It exhibits a spectacle truly distressing to the feelings of a benevolent mind, it calls innocence and virtue into a scene of suffering, and reputed guilt, in order to destroy the injurious effects of real vice. It pretends to free the world from the fatal effects of a primary apostasy, by the sacrifice of an innocent being. Evil has already been introduced into the world, and in order to remove it, a fresh accumulation of crimes becomes necessary. In plain terms, to destroy one evil, another must be committed. To teach mankind virtue, they are to be presented with the example of murder; to render them happy, it is necessary to exhibit innocence in distress; to provide for them the joys of Heaven, wretchedness is to be made their portion on earth. To make them love one another, they must be taught that the Deity, regardless of this principle, voluntarily sacrificed his only begotten Son. In fine, to procure for intelligent beings, the happiness suited to their nature, cruelty and vindictive malice must be exhibited for their contemplation. This doctrine presented in its true colours contains neither justice nor utility. Its principle is vicious, and its consequences are not beneficial. The reflecting mind which views the operation of causes and their natural effects, possesses a nice and accurate power of discrimination. Moral precision is an important object of attention, and although it traces the nature of the infinitely combined relations subsisting among beings of the same species, it cannot discern either the justice or the utility of the relation which suffering virtue can bear to the destruction of moral evil. No connection can be discovered between the exclamations of expiring innocence, and the triumphant march of vice over an apostate world. Does the suffering of the virtuous man destroy the evil habits or propensities of him who is vicious and abandoned, especially when he is told that these sufferings are to annihilate his own crimes? Can this induce the mind to exhibit any efforts wearing the appearance of reformation? Does it not rather contribute to the practice of vice, from the belief that the burden and effect must be sustained by another person? Yet this is the true ground on which this scheme of atonement is promulgated. It is exhibited as a substitute for moral perfection. It teaches man that his own virtues are insufficient for his felicity; that the cultivation of his faculties, and the discovery and practice of moral truth, can never lead to substantial happiness. This must be obtained from the sufferings and expiring groans of the Deity himself. But even on Christian principles, what useful purpose has this atonement answered? Though the believers of this religion have sacrificed the God of Nature, to gratify their pride, have they by this means accomplished their end? Have they established a sure foundation for the destruction of moral evil? Have they insured permanent happiness to every intelligent being? No; this desirable end is not completed. Sin, say they, is an infinite evil. Was the atonement infinite? Alas! No; for although Jesus Christ, who suffered, was equal to God himself, yet all of them acknowledge that it was the human, not the divine nature that partook of this suffering. If therefore, it was the human nature only that suffered, this suffering could make only a finite atonement, and if the sin was infinite, this atonement could not reach its nature or destroy its effects; for to have done this, the atonement must have been commensurate with the evil to be destroyed; but as the one is finite and the other infinite, no relation could have subsisted between them, and no beneficial effect has been, or can be produced from it. This method of destroying evil is an unfortunate one; it is essentially unjust in its principles, and useless in its effects; it professes to sacrifice an infinite being, but it denies the possibility of this sacrifice producing any thing more than a finite atonement. If an atonement was necessary, it ought to have been as extensive and complete in its nature, as the offences intended to be destroyed by its influence. But instead of this, every thing is reversed. According to believers themselves, this atonement has not reached the condition of more than one tenth part of the human race. The efforts of Trinitarian wisdom have all failed, and notwithstanding the pretended good news of the gospel, every living creature is destined to never ending torment. The elect themselves are incapable of escaping eternal damnation, for without an atonement, they cannot be saved, and the atonement that has been made is not equal to the crime committed. If, therefore, our hopes of salvation are to rest on this vicarious suffering, we shall be essentially disappointed, and endless misery must be the lot of man. Priests and fanatics of the world! is this your scheme of infinite benevolence? this your theme of divine eloquence? Is this the only way in which you can exhibit the perfections of your God, and adore his eternal wisdom? Are murder, carnage, and injustice, the objects in which you delight? Have you lost all attachment to moral virtue, all veneration for the dignity and faculties of your nature? Have you dismissed all respect for nature and for truth? Will you never learn wisdom from the book of nature, will you never derive instruction from the permanency of her laws? Is it only among miracles, ghosts, and crucified Gods that you delight to walk? Oh! prejudiced and superstitious man, look at the splendid beauties of nature, look at the vast machinery of the universe, and through these thou mayest discover the intelligent organizer of the whole, perfect in all his attributes, and worthy of thy adoration.

The next principle of discussion is, that of Christian faith; and this among the believers of this religion, has been considered as a great virtue. But is this substantially true? What is the real meaning of the word *Faith*? It is necessary to inquire concerning its true definition, and from this inquiry we shall be able to draw a conclusion whether or not the principle of faith is meritorious. Faith is an assent of the mind to the truth of a proposition supported by evidence. If the evidence adduced is sufficient to convince the mind, credence is the necessary result; if the evidence be insufficient, belief becomes impossible. In religion therefore, or in any other of the concerns of life, if the mind discerns that quantum of evidence necessary to establish the truth of any proposition, it will yield to the force and effect of the proofs which are produced; if, on the other hand, the intelligence of man does not discern the necessary influence of such evidence, infidelity will be the natural and unavoidable result. Why then is the principle of faith considered as a virtue? If a man beholds the sun in its meridian splendor, and declares the truth of this exhibition, is he meritorious in making this acknowledgment? If any truth in nature is well substantiated and supported by the testimony of his mind or his senses, does he deserve credit for his mental acquiescence? No. Why then have the christian world annexed to this principle of belief any degree of merit? Is necessary acquiescence a virtue? Does man become entitled to praise for the acknowledgment of facts guaranteed by his senses, or essentially supported through the channel of his mental faculties? Does truth really exist in the system of nature? And is this truth discoverable by the operations of the human mind? And shall man, notwithstanding this, arrogate to himself a high degree of importance, for the rejection of the splendid testimonies which are exhibited for his contemplation? No; after a full display of evidence, the mind must yield to its necessary and unavoidable influence; when therefore, the Christian religion represents faith as being meritorious, it loses sight of the natural operations of the human mind; it betrays an ignorance of nature, and becomes censurable by its deviation from the primary and essential arrangements. Yet in this holy book, we are told, that "he that believeth not shall be damned." But what are we to believe? Are we to believe that the Creator of the universe is the parent and friend of the whole human race? Are we to believe that his wisdom acts in coincidence with general felicity, or operates on the ground of universal happiness? Are we to believe that the establishment of general laws is sufficient for the well being of intelligent agents? Are we to believe the vast machinery of the universe to be under the guidance and direction of eternal perfection? Are we to believe that the primary principles of our nature are sufficient for our improvement and ultimate perfectibility? Are we to believe that the practice of moral virtue is essentially connected with the dignity and final improvement of the human species? Are we to believe that the establishment of good laws, and the exhibitions of moral energies are essentially interwoven with the permanent happiness of sensitive creatures? No! We are not permitted to believe this. What then is Christian belief? What are the dogmas and principles to which we are required to give an unqualified credence? However painful it may be to declare it, they are of the following nature:—That the great Creator of the world sacrificed his only begotten Son for the happiness of the human race; that he sent numerous prophets and apostles, to teach and instruct mankind; that they were charged with the disclosure of every species of celestial knowledge, relative to the future felicity of intelligent beings; that they were unwearied in their attention to enlighten and inform the human race; that they exhibited every possible effort for the accomplishment of this desirable end, and all this to no valuable purpose; that man is to be criminated for the bad conduct of a person who lived six thousand years ago; that he can be made happy only by a crucified God; that he can perform no virtue of himself, and yet, that without being perfectly holy, he cannot be happy; that he must give an unlimited credence to the greatest absurdities, and most palpable contradictions, and view the most immoral specimens of human actions as sanctioned by the Deity; that he must venerate the most senseless opinions, admire the most unexampled ignorance, and love the most detestable crimes; in fact, that he must believe in a book which contains, systematically considered, neither truth nor morality, neither purity of sentiment nor principle, neither propriety of arrangement, nor progression of human improvement; erroneous in all its primary establishments and vindictive in all its consequences; unjust in its origin and malevolent in all its subsequent movements; incorrect in its relations and impure in its intentions; destructive to science, an insult to morality, and essentially injurious to human felicity. This then is Christian faith. Great God of Nature! Must we then renounce the justifiable exercise of all our faculties, in order to be happy? To attain felicity, is it necessary that we believe in contradictions? Must we deem cruelty one of the attributes of divinity? Must the benevolent mind be called to the view of murder, in order to be fitted for the performance of its essential duties? Must injustice and revenge be interwoven with the morality of man? Shall we never be permitted to love truth, admire nature, and practise a pure and genuine morality? Oh, superstition! how much thou hast to answer for! Thine influence has corrupted the faculties of man, debased his heart, and rendered wretched the whole human race. Thou hast spread ruin, misery, and devastation over a beautiful and productive earth, and thou art deserving of the curses of every intelligent being in every part of the universe.

Eternal Damnation

Man is a being possessed of certain powers and faculties; of certain passions and propensities to actions, and these, by a primary law of nature, are subjected to the control of reason, and are to be directed by conscience or an internal moral sense of right and wrong. But what are these faculties, what these passions, which are essentially connected with the character and condition of intelligent agents? Our existence and all the properties of it are of a limited and finite nature; there is not a single quality of man, that is not imperfect; the parts of the aggregate of his life, do not constitute any thing like infinity. In all his movements, in all his energies, in all the capacities of his being, he is regulated by finite and not by infinite principles. He is incapable of any actions which do not result essentially from the faculties which he is possessed of; all his conduct must have a strict reference to the causes which have produced it, and every effect must bear a proportion to its productive cause. If the cause be limited and imperfect, the effect must also be imperfect, for the effect can never rise superior to the cause, which has given it birth. Before we speak, therefore, of an infinite sin, or an infinite evil, we should consider the capacity of those beings, to whom this evil is attributed; if the acting agents are infinite in their nature and character, the effects of their operations may be so too, but if they are finite, their actions can lay no claim to an infinite effect. Sin is the consequence of the infraction of moral law; if this infraction be made by an infinite being, the criminality would be like the being who made it, that is of an infinite quality; but if the infraction be made by an imperfect being, the criminality is finite, and limited in its essential nature. It follows of course, as man is a finite and imperfect agent, he is incapable of the performance of any infinite act; if he cannot do an infinite act, he is incapable of an infinite evil, and does not deserve an infinite punishment; consequently, the idea of eternal death is unjust and unreasonable. But further, if every sin were an infinite evil, which is the Christian doctrine, it would merit an infinite punishment; but if one sin deserves an infinite punishment, what must be the punishment of him who is guilty of ten thousand sins? According to this doctrine he must be liable to ten thousand infinite punishments, which is a physical and moral absurdity. This doctrine of eternal death or infinite punishment, disregards the nature of human actions, and every principle of distributive justice. It inflicts on the smallest offender, as great extent and severity of punishment as on the most abandoned

254   criminal. It goes to the destruction of all moral virtue, by inducing man to believe, that the commission of one vicious action is as odious in the sight of God, and deserves as much punishment as a thousand violations of moral rectitude. It destroys all relations between the actions of men and the beneficial arrangements of corrective improvement. It makes man infinite, and the Deity unjust; both of which are inconsistent with the nature of things and the principles of eternal truth.

Miracles

The productions of the earth are subject to no supernatural derangement; they are exhibited with a constancy and specific similarity which discard every idea of perversion in physical law, and present the material world as a theatre of certitude which the efforts of superstition cannot destroy. The tides of ebb and flow, and all the relative operations of nature are preserved entire in despite of the malignity of superstition. This vast whole, this extensive universe thus subjected to the operation of immutable laws, is, nevertheless, distorted and deranged by Christian theology; its author is insulted, and the scientific deductions of human intellect perverted or destroyed. Religion, not content with the consistency and harmony of Nature, has sought for redress in the violation of her laws, and nothing short of miracles could satisfy the extravagant desires of *pious and holy fanaticism*. . . .

A miracle is a violation of the laws of nature, by *supernatural power*. In the act of such violation, there must have been some great object in view, which could not otherwise be accomplished; the violation therefore must have been considered as the least of two evils, and the result as productive upon the whole, of the greatest possible good. But this represents an omnipotent GOD, surrounded with difficulties, and like imperfect creatures, disposed to make the best of a bad condition. It will be necessary for those who advocate the doctrine of miracles, to recur to the cause and primary establishment of the laws of nature. God is infinite in all his perfections; the laws of nature are an effect of the divine attributes, and must have been modified in the best possible manner, and to answer the best and wisest purposes. To alter, therefore, that which already had been done in the best possible manner, would be to make it worse, for no alteration or amendment could make that better which was already as good as it could be. If the world and the laws by which the world was governed, are the offspring of infinite wisdom, they must have been right in the first place, for it is a necessary character of infinite wisdom to perform whatever it does perform in the best possible manner. All alterations or violations in any system or set of laws, argues imperfection and want of discernment; but such imperfection and want of discernment cannot be the property of a perfect being. If God therefore is perfect, such perfection would enable him to conceive and execute with a masterly hand. The mechanic who builds a machine, frequently alters his plan, and is under the necessity of attending to amendments and repairs; but his ignorance was the ground work of this, and a competent knowledge of the principles by which the machine was constructed, would have precluded the necessity of subsequent correction and amendment. The Creator of the world knew perfectly well the force and effect of principle before it was applied to the accomplishment of the variegated motions and operations of existence; ignorance, therefore, could have no share in modifying the vast powers of the universe, or the immutable principles by which it is directed. Wisdom, power, and goodness, combined in the management of the whole, and consequently the whole is formed exactly in such a manner as these three leading perfections of the divine character at first intended. To work a miracle therefore, would answer no very valuable purpose, and is derogatory to the attributes of God, by which it is supposed to be wrought. To establish a system of religion by evidence drawn from miracles, is to establish it upon the ruin of the consistent harmony of the divine perfection; upon the ruin of all principle and all confidence. When the consistent character of the author of such religion is destroyed, the religion itself is not worth much. Either God did things in the first place as they ought to be done, or he did not; if he did them as they ought to be done, there could have been no need of alteration, and consequently there could have been no such thing as a miracle; if he did not, then he must have been either imperfect, or have acted inconsistent with good principle; in either of which cases, his character as God would be destroyed, and the perfection of his existence sacrificed upon the altar of human folly. Fanaticism, which attempts to exalt its God by making him work wonders, is as great an enemy to true Theism as the open and professed Atheist. A wonder working God, who violates his own laws, and acts inconsistently with the principles which he himself has established, is no God at all. It is an immoral phantom conjured up on the wild vagaries of a superstitious imagination. It is easy to perceive that if there be in nature, a perfect God, he cannot be the author of those marvellous and even ridiculous violations of the laws of nature detailed in the Old and New Testament. His character must be uniform, consistent and perfect, just and equitable, and in perfect coincidence with the immortal laws of the moral and physical world. All things it is said, are possible with God. This is one of the maxims of that religion which has perverted all the principles of truth and justice; but this maxim is not true; it is not possible, for instance, that God should destroy his own excellence; it is not possible that he should act inconsistently with the properties and principles of his nature. This extravagant assertion instead of exalting the character of the Creator, would absolutely destroy it, by causing him to act without rule and without justice. But superstition can never do enough for her God, until she has done a great deal too much. A consistent and immutable Deity, acting in strict conformity to the essential properties of his existence, would be, in the estimation of inconsistent superstition, an object far inferior to those wild and unruly divinities, who overturn states and empires, pervert the general order of nature, and occasionally, by way of amusement, drown the whole world, with all the inhabitants and animals therein existing. A man walking regularly upon the earth, and performing with fidelity all his moral duties, *is by no means an object of attachment*, but one walking upon the water, without doing any good, will draw forth the admiration of a gazing, foolish, and superstitious world. The passion for the marvellous has carried man from earth to heaven, and in the ranting fury of his zeal, he has supposed that his God would be pleased with all those moral distortions which at such unhappy moments agitated his own delirious mind. The idea of the existence of a miracle will be wholly destroyed by a just recurrence to the counterbalancing evidence, drawn from the experience of mankind. This experience bears testimony to the uniform operation of Nature's laws; it teaches man to repose in them unqualified confidence, and in all the common concerns of life, this confidence serves as the foundation of his courage, his activity, and his consolation. Here are then, two kinds of evidence opposed to each other; the one human experience, and other human testimony. Those who contend that miracles prove the divinity of the Christian religion, appeal to the testimony of witnesses to support the truth and existence of such miracles. Let this case be examined, and the superior weight of evidence will appear with convincing force. Believers declare that the miracles which were wrought to prove the truth of the holy Scriptures, were numerous and performed before great numbers of people. That the credit and veracity of these witnesses cannot be doubted; that they were honest and disinterested men; that they did not wish to be deceived themselves, nor could they possibly reap any advantage from deceiving others; that some of the eye witnesses were inspired men, in whom there was no guile, and that others were mere men of the world, whose feelings and interest would have rejected, if possible, the splendour of such supernatural evidence; that all these, however, yielded to the mighty energy of the mighty God; that they pronounced him a wonder working God, and that such marvellous facts had never before been presented to a wicked and apostate world. It is also declared and maintained, that the result of these pure and incorruptible witnesses has been transmitted down for more than two thousand years through the holy and incorruptible channel of the Church of Christ; that the present generation might as well doubt of the existence of Scipio or of Caesar, as to doubt of the existence of Jesus Christ and his apostles, and the miracles which by them were performed; that the unbeliever at this time, is working against all his own positions, destroying the nature of evidence, and unhinging the moral world. . . .

The Immorality of Christianity

The next point of examination, is the morality of the Christian religion. On this head, the advocates of this revealed system have made a mistake injurious to themselves, by extolling its morality above that of any other moral treatise; they have provoked inquiry and comparison, and the result serves only to diminish the pretended excellence of their scheme. It is not denied that this religion contains some good moral maxims. But it is denied that it contains any thing like a pure *system* of genuine morality. Its moral maxims are but thinly interspersed, and they are inaccurate and incomplete, trifling, and often without utility, destitute of justifiable application to the moral condition of intellectual life. All morality that is genuine, is drawn from the nature and condition of rational beings. It is calculated to preserve and augment their happiness, to raise and extend the dignity and utility of social existence. It assumes for its basis, the genuine principles of a reciprocal justice, and an extensive benevolence. While it regards the felicity of others, it also regards the preservation of our own life and happiness. But the moral doctrine concerning injuries, contained in the christian religion, is not established upon a principle of this mutual nature, but solicits an accumulation of insult, by commanding us after being smitten on one cheek to turn the other also. This is sacrificing the dignity of our character, and inviting fresh injuries. It is surrendering up the manly part of our nature, into the hands of him who is sure to trample it under foot. And again, it is said, "if any man will sue thee at the law, and take away thy coat, let him have thy cloak also"; that is, after thine enemy hath unjustly taken away a part of thy property, it becomes thy duty to bestow upon him the remainder. If thy coat is already gone, thou must give away the remainder of thy garments, and go naked thyself. If thine enemy do thee all possible injury, thou must in return exercise towards him sincere love and affection. If he persecute thee, thou shouldst bless him for his curses and persecutions. In short, to comply with the spirit of this morality, we must invert the order of nature, and bestow on crimes and continued abuse, the most endearing affections of our heart. Where is the believer who puts this morality in practice? It is not considered by every one as merely theoretical. Have you who are believers in this system, coats and other garments to bestow, in order to comply with its injunctions? Are you willing to surrender your natural dignity, to sink your nature to a level with the spaniel, in order to become a true christian? And can you with any appearance of truth and justice, advocate the purity and celestial nature of this species of moral maxims? It may reasonably be presumed that if one coat had been obtained through the channel of a law suit, another law suit would be necessary in order to obtain the cloak. And thus this celestial morality would become the cause of endless litigation. But if we should accede to the truth of the assertion, that all the maxims held as moral by the professors of christianity, were really and truly so, this would not prove the celestial origin of their religion. For if we attribute to them all the excellence which is contended for, they still fall below ancient and modern dissertations on this subject. This religion does not draw its morality from the right source. But the correct, the elegant, the useful maxims of Confucius, Antoninus, Seneca, Price and Volney, beautifully display its principles from the physical and moral organization of intelligent beings. The writings of these men are in the hands of the public, and may be perused by every one whose prejudices do not forbid it, and when examined with a spirit of candor, they will rise far superior to the boasted morality of the Christian system. But when the numerous, cruel and immoral maxims contained in the Bible, are placed in the balance, they greatly outweigh all its genuine morality, and the influence of this religion upon the human heart and human actions verifies the remark. . . .

When the human mind takes a retrospective view of past ages, through the mirror of history; when it calls up to its contemplation, the murderous devastations, the horrid wars and cruelties which have desolated the Christian world; when it beholds the faggot every where lighted up for the destruction of man; when gibbets, imprisonment, and persecutions are presented on every quarter, when it sees domestic peace and tranquillity tortured and almost annihilated, malevolence and sectarian spirit enkindling the most unbridled resentments to disturb the benevolent sentiments of the human heart; when, in fact, all Christendom exhibits a spectacle shocking to humanity, the weeping voice of Nature cries aloud, and demands a disclosure of the causes which have produced this general misery and distress. It asks in the name of Reason and Truth, whence all these calamities, whence these innumerable evils that have overwhelmed and laid waste a beautiful and productive earth? Where is the source of these human misfortunes? Where the fountain whence these miseries proceed? Righteous God of nature! What questions are these to ask in the face of the Christian church? But however painful the task, truth compels us to declare, that to this *holy* religion they are to be attributed. In this wonderful system of divine benevolence, we must seek for the origin. "Does the God of Nature then require devastation for homage, or conflagration for sacrifice? Would he have groans for hymns? Murderers to worship him, and a desert and ravaged world for his temple? Yet such, holy and faithful generations, are your works! these the fruits of your piety! You have massacred the people, reduced cities to ashes, destroyed all traces of cultivation, made the earth a solitude, and you demand the reward of your labours. For myself, I solemnly affirm by all laws, human and divine, by the laws of the human heart, that the hypocrite and the deceiver shall be themselves deceived. The unjust man shall perish in his rapacity, and the tyrant in his usurpation; the sun shall change his course, before folly shall prevail over wisdom and science, before stupidity shall surpass prudential economy in the delicate art of procuring to man his true enjoyments, and of building his happiness on a solid foundation" [Volney's *Ruins*].

. . . It is strange to observe, that in reasoning upon theological subjects, men are disposed to abandon the correct ground of moral decision, and contend that those actions which would be unjust in man, would nevertheless be just when performed by the Creator. This is a mode of reasoning which perverts all the faculties of our existence, destroys the moral excellence of Deity, and overturns the foundation of principle. In all beings that are intelligent, moral principle is the same; and God has no more right to violate it, than any other being. He is essentially bound by the properties of his existence, and his character cannot be sustained without an undeviating attention to the immutable principle of justice.

. . . The writings of Paul, that heated and fanatic zealot in the christian faith, are equally noxious to the cause of moral virtue, and are calculated to annihilate the most virtuous efforts of every individual. *"It is not of him that willeth nor of him that runneth; not of works lest any man should boast; of ourselves we can do nothing"*; together with a hundred other passages of a similar nature, which go directly to suppress all the elevated exertions of the human faculties, and if literally followed, would turn man from intelligent activity, to a state of brutal indolence. It is extremely destructive to the moral happiness of mankind to teach them the want of powers, or the inadequacy of those they possess; because the fact is otherwise, because it is a solemn truth that the powers of man are competent to provide for his happiness; they are equal to the exigencies of his existence. It is superstition that has made him a fool, it is religious tyranny that has enslaved his mind, perverted his faculties, and tarnished the glory of his intellectual energies. Christianity has taught him two awful and destructive lessons; first, that he is incapacitated for the performance of moral actions; and secondly, in case he *should* perform them, they would add no merit or superior excellence to his character; that his best righteousness is like filthy rags which God would treat with marked abhorrence.

The repetition of such discouraging impressions must necessarily work an effect remarkably injurious to the virtuous activity of the human race. It is in conformity to this immoral instruction, that we see fanatic Christians every where boasting of their own inability, and doing violence to that internal sentiment which would otherwise constantly impel them to the performance of acts of justice, benevolence, and universal charity. In addition to the pointed declarations of the *holy scriptures* against the power and practice of morality, the inventors and promoters of the Christian religion have set up various kinds of doctrines, which diminish the motives to good actions, and lead the uninstructed mind to repose confidence in something foreign from its own exertions and merit, such as atonement, baptism, faith, sacramental suppers, oblations, and ablutions, together with many other idle ceremonies and wild vagaries of a distempered and fanatic brain.

The idea that Jesus the son of Mary died for the sins of the world, and that henceforth moral virtue can have no saving efficacy, is among the most destructive conceptions by which the moral world has been insulted and perverted. The supernatural grace of God, which Christians for so many ages have been in search of, has hitherto eluded the grasp of all rational and philosophic men; and to those who pretend to be acquainted with this celestial gift, it has been at times more trouble than profit; since innumerable doubts have been created concerning its reality and modes of operation in the human heart.

The cursory survey that has been taken of the immoral precepts and principles contained in the *Old and New Testament*, clearly proves that these books are not of divine origin. The God of the Jews and Christians, according to their own description, is a changeable, passionate, angry, unjust, and revengeful being; infuriate in his wrath, capricious in his conduct, and destitute, in many respects, of those sublime and immutable properties which really belong to the Preserver of the universe. The characters spoken of in the scriptures, as the favourites of Heaven, such as Moses, Joshua, David, Solomon, Jesus, and Paul, are none of them good moral characters; it is not probable, therefore, that they were selected by the Creator as the organs of celestial communication. In the *Old Testament*, national and individual justice is disregarded, and God is made the accomplice of crimes which human nature abhors. The maxims of the *New Testament* are a perversion of all correct principles in a code of moral virtue. The whole system is calculated to take man out of himself, to destroy his confidence in his own energies, to debase his faculties, vitiate his social affections, and brutalize the most useful qualities of human existence. The highest dignity of the human race consists in the practice of an exalted virtue, in the exercise of a fine sympathetic benevolence, in reciprocating our feelings and affections, in promoting the justice and order of society, in relieving the unfortunate and supporting the cause of truth, in diminishing evil and augmenting good; in short, in promoting universally the science, the virtue, and happiness of the world. There is, however, no possibility of faithfully performing these duties while under the shackles of Jewish and Christian superstition. The remedy consists in a return to nature, and in elevating our views and conceptions above those theological absurdities which have degraded man to a level with the beast, and taught him to respect his civil and ecclesiastical tyrants as beings of an higher order, or celestial messengers from a vindictive and revengeful God.

Natural Morality

The Origin of Moral Evil

The facts in the physical world are, many of them, difficult of solution; those of the moral world have perplexed still more the operations of the human understanding. The subtilty, the abstruseness, the incognizable character of moral existence, place it beyond the power of clear intellectual perception, and the mind loses itself in those metaphysical combinations, whose successive variations are incalculable. But the difficulties which nature has thrown in the way of this inquiry, are much less numerous than those presented by superstition.

. . . Reason and theology, philosophy and superstition are at war upon this subject. The believers in the Christian religion, following the examples of their theological and fanatic predecessors, have searched the universe in quest of a satisfactory solution to that long altercated question, Whence came moral evil? One religious sectary, willing to screen the divinity from any just accusation relative to so nefarious a concern, has descended into hell, and discovered there all the characters and distorted machinery necessary to the production of such an effect; but here metaphysical and fanatic invention indulged itself in all the extravagance of delusion. It was necessary first to create this *infernal* country, and then to create inhabitants suited to the nature of the climate, and the unfortunate condition in which they were to reside. The idea of a Devil was accordingly formed, and the reality of his existence rendered an indubitable truth by the reiterated assertions of superstition. Ignorance and fanaticism greedily swallowed the foolish *infernal* dose which had been administered. There is a remarkable disposition in the human mind, to remove the point of intellectual difficulty, as far from the reality of the case as possible, and then it triumphantly imagines that a solution has been given. This is a fact particularly in theological inquiry, in which a few retrogressive efforts of the mind, have been considered as an ample illustration of all the difficulties relative to the subject of Theism, and the existence of the physical universe. Similar to this idea, is the doctrine concerning moral evil, and the disposition which theologians have exhibited to remove the burden from their own shoulders and place it upon the devil's back. The whole *infernal* machinery with which we are presented by superstition, serves only to detach the mind from the true and real source of moral evil. While reflection is directed to another world, it is incompetent to a clear view of the facts existing in this, and the habit of such reveries produces a fanatic delirium subversive of all correctness of judgment. The existence of hell and the beings that dwell therein, being only supported by what is called divine revelation, it follows of course, that if this revelation is not true, a belief in any thing that is a mere result of that system, cannot be substantially founded. Since then it is presumed, that in these chapters a competent refutation is given to the doctrine contained in the sacred books of the Jews and Christians, the idea of descending into hell, or having recourse to a devil, in search of moral evil, is futile and inconsistent. Another part of the Christian world, willing to avoid difficulties, which their antagonists had thrown in their way, abandoned the *infernal* abodes, and ascended into the celestial world, in quest of the origin of evil. They exhibited ingenious metaphysical reasoning upon the subject, declaring that God was the Creator of all things; that sin was something and not nothing, and therefore he must be the Creator of sin or moral evil. This puzzled the advocates of the *hell scheme*, and a clerical warfare was engendered concerning two theological opinions, neither of which had any kind of existence in the nature of things. After heaven and hell had been searched through and through to find something which did not belong to either of them, the terror struck inquirer, as if fatigued with his atmospheric journey, seated himself once more upon the earth, and saw, or might have seen in the very bosom of society, and the perverted character of man, a clear and satisfactory solution of that difficult question, which, for so long a time, had occupied his attention in distant regions. It is in this manner, that the plainest subject is rendered mysterious, when a superstitious religion is industriously employed in subverting the independent power of thought. It is neither in the upper nor lower regions; it is not in heaven nor in hell, that the origin of moral evil will be discovered; it is to be found only among those intelligent beings who exist upon the earth. *Man has created it, and man must destroy it.*

But it is necessary to exhibit the proofs of this last assertion, and convince Christian theology of the innumerable errors, which for ages past have been imposed upon a credulous and deluded world. What is it then that constitutes a moral evil? It is the violation of a law of justice or utility, by any one of the human species, competent to distinguish between right and wrong. We have no other cognizable idea upon this subject. Facts and practice are presented continually to the view of the human mind; the decision of a correct mind, is always according to the nature and character of the case. The character of a human being, is made either good or bad by the actions he commits. If these actions are conformable to the principles of justice and universal benevolence, they are with great propriety denominated good; if they are unjust, cruel and destructive to sensitive and intellectual life, they are denominated bad. There are certain fundamental laws, suitable for the government of rational beings, and it is a departure from these laws, that vitiates the human character. It is proved in another part of this work, that virtue and vice are personal qualities, and that they result from personal adherence to, or personal infraction of moral law. It is only necessary in this place, to call the attention once more to the nature of human actions, and to the characteristic difference between them, in order to establish the position principally assumed in this inquiry; for it ought to be recollected, that even if it *could* be proved, which by the way it cannot, that even a deity or a devil had violated moral law, this would not affect the decision upon the subject in regard to man; because that evil could not be transferred from a different kind of beings in the other world, to those who exist upon earth. As the moral properties of all intelligent agents are personal; are essentially their own and not another's, as there can be no justifiable transfer between man and man, so it follows that there can be none between man and devil. Every intellectual being must depend upon himself; must rest upon his own energies and be responsible for himself.

. . . Reason, or the intellectual powers of man, must eventually become both the deposit and the guardian of the rights and happiness of human existence. Reason has already acquired such strength and so far unfolded its powers, that it has already sealed the future destiny of the human race. It is the peculiar office of reason to look to the utter demolition of the ancient regimen of church and state. These twin sisters of iniquity are the moral giants, which have stalked with huge devastation over the face of the whole globe. Political despotism and supernatural religion have done more to render the human race vicious and depraved, than all other causes conjointly combined. If the passions of man and the impulses of his nature have frequently produced a moral eccentricity in his conduct, it is certain that a corrupt government and a corrupt religion have rendered him habitually wicked; have perverted all the conceptions of the mind upon moral and political subjects, and brutalized his intellectual existence. The most important step which can be taken for the extermination of vice and misery, is to destroy the artificial causes by which such evils are perpetuated. If other causes should be found to exist in the constitution of nature, they will be progressively removed by the light and power of science, and a more comprehensive view of the true interest of the human species. But efforts tending to make the individuals of a nation virtuous and happy, will never succeed extensively till the civil and religious tyranny under which they groan shall be completely annihilated.

. . . Despotism gives no encouragement to any kind of improvement, and the hope of human amelioration from this quarter will ever prove to be fallacious. Reason, righteous and immortal reason, with the argument of the printing types in one hand, and the keen argument of the sword in the other, must attack the thrones and the hierarchies of the world, and level them with the dust of the earth; then the emancipated slave must be raised by the power of science into the character of an enlightened citizen; thus possessing a knowledge of his rights, a knowledge of his duties will consequently follow, and he will discover the intimate and essential union between the highest interests of existence, and the practice of an exalted virtue. If civil and ecclesiastical despotism were destroyed, knowledge would become universal, and its progress inconceivably accelerated. It would be impossible, in such a case, that moral virtue should fail of a correspondent acceleration, and the ultimate extirpation of vice, would become an inevitable consequence. Ages must elapse before the accomplishment of an object so important to the elevated concerns of intelligent life; but the causes are already in operation, and nothing can arrest or destroy the benignant effects which they are calculated to produce. The power of reason, the knowledge of printing, the overthrow of political and ecclesiastical despotism, the universal diffusion of the light of science, and the universal enjoyment of republican liberty; these will become the harbingers and procuring causes of real virtue in every individual, and universal happiness will become the lot of man.

Morality Is Not Based on the Divine

If a thousand Gods existed, or if nature existed independent of any; the moral relation between man and man would remain exactly the same in either case. Moral principle is the result of this relation, it is founded in the properties of our nature and it is as indestructible as the basis on which it rests. If we could abandon for a moment every theistical idea, it would nevertheless remain substantially true, that the happiness of society must depend upon the exercise of equal and reciprocal justice. It would also be true, that benevolence is an amiable trait in the character of man; that the cultivation of his faculties is a duty imposed on him, because the faithful performance of his duty extends the circle of his real felicity; that vice is the bane of individual and social existence; that truth is to be preferred to falsehood, activity to indolence, temperance to debauchery, and generally, that science and virtue claim preeminently over ignorance and vice, the universal attachment of the human race. All these, and many other particulars of a like nature, would stand as immortal monuments of the real nature of moral principles, even after cultivated intellect shall have performed the last solemn act of duty relative to the ancient regimen, and shall have recalled bewildered man to the happy contemplation of the laws and immutable energies of the physical universe. If this be true, in regard to the essential nature of theological ideas, how much more powerfully will it hold upon every sectarian modification of the subject. If pure theism be independent of morality, and morality independent of that, because it rests upon the relations and the properties of human life, then it will be easy to conceive that the subordinate descriptions of sectarian theology, must be still more unconnected with the present subject. The character, however, of all the Gods of antiquity, is, of itself, a sufficient consideration to exclude them from any participation in the concerns of an exalted virtue. The Jewish God commands theft and murder; he puts a lying spirit into the mouth of his prophets; he repents and grieves for his past conduct; he is a God of fury, wrath, and vengeance. These actions and qualities are all attributed to him in the Old Testament! Is it possible that any man of common sense can believe, that moral principles which are so important to the best interests of human society, should be placed upon such an immoral and vindictive foundation? Can any one imagine that a being, so destitute of moral justice and benevolence himself, could serve as a solid basis on which to rest these qualities in human nature? No, this sectarian God, this malignant phantom of former ages, this compound of weakness and wickedness, is calculated to subvert all moral principle, both in theory and practice, and present the moral world in the full exercise of the most detestable passions.

The wrathful and unrelenting character of the christian divinity, is not less hostile to the immaculate principles of a sound and excellent morality; imbittered in his anger, and infuriate in his vengeance, he lays his hand upon his innocent son, and offers him up a living sacrifice for the purposes which reason abhors, and justice utterly disclaims. Under the modification, name and character of the Holy Ghost, this being introduces himself to a woman, and violates those correct and delicate sentiments which ought to guide an intelligent being in cases of this kind. Under the name and character of Jesus Christ, he exhibits the most flagrant departures from the purity of moral sentiment and moral practice. . . . The sectarian divinity, which christianity presents to us, is represented as a consuming fire, as a being possessing fiery indignation and an uncontrollable vengeance; as a being who disregards all just discrimination upon the subject of moral principle. He declares in some parts of the New Testament, that every thing shall be regulated by his arbitrary will without regard to the nature or character of the case. *He will have mercy on whom he will have mercy, and whom he will he hardeneth.* (See Rom. chap. 9th, etc.) Is it possible that even a christian believer can suppose for a single moment, that the principles of genuine morality can rest upon such an arbitrary basis? No, a divinity of immoral description is the bane of moral virtue. The purest theism is independent of morality, and morality is independent of that; much less then can the corrupt and vitiated conceptions of barbarous ages be produced in support of a principle which could not exist without the intellectual faculties of man, and which cannot be destroyed while these faculties exist. The principle and the practice of immortal virtue, will long remain after the plundering and bloody theology of Moses, Jesus, and Mahomet, has ceased to afflict the human race. The essential principles of morality are founded in the nature of man, they cannot be annihilated, they are as indestructible as human existence itself.

Universal Benevolence

The sentiment which includes the whole sensitive and intelligent world, within the sphere of its benignant operations, is justly denominated universal benevolence. Every organized being, whether of a high or low station in animal existence, is susceptible of pleasure and pain; they are all alternately affected by the wishes, the passions, and the conduct of each other, and this influence is extended much farther than at first view would strike the mind of the most correct and accurate observer. The universe is a vast assemblage of living creatures, whose relations are reciprocal and reciprocated under a thousand different forms, and supported by a thousand different ligaments of an imperceptible nature. The parts are interested in the whole, and the whole is interested in the preservation and diversified modification of the parts. Nothing is foreign or irrelative in the vast fabric to which we belong. Union is most intimate, and the intellectual destiny which awaits the human race, will ultimately disclose the consoling secret, that man's highest happiness consists in perspicuously discovering his true connection with nature, and the eternal duration of this connection. The circumscribed condition of man's excellence, his wants, his social duties, his appetites, and his passions, constitute a considerable drawback upon the comprehensive conceptions, which he would otherwise have been capable of forming concerning his relationship with nature, and the ultimate destination to which the powers of nature have devoted the component and immortal parts of his existence. The intellectual properties of man are, however, capable of being expanded so far as to indulge an opinion subversive of those narrow views which have excited sentiments of hostility between individuals and nations whose interests were the same, and whose duties ought to have been universally reciprocated. It is, no doubt, extremely natural and even absolutely necessary that each individual should feel an anxiety extremely impulsive respecting the preservation of his own existence, and the means by which it is to be rendered tranquil and comfortable; but this sensation, the first which is experienced by a sensitive creature, does not preclude that expansion of mind which would benevolently extend the circle of man's moral affections and duties, and which also prepares for himself an additional portion of exalted enjoyment. Sensation alone, or in other words mere animal existence, must be deprived in a high degree of the power and the pleasure of reciprocating those sentiments of moral sympathy, to which intelligent man is indebted for his highest happiness. The gradual increase of the capacity of sensation constitutes a continual approach toward the possession of those properties on which the sublimity of thought depends, and by which human reason recognizes the benefit of benevolent reciprocation. It is, however, denied by some, that man possesses any other qualities than those which are merely selfish or individual; that his sensual impulses repel every sentiment of comprehensive kindness and affection; that in every respect he is a being of insulated nature and character, and that the powers and properties of his existence are necessarily in a high degree hostile to the interest and well being of others. Two points of prominent and conspicuous importance invite the activity of mind in the solution of the present difficulty. The one point is the physical relation of man to all existence; the other is his moral relation to his own species and to all other inferior animals. The component parts of which man is formed, are all drawn from the great fountain of existence; they are essentially material in their nature, and destined to return to the source from which they sprang. Organized matter cannot lay claim to a preeminent essence; it is modification and refinement which produce visible exaltation, and not the native properties contained in the substance of which man is composed. The constant interchange of matter with matter, is a primary and immutable law of nature, and should teach man through the channel of observation the ultimate destiny that awaits him, it should teach him that the pain which he inflicts upon sensitive existence will return upon himself with interest, and will pave the way for eternizing a system of misery fatal to the sensations of the whole animal world. Humanity has lessons of a different kind, pregnant with salutary instructions calculated to enforce conviction upon the intellectual powers of man. The spiritualization of human existence has made man a fool, it has taught him to spurn at matter, to condemn its power and ridicule its essence; whereas on the contrary, sound philosophy, which unfolds the connection between man and nature, is calculated to produce in the mind sentiments of respect and tranquillity; respect for the aggregate of existence to which he belongs, and tranquillity at the idea of an eternal interest in this indestructible mass. The successive changes through which he is destined to pass, and the impossibility of relinquishing his connection with nature should inspire him with feelings of universal sympathy, and with sentiments of universal benevolence. Human reason has an important duty to perform in the institutions which it establishes; for these institutions will effect in succession, all the portions of matter destined to pass through an organized predicament. It is, no doubt, difficult to convince the human understanding of this physical or universal connection, or to make man see his true interest in this respect. It is, nevertheless, a solemn and philosophic truth that our sensations are, at this moment, suffering under the cruel lash of ancient institutions; that the whole animal world are reciprocating with each other a system of extensive and perpetual wretchedness resulting principally from that contempt which has been thrown upon the capacity of material substance, and our ignorance of an important and an indestructible connection with the great body of nature. If man had a comprehensive view of the successive changes of his existence, and a correct idea of the nature of sensation continually resulting from the renovation of organic forms, sympathy or universal benevolence, would become irresistibly impressive upon his moral powers, and form the basis of his subsequent conduct.

In the second place, man's moral relation to his own species, and to all other inferior animals, furnishes cogent evidence in favour of moral sympathy or universal benevolence. If the subject of man's physical connection presents us with some philosophical difficulties, the repeated and frequent necessity of performing his moral duties, will furnish a mass of instruction adequate to every important decision. The single idea of establishing the doctrine of perpetual reprisals, ought to constitute an ample refutation of those selfish opinions which regard only the individual to the exclusion of all the other members of society. It is the interest as well as the duty of every man to be just and benevolent; an opposite conduct would become the signal of universal discord, and the selfish principle which at first had for its object the preservation of self, would become the procuring cause of self destruction. The powers and the properties of human existence are of a similar nature, and require a correspondent method of treatment; beside, the intimate connection which subsists between us in this respect, our enjoyments and our capacity of enjoying, are augmented by every effort which the mind makes in a comprehensive system of philanthropy. The narrow prejudice which makes one man the enemy of another and one country the enemy of another, is not only disgraceful, but subversive of the best interests of human society. Political governments, and the prejudices which have been created and nurtured by these governments, have set individuals and nations in battle array against each other, without any good or substantial reason whatever. What is there in the nature of the case which should make a Frenchman and an Englishman hostile to each other? Are they not both men, possessed of similar faculties, equally indebted to nature for the resources of their felicity, and capable of being made happy or miserable by the operation of the same causes? Yes, and it is the iniquity of corrupt government which has perverted those sentiments of the human heart by which one human being is bound to another in a general system of interest, sympathy and universal benevolence. This principle should also be extended to the whole animal world, so as to exclude acts of cruelty, and annihilate every species of injustice. The child that is permitted in early life to run a pin through a fly, is already half prepared to run a dagger through the heart of his fellow creature! It is the duty of parents and the business of instruction, to correct the ferocious errors of former ages, and inspire society with sentiments of sympathy and universal goodness. But to do this with effect, our political institutions must be changed, and placed upon the broad basis of universal liberty and universal justice. This will be a work of time, but it is as certain in the ultimate issue of things, as the progress of the earth around the sun, or the general revolution of the planetary system. The individual that withholds his intellectual contribution in this respect is either grossly ignorant, or a wicked traitor in the great cause of human existence.

Moral Principle

In the sacred writings of the Jews and Christians; in all ancient theological compositions, the idea of correct moral principle, had been so frequently abandoned, and so grossly violated, that the energy of thought, for many ages, was inadequate to an upright and full investigation of the nature of human actions. The subject is, no doubt, connected with considerable difficulties; but these difficulties have been essentially augmented by the rubbish with which superstition has covered the moral character of man. The proofs of any inquiry, which relate to moral principle, adhere so closely to the realities of physical and intellectual existence, that the errors of an upright and intelligent mind, can never assume a frightful and destructive character. They will be continually modified, and undergo frequent corrections by the new information of which the mind is continually susceptible. Moral science cannot, perhaps, be reduced to absolute certitude, or become susceptible of absolute perfection; it is in its nature progressive, and the infinite diversity of sensations, which constitute the essential basis of all our intellectual combinations and deductions, will furnish, at least, a suspicion, that the decisions of the mind upon this subject, ought frequently to be reexamined and subjected to a new and more accurate scrutiny. All the theological systems, that ever have been written, have never thrown a particle of light upon this most interesting inquiry; they have established precepts, some few of which are good, and others extremely immoral; but no analysis of the physical or moral powers of man has ever been exhibited; no development of the principle of causation, or the nature of those effects, which have essentially resulted from the constitution of animal or intellectual existence. In all these cases, supernatural theology has prudently observed an absolute silence, probably from a consciousness of the most profound ignorance. This single truth, of itself, evinces the moral deficiency of supernatural religion, and the necessity of returning to the basis of nature for a correct development of principle. Every thing that is discordant to this, has been established by the force of authority, and the reasonableness of such establishment, has never been a ground of serious inquiry.

If it should be objected, that it is impossible, even upon the basis of nature, to find an universal standard of morality, it will nevertheless appear, that a continual approach toward such a standard, must be far preferable to those arbitrary decisions, which theology has made upon this subject. There can be no internal force or excellence connected with a system established solely by external power, without reference to the essence, or character of the principles, which constitute the body of such a system. The internal excellence of the principle itself, together with capacity of mental discernment, is essential to the ultimate benefit, which may be expected from the natural operation of legal codes. But there is no better method of rendering a principle intelligible, than by shewing that it is consistent with nature, that it has resulted from her laws, that it is useful in its effect, that it is capable of being reduced to practice; in a word, that it is suited to the powers, condition, and character of the human species. There is another previous consideration also, which ought to be taken into the account before we shall be able to comprehend the essence of moral principle, or to understand the nature of those duties, which result from our original constitutions. That intellectual part of man, which supernatural theology has denominated a soul, has been viewed separate and distinct from the body, as a kind of spiritual and celestial inhabitant of a mean and material tenement; that their union would be of short duration, and that their final destination was extremely different. This led to reasonings and conjectures, that were erroneous; for as the corporeal sensations were entirely excluded from a participation in the cause, by which moral influence was produced, an accurate knowledge of the sources of action, was necessarily excluded, and spiritual mystery was substituted for philosophic demonstration. The human mind is incapable of forming any conception of that which is not material; man is a being whose composition is purely physical, and moral properties or intellect, are the necessary results of organic construction. To ascertain, therefore, the foundation of moral principle, it is necessary to revert to the physical constitution of human nature, it is necessary to go to the source of sensation, to the cause of impressions, and the diversity of these impressions; to the universality of the fact, that all human nature possesses the same, or similar sensations, together with all the other additional circumstances resulting from the subsequent intellectual combinations of our existence. All human beings are susceptible of pain, they are also, all susceptible of pleasure; they are all possessed of the same senses, subjected to the same wants, exhibit the same desires, and are satisfied with the same enjoyments. These positions cannot be controverted, they are true in the general features of their character, and the inconsiderable deviations resulting from the variations of animal structure, cannot, in any eminent degree, shake the rectitude or universality of these positions. The modification of the principle of animal structure in intelligent existence, is, no doubt, diversified by a nice and inscrutable gradation, but the aggregate amount of organic result must be nearly the same, and though the animal sensation were to vary in a still higher degree, yet it would, nevertheless, be substantially true, that certain comprehensive axioms might be laid down, which would necessarily include within the sphere of their imperious effect, every possible diversification of the sensitive faculties of human nature. That happiness is to be preferred to misery, pleasure to pain, virtue to vice, truth to falsehood, science to ignorance, order to confusion, universal good to universal evil, are positions which no rational being can possibly controvert. They are positions to which mankind, in all ages and countries, must yield assent. They are positions, the truth of which, is never denied, the essence of which, is never controverted; it is the form and application only, which has been the cause of social contention, and not the reality or excellence of the axioms themselves. The universality of the principle of sensation, generates universal capacity of enjoying pleasure, and suffering pain; this circumstance modifies the character of human actions, and renders it necessary that every man should regard every other man with an eye of strict justice, with a tender and delicate sensibility, with a constant reference to the preservation of his feelings, and the extension of his happiness; in a word, that the exercise of eternal justice should be constantly reciprocated by all the individuals of the same species. If I assume to myself the pretended right of injuring the sensations, the moral sentiments, or general happiness of my neighbour, he has, undoubtedly, an equal right to commit the same violence upon me; this would go to the destruction of all right, to the total subversion of all justice; it would reduce society instantly to a state of warfare, and introduce the reign of terror and of misery. It is a contradiction in terms to assert that any man has a right to do wrong; the exercise of such a pretended right, is the absolute destruction of all right, and the first human being who commits violence, has already prepared for himself a hell of retaliation, the justice of which, his own mind can never deny. It is, therefore, inconsistent with truth to say, that there is no such thing as a general standard of moral principle; this standard has a real existence in the construction of our nature; it is ascertained and regulated by the rule of reciprocal justice. It is absolute in the most important duties of human life; but in other cases of less weight and magnitude, it is discovered, by the calculations of judgment, by the process of the understanding, and will sometimes vibrate between the impressions of sense, and the subtile combinations which constitute an ultimate moral decision. If it be objected upon the suggestion of this idea, that the system of natural morality, is less perfect than that which has been revealed, the true answer is, that revealed morality, in the most intelligible cases, is incorrect and absurd: and in the more refined cases of difficulty, a total ignorance is manifested, so that it is evident, upon the very face of the record, that the subject of moral principle, in its subtile discriminations, was never examined or understood by Theological writers. The boasted maxim of the Christian religion, "All things whatsoever ye would that men should do to you, do ye even so to them," is incorrect in point of phraseology, and in point of principle does not exceed any of the moral writers of antiquity, who lived many hundred years before Jesus Christ. If this scriptural declaration means to establish the doctrine of reciprocal justice, it is incontrovertibly right; but the idea of placing the essence of virtue in the *wishes* of the human heart, is not very correct. It is very possible that one human being may desire another to do unto him many things which ought not to be done, and which are, in their own nature, improper or immoral. To say, therefore, that our desires should constitute the basis of moral decision, is a declaration not consistent with truth, and which, in many cases, would subvert the very essence of moral principle. There is a fitness of suitableness in the thing itself, united with the consideration of the good or bad effect that would be produced, which ought to become the ground of uniform and universal judgment in the human mind. My neighbour may wish me to do unto him an act of serious and substantial injury, which being performed, ought to be returned to me in manner and form exactly the same; and thus, by an adherence to this maxim as it is now stated, a double injury would be produced, and the foundation of virtue be shaken to the centre. But waiving any criticism of this kind, and giving to this scripture declaration the full extent of what is contended for, it is, nevertheless, no more than a plain maxim of justice, which had been known and practised, in a greater or less degree, at all times and in all countries. All the local and unjust institutions of mankind in former ages, have not destroyed the essential relation which man bears to man, nor have they been able, wholly to efface a knowledge of those duties, which result from these relations, and from the powers and principles of human existence. The more the subject of moral principle is examined, the more it will appear that there are certain general features in it, which the experience of man has partially recognized, and being fully developed and reduced to practice, would constitute a solid foundation for human felicity. The approach to such a standard of perfection, will be gradual and slow, but it must, nevertheless, from the very nature of man, be constant and certain. The following, says Volney, is conceived to be the primordial basis, and physical origin of all justice and right; whatever be the active power, the moving cause that directs the universe, this power having given to all men the same organs, the same sensations, and the same wants, has thereby declared, that it has also given them the same rights to the use of its benefits, and that in the order of nature, all men are equal. Secondly, inasmuch as this power has given to every man the ability of preserving and maintaining his own existence, it clearly follows, that all men are constituted independent of each other, that they are created free, that no man can be subject, and no man sovereign, but that all men are the unlimited proprietors of their own persons. Equality, therefore, and liberty, are two essential attributes of man, two laws of the divinity, not less essential and immutable, than the physical properties of inanimate nature; again, from the principle that every man is the unlimited master of his own person, it follows that one inseparable condition in every contract and engagement is the free and voluntary consent of all the persons therein bound; farther, because every individual is equal to every other individual, it follows that the balance of receipts and payments in political society, ought to be rigorously in equilibrium with each other; so that from the idea of equality, immediately flows that other idea, equity and justice.

Again, the same author observes, that there existed in the order of the universe, and in the physical constitution of man, eternal and immutable laws, which waited only his observance to render him happy. O men of different climes! look to the heavens that give you light, to the earth that nourishes you; since they present to you all the same gifts; since the power that directs their motion has bestowed on you the same life, the same organs, the same wants, has it not also given you the same right to the use of its benefits? Has it not hereby declared you to be all equal and free? What mortal then shall dare refuse to his fellow creature, that which is granted him by nature? O nations, let us banish all tryanny and discord! let us form one society, one vast family; and since mankind are all constituted alike, let there henceforth exist but one law, that of nature; one code, that of reason; one throne, that of justice; one altar, that of union. The foregoing impressive sentiments of this celebrated writer, disclose with clearness to the view of the human mind, the nature of moral principle and the foundation of all right and virtue. It is the reciprocation of sensation, the mutuality of condition, of powers and wants, that constitute the immortal basis of justice, and lead to the establishment of rules, whose operation must ever be in strict coincidence with the happiness of the human species. The exceptions to those fundamental principles are so few, and so unimportant, as to form no strong objection against the general assertion, that there exist in the constitution of human nature, those essential properties which confer upon man the character of moral agent. To controvert, therefore, the existence of these moral principles, or the idea of a general standard in the morality of human actions, is to fly in the face of all experience, to oppose the universal consciousness of the human understanding, and deny the most conspicuous facts connected with the life of man.

The Religion of Nature

. . . It is this religion which, at the present period of the world, creates such frightful apprehensions in the household of faith, and threatens to shake to the centre, the chief corner stone on which the Church is built. These apprehensions are daily disclosed by Christian professors, and they depict in such strong colours, the fatal effects of Deism, that ignorant fanaticism believes it to be an immoral monster, stalking with gigantic strides over the whole civilized world, for the detestable purpose of producing universal disorder, and subverting all the sound principles of social and intelligent existence. Such are the horrid ideas which the enemies of this pure and holy religion are every where propagating amongst their credulous and deluded followers. This circumstance renders it necessary, that the true idea of Deism be fairly stated, that it may be clearly understood by those whose minds have hitherto been darkened by the mysteries of faith. Deism declares to intelligent man the existence of one perfect God, Creator and Preserver of the Universe; that the laws by which he governs the world, are like himself immutable, and of course, that violations of these laws, or miraculous interference in the movements of nature, must be necessarily excluded from the grand system of universal existence; that the Creator is justly entitled to the adoration of every intellectual agent throughout the regions of infinite space; and that he alone is entitled to it, having no copartners who have a right to share with him the homage of the intelligent world. Deism also declares, that the practice of a pure, natural, and uncorrupted virtue, is the essential duty, and constitutes the highest dignity of man; that the powers of man are competent to all the great purposes of human existence; that science, virtue, and happiness, are the great objects which ought to awake the mental energies, and draw forth the moral affections of the human race.

These are some of the outlines of pure Deism, which Christian superstition so dreadfully abhors, and whose votaries she would willingly consign to endless torture. But it is built upon a substantial foundation, and will triumphantly diffuse happiness among the nations of the earth, for ages after Christian superstition and fanaticism have ceased to spread desolation and carnage through the fair creation of God.

In surveying the history of man, it is clearly discovered, that the miseries and misfortunes of his existence are, in a high degree, the result of his ignorance and his vices. Ignorance renders him savage and ferocious; while science pours into his mind the benign sentiments of humanity, and gives a new colouring to his moral existence. Reason, which every kind of supernatural theology abhors; reason, which is the glory of our nature, is destined eventually, in the progress of future ages, to overturn the empire of superstition, and erect upon its ruins a fabric, against which the storms of despotism may beat in vain; against which superstition may wreak her vengeance without effect, from which she will be obliged to retire in agonizing tortures. It has been the opinion of some honest and intelligent minds, that the power of intellect is inadequate to the moral and political emancipation of man. This opinion, though sometimes it is found to be operative upon benevolent hearts, seems, however, to be at war with the intellectual structure of our existence, and the facts furnished by modern history. In the great question which relates to human improvement, the cause which is productive of thought, cannot, in any high degree, be included as influencing the final decision. It is probable, however, that the opinion which refers intellect to organic material combination would favour most an unlimited improvement of the human species. If thought to be an effect of matter finely organized, and delicately constructed, the best method of augmenting its power would be, to preserve the whole human system in the most pure, regular, and natural mode of operation. Parents and instructors, in this respect, are capable of doing great injury, or of producing most important benefits to future ages.

The science of the world has been, in some measure, diminished by the propagation of an opinion, that there are only a few human beings who are possessed of what is called genius, to the exclusion of all the rest. This looks too much like mystery, and seems to include in it the idea that mind is sent from heaven, to occupy for a short time, a miserable and material tenement, and then return to its native home. It ought to be recollected that earth is the abode of man, and that of this the materials of his existence are composed, all are confined to this place of residence, and to the amelioration of sensitive and intelligent life, all his labours ought to be directed. He should learn to respect, and not despise his reason. He should learn to consider moral virtue, as the greatest good, as the most substantial joy of his existence. In order, however, to be eminently good, a full scope must be given to the operation of intellectual powers, and man must feel an unqualified confidence in his own energies. The double despotism of Church and state, has borne so hard upon human existence, that man is sunk beneath its dreadful weight; but resuscitated nations are about to teach kings and tyrants, a lesson awfully impressive, in regard to the destiny which awaits the aggregate injustice of the world. The period is at hand, in which kings and thrones, and priests and hierarchies, and the long catalogue of mischiefs which they have produced, shall be swept away from the face of the earth and buried in the grave of everlasting destruction. Then will arrive the era of human felicity, in which the heart of unfortunate man shall be consoled; then will appear the moment of national consolation, and universal freedom; then the empire of reason, of science, and of virtue, will extend over the whole earth, and man, emancipated from the barbarous despotism of antiquity, will assume to himself, his true predicament in nature, and become a standing evidence of the divinity of thought and the unlimited power of human reason.

. . . In examining the vast machinery of the universe, presented for our contemplation, by the great Creator, the human mind is lost in a labyrinth of reflection, and swallowed up in the most profound meditations! We behold on every side, the most ineffable beauties and the most astonishing wonders; the most splendid exhibitions of eternal wisdom, the most unbounded displays of infinite benevolence, and the most testimonies of an incomprehensible power. In this vast system, there are many things inexplicable to man; many events beyond the power of human solution, and many arrangements incomprehensible by the most scrutinizing efforts of human wisdom. But man should consider himself as an unit in the totality of existence; as a part of a widely extended whole, bearing a relation to every other part, and every other part bearing a relation to his own modification of life. He should reflect that the world is governed by general and immutable laws, and that the immutable operation of these laws produces perpetual mutability in the infinitely diversified parts and portions of the great fabric of nature. He ought to learn that change is the eternal order in the established arrangements of the world, and he ought not to be excluded from the general influence of fundamental laws established by eternal wisdom. He should learn to be reconciled to his fate, and consider death as a necessary and justifiable appendage of the present modification of existence. He should be taught to love and practice virtue, but not through the fear of an eternal hell; but because it is useful to society, and contributes to his individual happiness. He should be taught to revere the power, which animates and enlivens the great system of nature; but not to fear God on the one hand, nor flatter him on the other, with an expectation of obtaining his favour. He should disregard all ideas of ghosts, demons, and malignant spirits, and reason on the cognizable properties of real existence. The mind of man should be elevated above the practice of vice, above the frowns of fortune, and the fears of death. He ought to be the strong advocate of nature, *and have confidence in his own energies*, his principles should be just and correct, his actions strictly moral, and his sentiment in coincidence with the system of benevolence and utility. No bugbears of superstition, no ghosts of fanaticism, no demons of hell

should be permitted to disturb his brain; but rising above all vice and all prejudice, he should consider himself as an associated being, and live for the benefit
of himself and his fellow creatures.

Principles of the Deistical Society
of the State of New York

Proposals for forming a society for the promotion of moral science and the
religion of nature—having in view the destruction of superstition and fanaticism—tending to the development of the principles of a genuine natural
morality—the practice of a pure and uncorrupted virtue—the cultivation of
science and philosophy—the resurrection of reason, and the renovation of the
intelligent world.

At a time when the political despotism of the earth is disappearing, and man
is about to reclaim and enjoy the liberties of which for ages he has been deprived, it would be unpardonable to neglect the important concerns of intellectual and moral nature. The slavery of the mind has been the most destructive of all slavery; and the baneful effects of a dark and gloomy superstition have
suppressed all the dignified efforts of the human understanding, and essentially
circumscribed the sphere of intellectual energy. It is only by returning to the
laws of nature, which man has so frequently abandoned, that happiness is to be
acquired. And, although the efforts of a few individuals will be inadequate to
the sudden establishment of moral and mental felicity; yet, they may lay the
foundation on which a superstructure may be reared incalculably valuable to
the welfare of future generations. To contribute to the accomplishment of an
object so important, the members of this association do approve of the following fundamental principles:—

1. That the universe proclaims the existence of one supreme Deity, worthy
of the adoration of intelligent beings.

2. That man is possessed of moral and intellectual faculties sufficient for the
improvement of his nature, and the acquisition of happiness.

3. That the religion of nature is the only universal religion; that it grows out
of the moral relations of intelligent beings, and that it stands connected with
the progressive improvement and common welfare of the human race.

4. That it is essential to the true interest of man, that he love truth and
practise virtue.

5. That vice is every where ruinous and destructive to the happiness of the
individual and of society.

6. That a benevolent disposition, and beneficent actions, are fundamental
duties of rational beings.

7. That a religion mingled with persecution and malice cannot be of divine
origin.

8. That education and science are essential to the happiness of man.

9. That civil and religious liberty is equally essential to his true interests.

10. That there can be no human authority to which man ought to be amenable for his religious opinions.

11. That science and truth, virtue and happiness, are the great objects to which the activity and energy of the human faculties ought to be directed.

Every member admitted into this association shall deem it his duty, by every suitable method in his power, to promote the cause of nature and moral truth, in opposition to all schemes of superstition and fanaticism, claiming divine origin.

Philip Freneau

*The Reasoning Power, Celestial Guest,
the Stamp upon the Soul Impress'd*

Philip Freneau (1752–1832) is popularly remembered as the "poet of the American Revolution" and the "founder of American poetry." Both these titles could be debated: Joel Barlow, for example, might be equally in the running for the first, Anne Bradstreet for the second. But one unbestowed honorific Freneau indisputably deserves is "poet of American deism." More than any other Early Republic bard, he captured and celebrated in his verse the themes of Enlightenment rational religion. It is arguable that his influence was more pervasive than even Paine's or Palmer's, especially since he was less controversial. Many Early Republic readers (like readers today) may have been reluctant to plow through lengthy and demanding philosophical defenses of deism, but few could resist glancing at short and pithy poems scattered throughout newspapers and journals.

Of all the American deists, Freneau's beginnings were the most propitious. He was born in New York City, on 2 January 1752, into a prosperous and cultured family. Young Freneau grew up surrounded by books, art, and intelligent conversation. Privately educated by tutors, he entered the College of New Jersey (Princeton) at fifteen, where he enjoyed a distinguished career during his four-year stint.

Even as a student, Freneau's interests clearly ran toward writing. When the American Revolution erupted shortly after his graduation, he supported the cause by penning no less than eight satirical pamphlets aimed at the British and Tories. But wanderlust soon overwhelmed revolutionary fervor, and in 1776 Freneau sailed to Santa Cruz, where he remained for almost three years. There he wrote some of his best poetry, including "The Jamaica Funeral" and "The House of Night," each of which served as exemplars for the later romantic poets.

Freneau briefly returned to the United States in 1778 but quickly shipped out again for the West Indies. Luck was against him. The frigate on which he was a passenger was captured by a British man-of-war, and for a time Freneau was remanded to a prison ship in New York harbor. After nearly dying from ill treatment and privation, he was finally released. In 1781 he dramatically described his ordeal in the masterful *British Prison-Ship; A Poem, in Four Cantoes.*

During the next four years, Freneau was an employee of the Philadelphia

Post Office. Although he appears to have despised his job, it left him enough spare time to versify, and a steady stream of his poetry appeared in newspapers and journals. His passion for the ocean and adventure once more proved irresistible, however, and in 1784 he took to sea again, only returning to the United States five years later. In 1789, having finally exhausted his wanderlust (and, incidentally, having written some of his best seafaring poetry), he married and threw himself into journalism and governmental work. He edited several newspapers, including the anti-Federalist *Aurora*, served in the Department of State during Jefferson's administration, and finally retired to a New Jersey farm to devote himself to poetry. In December 1832, while returning home from a country store, he was caught in a sudden blizzard, lost his way, and perished. It was an appropriately romantic end for a man who his entire life had relished the unexpected.

Although Freneau had briefly studied for the ministry following his graduation from Princeton, he was by temperament and intellectual conviction ill suited for the clerical life. In company with the other American deists, he had imbibed early on the New Learning of Locke and Newton, becoming convinced that the only worship worthy of humans was one based on a rational investigation of nature and morality. His deistic writings, prose as well as poetry, reflect that belief. Interestingly, Freneau did not tend to be as anticlerical as his fellow deists, although he did lambast what he took to be priestly hypocrisy in several of his pieces. He was more concerned with lyrical celebrations of nature's God than with vindictive diatribes against supernaturalist dogma. Nor did he militantly propagandize for deism. Although an acquaintance of Palmer's, a correspondent of Paine's, and a sometime member of the New York Deistical Society, Freneau by and large preferred the contemplative to the activist life, at least when it came to religious matters. Indeed, most of his deistic poetry, although written throughout his entire career, was only published late in life.

The selections from Freneau here include both prose and poetry. The verse generally centers on the key deistic concepts of God, nature, reason, and morality. "Reflections on the Constitution, or Frame of Nature," argues, along lines reminiscent of Ethan Allen's *Reason the Only Oracle*, that God's revelation is nature and nature's laws: "THOU, nature's self art nature's God / Through all expansion spread abroad, / Existing in the eternal scheme, / Vast, undivided, and supreme." "On a Book Called Unitarian Theology," "On the Uniformity and Perfection of Nature," and "On the Universality, and Other Attributes of the God of Nature" all echo the claim that God is revealed through the constant and immutable laws of nature. In addition, the first, with its reiteration of a sun metaphor, hints at an almost platonic relationship between the divine Mind and the created world. The second insists, in typical deistic fashion, that the doctrine of miracles, if taken seriously, demolishes the integrity of nature as well as the dignity of God: "Could [Nature] descend from that great plan / To work unusual things for man, / To suit the insect of an hour— / This would betray a want of power."

In "On the Powers of the Human Understanding," "On Superstition," and "Belief and Unbelief," Freneau considers the nature of rationality. The first argues that human reason will continue to evolve, perhaps even after death, more and more closely approximating the divine Reason of which it is a reflection. The second claims that "true" religion is "on nature and reason built," but that sectarian bigotry and ignorance reduces it to an irrational system that encourages error and anxiety. Only when humans "No more fictitious gods revere, / Nor worship what engenders fear," will religious sensibility resume its original purity. "Belief and Unbelief" argues, a la Volney, for the relativity of sectarian doctrines and concludes by suggesting that faith, properly understood, is inductive rather than mysteriously supernatural: "Nor can conviction bind the heart / Till evidence has done its part: / And, when that evidence is clear, / Belief is just, and truth is near."

"Science, Favourable to Virtue," "On False Systems of Government," "The New Age," "On the Abuse of Human Power," "On the Religion of Nature," "On the Evils of Human Life," "On Happiness," and "The Millennium" each reveal Freneau's deistic conviction that morality is the supreme goal of natural religion, that it is properly based on reason's control of the passions, and that it enhances social utility as well as individual felicity. Rational religion, then, encourages the progress of the natural sciences, because they are the vehicles best suited to cultivate human reason and promote morality. Moreover, freedom of conscience and release from political oppression and social inequality are requisite conditions for the flourishing of human reason. Finally, in lines that recall Pope's "All that is, is right," Freneau argues that evil does not arise from natural law, which necessarily reflects divine goodness and providence, but rather from human error and prejudice. If humans but regulate their behavior to conform to the lessons of nature, evil can be extirpated. This is because "That moral track to man assign'd" is "A transcript from the all-perfect mind."

The prose pieces reprinted here are delightful illustrations of Freneau at his satirical best. They also contain two of his infrequent assaults on institutionalized Christianity and the clergy. As mentioned, Freneau rarely employed his pen directly against revealed religion but instead concerned himself with highlighting the positive attributes of deism. Occasionally, however, exasperated by what he interpreted as egregious abuses or absurdities on the part of the Christian establishment, he entered the fray—although even then he usually dressed his criticisms in humor rather than invective. His prods were indirect stabs rather than frontal attacks. As such, they were probably more effective than the angry recriminations of a Paine or Palmer. They encouraged readers to laugh at supernaturalist doctrine, sectarian rituals, and stuffy clergy. And humor, after all, is a sure antidote to authoritarianism: One cannot take seriously what one finds laughable.

The first selection is part of a series entitled "Letters on Various Interesting and Important Subjects," which Freneau ran in his *Aurora*. It is both a defense of the ideals of the French Revolution and a slap at the perceived hypocrisy of American religionists. The protagonist in the little vignette is Robert Slender, a homespun philosopher whom Freneau frequently used as his mouthpiece. Robert is everyman, a seemingly naive, nonbookish character who disingenuously trusts common sense and experience and is consequently always finding himself on the wrong side of his more "learned" clerical neighbors. His ability to cut through the sophistries of theological nonsense calls to mind the disarmingly acute innocence of two of Franklin's "commonplace" philosophers: Poor Richard and Silence Dogood.

In this piece, Robert finds himself perplexed about the correct definitions of "orthodoxy" and "heterodoxy." Before the French Revolution (which Freneau always fervently admired), the Calvinist clergy had never missed a chance to blast from the pulpit Catholicism and papacy. Such denunciations, Robert had been led to believe, were "orthodox." But now that France has overthrown the monarchy, established democracy, and broken the hegemony of the church, Robert is puzzled to discover that the American clergy praises Catholicism, defends the pope, and adulates such non-Protestant enemies of liberalism as "Suwarrow" (a reference to the Russian field marshal Suvarov, who was instrumental in savagely breaking the back of the democratic Polish insurrection in 1794). This reversal is now likewise "orthodox." How?

The cleric to whom Robert addresses his question proceeds to explain away the "merely apparent" discrepancy by leading Slender through a hilarious maze of sophisms. But the real explanation for the about-face is obvious: Whenever established Christianity feels itself threatened by either political liberalism or rational religion, it expeditiously aligns itself with what was previously condemned as heretical. When Slender mildly suggests that such a move is less than consistent, the clergyman who is instructing him sternly thunders, "I hope . . . you don't pretend to argue religion *with me!*" and declares poor Robert anathema.

The second prose selection is from "The Voyage of Timberoo-Taho-Eede, an Otaheite Indian." In it, Freneau pokes fun at both Christian ritual and values. The story is a report from an Otaheite sent as an emissary to New England. He tells his curious chief that the religion of the foreigners he visited is bizarre, holding as it does that the deity is both one and three persons and that God, though eternal, was murdered. The adherents of this religion indulge in every species of wickedness, including slavery; they are "intolerably proud, selfish, vain, malevolent, and lazy"; and they appear to worship "little plates of metal" which they hoard. The emissary concludes his report by assuring his chief that the Otaheite priest attempted to instruct the foreigners in the one true Otaheite religion but barely escaped being soundly drubbed for his pains. This leads him to surmise that "these people seem to be under some indissoluble obligation to believe only what has previously been believed for them by their progenitors"—a subtle jab at religious bigotry that reminds one of the eloquent opening stanza of Freneau's "On the Abuse of Human Power": "Must man at that tribunal bow / Which will no range to thought allow, / But his best powers would sway or sink, / And idly tells him what to THINK."

On the Powers of the Human Understanding

This human mind! how grand a theme:
Faint image of the Great Supreme,
   The universal soul,
That lives, that thinks, compares, contrives;
From its vast self all power derives
   To manage or control.

What energy, O soul, is thine:
How you reflect, resolve, combine;
   Invention all your own!
Material bodies changed by you
New modes assume, or natures new,
   From death or chaos won.

To intellectual powers, though strong,
To moral powers a use belong
   More noble and refined;
These lift us to the power who made,
Illume what seems to us all shade,
   The part to man assigned.

Both nurtured in the heart of man
Serve to advance his social plan,
   And happier make his race;
Hence Reason takes her potent sway,
And *grovelling passions* bids obey
   That harm us and debase.

O ye, who long have walked obscure;
Forever must those clouds endure
   Which darken human bliss?
Though for some better state designed,
Is there not rigour in the mind
   To make a heaven of this—

Eternal must that progress be
Which Nature through futurity
   Decrees the human soul;
Capacious still, it still improves
As through the abyss of time it moves,
   Or endless ages roll.

Its knowledge grows by every change;
Through science vast we see it range
   That none may here acquire;
The pause of death must come between
And Nature gives another scene
   More brilliant, to admire.

Thus decomposed, or recombined,
To slow perfection moves the mind
   And *may* at last attain
A nearer rank with that first cause
Which distant, though it ever draws,
   Unequalled must remain.

Its moral beauty thus displayed
In moral excellence arrayed
   Perpetually it shines:
Its heaven of happiness complete
The mass of souls united meet
   In orbs that heaven assigns.

Reflections on the Constitution, or Frame of Nature

From what high source of being came
This system, Nature's aweful frame;
This sun, that motion gives to all,
The planets, and this earthly ball:

This sun, who life and heat conveys,
And comforts with his cheering rays;
This image of the God, whose beam
Enlivens like the GREAT SUPREME.

We see, with most exact design,
The WORLD revolve, the planets shine,
In nicest order all things meet,
A structure in ITSELF complete.

Beyond our proper solar sphere
Unnumbered orbs again appear,
Which, sunk into the depths of space,
Unvarying keep their destined place.

Great Frame! what wonders we survey,
In part alone, from day to day!
And hence the reasoning, human soul
Infers an author of the whole:

A power, that every blessing gives,
Who through eternal ages lives,
All space inhabits, space his throne,
Spreads through all worlds, confined to none;

Infers, through skies, o'er seas, o'er lands
A power throughout the whole commands;
In all extent its dwelling place,
Whose mansion is unbounded space.

Where ends this world, or when began
This spheric point displayed to man?—
No limit has the work divine,
Nor owns a circumscribing line.

Beyond what mind or thought conceives,
Our efforts it in darkness leaves;
And Nature we, by Reason's aid,
Find boundless as the power that made.

THOU, nature's self art nature's God
Through all expansion spread abroad,
Existing in the eternal scheme,
Vast, undivided, and supreme.

Here beauty, order, power, behold
Exact, all perfect, uncontrouled;
All in its proper place arranged,
Immortal, endless, and unchanged.

Its powers, still active, never rest,
From motions, by THAT GOD impressed,
Who life through all creation spread,
Nor left the meanest atom dead.

Science, Favourable to Virtue

The mind, in this uncertain state,
Is anxious to investigate
All knowledge through creation sown,
And would no atom leave unknown.

So warm, so ardent in research,
To wisdom's *source* she fain would march;
And find by study, toil, and care
The secrets of all nature *there*.

Vain wish, to fathom all we see,
For nature is all mystery;
The mind, though perched on eagle's wings,
With pain surmounts the scum of things.

Her knowledge on the surface floats,
Of things supreme she dreams or dotes;
Fluttering awhile, she soon descends,
And all in disappointment ends.

And yet this proud, this strong desire,
Such ardent longings to aspire,
Prove that this weakness in the mind
For some wise purpose was designed.

From efforts and attempts, like these,
Virtue is gained by slow degrees;
And science, which from truth she draws,
Stands firm to Reason and her cause.

However small, its use we find
To tame and civilize mankind,
To throw this brutal instinct by,
To honour Reason, ere we die.

The lovely philanthropic scheme
(Great image of the power supreme,)
On growth of science must depend;
With this all human duties end.

On a Book Called Unitarian Theology

In this choice work, with wisdom penned, we find
The noblest system to reform mankind,
Bold truths confirmed, that bigots have denied,
By most perverted, and which some deride.
   Here, truths divine in easy language flow,
Truths long concealed, that now all climes shall know:
Here, like the blaze of our material *sun*,
Enlightened *Reason* proves, that GOD IS ONE—
As that, concentered in itself, a sphere,
Illumines all Nature with its radiance here,
Bids towards itself all trees and plants aspire,
Awakes the winds, impels the seeds of fire,
And still subservient to the Almighty plan,
Warms into life the changeful race of man;
So—like the sun—in heaven's bright realms we trace
One POWER OF LOVE, that fills unbounded space,
Existing always by no borrowed aid,
Before all worlds—eternal, and not made—
To THAT indebted, stars and comets burn,
Owe their swift movements, and to THAT return!
Prime source of wisdom, all-contriving mind,
First spring of REASON, that this globe designed;
Parent of order, whose unwearied hand
Upholds the fabric that his wisdom planned,
And, its due course assigned to every sphere,

Resolves the seasons, and sustains the year!—
    Pure light of TRUTH! where'er thy splendours shine,
Thou art the image of the power divine;
Nought else, in life, that full resemblance bears,
No sun, that lights us through our circling years,
No stars, that through yon' charming azure stray,
No moon, that glads us with her evening ray,
No seas, that o'er their gloomy caverns flow,
No forms beyond us, and no shapes below!

    Then slight—oh slight not, this instructive page,
For the mean follies of a dreaming age;
Here to the truth, by REASON's aid aspire,
Nor some dull preacher of romance admire;
See ONE, SOLE GOD, in these convincing lines,
Beneath whose view perpetual day-light shines;
At whose command all worlds their circuits run,
And night, retiring, dies before the sun!

    Here, MAN *no more disgraced by Time appears,*
Lost in dull slumbers through ten thousand years;
Plunged in that gulph, whose dark unfathomed wave
Men of all ages to perdition gave;
An empty dream, or still more empty shade,
The substance vanished, and the form decayed!—

    Here Reason proves, that when this life decays,
Instant, new life in the warm bosom plays,
As that expiring, still its course repairs
Through endless ages, and unceasing years.

    Where parted souls with kindred spirits meet,
Wrapt to the bloom of beauty all complete;
In that celestial, vast, unclouded sphere,
Nought there exists but has its image here!
All there is MIND!—That INTELLECTUAL FLAME,
From whose vast stores all human genius came,
In which all Nature forms or REASON's plan—
FLOWS TO THIS ABJECT WORLD, AND BEAMS ON MAN!

On False Systems of Government, and the Generally Debased Condition of Mankind

Does there exist, or will there come
An age with wisdom to assume,
    The RIGHTS by heaven designed;

The Rights which man was born to claim,
From Nature's God which freely came,
   To aid and bless mankind.—

No monarch lives, nor do I deem
There will exist one crown supreme
   The world in peace to sway;
Whose first great view will be to place
On their true scale the human race,
   And discord's rage allay.

REPUBLICS! must the task be your's
To frame the code which life secures,
   And RIGHT from man to man—
Are you, in Time's declining age,
Found only fit to tread the stage
   When tyranny began?

How can we call those systems just
Which bid the few, the proud, the first
   Possess all earthly good;
While millions robbed of all that's dear
In silence shed the ceaseless tear,
   And leeches suck their blood.

Great orb, that on our planet shines,
Whose power both light and heat combines
   You should the model be;
To man, the pattern how to reign
With equal sway, and how maintain
   True human dignity.

Impartially to all below
The solar beams unstinted flow,
   On all is poured the RAY,
Which cheers, which warms, which clothes the ground
In robes of green, or breathes around
   Life;—to enjoy the day.

But crowns not so;—with selfish views
They partially their bliss diffuse
   Their *minions* feel them *kind*;—

And, still opposed to human right,
Their plans, their views in *this* unite,
   To embroil and curse mankind.

Ye tyrants, false to HIM, who gave
Life, and the virtues of the brave,
   All worth we own, or know:—
Who made you great, the lords of man,
To waste with wars, with blood to stain
   The Maker's works below?

You have no iron race to sway—
Illume them well with Reason's ray;
   Inform our active race;
True honour, to the mind impart,
With virtue's precepts tame the heart,
   Not urge it to be base;

Let laws revive, by heaven designed,
To tame the tiger in the mind
   And drive from human hearts
That love of wealth, that love of sway,
Which leads the world too much astray,
   Which points envenomed darts:

And men will rise from *what they are*,
Sublimer, and superior, far,
   Than SOLON guessed, or PLATO saw;
All will be just, all will be good—
That harmony, "*not understood*,"
   Will reign the general law.

For, in our race, deranged, bereft,
The parting god some vestige left
   Of worth before possessed;
Which full, which fair, which perfect shone,
When love and peace, in concord sown,
   Ruled, and inspired each breast.

Hence, the small GOOD which yet we find,
Is *shades* of that prevailing mind
   Which sways the worlds around:—

Let *these* depart, once disappear,
And earth would all the horrors wear
    In hell's dominions found.

Just, as yon' tree, which, bending, grows
To chance, not fate, its fortunes owes;
    So man from some rude shock,
Some slighted power, some hostile hand,
Has missed the state by Nature planned,
    Has split on passion's rock.

Yet shall that tree, when hewed away
(As human woes have had their day)
    A new creation find:
The infant shoot in time will swell,
(Sublime and great from that which fell,)
    To all that heaven designed.

What is this earth, that sun, these skies;
If all we see, on man must rise,
    Forsaken and oppressed—
Why blazes round the eternal beam,
Why, Reason, art thou called supreme,
    Where nations find no rest.—

What are the splendours of this ball—
When life is closed, what are they all?
    When *dust to dust returns*
Does power, or wealth, attend the dead;
Are captives from the contest led—
    Is homage paid to urns?

What are the ends of Nature's laws;
What folly prompts, what madness draws
    Mankind in chains, too strong:—
Nature, *to us*, confused appears,
On little things she wastes her cares,
    The great *seem sometimes* wrong.

The New Age: Or, Truth Triumphant

In reason's view the times advance
   That other scenes to man disclose,
When nature to her children grants
   A smiling season of repose;
      And better laws the wise will trace,
      To curb the wicked of our race.

Those happy ages, years of bliss,
   Had many an ancient sage foretold,
Who, if they err'd or aught amiss,
   Predicted of this age of gold,
      It was, that crowns and courts and kings
      Would still attend this charge of things.

Strange thought, that they whose god is gain,
   Who live by war, who thrive on blood,
Of half that live the curse the bane,
   Could ever rule among the good:
      These did some hateful fiend engage
      To banish peace and vex the age.

Man to be happy, as he may
 As far as nature meant him here,
Should yield to no despotic sway
 Or systems of degrading fear;
  And sovereign man, new modell'd now,
  To sovereign man alone should bow.

The civil despot, once destroy'd,
   With all his base, tyrannic laws,
The mind of man will be employ'd
   In aiding virtue and her cause:
      Enlighten'd once, inform'd and free,
      The mind admits no tyranny.

I saw the blest benignant hour
   When the worst plague of human race,
Dread superstition, lost her power,
   And, with her patrons, black and base,

Fled to the darkest shades of hell,
And bade at least one world farewell.

Fanatic flames extinguish'd all
  The energy of thought will rise:
I see imposture's fabric fall,
  Each wicked imp of falsehood dies;
    And sovereign truth prevails at last
    To triumph o'er the errors past.

The moral beauties of the mind
  If man would to a blessing turn,
And the great powers to him assign'd
  Would cultivate, improve, adorn:
    The sun of happiness, and peace
    Would shine on earth and never cease.

On Superstition

Implanted in the human breast,
Religion means to make us blest;
On reason built, she lends her aid
To help us through life's sickening shade.

But man, to endless error prone
And fearing most what's most unknown,
To phantoms bows that round him rise,
To angry gods, and vengeful skies.

Mistaken race, in error lost,
And foes to them who love you most,
No more fictitious gods revere,
Nor worship what engenders fear.

O Superstition! to thy sway
If man has bow'd and will obey,
Misfortune still must be his doom
And sorrow through the days to come.

Hence, ills on ills successive grow
To cloud our day of bliss below;

Hence wars and feuds, and deadly hate,
And all the woes that on them wait.

Here moral virtue finds its bane,
Hence, ignorance with her slavish train.
Hence, half the vigor of the mind
Relax'd, or lost in human kind.

The social tie by this is broke
When we some tyrant god invoke:
The bitter curse from man to man
From this infernal fiend began.

The reasoning power, celestial guest,
The stamp upon the soul impress'd;
When Superstition's awe degrades,
Its beauty fails, its splendor fades.

O! turn from her detested ways,
Unhappy man! her fatal maze;
The reason which he gave, improve,
And venerate the power above.

On the Abuse of Human Power, As Exercised over Opinion

What human power shall dare to bind
The mere opinions of the mind?
Must man at that tribunal bow
Which will no range to thought allow,
But his best powers would sway or sink,
And idly tells him what to THINK.

Yes! there are such, and such are taught
To fetter every power of thought;
To chain the mind, or bend it down
To some mean system of their own,
And make religion's sacred cause
Amenable to human laws.

Has human power the simplest claim
Our hearts to sway, our thoughts to tame;

Shall she the rights of heaven assert,
Can she to falsehood truth convert,
Or truth again to falsehood turn,
And at the test of reason spurn?

All human sense, all craft must fail
And all its strength will nought avail,
When it attempts with efforts blind
To sway the independent mind,
Its spring to break, its pride to awe,
Or give to private judgment, law.

Oh impotent! and vile as vain,
They, who would native thought restrain!
As soon might they arrest the storm
Or take from fire the power to warm,
As man compel, by dint of might,
Old darkness to prefer to light.

No! leave the mind unchain'd and free,
And what they ought, mankind will be,
No hypocrite, no lurking fiend,
No artist to some evil end,
But good and great, benign and just,
As God and nature made them first.

On the Uniformity and Perfection of Nature

On one fix'd point all nature moves,
Nor deviates from the track she loves;
Her system, drawn from reason's source,
She scorns to change her wonted course.

Could she descend from that great plan
To work unusual things for man,
To suit the insect of an hour—
This would betray a want of power.

Unsettled in its first design
And erring, when it did combine
The parts that form the vast machine,
The figures sketch'd on nature's scene.

Perfections of the great first cause
Submit to no contracted laws,
But all-sufficient, all-supreme,
Include no trivial views in them.

Who looks through nature with an eye
That would the scheme of heaven descry,
Observes her constant, still the same,
In all her laws, through all her frame.

No imperfection can be found
In all that is, above, around,—
All, nature made, in reason's sight
Is order all, and *all is right.*

On the Universality, and Other Attributes of the God of Nature

All that we see, about, abroad,
What is it all, but nature's God?
In meaner works discover'd here
No less than in the starry sphere.

In seas, on earth, this God is seen;
All that exist, upon him lean;
He lives in all, and never stray'd
A moment from the works he made:

His system fix'd on general laws
Bespeaks a wise creating cause;
Impartially he rules mankind,
And all that on this globe we find.

Unchanged in all that seems to change,
Unbounded space is his great range;
To one vast purpose always true,
No time, with him, is old or new.

In all the attributes divine
Unlimited perfections shine;
In these enwrapt, in these complete,
All virtues in that centre meet.

This power who doth all powers transcend,
To all intelligence a friend,
Exists, the *greatest and the best*
Throughout all worlds, to make them blest.

All that he did he first approved
He all things into *being* loved;
O'er all he made he still presides,
For them in life, or death provides.

On the Religion of Nature

The power, that gives with liberal hand
    The blessings man enjoys, while here,
And scatters through a smiling land
    The abundant products of the year;
        That power of nature, ever bless'd,
        Bestow'd religion with the rest.

Born with ourselves, her early sway
    Inclines the tender mind to take
The path of right, fair virtue's way
    Its own felicity to make.
        This universally extends
        And leads to no mysterious ends.

Religion, such as nature taught,
    With all divine perfection suits;
Had all mankind this system sought
    Sophists would cease their vain disputes,
        And from this source would nations know
        All that can make their heaven below.

This deals not curses to mankind,
    Or dooms them to perpetual grief,
If from its aid no joys they find,
    It damns them not for unbelief;
        Upon a more exalted plan
        Creation's nature dealt with man—

Joy to the day, when all agree
   On such grand systems to proceed,
From fraud, design, and error free,
   And which to truth and goodness lead:
     Then persecution will retreat
     And man's religion be complete.

On the Evils of Human Life

To him who rules the starry spheres,
No evil in his works appears:
Man with a different eye, surveys,
The incidents in nature's maze:
   And all that brings him care or pain
   He ranks among misfortune's train.

The ills that God, or nature, deal,
The ills we hourly see, or feel,
The sense of wretchedness and woe
To man may be sincerely so;
   And yet these springs of tears and sighs
   Be heaven's best blessings in disguise.

Some favorite late, in anguish lay
And agonized his life away:
You grieved—to be consoled, refused,
And heaven itself almost accused
   Of cruelty, that could dispense
   Such tortures to such innocence.

Could you but lift the dreary veil,
And see with eyes or mind less frail
The secrets of the world to come,
You would not thus bewail *his* doom,
   To find on some more happy coast
   More blessings, far, than all he lost.

The seeming ills on life that wait
And mingle with our best estate,
Misfortune on misfortune grown,

And heaviest most, when most alone;
Calamities, and heart oppress'd—
These all attend us, for the best.

Learn hence, ye mournful, tearful race,
On a sure ground your hopes to place;
Immutable are nature's laws;
And hence the soul her comfort draws
That all the God allots to man
Proceeds on one unerring plan.

Hold to the moral system, true,
And heaven will always be in view;
O man! by heaven this law was taught
To reconcile you to your lot,
To be your friend, when friendship fails,
And nature a new being hails.

Belief and Unbelief: Humbly Recommended to the Serious Consideration of Creed Makers

What some believe, and would enforce
Without reluctance or remorse,
Perhaps another may decry,
Or call a fraud, or deem a lie.

Must he for that be doom'd to bleed,
And fall a martyr to some creed,
By hypocrites or tyrants framed,
By reason damn'd, by truth disclaim'd?

On mere belief no merit rests,
As unbelief no guilt attests:
Belief, if not absurd and blind,
Is but conviction of the mind,

Nor can conviction bind the heart
Till evidence has done its part:
And, when that evidence is clear,
Belief is just, and truth is near.

In evidence, belief is found;
Without it, none are fairly bound
To yield assent, or homage pay
To what confederate worlds might say.

They who extort belief from man
Should, in the out-set of their plan,
Exhibit, like the mid-day sun
An evidence denied by none.

From this great point, o'erlook'd or miss'd,
Still unbelievers will exist;
And just their plea; for how absurd
For evidence, to take *your word*!

Not to believe, I therefore hold
The right of man, all uncontrol'd
By all the powers of human wit,
What kings have done, or sages writ;

Not criminal in any view,
Nor—man!—to be avenged by you,
Till evidence of strongest kind
Constrains assent, and clears the mind.

On Happiness, as Proceeding from the Practice of Virtue

This truth, upon the soul impress'd,
Has been by every age confess'd,
That in the course of human things
Felicity from virtue springs.

Where vice prevails, or baseness sways,
Remorse and pain the fault repays,
The man of vice has no resource,
But even in pleasure finds a curse.

If happiness can be sincere
A virtuous conduct makes it here,
That moral track to man assign'd
A transcript from the all-perfect mind.

Should virtue sometimes fail of bliss,
Plung'd in misfortune's dark abyss,
Still, in the event she would not fall,
But rise, triumphant o'er it all.

Should life's whole course replete with ill,
To virtue prove a bitter pill;
Another life has heaven design'd
Where she her due rewards will find.

Nay, though through life perplex'd and pain'd
And though no other life remain'd;
A life well spent itself would prove
A due reward from HIM above.

And to be conscious we have done
The worthy part, though frown'd upon,
Can every seeming ill destroy
And grief and sadness change to joy.

The Millennium—To a Ranting Field Orator

With aspect wild, in ranting strain
    You bring the brilliant period near,
When monarchy will close her reign
    And wars and warriors disappear;
        The lion and the lamb will stray,
        And, social, walk the woodland way.

I fear, with superficial view
    You contemplate dame nature's plan:—
She various forms of being drew,
    And made the common tyrant—man:
        She form'd them all with wise design,
        Distinguish'd each, and drew the line.

Observe the lion's visage bold
    His iron tooth, his murderous claw,
His aspect cast in anger's mould;
    The strength of steel is in his paw:
        Could he be meant with lambs to stray
        Or feed along the woodland way?

Since first his race on earth began
   War was his trade and war will be:
And when he quits that ancient plan
   With milder natures to agree,
     He will be changed to something new
     And have some other part to do.

One system see through all this frame,
   Apparent discord still prevails;
The forest yields to active flame,
   The ocean swells with stormy gales;
     No season did the God decree
     When leagued in friendship these should be.

And do you think that human kind
   Can shun the all-pervading law—
That passion's slave we ever find—
   Who discord from their nature draw;
     Ere discord can from man depart
     He must assume a different heart.

Yet in the slow advance of things
   A time may come our race may rise,
By reason's aid to stretch their wings,
   And see the light with other eyes;
     And when the ancient mist is pass'd;
     To find their nature changed at last.

The sun himself, the powers ordain,
   Should in no perfect circle stray;
He shuns the equatorial plane,
   Prefers an odd serpentine way,
     And lessens yearly, sophists prove,
     His angle in the voids above.

When moving in his ancient line,
   And no oblique ecliptic near,
With some new influence he may shine
   But you and I will not be here
     To see the lion shed his teeth
     Or kings forget the trade of death—

Letters on Various Interesting
and Important Subjects: Letter 13

Some time ago, I thought that I had gained such an entire mastery over my fears that the whole troop, so remarkable for printer-flogging here or elsewhere, could not make me tremble—and so I walked about in open day, ventured even to talk in favour of the Aurora in the little beerhouse at the corner, and indeed was so fool-hardy as to assert that the clergy were now behaving in the most inconsistent manner by praying for the success of Suwarrow, the pope, and the re-establishment of the Romish religion, for the downfall of which they, and their fathers before them in the church, have prayed heartily for at least these two hundred years—But this conduct raised such a buzz about my ears that I have been forced to run away in good earnest. What chiefly led to this was the following—One day, having gained a little time, I took my stick in my hand, adjusted my wig, and walked out to see an acquaintance. Who happened to be there, as ill luck would have had it, but his reverence—So after some chit chat about dry weather, water works, sickness, and some thoughts on death, which I thought made the parson's face longer than ordinary, though it is not short at any time, he thus addressed me—So Robert, I am informed that the reason why you no longer attend to hear God's word preached on the Sabbath is because you neither like our prayers nor our preaching. I confess, Mr. Editor, I knew not what to say—I looked on the one side, and then on the other, rose from my chair, spit in the sand box, and threw a segar I had but just lighted into the fire. —I had never contradicted the clergy because my good father had often said to me, "Robert, never meddle with the clergy—they are edge-tools"; but father's advice had slipped out of my memory at that time—so, giving three pretty loud hems, by way of practice, I answered—And pray your reverence, said I, can I have a better reason? If, Robert, answered he, our preaching or praying were not *orthodox*, then you would have a right to quit us and go elsewhere; but what fault have you?—Why sir, said I, as to what is *orthodox*, and what do you call it, the other dox—Heterodox, replied he—Aye, aye, says I, that's it; I never clearly knew what they meant—I have but a poor head at best, and these are hard words—I would be much obliged to your reverence to tell me what they mean, and then I will try to answer your question. The parson, putting on one of his airs, went on thus: I am astonished, Robert, to hear you talk thus—You have appeared in public, censured men and measures in that democratical sheet called the Aurora, and your name is familiar in every company. Some say you're a man of sense; others, that you are a fool; yet both laugh at your productions; and *you ask* what is the meaning of two plain *English* words.—They may be *English* or *Spanish* for me, said I, much ashamed of my own ignorance; but if you please to tell me, I'll thank you kindly sir, and if I can I won't forget what you say.— Why, said he, with a smile of superior wisdom, orthodoxy is the whole body of principles taught in *our church*—and every opinion contrary thereto is hetero-dox—So, said I, this is indeed to me very strange—but I'll remember it—But, added I, can a principle be heterodox one year and orthodox another year?—No sir, answered his reverence, with much authority; orthodoxy is ever the same; the principles I have the honour to preach were taught by Christ, his apostles, and so on to the present day, without the smallest alteration.—It may be so, answered I; I have but a poor brain—but I confess I think it otherwise. And pray, sir, said the parson, what is this great fault that we have been guilty of, and of which your wise head is so full?—Sir, says I, before you came to preach at our church, the reverend Dr. **** never went into the pulpit but he prayed for the fall of Antichrist, that man of sin, and this I think was orthodox praying—He preached very often against the errors of the church of Rome, and from the prophecies proved that the Pope was Antichrist; and this, because you know it was taught in *our church*, was orthodox preaching—Now sir, you pray for the re-establishment of the Romish religion, and preach that the French have committed a damning sin in pulling Antichrist from his chair, converting images into money, consecrated bells into democratic cannon, shutting up the nunneries, and sending the poor girls into the world to answer the end of their creation—Now sir, is this also orthodoxy? Undoubtedly sir, answered he, for you know it is taught in our church. But, says I, how sir can this be? You told me but just now that orthodoxy did not change, but was always the same—I acknowledge, said his reverence, that you have, Robert, stumbled on something like a contradiction, and it deserves a reply. We prayed for the downfall of the Pope because we thought religion would be benefitted by it—we now see that religion is much hurt by it, and therefore we wish it restored—If indeed God had brought down Antichrist in *some other way*, and established the true Calvinistic Presbyterian religion in its room, then we would not have desired its restoration—*and this is orthodox*. It may be orthodox, said I, for ought I know to the contrary, but one thing I'll venture to say, that it is neither agreeable to Judaism or Christianity—I hope, Robert, said his rever-ence, you don't pretend to argue religion *with me!*—God forbid sir, says I; excuse me for speaking rashly; but if you please sir, I'll tell you a story—Let's hear it, says he; but I tell you aforehand, there must be nothing about the French in it, for I hate them heartily—Indeed, said I, there is not one word about the French in it, for I believe it is somewhere in the Bible or Testament—Once upon a time, there was a very great man, but he was not a Jew, who had the bad fortune to be afflicted with the leprosy—all the doctors in his own country were consulted in vain, and he was pronounced incurable. At length he was informed that in the land of Jewry there lived a very good man who could cure him in an instant. The great man set forward immediately on his journey. His equipage was splendid—his retinue numerous. He arrived—the man of God paid no respect to him, although he was very great—but sent him word to go and wash himself a number of times in the river Jordan. The great man was enraged. Are not, said he, the rivers of my own country much better than the rivers of Israel? I thought he would have come out to me—put his hand on the place, called on God, and so healed me. However, being a man of some sense, and having some wise men about him, he was induced to obey the prophet. He did so, and was cured. You have my story. I can make nothing of it, said the parson. Well, said I, I'll apply it. God had his way (like the prophet) of bringing down Antichrist; but you, like the great man, say his way was not a good way, and if he had taken counsel with the very wise Christians of the day, they would have taught him that it would have been much better to have left him standing than to have made use of such instruments; and now you would instruct him to govern his providential dispensations by your advice, and once more erect spiritual Babylon, bring back the images, catch the poor nuns, and shut them once more in their cells. As I said this, his reverence leaped to his feet. I declare, Robert, said he, you are unfit to live in society; 'tis such men as you who are bringing the curse of God on our city. I pronounce you an infidel, a despiser of the clergy, constituted authorities, holy customs, and a dangerous man in society, and I hope we shall shortly have it in our power to lay such fault-finding, ignorant fellows by the heels, that so they may learn to reverence the most useful and honourable of all men, the clergy. Having said this, he stalked out of the house with great consequence. Shortly after I took my leave. The story ran like lightning—Robert Slender is an infidel, said one— Why, he argued with the Reverend _____, and the parson told him he ought to be imprisoned for the good of society. Mrs. Slender went to visit her neighbour—I am very sorry, says Goody Rattle, that it is so bad. What's the matter, said she? Why, I need not hide it—Mr. Slender is an infidel—a speaker against the clergy—a puller down of religion—and his reverence says so!—In short, I had once more to shut myself up in the house; and I have moved into the country among my friends till the story blows over.

The Voyage of Timberoo-Taho-Eede, an Otaheite Indian

. . . Their places of worship are far superior in point of size to any thing of the same sort in your majesty's island of Otaheite. But we gained, while amongst them, a very imperfect idea of their religion, owing to our not staying long enough to acquire a perfect knowledge of their language. We found out, however, with some difficulty, that they worship three Gods, first, second, and third, whom they yet hold to be only one and the same. If we comprehended them aright, they asserted that the second one formerly came down from the clouds, and was put to death for the offences of the island. This, may it please your majesty, appeared to us a very strange conceit; but, if the matter has been really so, your slave is inclined to think, that it is high time for some benevolent divinity to descend upon the island a second time, as it is at present overrun with every species of wickedness; particularly injustice, falsehood, and cruelty. The white people are intolerably proud, selfish, vain, malevolent, and lazy; and are supported by a miserable race of black slaves, whom they steal away from a distant country, and force them to undergo the severest labours. The slightest punishments inflicted for the slightest offences upon these wretched men, are infinitely more severe than your majesty would think due to the crime of high treason itself.

But, we must do the white men the justice to say, that they did not seem at all urgent that we should be acquainted with the particulars of their religion; nor did the priests themselves take much notice of us. The reason given us for this conduct was very odd. A man in *red* told us, that the high priest of the island and his deputies never took any notice of those, who had not in their possession considerable quantities of *small circular plates of yellow metal*. There was some superstition in this matter, which we never could unravel. Possibly, sir, these little plates of metal may be the image or sign of *their god*, as *Tieraboo*, my first lieutenant, has more than once told me, that he saw the representation of a man's head on one of them. Be the matter as it may, the islanders are so amazingly tenacious of these trinkets, that we never could lay our fingers on a single one of them to bring away only for your majesty's inspection.

. . . The worship in their churches consists principally in gazing upon each others faces. We went to these places several times, but gained very little instruction. A man in black had a good deal to say from an elevated station, but we could make nothing of his discourse. Another sat a few steps below him, who at certain intervals opened his mouth very wide, uttering strange and dismal noises, in which the greatest part of the assembly joined him. Towards the conclusion of the service we saw several old men coming towards us with long black sticks, polished very nicely, which we supposed were to chastise those who had been inattentive to the words of the man in black. From one end of each of these sticks was suspended a small black cap. —As far as we could perceive, the inattentive persons had no other way to avoid being beaten than by throwing a piece of metal into one of these caps, which in an instant pacified the chastiser. As we had nothing wherewith to make atonement, we fled with precipitation before the black stick had reached us. Our own priest, after he had gained some little knowledge of the barbarian language, did his endeavour not only to convince the citizens and islanders in general of their being under the influence of a false religion, but also offered to instruct them in the true faith and enlightened theology of our own country. We are sorry to inform your sublime majesty, that his success was by no means answerable to his labours, and it was with some difficulty he escaped three or four sound drubbings from the priests of the infidels, for even attempting to make converts. —These people seem to be under some indissoluble obligation to believe only what has previously been believed for them by their progenitors. . . .

The Temple of Reason
In Defence of Pure Religion

Elihu Palmer, along with a group of like-minded religious and political radicals, founded the Deistical Society of New York in the winter of 1796–97 for the grandiose purpose of systematically "promoting the cause of nature and moral truth" and "opposing . . . all schemes of superstition and fanaticism." The fraternity initially limited its activities to regular private meetings and occasional public lectures. But as popular interest in its tenets grew, the Deistical Society decided to appeal to a larger audience. On 8 November 1800 it proudly launched a weekly entitled *The Temple of Reason*.

The newspaper's first editor, Dennis Driscoll, was one of those curiously ephemeral Early Republic deists who suddenly emerged from obscurity and just as quickly faded back into it. We know nothing about him except that he had immigrated from Ireland shortly before *The Temple*'s inauguration and that he was a defrocked Jesuit. He rather clumsily nurtured the society's fledgling weekly until 7 February 1801, when he sadly announced in its columns "the necessity of suspending the publication for a moment" and urgently pled that those "indebted to the paper will immediately come forward and pay what they owe."

The Temple's momentary suspension stretched into almost three months, until Palmer—Driscoll having left the scene—relocated its offices to Philadelphia and assumed the editorship. The first issue of the reborn *Temple* appeared on 22 April 1801. The paper continued in print, albeit sporadically toward the end, until 19 February 1803, when it again and finally shut down its presses. Although it appears to have drawn a wide readership throughout the middle Atlantic and New England states, it was plagued by chronic financial embarrassment.

Despite its short and debt-ridden existence, the weekly quickly became infamous as a bastion of "infidelity." Its notoriety eventually even prompted the appearance in Baltimore of *The Temple of Truth*, a periodical that ran from 1 August to 31 October 1801 and was edited by John Hargrove, whose express purpose was to provide an antidote to the "gross and ungenerous mistatement of the Scriptures" perpetrated by the "atheistic" *Temple of Reason*. There was good cause for Hargrove's (and others') concern. *The Temple*'s inaugural issue unabashedly proclaimed its militancy in political as well as religious matters, insisting that religious bigotry was the bane of both spiritual and

social progress. It ran didactic pieces on rational religion, astronomy ("of sciences . . . the most sublime and best calculated to elevate mens minds to a
proper understanding of the Creator and themselves"), and ethics, in addition
to the standard deistic critiques of Christianity. Moreover, it regularly provided
its readers with serializations from the writings of British and European freethinkers such as Jeremy Bentham, Locke, Hume, Voltaire, Volney, Helvétius,
and d'Holbach. The prose in *The Temple* was complemented by poetry—most
of it execrable, although charmingly fervent—and occasionally nestled within
its pages were brief communications on political events of the day. As Palmer
emphasized in the 22 April 1801 issue, *The Temple* sought to be more than
merely a religious periodical. Its intention was to combine "Politics with Pure
Religion. . . . Contrary to the opinion of most men, we hold, that Deism and
Liberty should go hand in hand." Finally, *The Temple*—especially after Palmer
assumed its editorship—served as a ready means to advertise the public lectures
for which the Deistical Society had become notorious. The following an-
nouncement, for example, appeared in issue after issue and reflected the militancy of *The Temple* as well as its broad scope of concerns.

> Mr. Palmer, still continues to deliver public discourses every Sunday
> evening at six o'clock, at Lovett's long room in Broadway. The object
> of these discourses, is to disclose and mark with discriminating preci-
> sion, moral principles by which human existence ought to be gov-
> erned—To develope some of the fundamental rules and laws of physical
> philosophy and astronomy—To prove that God is immutable, and that
> the working of miracles is inconsistent with the nature of his charac-
> ter—That a religion built upon a miraculous foundation is false—That
> Christian superstition has been one of the most scourges of the human
> race—That the powers of men are competent for human happiness—
> That the triumphant reign of pure morality and sound philosophy can
> alone restore to the species that dignity, energy and virtue, which super-
> stition for ages past has destroyed.

The selections here are culled from original articles in *The Temple* written
by Driscoll, Palmer, and their fellow American deists. As the newspaper entered
its last year and a half, fewer original pieces and more serialized ones from
European freethinkers filled its pages—to such an extent that there is little in
the periodical after late 1801 truly representative of the American deistic tradition.

Driscoll probably wrote or at least collaborated in the composition of "To
the American Reader" and "The Deists Creed." Both are conventional statements of deism's insistence on the natural and constitutional primacy of freedom
of conscience, as well as the superiority of naturalistic religion and morality.

"A Demonstration of the Being and Attributes of God," which appeared in *The Temple*'s first and second issues, is particularly interesting. Although published anonymously, it was probably largely or solely written by Driscoll, whose Jesuit training in Ireland would have centered around Thomistic scholasticism. Certainly more Thomistic elements emerge in this short catechism than in any other American deistic tract. Driscoll defends natural theology, but in a way more reminiscent of Catholic natural law than of Enlightenment rationalism. In discussing "proofs" for God's existence, he appeals to arguments from causation and necessity that are almost identical to Aquinas's second and third demonstrations in the *Summa Theologiae* (part I, question 2, article 3). Moreover, again, in keeping with the Thomistic tradition, Driscoll argues that God's essence or substance is intrinsically unknowable, even though divine attributes such as eternity, immutability, freedom, intelligence, goodness, and so on are logically deducible. In good deistic form, however, Driscoll parts company with Thomistic natural theology in his insistence that God is unitary rather than triune. He also relies more heavily than did Aquinas on design arguments in his analysis of divine attributes. "A Demonstration," then, is one of the most remarkable mixtures of orthodox natural theology and deistic rationalism to appear in the American tradition.

There is no clue as to who wrote "An Ode to Reason" and "A New Hymn for The Temple of Reason," although the two poems' clumsiness suggests an amateur author or authors. The former deprecates religious superstitions, concluding that "the philosophic eye" can "Discern in them aught but a lie." The latter deplores the irrationality of a Triune, dying God and applauds the normative and philosophical superiority of a naturalistic Creator "Who hung the Starry Worlds on high, / Whose wisdom shines through all his ways, / Whose goodness is for ever nigh."

"Christian Morality Compared with That of the Pagan Philosophers" and "Natural Ideas Opposed to Supernatural" are also anonymous, but it is likely they were contributed by Palmer. They are written in his style and reflect many of the central themes in the *Principles of Nature*. The first piece argues that the best of Christian morality was anticipated by pagan philosophers such as Plato and Cicero. Consequently, it is unwarranted to claim that scriptural moral principles are revelatory in origin or even unique. Indeed, Palmer goes so far as to call Jesus a "sincere and good Deist" whose original religion of nature was debased by subsequent supernaturalism. In the second piece, Palmer elucidates what for him and other deists was a recurring theme: that supernaturalism is bred from ignorance and fear, encourages ecclesial and social oppression, and impedes the progress of the individual as well as society. As such, orthodox theology is the "Kingdom of Darkness" that "has for its object only things incomprehensible," mutating light into darkness and good sense into madness. Such a "science," he concludes, "is a continual insult to the reason of man."

To the American Reader (8 November 1800)

The torrents of illiberal reflections and unqualified abuse poured forth every day, through the channels of bigotry and intolerance, against Deists, have provoked this publication. It is the settled maxim of the philosophic Deist, to let all men rest in peace and enjoy their speculative opinions, however absurd, without animosity or persecution: But it is, unfortunately, the settled maxim and practice of others, to abuse and revile all those who are not of their creed. This is certainly, a perverse disposition, and has ever been productive of very many evils to society. In justice to what we conceive, and are convinced, to be the Truth, we can no longer remain silent. We are determined to shew to the world, the purity of our doctrines and the soundness of our principles, exposing at the same time, the corruption of those of our adversaries.

If we were to conclude from the intemperance of over-heated bigots, whose constant study is to denounce and cry down Deism in America; we must think that the inquisition had been established, with all its terrors in the United States; and that the christian religion, in all its sects and branches, had been placed under its *holy protection*. But fortunately for the peace and prosperity of America, *Mahometism* is as much *established by law*, there, as christianity. The immortal framers of the constitution, wisely thought, that in matters of religion, all men have an equal right to private and public opinion; and therefore, left them all on the same level— On this level we stand; and if we shew our religion to be superior to that of others, it shall be by the force of Reason, not by scurrility, deception, or persecution.

. . . The Temple of Reason is not dedicated wholly to the investigation and defence of pure religion; in it will be found philosophical enquiries and moral disquisitions also.

The Deists Creed (8 November 1800)

I believe that there is one, eternal, infinite, intelligent, all-powerful and wise Being, the creator, preserver and governor of all things. That this supreme cause is a Being of infinite justice, goodness and truth, and all other moral as well as natural perfections. That he made the world for the manifestation of his power and wisdom, and to communicate his goodness and happiness to his creatures; that he preserves it by his continual all-wise providence, and governs it according to the eternal rules of infinite justice, equity, goodness, mercy and truth; That all created rational beings, depending continually upon him, are bound to adore, worship and obey him; and to praise him for all things they enjoy; That they are all obliged to promote in their proportion and according to the extent of their several powers and abilities, the general good and welfare of those parts of the world, wherein they are placed; in like manner as the divine goodness is continually promoting the universal benefit of the whole; That men in particular are every one obliged to make it their business by an

310 universal benevolence, to promote the happiness of all others; That in order to do this, every man is bound always to behave himself so towards others, as in reason he would desire they should in like circumstances deal with him; That therefore he is obliged to obey and submit to his superiors in all *just* and *right* things, for the preservation of society and the peace and benefit of the community; to be just, honorable, equitable and sincere in all his dealings with his equals, for the making inviolable the everlasting rule of righteousness, and maintaining an universal trust and confidence, friendship and affection amongst men; and towards his inferiors, to be gentle, easy and affable, charitable and willing to assist as many as stand in need of his help, for the promotion of universal love and benevolence amongst mankind, and in imitation of the goodness of God, who preserves and does good to all creatures, which depend entirely upon him for their very being and all that they enjoy: That in respect of himself, every man is bound to preserve as much as in him lies, his own being and the right use of all his faculties, so long as it shall please God who appointed him his station in this world, to continue him therein: That therefore he is bound to have an exact government of his passions, and carefully to abstain from all debaucheries and abuses of himself, which tend either to the destruction of his own being, or to the disordering of his faculties, and disabling him from performing his duty, or hurrying him into the practice of unreasonable and unjust things; Lastly, that according as men regard or neglect these observations, so they are proportionably acceptable or displeasing to God, who being supreme governor of the world, cannot but testify his favor or displeasure at some time or other; and consequently, since this is not done in the present state, therefore there must be a future state of rewards and punishments in a life to come.

All this reason tells me, and all this I do firmly believe. Now if men will act up to the foregoing Creed, they must be more happy, wise and virtuous, than the most exact observer of what is called divine revelation, in as much as they are free from idolatry and superstition, the disgrace of religion, and the gangrene of morality.

Such is the God that all enlightened Deists do worship in SPIRIT and in TRUTH—And such is the simple religion of nature, worthy of rational creatures, and becoming the majesty of a pure spirit, all-wise and omnipresent. Any other oblations are childish—Any other offerings are ridiculous—Any other incense is gross and unbecoming. *Cakes* are for children; *Wine* for drunkards; bullocks, rams and calves for epicures; but the holy and spiritual God of nature delighteth not in such mean and puerile ceremonies; nor can philosophers be so foolish or absurd as to offer them. The finest and most acceptable victim that can be presented to the Father of the Universe, is a grateful heart and a virtuous mind—and the priest the highest in his favor, must be an Honest Man.

A Demonstration of the Being and Attributes of God
(8 and 15 November 1800)

I. First then, it is absolutely and undeniably certain, that something has existed from all eternity. This is so evident and undeniable a proposition, that no Atheist in any age has ever presumed to assert the contrary; and therefore there is little need of being particular in the proof of it. For since something now is, 'tis evident that something always was: Otherwise the things that now are, must have been produced out of nothing, absolutely and without cause: Which is a plain contradiction in terms. For, to say a thing is produced, and yet that there is no cause at all of that production, is to say that something is effected, when it is effected by nothing; that is, at the same time when it is not effected at all. Whatever exists, has a cause, a reason, a ground of its existence; (a foundation, on which its existence relies; a ground or reason why it doth exist, rather than not exist;) either in the necessity of its own nature, and then it must have been of itself eternal: Or in the will of some other Being; and then that other Being must, at least in the order of nature and causality, have existed before it.

That something therefore has really existed from eternity, is one of the most certain and evident truths in the world; acknowledged by all men, and disputed by none. Yet as to the manner how it can be; there is nothing in nature more difficult for the mind of man to conceive, than this very first plain and self evident truth. For, how any thing can have existed eternally; that is, how an eternal duration can be now actually past; is a thing utterly as impossible for our narrow understandings to comprehend as any thing that is not an express contradiction can be imagined to be: And yet to deny the truth of the proposition, that an eternal duration is now actually past; would be to assert something still far more unintelligible, even a real and express contradiction.

II. *There has existed from eternity, some one unchangeable and independent Being.*

Either there has always existed some one unchangeable and independent Being, from which all other Beings have received their original; or else there has been an infinite succession of changeable and dependent Beings, produced one from another in an endless progression, without any original cause at all. According to this latter supposition; there is nothing, in the universe, self-existent or necessarily-existing. And if so; then it was originally equally possible, that from eternity there should never have existed any thing at all; as that there should from eternity have existed a succession of changeable and dependent Beings. Which being supposed; then, What is it that has from eternity determined such a succession of Beings to exist, rather than that from eternity there should never have existed any thing at all? Necessity it was not; because it was equally possible, in this supposition, that they should not have existed at all.

Chance, is nothing but a mere word, without any signification. And other Being, 'tis supposed there was none, to determine the existence of these. Their existence therefore was determined by nothing; neither by any necessity in the nature of the things themselves, because 'tis supposed that none of them are self existent; nor by any other Being, because no other is supposed to exist. That is to say; Of two equally possible, (viz. whether any thing or nothing should from eternity have existed) the one is determined, rather than the other, absolutely by nothing: Which is an express contradiction. And consequently, as before, there must on the contrary, of necessity have existed from eternity, some one immutable and independent Being. Which, what it is, remains in the next place to be enquired.

III. *That unchangeable and independent Being, which has existed from eternity, without any external cause of its existence; must be self-existent, that is, necessarily-existing.* For whatever exists, must either have come into Being out of nothing, absolutely without cause; or it must have been produced by some external cause; or it must be self existent. Now to arise out of nothing, absolutely without any cause; has been already shewn to be a plain contradiction. To have been produced by some external cause, cannot possibly be true of every thing; but something must have existed eternally and independently; as has likewise been shewn already. It remains therefore, that that Being which has existed independently from eternity, must of necessity be self-existent. Now to be self-existent, is not, to be produced by itself; for that is an express contradiction. But it is, (which is the only idea we can frame of self-existence; and without which, the word seems to have no signification at all:) It is, I say, to exist by an absolute necessity originally in the nature of the thing itself. And this necessity must be antecedent; not indeed in time, to the existence of the being itself; because that is eternal: But it must be antecedent in the natural order of our ideas, to our supposition of its Being. That is; This necessity must not barely be consequent upon our supposition of the existence of such a being; (for then it would not be a necessity absolutely such in itself, not be the ground or foundation of the existence of any thing, being on the contrary, only a consequent of it) but it must antecedently force itself upon us, whether we will or no, even when we are endeavoring to suppose that no such Being exists.

From this Third Proposition, it follows:

1st. *That the only true idea of a self-existent or necessarily-existing Being, is the idea of a Being, the supposition of whose not-existing is an express contradiction.*

If any one now asks, what sort of idea the idea of that Being is, the supposition of whose not existing is thus an express contradiction: I answer, 'tis the first and simplest idea we can possibly frame; an idea necessarily and essentially included or pre-supposed, as a *sine qua non*, in every other idea whatsoever; an idea, which (unless we forbear thinking at all) we cannot possibly extirpate or remove out of our minds; of a most simple Being, absolutely eternal and infinite, original and independent. For, that he who supposes there is no original independent Being in the Universe, supposes a contradiction; has been shewn already.

2d. From hence it follows, that *there is no man whatsoever, who makes any use of his reason, but may easily become more certain of the Being of a supreme independent cause, than he can be of any thing else besides his own existence.* For how much thought soever it may require to demonstrate the other attributes of such a Being, as it may do to demonstrate the greatest mathematical certainties: (of which more hereafter). Yet, as to its existence; that there is something eternal, infinite, and self-existing, which must be the cause and original of all other things; this is one of the first and most natural conclusions, that any man, who thinks at all, can frame in his mind: And no man can any more doubt of this, than he can doubt whether twice two be equal to four.

3d. Hence we may observe, that our first certainty of the existence of God, does not arise from this, that in the idea our minds frame of him, (or rather in the definition that we make of the word, God, as signifying a Being of all possible perfections) we include self-existence: But from hence, that it is demonstrable both negatively, that neither can all things possibly have arisen out of nothing, nor can they have depended one on another in an endless succession; and also positively, that there is something in the Universe, actually existing without us, the supposition of whose not existing plainly implies a contradiction.

4th. From hence it follows, that *the material World cannot possibly be the first and original Being, uncreated, independent, and of itself eternal.* For since it hath been already demonstrated, that whatever Being hath existed from eternity, independent, and without any external cause of its existence, must be self-existent; and that whatever is self-existent, must exist necessarily by an absolute necessity in the nature of the thing itself: It follows evidently, that unless the material World exists necessarily by an absolute necessity in its own nature, so as that it must be an express contradiction to suppose it not to exist; it cannot be independent, and of itself eternal. Now, that the material World does not exist thus necessarily, is very evident. For absolute necessity of existing, and a possibility of not existing, being contradictory ideas; 'tis manifest the material world cannot exist necessarily, if without a contradiction we can conceive it either not to be, or to be in any respect otherwise than it now is: Than which nothing is more easy. For whether we consider the form of the World, with the disposition and motion of its parts; or whether we consider the matter of it, as such, without respect to its present form; every thing in it, both the whole and every one of its parts, their situation and motion, the form and also the matter, are the most arbitrary and dependent things, and the farthest removed from necessity, that can possibly be imagined.

IV. *What the substance or essence of that Being, which is self-existent, or nec-essarily-existing, is; we have no idea, neither is it at all possible for us to compre-hend it.* That there is such a Being actually existing without us, we are sure, (as I have already shewn) by strict and undeniable demonstration. Also what it is not; that is, that the material World is not it, as modern Atheists would have it; has been already demonstrated. But what it is, I mean as to its substance and essence: This we are infinitely unable to comprehend. Yet this does not in the least diminish the certainty of the demonstration of its existence. For 'tis one thing, to know certainly that a Being exists; and another, to know what the essence of that Being is. And the one may be capable of the strictest demon-stration, when the other is absolutely beyond the reach of all our faculties to understand. A blind or deaf man has infinitely more reason to deny the Being, or the possibility of the Being, of light or sounds; than any Atheist can have to deny, or doubt of, the existence of God. For the one can at the utmost have no other proof, but credible testimony, of the existence of certain things, whereof 'tis absolutely impossible that he himself should frame any manner of idea, not only of their essence, but even of their effects or properties: But the other may, with the least use of his reason, be assured of the existence of a Supreme Being, by undeniable demonstration; and may also certainly know abundance of its attributes, (as shall be made appear in the following proposi-tions) though its substance or essence be entirely incomprehensible.

V. *Though the substance or essence of the self-existent Being, is itself absolutely incomprehensible to us; yet many of the essential attributes of his nature, are strictly demonstrable, as well as his existence.* Thus, in the first place, the self existent Being must of necessity be eternal. The ideas of eternity and self-existence are so closely connected, that because something must of necessity be eternal independently and without any outward cause of its Being, therefore it must necessarily be self-existent; and because 'tis impossible but something must be self existent, therefore 'tis necessary that it must likewise be eternal. To be self existent, is (as has been already shewn) to exist by an absolute necessity in the nature of the thing itself. Now this necessity being absolute, and not depending upon any thing external, must be always unalterably the same: Nothing being alterable, but what is capable of being affected by somewhat without itself. That Being therefore, which has no other cause of its existence, but the absolute necessity of its own nature; must of necessity have existed from everlasting, without beginning; and must of necessity exist to everlasting without end.

As to the manner of this eternal existence; 'tis manifest, it herein infinitely transcends the manner of the existence of all created Beings, even of such as shall exist forever; that whereas 'tis not possible for their finite minds to com-prehend all that is past, or to understand perfectly all things that are at present, much less to know all that is future, or to have entirely in their power any thing that is to come; but their thoughts, and knowledge, and power, must of necessity have degrees and periods, and be successive and transient as the things themselves: The eternal, supreme cause, on the contrary, (supposing him to be an intelligent Being, which will hereafter be proved in the sequel of this discourse) must of necessity have such a perfect, independent and unchangeable comprehension of all things, that there can be no one point or instance of his eternal duration, wherein all things that are past, present, or to come, will not be as entirely known and represented to him in one single thought or view: and all things present and future, be equally and entirely in his power and direction; as if there was really no succession at all, but all things were actually present at once. Thus far we can speak intelligibly concerning the eternal duration of the self-existent Being.

VI. *The self-existent Being must of necessity be infinite and omnipresent.* The idea of infinity or immensity, as well as of eternity, is so closely connected with that of self-existence that because 'tis impossible but something must be infinite, independent and of itself, (for else it would be impossible there should be any infinite at all, unless an effect could be perfecter than its cause;) therefore it must of necessity be self existent: And because something must of necessity be self existent, therefore 'tis necessary that it must likewise be infinite. To be self-existent, (as has already been shewn) is to exist by an absolute necessity in the nature of the thing itself. Now this necessity being absolute in itself, and not depending on any outward cause: 'tis evident it must be everywhere, as well as always, unalterably the same. For a necessity which is not everywhere the same, is plainly a consequential necessity only, depending upon some external cause, and not an absolute one in its own nature: For a necessity absolutely such in itself, has no relation to time or place, or any thing else. Whatever therefore exists by an absolute necessity in its own nature must needs be infinite as well as eternal. To suppose a finite Being, to be self existent; is to say that 'tis a contradiction for that Being not to exist, the absence of which may yet be conceived without a contradiction. Which is the greatest absurdity in the world. For if a Being can without a contradiction be absent from one place, it may without a contradiction be absent likewise from another place, and from all places: And whatever necessity it may have of existing, must arise from some external cause, and not absolutely from itself; and consequently, the Being cannot be self existent.

From hence it follows.

1st. That the infinity of the self-existent Being; must be an infinity of fullness as well as of immensity; that is, it must not only be without limits, but also without diversity, defect, or interruption.

2d. From hence it follows, that the self-existent Being, must be a most simple, unchangeable, incorruptible Being; without parts, figure, motion, divisibility, or any other such properties as we find in matter. For all these things do plainly and necessarily imply finiteness in their very notion, and are utterly inconsistent with complete infinity.

'Tis evident therefore, that the self existent Being must be infinite in the strictest and most complete sense. But as to the particular manner of his being infinite or every where present, in opposition to the manner of created things being present in such or such finite places; this is as impossible for our finite understandings to comprehend or explain, as it is for us to inform an adequate idea of infinity. Yet that the thing is true, that he is actually omnipresent, we are as certain, as we are that there must something be infinite; which no man, who has thought upon these things at all, ever denied.

VII. *The self-existent Being, must of necessity be but one.* This evidently follows from his being necessarily existent. For necessity absolute in itself, is simple and uniform and universal, without any possible difference, deformity, or variety whatsoever: And all variety or difference of existence, must needs arise from some external cause, and be dependent upon it, and proportionable to the efficiency of that cause, whatsoever it be. Absolute necessity, in which there can be no variation in any kind or degree, cannot be the ground of existence of a number of Beings, however similar and agreeing: Because, without any other difference, even Number is itself a manifest deformity of inequality (if I may so speak) of efficiency or causality.

VIII. *The self existent and original cause of all things, must be an intelligent Being.* In this proposition lies the main question between us and the Atheists. For that something must be self-existent; and that that which is self existent, must necessarily be eternal and infinite and the original cause of all things, will not bear much dispute. But all Atheists, whether they hold the World to be of itself eternal both as to the matter and form, or contingent, or whatever hypothesis they frame: have always asserted and must maintain, either directly or indirectly, that the self-existent Being is not an intelligent Being, but either pure unactive matter, or (which in other words is the very same thing) a mere necessary agent. For a mere necessary agent must of necessity either be plainly and directly in the grossest sense unintelligent; which was the ancient Atheists notion of the self existent Being: Or else its intelligence, (which is the assertion of Spinoza, and some moderns) must be wholly separate from any power of will and choice; which, in respect of any excellency and perfection, or indeed to any common sense, is the very same thing as no intelligence at all.

Now that the self existent Being is not such a blind and unintelligent necessity, but in the most proper sense an understanding and really active Being; does not indeed so obviously and directly appear to us by considerations a priori; because, (through the imperfection of our faculties) we know not wherein intelligence consists, nor can see the immediate and necessary connexion of it with self-existence, as we can that of eternity, infinity, unity, etc. But a posteriori, almost every thing in the world, demonstrates to us this great truth; and affords undeniable arguments, to prove that the world, and all things therein, are the effects of an intelligent and knowing Cause.

IX. *The self existent and original cause of all things, is not a necessary agent, but a Being indued with liberty and choice.* The contrary to this proposition, is the foundation and the sum of what Spinoza and his followers have asserted concerning the nature of God. What reasons or arguments they have offered for their opinion, I shall have occasion to consider briefly in my proof of the proposition itself. The truth of which appears, in that it is a necessary consequence of the foregoing proposition. For intelligence without liberty, (as I there hinted) is really (in respect of any power, excellence, or perfection) no intelligence at all. It is indeed a consciousness, but it is merely a passive one; a consciousness, not of acting, but purely of being acted upon. Without liberty, nothing can in any tolerable propriety of speech, be said to be an agent, or cause of any thing. For to act necessarily, is really and properly not to act at all, but only to be acted upon.

X. *The self-existent Being, the supreme cause of all things, must of necessity have infinite power.* This proposition is evident and undeniable. For since nothing (as has been already proved) can possibly be self-existent besides himself; and consequently all things in the Universe were made by him and are entirely dependent upon Him; and all the powers of all things are derived from Him, and must therefore be perfectly subject and subordinate to Him; 'Tis manifest that nothing can make any difficulty or resistance to the execution of his will; but he must of necessity have absolute power to do every thing he pleases, with the perfectest ease, and in the perfectest manner, at once and in a moment, whenever he wills it.

1st. That infinite power reaches to all possible things; but cannot be said to extend to the working any thing which implies a contradiction: As, that a thing should be and not be at the same time; that the same thing should be made and not be made, or have been and not have been; that twice two should not make four, or that which is necessarily false should be true. The reason whereof is plain: Because the power of making a thing to be, at the same time that it is not; is only a power of doing that which is nothing, that is, no power at all.

2d. Infinite power cannot fail to extend to those things, which imply natural imperfection in the Being to whom such power is ascribed: As, that it should destroy its own Being, weaken itself, or the like. These things imply natural imperfection, and are by all men confessed to be such as cannot possibly belong to the necessary self existent Being. There are also other things which imply imperfection in another kind, viz. moral imperfection: Concerning which, Atheism takes away the subject of the question, by denying wholly the difference of moral good and evil; and therefore I shall omit the consideration of them, 'til I come to deduce the moral attributes of God.

XI. *The supreme cause and author of all things, must of necessity be infinitely wise.* This proposition is evidently consequent upon those that have already been proved: And those being established, this, as admitting no further dispute, needs not to be insisted upon. For nothing is more evident, than that an infinite, omnipresent, intelligent Being, must know perfectly all things that are; and that He who alone is self existent and eternal, the sole cause and author of all things, and on whom they continually depend; must also know perfectly all the consequences of those powers, that is, all possibilities of things to come, and what in every respect is best and wisest to be done: And that, having infinite power, he can never be controuled or prevented from doing what he so knows to be fittest. From all which, it manifestly follows, that every effect of the supreme cause, must be the product of infinite wisdom. More particularly: The supreme Being, because he is infinite, must be every where present: And because he is an infinite mind or intelligence, therefore wherever he is, his knowledge is, which is inseparable from his Being, and must therefore be infinite likewise. And wherever his infinite knowledge is, it must necessarily have a full and perfect prospect of all things, and nothing can be concealed from its inspection: He includes and surrounds every thing with his boundless presence; and penetrates every part of their substance with his all seeing eye: So that the inmost nature and essence of all things, are perfectly naked and open to his view; and even the deepest thoughts of intelligent beings themselves, manifest in his sight. Further: All things being not only present to him, but also entirely depending upon him, and having received both their being itself, and all their powers and faculties from him; 'tis manifest that, as he knows all things that are, so he must likewise know all possibilities of things, that is, all effects that can be. For, being himself alone self-existent, and having alone given to all things, all the powers and faculties they are endued with; 'tis evident he must of necessity know perfectly what all and each of those powers and faculties, which are entirely from himself, can possibly produce: And seeing at one boundless view, all the possible compositions and divisions, variations and changes, circumstances and dependences of things; all their possible relations one to another, and their dispositions or fitnesses to certain and respective ends; he must, without possibility of error, know exactly what is best and properest in every one of the infinite possible methods of disposing things; and understand perfectly how to order and direct the respective means, to bring about what he knows to be, in its kind, or in the whole, the best and fittest in the end. And having before shown, (which indeed is also evident of itself) that the supreme cause is moreover all-powerful; so that he can no more be prevented by force or opposition, than he can be hindered by error or mistake, from effecting always what is absolutely fittest and wisest to be done: It follows undeniably, that he is actually and effectually, in the highest and most complete sense, infinitely wise; and that the world and all things therein, must be and are effects of infinite wisdom. This is demonstration a priori. The proof a posteriori, of the

infinite wisdom of God, from the consideration of the exquisite perfection and
consummate excellency of his works; is no less strong and undeniable. But I
shall not enlarge upon this argument, because it has often already been accurately and strongly urged, to the everlasting shame and confusion of Atheists,
by the ablest and learned writers both of ancient and modern times. I shall here
observe only one thing; that the older the world grows, and the deeper men
enquire into things, and the more accurate observations they make, and the
more and greater discoveries they find out; the stronger this argument continually grows: Which is a certain evidence of its being founded in truth. If Galen,
so many ages since, could find in the construction and constitution of the parts
of a human body, such undeniable marks of contrivance and design, as forced
him them to acknowledge and admire the wisdom of its author; what would
he have said if he had known the late discoveries in anatomy and physic, the
circulation of the blood, the exact structure of the heart and brain, the uses of
numberless glands and valves for the secretion and motion of the juices of the
body; besides several veins and other vessels and receptacles not at all known,
or so much as imagined to have any existence, in his days; but, which now are
discovered to serve the wisest and most exquisite ends imaginable? If the arguments against the belief of the being of an all-wise creator and governor of the
world, which Epicurus and his follower Lucretius drew from the faults which
they imagined they could find in the frame and constitution of the earth, were
so poor and inconsiderable, that, even in that infancy of natural philosophy, the
generality of men contemned and despised them as of no force; How would
they have been ashamed, if they had lived in these days: when those very
things, which they thought to be faults and blunders in the constitution of
nature, are discovered to be very useful and of exceeding benefit to the preservation and well-being of the whole? And, to mention no more: If Tully, from
the partial and very imperfect knowledge in astronomy, which his times afforded, could be so confident of the heavenly bodies being disposed and
moved by a wise and understanding mind, as to declare, that, in his opinion,
whoever asserted the contrary, was himself void of all understanding; What
would he have said, if he had known the modern discoveries in astronomy? The
immense greatness of the world; (I mean of that part of it which falls under our
observation) which is now known to be as much greater than what in his time
they imagined it to be, as the world itself, according to their system, was greater
than Archimedes' sphere? The exquisite regularity of all the planets' motions,
without epicycles, stations, retrogradations, or any other deviation or confusion whatsoever? The inexpressible nicety of the adjustment of the primary
velocity and original direction of the annual motion of the planets, with their
distance from the central body and their force of gravitation towards it? The
wonderful proportion of the diurnal motion of the earth and other planets
about their own centers, for the distinction of light and darkness; without that

monstrously disproportionate whirling of the whole heavens, which the ancient astronomers were forced to suppose? The exact accommodation of the densities of the planets, to their distances from the sun, and consequently to the proportion of heat which each of them is to bear respectively; so that neither those which are nearest to the sun, are destroyed by the heat; nor those which are farthest off, by the cold; but each one enjoys a temperature suited to its proper uses, as the earth is to ours? The admirable order, number, and usefulness of the several moons (as I may very properly call them,) never dreamt of by antiquity, but now by the help of telescopes clearly and distinctly seen to move about their respective planets; and whose motions are so exactly known, that their very eclipses are as certainly calculated and foretold, as those of our own moon? The strange adjustment of our moon's motion about its own center once in a month, with its motion about the earth in the same period of time, to such a degree of exactitude, that by that means the same face is always obverted to the earth without any sensible variation? The wonderful motions of the comets, which are now known to be as exact, regular, and periodical, as the motions of other planets? Lastly, the preservation of the several systems, and of the several planets and comets in the same system, from falling upon each other; which in infinite past time, (had there been no intelligent governor of the world) could not but have been the effect of the smallest possible resistance made by the finest aether, and even by the rays of light themselves, to the motions (supposing it possible there ever could have been any motions) of those bodies; What, I say, would Tully, that great master of reason, have thought and said; if these and other newly discovered instances of the inexpressible accuracy and wisdom of the works of God, had been found out and known in his time? Certainly Atheism, which then was altogether unable to withstand the arguments drawn from this topic; must now, upon the additional strength of these latter observations, (which are every one an unanswerable proof of the incomprehensible wisdom of the Creator) be utterly ashamed to shew its head. We now see with how great reason the author of the book of Ecclesiasticus, after he had described the beauty of the sun and stars, and all the then visible works of God in heaven and earth; concluded, chap. xliii, v. 31, (as we, after all the discoveries of later ages, now no doubt still truly say) There are yet hid greater things than these, and we have seen but a few of his works.

The supreme cause must in the first place be infinitely good; that is, he must have an unalterable disposition to do and to communicate good or happiness: Because, being himself necessarily happy in the eternal enjoyment of his own infinite perfections, he cannot possibly have any other motives to make any creatures at all, but only that he may communicate to them his own perfections; according to their different capacities, arising from that variety of natures, which it was fit for infinite wisdom to produce; and according to their different improvements, arising from that liberty which is essentially necessary to the constitution of intelligent and and active beings. That he must be infinitely good, appears likewise further from hence; that being necessarily all sufficient, he must consequently be infinitely removed from all malice and envy, and from all other possible causes or temptations of doing evil; which 'tis evident, can only be effects of want and weakness, of imperfection or depravation. Again; The supreme cause and author of all things, must in like manner be infinitely just: Because, the rule of equity being nothing else but the very nature of things, and their necessary relations one to another; and the execution of justice, being nothing else but a suiting the circumstances of things to the qualifications of persons, according to the original fitness and agreeableness, which I have before shewn to be necessarily in nature, antecedent to will and to all positive appointment; 'tis manifest, that He who knows perfectly this rule of equity, and necessarily judges of things as they are; who has complete power to execute justice according to that knowledge, and no possible temptation to deviate in the least therefrom; who can neither be imposed upon by any deceit, nor swayed by any bias, nor awed by any power; must of necessity, do always that which is right; without iniquity, and without partiality; without prejudice, and without respect of persons. Lastly, That the Supreme Cause and Author of all things, must be true and faithful, in all his declarations and all his promises; is most evident for the only possible reason of falsifying, is either rashness or forgetfulness, inconstancy or impotency, fear of evil, or hope of gain; from all which, an infinite wise, all-sufficient and good Being, must of necessity be infinitely removed; and consequently, as 'tis impossible for him to be deceived himself, so neither is it possible for him in any wise to deceive others. In a word: All evil and all imperfections whatsoever, arise plainly either from shortness of understanding, defect of power, or faultiness of will; And this last, evidently from some impotency, corruption, or depravation; being nothing else, but a direct choosing to act contrary to the known reason and nature of things. From all which, it being manifest that the supreme cause and author of all things, cannot but be infinitely removed; it follows undeniably, that he must of necessity be a Being of infinite goodness, justice and truth, and all other moral perfections.

To this argumentation a priori, there can be opposed but one objection that I know of, drawn on the contrary a posteriori, from experience and observation of the unequal distributions of Providence in the world. But (besides the just vindication of the wisdom and goodness of Providence in its dispensations, even with respect to this present world only, which Plutarch and other heathen writers have judiciously made) the objection itself is entirely wide of the question. For concerning the justice and goodness of God, as of any governor whatsoever, no judgment is to be made from a partial view of a few small portions of his dispensations, but from an entire consideration of the whole;

and consequently, not only the short duration of this present state, but moreover all that is past and that is still to come, must be taken into the account:
And then every thing will clearly appear just and right.

From what has been said upon this argument, we may see how it comes to
pass, that though nothing is so certain and undeniable as the necessary existence of God, and the consequent deduction of all his attributes; yet men, who
have never attended to the evidence of reason, and to the notions that God
hath given us of himself, may easily be in great measure ignorant of both. That
the three angles of a triangle are equal to two right ones, is so certain and
evident, that whoever affirms the contrary, affirms what may very easily be
reduced to an express contradiction. Yet whoever turns not his mind to consider it at all, may easily be ignorant of this and numberless other of the like
mathematical and most infallible truths.

Yet the notices that God has been pleased to give us of himself, are so many
and so obvious; in the constitution, order, beauty, and harmony of the several
parts of the world; in the frame and structure of our own bodies, and the
wonderful powers and faculties of our souls; in the unavoidable apprehensions
of our own minds, and the common consent of all other men; in every thing
within us, and in every thing without us: That no man of the meanest capacity
and greatest disadvantages whatsoever, with the slightest and most superficial
observations of the works of God, and the lowest and most obvious attendance
to the reason of things, can be ignorant of Him; but he must be utterly without
an excuse. Possibly he may not indeed be able to understand, or be affected by
nice and metaphysical demonstrations of the being and attributes of God; But
then, for the same reason, he is obliged also not to suffer himself to be shaken
and unsettled, by the subtle sophistries of Sceptical and Atheistical men; which
he cannot perhaps answer, because he cannot understand. But he is bound to
adhere to those things which he knows, and those reasonings he is capable to
judge of, which are abundantly sufficient to determine and to guide the practice of sober and considering men.

An Ode to Reason (8 November 1800)

REASON DIVINE! thou gift of Heaven,
The greatest gift that e'er was given,
In human hearts resume thy throne,
Let all to thee subjection own.
To search for wisdom, be our pride,
And thou! O thou! our only guide:
Aided by thee our breasts shall burn
With indignation just, and spurn
At all the slavish fearful fools

Of priests, as well as priestly tools;
Nor dread the sceptr'd tyrant's frown;
(For tyrants, reason's sons disown.)
With perseverance, strong we'll grow,
And like a river onward flow,
Whose steady course obstructions brave,
Until it meets great ocean's wave.

For long have priests devoid of shame
Abused—Nay, spurned thy sacred name!
Their *triple Gods*, these Gods but *one*,
Their *married Virgin*, and her son;
How *snakes* could *speak*, and *asses* too,
What wond'rous feats some fish could do,
Could swallow *prophets* and could bring
The *cash* for *taxes* to a King!
How Moses over Egypt's land,
Dispers'd the *frogs* by his command;
How *fleas* and *lice* came at his call,
And plagu'd Egyptians one and all,
How *coat* and *shoes* for forty year
Though always *worn*—did never wear.
How gen'ral Joshua *stopt* the sun,
Until his men the battle won.
How gates and bulwarks kiss'd the ground,
When nought but *horns* and *trumpets* sound.
How *Endor's witch* could raise the *dead*,
And make heroic Saul afraid.
How Babylon's king with pride so full
Became at last a *lusty bull*!
And thus for seven long years remain'd
E're he again his shape regain'd;
(What pity kings of modern days
Could not be sent as long to graze.)
How God bid one go eat his bread,
Bespread with t____d in butter's stead,
But when at this his heart did spurn
Cow's *dung*, God said, would serve the turn,
Such foolish, childish tales as these,
A barbarous race of men might please,
But sure such tales can never claim

From Reason's sons, of Truth the name;
Nor can the philosophic eye
Discern in them aught but a lie.
Though raging priests aloud proclaim,
Damnation, Hell and endless flame,
To ev'ry son of man who dare
But doubt what they solemnly swear;
The God of Nature says not so,
He ne'er can doom a man to woe,
For disbelieving when he's told
That silver is as yellow's gold;
And sure where common sense prevails,
As foolish are those *bible tales.*

Fair Reason needs no aids like these,
Her simple rules are rules of ease.
To view the Universe around,
That work of Wisdom most profound!
The varying seasons as they go,
The summer's heat—the winter's snow;
These—these the *Mighty God* proclaim;
These cry aloud his mighty name;
These teach us equal love to shew
To wipe the tear of human woe,
To give misfortune quick relief,
To cheer the heart oppress'd with grief:
In short—Do ev'ry good we can
To all our brethren—fellow man.

Christian Morality Compared with That
of the Pagan Philosophers (29 November 1800)

Far be it from us to find fault with christian morality, though some of its principles may be so *refined*, as that men in the present state of affairs, are not able fully to comply with them. We appeal to the sense, experience and practice of the most canting christians, how far *they* return good for evil—forgive their enemies, and reduce certain other precepts to operation, which they so earnestly recommend by the authority of Jesus Christ: All we wish to insist on and shew in this place is, that this branch of *divine* revelation is not of so modern a date as it is pretended.

The best morality of the new testament has been long known, taught and practiced before Jesus Christ or his disciples; and therefore cannot possibly be considered as immediate and divine revelation, communicated to us by God the Son.

The advocates for revelation will not allow, nor do we want them to allow it, that Socrates, Plato, Cicero, Epictetus and many other philosophers in and before their times, had been *inspired*, by God the Holy Ghost!—It was not at all necessary: they had their morality from reason and their predecessors; for moral truths are as old as the creation: Christ may *refine* on them, but he did not invent, nor was he the first to promulgate them. The striking likeness that appears between the morality of the gospel, and that of Socrates and Plato, even in the most refined parts, shews that Jesus Christ was acquainted with the works of these Greek philosophers, and that he wished to introduce them among his country-men the Jews, who, it would appear from their own history even, had much need of them.

We may as well suppose and believe that Christ had travelled for his information, during the time there is no account of him in Judea, as that Solon, Lycurgus, and many other eminent patriots and philosophers of antiquity, had done the same for the benefit and improvement of their countries. It is somewhat more rational, and indeed more probable, to think that Jesus Christ had drawn his knowledge and morality from Greece and Egypt, than immediately from the celestial regions.

Having made these preliminary observations, leaving the reflecting reader to make many more to the same purpose, we shall quote a few moral precepts from some of the ancient philosophers, and then leave others to compare them with corresponding passages in the new testament.

Plato tells us in his *Apology*, that Socrates did nothing else but go continually about, persuading both old and young, not to be so much solicitous to gratify the appetites of the body: or to heap up wealth; or gain any outward advantage whatever; as to improve the mind by the continual exercise of all virtue and goodness; teaching them a man's true value did not arise from riches, or from any outward circumstances in life; but that true riches and every real good, whether public or private, proceeded wholly from virtue.

It would be tedious to cite all the passages in the new testament, that are in sense, and nearly in expression, the same as this in Plato—To the sagacious reader it will certainly appear plain, that in his moral system, Jesus Christ had taken Socrates and Plato for his masters and models; and he could not have taken better.

Plato in *Critone*, says that no one ought to do willingly any hurt or mischief to any man; no, not even to those that have first injured him; but ought, for the public benefit, to endeavor to appease with gentleness, rather than exasperate with retaliations.— Here we have forgiveness to our enemies, and a return of good for evil preached about four hundred years before Christ was born! and now what becomes of Christian morality, and the *new* commandments?

For a full and satisfactory elucidation of this subject, we must refer our readers to the works of Plato, which we could wish to be more generally known, that the public may see how clearly this illustrious philosopher and his master Socrates, treated of the existence of one God, of moral philosophy and the immortality of the soul. The new testament appears, as to these three subjects, to be a mere copy of Plato's works.

It is evident, says Cicero, every man is bound by the law of his nature, to look upon himself as a part or member of that one universal body or community, which is made up of all mankind; to think himself born to promote the public good and welfare of all his fellow creatures; and consequently, obliged, as the necessary and only effectual means to that end, to embrace them all with universal love and benevolence; so that he cannot without acting contrary to the reason of his own mind, do willingly any hurt or mischief to any man—And to comprehend all in one word—for man to love his neighbour as himself: Thus far Cicero, who has expressed himself as distinctly on this head, as any Philosopher of the present day could possibly do.

As morality in its full extent, and in its *niceties* and refinements, has been known and taught many centuries before the christian era, it is evidently false to say, that it forms a part of divine revelation. The blindest bigots must see the truth of this and feel its force; let us not hear them any longer therefore, insult our understanding with the *unparalleled* purity of *their* morality, or with its *novelty* either. Until now, their best and only excuse could have been their *ignorance*; but if they still persist in their error, we shall very justly say to them, what the Jewish writer had said to his countrymen, "They have eyes, and they cannot see—ears, and they cannot hear!"

Having shewn that Christ's moral system is not by *divine revelation*, we shall soon shew also, that there is *nothing new* in the *theoretic* or *mysterious* part of his religion, or the religion of his disciples and followers rather; for we are decidedly of opinion, and we have published our reasons for thinking so, that Christ was a sincere and good Deist: hence we must conclude, that Pagan theology had been introduced in *his name*, and that after his death. We say, Pagan theology; for we shall prove that the Egyptians, Greeks and Romans, long before the birth of Christ, had believed dogmas similar to those of the new testament—whether of Trinities, incarnations, metamorphoses—celestial love-intrigues—whether of feasts of bread and wine—of transfigurations—resurrections, ascensions to heaven, etc. etc. All these extravagant fables calculated to subjugate the mind to sacerdotal influence, to ignorance, blind obedience and superstition, were well known and successfully practiced, before Paul figured away in Asia, or Peter in Rome. And of course, cannot be *new*, or of *divine origin*, as pretended by the advocates for christianity.

A New Hymn for the Temple of Reason
(16 September 1801)
While others sing a Triune God,
Of Three in one—and one in three;
In Reason's Temple we have trod,
And sing alone a Deity.

We sing the great Creator's praise,
Who hung the Starry Worlds on high,
Whose wisdom shines through all his ways,
Whose goodness is for ever nigh.

While others sing a changing God,
And make his wrath and love their theme;
In Reason's Temple we have trod,
And sing a God thats e'er the same.

E'en let them sing a Dying God,
And to his blood for shelter fly;
In Reason's Temple we have trod,
And say a God could never die.

Yet when they sing th' atoning blood
Of him who knew himself no sin,
We ask, (tho' long their faith has stood,)
Could reason e'er such faith begin?

Tho' bold fanatics sing aloud
Of love from God to them alone,
And deal damnation to the crowd;
A God so partial we disown.

Then lift ye sad unhappy souls,
With hopes of heaven—and fears of hell;
The knell of superstition tolls,
'Tis reason tolls her passing knell.

Natural Ideas Opposed to Supernatural (30 December 1801)

When we coolly examine the opinions of men, we are surprised to find, that in those, which they regard as the most essential, nothing is more uncommon than the use of common sense; or, in other words, a degree of judgment sufficient to discover the most simple truths, to reject the most striking absurdities, and to be shocked with palpable contradictions. We have an example of it in theology, a science revered in all times and countries, by the greatest number of men; an object they regard as the most important, the most useful, and the most indispensable to the happiness of societies. Indeed, with little examination of the principles, upon which this pretended science is founded, we are forced to acknowledge, that these principles, judged incontestable, are only hazardous suppositions, imagined by ignorance, propagated by enthusiasm or knavery, adopted by timid credulity, preserved by custom, which never reasons, and revered solely because not understood. Some, says Montaigne, make the world think, that they believe what they do not; others, in greater number, make themselves think, that they believe what they do not, not knowing what belief is.

Restless meditations upon an object, impossible to understand, in which, however, he thinks himself much concerned, cannot but put a man in a very ill humor and produce in his head dangerous transports. Let interest, vanity and ambition, cooperate ever so little with these dispositions, and society must necessarily be disturbed.—This is the reason that so many nations have often been the theatres of the extravagances of senseless dreamers, who, believing or publishing their empty speculations as eternal truths, have kindled the enthusiasm of princes and people, and armed them for opinions, which they represented as essential to the glory of the Deity, and the happiness of empires. In all parts of our globe, intoxicated fanatics have been seen cutting each other's throats, lighting funeral piles, committing without scruple and even as a duty, the greatest crimes, and shedding torrents of blood.

Fierce and uncultivated nations, perpetually at war, have in their origin under divers names, adored some God, conformably to their ideas; that is to say, cruel, carnivorous, selfish, blood-thirsty. We find, in all religions of the earth, a God of armies, a jealous God, an avenging God, a destroying God, a God, who is pleased with carnage, and whom his worshippers, as a duty, serve to his taste.—Lambs, bulls, children, men, heretics, infidels, kings, whole nations are sacrificed to him. Do not the zealous servants of this so barbarous God, even think it a duty to offer up themselves as a sacrifice to him? We every where see madmen, who, after dismal meditations upon their terrible God, imagine, that to please him, they must do themselves all possible injury, and inflict on themselves for his honor invented torments. In short, the gloomy ideas of such a divinity, far from consoling men under the evils of life, have every where disquieted and confused their minds, and produced follies destructive to their happiness.

Infested with frightful phantoms, and guided by men, interested in perpetuating its ignorance and fears, how could the human mind have made any considerable progress? Man has been forced to vegetate in his primitive stupidity: nothing has been offered to his mind, but stories of invisible powers, upon whom his happiness was supposed to depend. Occupied solely by his fears, and unintelligible reveries, he has always been at the mercy of his priests, who have reserved to themselves the right of thinking for him, and directing his actions.

Thus man has been, and ever will remain, a child without experience, a slave without courage, a stupid animal, who has feared to reason, and who has never known how to extricate himself from the labyrinth, where his ancestors had strayed. He has believed himself forced to groan under the yoke of his gods, whom he has known only by the fabulous accounts of his ministers, who, after having bound him with the cords of opinion, have remained his masters; or rather have abandoned him, defenceless, to the absolute power of tyrants no less terrible than the gods, whose representatives they have been upon earth.

Crushed under the double yoke of spiritual and temporal power, it was impossible for the people to know and pursue their happiness. As religion, politics, and morality became sanctuaries, into which the ungodly were not permitted to enter, men had no other morality, than what their legislators and priests brought down from the unknown regions of the Empyrean. The human mind, confused with its theological opinions, forgot itself, doubted its own powers, mistrusted experience, feared truth, disdained its reason, and abandoned her direction, blindly to follow authority. Man was a mere machine in the hands of his tyrants and priests, who alone had the right of directing his actions: always led like a slave, he ever had his vices and character. These are the true causes of the corruption of morals, to which superstition ever opposes only ideal barriers, and that without effect. Ignorance and servitude are calculated to make men wicked and unhappy. Knowledge, reason and liberty, can alone reform them, and make them happier; but every thing conspires to blind them, and confirm their errors. Priests cheat them, tyrants corrupt, the better to enslave them. Tyranny ever was, and ever will be, the true cause of the corruption of morals, and the habitual calamities of men; who, almost always fascinated with religious notions, and metaphysical fictions, instead of turning their eyes to the natural and obvious causes of their misery, attribute their vices to the imperfection of their nature, and their unhappiness to the anger of the gods. They offer up to heaven vows, sacrifices and presents, to obtain the end of their sufferings, which, in reality, are chargeable only to the negligence, ignorance and perversity of their guides, the folly of their institutions, their silly customs, false opinions, irrational laws, and above all, to the want of knowledge. Let men's minds be filled with true ideas; let their reason be cultivated; let justice govern them; and there will be no need of opposing to the passions, such a feeble barrier, as a fear of devils. Men will be good, when they are well instructed, well governed, and when they are punished or despised for the evil and justly rewarded for the good, they do to their fellow creatures.

330   In vain should we attempt to cure men of their vices, unless we begin by curing them of their prejudices. It is only by shewing them the truth, that they will know their dearest interests, and the motives that ought to include them to do good. Fatigued with an inconceivable theology, ridiculous fables, impenetrable mysteries, puerile ceremonies, let the human mind apply itself to the study of nature, to intelligible objects, sensible truths, and useful knowledge. Let the vain chimeras of men be removed and reasonable opinions will soon come of themselves, into those heads, which were tho't to be forever destined to error.

To learn the true principles of morality, men have no need of theology, of revelation, or gods: They have need only of reason. They have only to enter into themselves, to reflect upon their own nature, consult their sensible interests, consider the object of society, and of the individuals, who comprise it; and they will easily perceive, that virtue is the interest, and vice the unhappiness of beings of their kind. Let us advise men to abstain from vice and crimes; not because they will be punished in the other world, but because they will suffer for it in this. —There are, says a great man, means to prevent crimes—these are punishments; there are those to reform manners—these are good examples.

Truth is simple; error is complex, uncertain in its progress, and full of windings. The voice of nature is intelligible; that of falsehood is ambiguous, enigmatical, mysterious; the way of truth is straight; that of imposture crooked and dark. Truth, forever necessary to man, must necessarily be felt by all upright minds; the lessons of reason are formed to be followed by all honest men.— Men are unhappy only because they are ignorant; they are ignorant only because every thing conspires to prevent their being enlightened: they are so wicked only because their reason is not yet sufficiently unfolded.

By what fatality, then, have the first founders of all sects given to their gods the most ferocious characters, at which nature recoils? Can we imagine a conduct more abominable, than that ascribed by Moses to his God, towards the Egyptians, where that assassin proceeds boldly to declare, in the name, and by the order of *his God*, that Egypt shall be afflicted with the greatest calamities, that can happen to man. Of all the different ideas, which they wish to give us of a Supreme Being, of a God, creator and preserver of men, there are none more horrible, than those of these imposters, who believed themselves inspired by a divine spirit.

Why, O theologians! do you presume to rummage in the impenetrable mysteries of a first being, whom you call inconceivable to the human mind? You are the first blasphemers, in attributing to a Being, who must be infinitely perfect, so many horrors, committed towards creatures, whom he has made out of nothing.

There is a science, that has for its object only things incomprehensible. Contrary to all other sciences, it treats only of what cannot fall under our

senses. Hobbes calls it the Kingdom of Darkness. It is a country, where every $\qquad$ *331*
thing is governed by laws, contrary to those which mankind are permitted to
know in the world they inhabit. In this marvelous region, light is only darkness;
evidence is doubtful or false; impossibilities are credible; reason is a deceitful
guide; and good sense becomes madness. This science is called theology, and
this sort of theology is a continual insult to the reason of man.

Prospect; or, View of the Moral World

Virtue, the Highest Dignity of Man

When *The Temple of Reason* printed its last issue on 19 February 1803, it promised its readers that a new periodical would soon take its place. Unhappily, logistic and financial problems delayed the appearance of its successor, *Prospect; or, View of the Moral World*, for almost a year. But the new weekly was well worth the wait. When the inaugural issue finally appeared on 10 December 1803, it was clear the publication was a cut above *The Temple*. The reason for the *Prospect*'s superiority was not hard to discern: It was edited and for the most part written by the tireless and brilliant Elihu Palmer.

The *Prospect*'s first issue declared that "the period has at length arrived in which the civilized world has recognized the necessity of moral principles to regulate the conduct of intelligent beings," and it proudly announced that the paper's primary goal would be to elucidate the foundations and nature of those principles. It was as good as its word. Until it ceased publication on 30 March 1805, the *Prospect* ran articles on religion, biblical criticism, ethics, natural philosophy, politics, economics, and literature that for the most part revolved around the themes of moral progress and human improvement. The necessary conditions for such improvement were rational standards of behavior as well as thought. These standards in turn, so the *Prospect* assured its audience, were derivable from the investigation of natural philosophy, or science. Reason, "the highest and noblest faculty of man," had the power to throw off the "shackles of prejudice" and the "trammels of superstition." As such, reason was not merely a tool for the promotion of commerce, social utility, and the conquest of nature. It also served as the catalyst for human liberty, freedom of conscience, rational religion, and moral perfection. As Palmer so eloquently says in "Moral Philosophy" (31 December 1803), "The true point of wisdom is to regulate conduct by principle, to control passion by reason, elevate the mind above common prejudices, to discard superstition, to love truth, and practice an incorruptible virtue."

The *Prospect*'s acuteness, diversity, and sheer readability quickly earned it a circulation far surpassing that of *The Temple*. Subscription agents in New York, Newburgh, Philadelphia, and Baltimore were kept busy throughout the paper's sixteenth-month history. Although the number of paid subscribers ultimately proved insufficient to keep the weekly afloat, Palmer's words were undoubtedly read and discussed by thousands of nonsubscribers. When he boasts in the 16 June 1804 issue that there were "thousands and tens of thousands of deists in the United States and Europe," he may have been guilty of hyperbole. But it is more than likely that the *Prospect* was followed with interest by what for the times represented a huge readership. In quality as well as popularity, then, the *Prospect* was the most successful of all Early Republic deistic papers.

The *Prospect* was also the most militant of the deistic newspapers. It repeatedly denounced the "double despotism" of church and state—one of Palmer's favorite themes—claiming that oppressive political structures worked hand-in-hand with ecclesial authority to encourage fear, superstition, ignorance, and social tractability. It ran a series of devastating textual analyses of Scripture, written completely by Palmer and covering Genesis and Exodus in minute detail, which underscored logical and ethical inconsistencies and absurdities in Holy Writ. It was unabashedly anticlerical, arguing that "the clergy have always found it to their advantage to keep the people in utter ignorance, and it has been a part of their profession from those of Apollo to the present day" to inflict "misery and distress . . . upon the human race" (25 February 1804, 28 January 1804). And it continuously reaffirmed, in both prose and poetry, the superiority of deism's rational religion over the supernaturalist dogma of traditional Christianity. Unlike many of the earlier "moderate" deists, Palmer was convinced that the lay reader was intelligent and emotionally stable enough to throw off the orthodox "shackles of prejudice" without succumbing to despair and nihilism, and the straightforward militancy of the *Prospect* reflects that confidence.

In the selections from the *Prospect* included here, Palmer criticizes traditional Christian doctrines such as faith, miracles, and revelation by claiming that they are either unjust or irrational and hence unworthy of both humans and the divine: "God will not reveal that which is unjust, and to reveal that which is unintelligible would be of no use" (7 April 1804). In "Laws of Nature" (28 April 1804), he defends a Baconian model of inferential generalization, arguing that observation of experience and the logical deduction from it of uniform patterns is an appropriate methodology for the human as well as the physical sciences. In "More of Human Reason" (28 July 1804), he suggests that Christianity's insistence that human reason is corrupt and thus insufficient as an epistemological standard is self-contradictory and absurd. If human reason is too corrupt to rationally assent to the proposition that reason is untrustworthy, then humans cannot properly believe it; if the proposition *can* be rationally grasped, then reason is *not* corrupt. Instead of attempting to replace reason, "Heaven's best gift to man," with theological sophisms that deny its sufficiency, humans would be better served if, like "The Indian Student" (24 November 1804), they bowed only to "Nature's God" by trusting both their experience of physical reality and their logical deductions from it. To decry reason and instead rest content on emotionalism is to sink into the subjectivistic trap of "enthusiasm" (2 February 1805), a surrender that breeds intellectual passivity as well as doctrinal dogmatism.

Especially interesting are two articles criticizing church and state relations: "Remarks" (25 January 1805) and "For the *Prospect*" (30 March 1805). The first piece is a blast against secular antiblasphemy laws. In a discussion reminiscent of Volney's comparative analysis of credal differences, Palmer argues that blasphemy is contextually defined: What constitutes an instance of it depends on the religious perspective to which a particular sect subscribes. Let each person look to his or her own conscience as a guide, and "let legislators look to the morals, the science, and the virtues of society—with theology they have nothing to do."

In "For the *Prospect*," Palmer assails the legal requirement of oath taking as a necessary condition for testimony in courts of law. When confronted with the obligation to swear to tell the truth "so help me God," a potential witness who is also an unbeliever is forced either to pretend allegiance to a God in which he or she does not believe, or to refrain from participating in the legal process. Both options, Palmer claims, constitute unwarranted coercion and are founded on a bigoted assumption by the establishment that non-Christians are innately untrustworthy. But, as Palmer so eloquently argued in *Principles of Nature*, ethics has no necessary foundation in religious belief. For the state to presume otherwise is to dangerously allow ecclesial superstition to poison what are properly secular proceedings. Such a move is not only ethically unacceptable but also, in the truest sense of the word, blasphemous, attempting as it does to usurp in the interests of the state what are rightly matters of private conscience.

Competency of the Human Powers (10 December 1803)

A survey of the infancy of man and of the imbecilities to which he is subjected, seems to form in some measure an objection against the admissions of an opinion pre-eminently important in the general improvement of the world. If superstition be permitted to depreciate human energy and calumniate its character for activity, it will by this coalition, with native weakness, form an insurmountable barrier to the progress of knowledge among the nations of the earth. The strength of our faculties is diminished by fear or augmented by moral encouragements, when impressions are frequently made unfavorable to the right as well as the real exercise of rational powers; it creates in individuals a consciousness, or rather a belief of self-sufficiency. This becomes the generating cause of a thousand subsequent mischiefs; for when a man is once impressed with an idea that he is either weak or foolish, or that it is a crime to bring his faculties, small as they are, to bear upon the high sounding topics of theological doctrines, he trembles at the idea of intellectual efforts, and cries out in the language of revealed theology, *Lord, what is man!* It is a point of policy in the hierarchy to cherish this submissive temperament, and cultivate in the soul of man the divine virtue of humility. If the enemies of truth and free discussion upon religious subjects, have discovered an interest in human degradation, philosophers and philanthropists have recognized in the exaltation of human power, man restored to his true dignity and in the full possession of those moral pleasures to which his nature and his station in existence furnish so indisputable a claim; the zeal and exertions of great and good men during the last century, were directed to the important subject of giving a new elevation to the powers of man; they directed him to contemplate his organization, to mark the slow but certain expansion of his faculties, to take a retrospective and comparative view of what he was in early life, and what relation his intellectual properties bore to the whole visible universe. In this train of instruction and reflection, he learnt duly to appreciate the energies of his existence, he saw the whole moral and physical world subjected to the electric movements of mind, the revolution of the planets were calculated, their relative distances and magnitudes ascertained, and the universal harmony of the solar system disclosed for the contemplation of an astonished world! But the full recognition of human competency did not result solely from these splendid and majestic facts;—another circle of science more circumscribed it is true, but more important to the real interests of society, gave fresh testimony in favor of the strength and all-sufficiency of our mental powers. The double despotism of the world had taught man the shameful maxim that his mind and body might be rightfully held in subjection by others; the power of thought revived the discriminative considerations essential to moral science, and society witnessed a new era in the history of its existence. The rules, principles, laws, customs, and constitutions necessary to peace and social happiness, were demonstrated to result from the inherent character, and to be essentially interwoven with the rational constitution of intelligent beings. Superstition declared that man could accomplish nothing; experience taught him that he could accomplish every thing necessary to his real felicity, and that if it were not for the institutions of supernatural theology, he might have seen himself surrounded with more comforts, and his life abundantly more tranquil. —When reason, the highest and noblest faculty of man, asserted the right of moral decision upon questions of vast importance, the church and its coadjustors issued a writ of proscription and combined ecclesiastical and military power for the completion of their iniquitous design. The history of the church in Europe furnishes ample verification to this remark. Galileo, who only asserted that the earth is round, together with an hundred other philosophers bold in the cause of truth, suffered imprisonment or death under the vindictive cruelty of clerical domination. But if St. Paul, who is a great stickler for the incapacity of man, for he says of *ourselves we*

336 *can do nothing,* together with thousands of adherents to christianity, should labour to demonstrate the incompetency of human powers, let it be remembered that the period is past for this doctrine to obtain celebrity—the realization of the fact is an ample refutation to such destructive calumnies. The arts, the sciences, all the comforts of human life, bear testimony to the solemn truth, and if we still suffer evils the fault is our own—it ought not to be charged upon nature or nature's God.

Explanation of the Principles of Deism (17 December 1803)

Principles, opinions, and doctrines are frequently considered in a destructive point of light, because they are not well understood. It is a duty which the mind owes to the dignity of its character, to examine and discriminate previous to an ultimate decision, by which sentiments are to be condemned or applauded. Deism is a word which sounds terrible in the ears of those who have been accustomed from early life to contemplate theological opinions, of a nature entirely opposite. Prejudices are in some measure unavoidable appendages of imperfect powers, and when reiterated efforts are made for the purpose of exciting a rancourous spirit against any particular opinions, the mind loses that just equilibrium which leads to fair inquiry, and honest judgment. It hence becomes necessary in developing the principles of a subject that has received any considerable share of popular odium, to state with simplicity, and delineate with correctness the prominent features of such principles. With a view to this point, we proceed to explain the properties of a subject, which has so often excited in christian minds such extreme abhorrence—in doing this there is no intention to impose a creed upon men whose sentiments are similar—we know that among those who believe that the religion of nature is the only true religion, there are shades of difference in their opinions, but these differences are inconsiderable—less, much less, than those which are every day exhibited in every part of the christian world. Be this as it may, however, we have an unquestionable right to state our ideas upon this interesting subject, conceding to all others the same right. "Deism declares to intelligent man the existence of one perfect God, creator and preserver of the universe—that the laws by which he governs the world, are like himself immutable, and of course, that violations of these laws, or miraculous interferences in the movements of nature, must be necessarily excluded from the grand system of universal existence—that the creator is justly entitled to the adoration of every intellectual agent throughout the regions of infinite space—and that he alone is entitled to it, having no copartners who have a right to share with him the homage of the intelligent world. Deism also declares that the practice of a pure, natural, and uncorrupted virtue is the essential duty, and constitutes the highest dignity of man.

That the powers of man are competent to all the great purposes of human existence—that science, virtue and happiness are the great objects which ought to awake the mental energies, and draw forth the moral affections of the human race.

These are some of the outlines of pure Deism, which christian superstition so dreadfully abhors, and whose votaries she would willingly consign to endless torture. But it is built upon a staunch foundation, and will triumphantly diffuse happiness among the nations of the earth, for ages after christian superstition and fanaticism have ceased to spread desolation and carnage through the fair creation of God."

Aphorisms (17 December 1803)

Man is born ignorant—it is the expansion of his intellectual powers that constitutes his glory and his happiness.

Science is the sun of the moral world; when its rays shall have penetrated the darkness of every understanding, a new era will be commenced in history, and man will become universally the friend of sensative existence.

Superstition has shed the blood of millions—she must answer for her crimes at the bar of reason, and there she will receive a condemnatory sentence—depart ye cursed and trouble the world no more.

If the murders which have been committed in the name of religion could be placed distinctly before the minds of believers, it would at least induce this interrogatory—is that religion holy and divine whose effects have been so destructive among the human race?

The energy of thought will one day teach fanaticism that her native home is hell!

War is the curse and scourge of the world—yet revealed religion has generated more wars than any other cause by which they have been produced.

We look at all mankind through the mirror of history—but he who reads history without discriminative reflection, might as well pass away his existence under the influence of the morphean God.

Why does superstition calumniate philosophy? *Answer,* because philosophy teaches the purest morals.

Philosophy labors to convince by mild and peaceful means—religious fanaticism by fire and faggot.

338 Philosophy teaches that belief must be founded upon evidence—christianity destroys this moral axiom, in the sentence, he that believeth not shall be damned.

If meekness consist in murder, then was Moses a meek man.

Human merit is in proportion to talents and virtues—celestial merit cannot be transferred from heaven to earth.

"The unjust man shall perish in his rapacity, and the tyrant in his usurpation."

Moral Philosophy (31 December 1803)

The conduct of human beings ought to be regulated by principles just and useful. The source of these principles is essentially interwoven with the character of man; his moral position in life, his powers and the general properties of his existence constitute the fundamental basis of enquiry and deduction. Theological superstition has taught lessons of dreadful heresy—it has instructed man to believe that he ought to depart from the present world to procure for himself joys suitable to the character of his present existence. The philosophy of which we speak has provided for man a variety of comforts in his present predicament, and this philosophy instructs him to diminish by intellectual exertion, the force of evil by which his life is afflicted. It teaches him that the ills of life are not always real but frequently fabricated from causes of a trifling nature. There is not perhaps on earth a human being who does not make more of his misfortunes than he ought—there is not one who does not magnify beyond the reality!— The human imagination is always awake, it is perpetually active, and to its combinations, conjectures, and anticipations, there seems to be no fixed termination. An evil apprehended, but not yet realised, often assumes a shape as terrific as the most dreadful calamity, which has already burst in thunder upon the world. Earthquakes and volcanos sometimes happen— they happen really in the order of the universe—but how much more frequent are they in the imaginary apprehensions of human beings. The true point of wisdom is to regulate conduct by principle, to control passion by reason, elevate the mind above common prejudices, to discard superstition, to love truth, and practice an incorruptible virtue.

Religious Self-Conceit (21 January 1804)

The very worst effect of an excessive self-love is the over-weening conceit of one's self, relatively to devotion, and the punctual discharge of religious duties. This is sure to declare itself in a contempt of every one who does not make the same parade of sanctimony. Not a day passes in which people of this cast do not sacrifice some innocent victim at the altar of their malignant passions. Surmise is their very food, slander their delight, altercation the whetstone of their wit, rancour the fire which animates their discourse, and revenge the mobile of their actions. For gluttony, imperiousness, avarice, and cruelty, they are noted—the loss of a dollar sets their soul in an uproar, and under the cloak of devotion they trample on common probity. But they indeed distinguish themselves by a strict attendance on divine service, and their preparations at the approach of high festivals. The word christianity is perpetually on their tongues—in visiting the sick they affect an agonizing tenderness—they pay a most profound respect to the clergy, and sigh and groan about the spread of infidelity: but after all their hypocrisy, these hypocrites deceive their own consciences more than the world—they are the detestation of the truly good, and men of common under-standing laugh at their farcical sanctimoniousness.

On the Christian Religion (28 January 1804)

The Christian System, from the day of its birth, appears to have opened to the world a new and melancholy scene of contention, animosity and bloodshed. During its three first centuries it was frequently and severely persecuted, even to the destruction of millions of its devotees. Either from state policy, or otherwise, about this time it began to be encouraged and was afterwards em-braced by the Roman emperors, who then gave laws to all the christian world. Thus were the christians reconciled to their enemies and relieved from former sufferings: having now no external persecutions, the system soon furnished the means of converting friends into enemies—they split and were divided by its mysteries, and the sword of enthusiasm was drawn to explain them. —So great were the massacres, carnage, and distress occasioned thereby, that even in the days of the greatest superstition it was made a question, whether their existing notions of religion had not done the world more harm than good: and a great defender of christianity has long since acknowledged, that the mischiefs attend-ing the christian system had cost the lives of fifty millions of the human race. Oh! that the cause had never existed—these horrid effects could not have taken place. Ambition, intrigue and fanatical madness in the priests, and big-otry and superstition in the people, led on these dreadful and savage barbarities which distracted and almost desolated the christian world.

It is well known that priestcraft is an imposition of early date. Cato, the great Roman orator was surprised that two priests could possibly meet without bursting into fits of laughter—but tears of blood would not have atoned for the misery and distress they brought upon the human race. Dark and mysterious things are the essence of imposition. The craft and secrecy practised by the clergy of Rome, served to obscure the avenues of light, to encourage supersti-tion and religious bigotry, and became a lasting source of corruption, imposi-tion and pious fraud. Hence, the sale of pardons and dispensations, the forgiving of sins, and praying the souls of the dead out of purgatory: besides public worship was at all times administered in a foreign language. None were permitted to read the bible, and to be detected with it, in their known language, was a criminal matter in the people. Hence, they became the ignorant dupes, the slaves, and mere sport of the priests; and thus the priests became superior to check restraint or responsibility—fraud, tyranny, and imposition appears to have reigned triumphant!

The privilege of forgiving sin, must have been a most sublime acquisition to these holy fathers. Hence, were they deified by the very means adopted for their lucrative purposes, their lust, and ambition:—"*Whosoever sins ye remit, they are remitted unto them—and whosoever sins ye retain, they are retained.*" John, xx. 23. The Sovereign Ruler of the universe gave being to man, he called forth the globe we inhabit, and gave existence to numerous worlds that surround us; directing their order and course, all firmly supported without visible agency or apparent foundation; yet permanently secure, and free from clashing or confusion. —The author of such wisdom and power could not act inconsistently: we know that he gave us reason for our guide; consequently, we cannot know, nor ought we to believe, that he gave us this system of religion which in fact is diametrically opposite to reason. His wisdom and power must have been competent to the support of his rational creation, able to affect their ultimate and lasting good, without the necessity of a miraculous conception, divine suffering, or the eternal damnation of any individual.

The common opinion of christians in these matters is nothing more, than the result of that pride and prejudice, which originated in deception and intrigue. They have no foundation in nature or reason, and ought to be rejected as inconsistent and contradictory to the wisdom, the power, and justice of the great and eternal Source of Nature.

The supposed Saviour must either have been of the divine essence or of the human. If of the divine essence, it was impossible he could have suffered, and being of the human, it was equally impossible that his sufferings should redeem the sins of the world, or the sins of any part thereof:—God could not have suffered, nor could man have redeemed us.

We are told in Scripture, that not many wise, not many mighty are called; that God has chosen the weak things to confound the strong, and foolish things to confute the wise. "*I thank thee, O Father! Lord of heaven and earth, because thou hast hid these things from the wise and prudent, and hast revealed them unto babes.*" These texts, thus disguised, are the great support, the joy, and comfort of the bigot—but divest them of mystery and they appear less flattering, viz. the weak and foolish things are the most suitable objects of craft and imposition, they can believe every thing that is inconsistent with reason, that radical and powerful enemy of revelation.

The wise and prudent, when divested of prejudice and interest, will recur to reason as their safest guide. They must be fairly convinced before they assent to matters of importance. They have no interest in deceiving or in being deceived: they endeavor to avoid the one and guard against the other. They see, they know, and regret, that mankind have been long duped and imposed upon. They consider the inhabitants of the whole world as one great family of the deity, and that the precepts necessary for one part extend universally to all. They regret that the pretended holiness of religion is frequently made a pretext for war. That this idle pretence has quietly excused for the murder of millions of the human race.—"*And truly the Son of Man goeth as it was determined, but woe unto that man by whom he is betrayed.*" Thus it was decreed by God that Jesus should be betrayed by a certain man, and that as a reward for performing the divine will, this man was doomed to eternal punishments. "*Those that thou gavest me have I kept, and none of them is lost but the son of perdition, that the scriptures might be fulfilled.*"

Communication on Science from "A Subscriber"
(25 February 1804)

Science gives activity to the human mind, expands the intellect, raises and exalts the understanding: the scientific character is placed above all vulgar prejudice, he surveys the wonders of creation with an inquisitive eye—he beholds the order and regularity of the different planets—studies the laws by which they are governed, and admires the wisdom of the great author of nature, displayed in all his wondrous works. 'Tis owing to science that men are enabled to throw off the shackles of prejudice, divest themselves of the trammels of superstition, and erect the religion of *nature* on the firm basis of truth. To science we owe the dissipation of *error*, the extension of human happiness, and the consequent prevalence of *liberty*. 'Tis the object of tyrants to keep their subjects in blindness, to make ignorance the subject of panegyric, and science that of contempt. They endeavour to create prejudice in all minds against it; the literati they hold up as men devoid of principle or of virtue, for well do they know that as soon as the mind is enlightened their power receives a deadly blow. The annihilation thereof is the consequence they expect if men are suffered to think for themselves, to investigate the conduct and motives of their rulers. If we examine history, if we study the progress of mankind from the barbarous to the civilized state, we shall immediately discover that as men are involved in ignorance and superstition, they are subjected to the uncontrolled force of tyrannic sway: a tyrant rules them with a rod of iron or thunders over their heads the terrors of excommunication and eternal misery: —The imposters who have governed mankind, were well acquainted with this. Zoroaster, Mahomet, and Christ, owe their success to the universal prevalence of Ignorance. The power of the Pope depended altogether upon the ignorance and superstition of the people, it was owing to this cause that he could denounce

342 vengeance against his enemies, and hurl his anathemas and excommunications against both the princes and their subjects. The catholics were buried in the profoundest ignorance, believing that if he pronounced judgment upon them, their eternal doom was fixed, that his was the power to exalt them to heaven, or make them undergo eternal misery. The clergy have always found it to their advantage to keep the people in utter ignorance, and it has been a part of their profession from those of Apollo to the present day; but happily for mankind they have not been latterly so successful, learning has revived, philosophy has burst asunder the bands of prejudice, dissipated error, promoted happiness, and enabled the votaries of science to behold with astonishment the degradation of their species.

Many and important advantages have been derived therefrom—it was owing to science that the enlightened mind of Columbus gave to the astonished eye of Europe the western hemisphere, his expansive mind was thereby capacitated to conceive and execute a design that has changed the condition and situation of half the inhabitants of the globe. 'Tis owing to science that mankind are enabled to draw down the lightning from the clouds and conduct it harmless to the earth—to it we owe the extension of commerce, the progress of civilization and the increase of humanity—by it we are enabled to assume almost a portion of the divinity to create earthquakes, to decompose and recombine, to pursue our way over the pathless ocean, and to ride on the wings of the wind.

Miracles (31 March 1804)

Suppose for instance, that a miracle-monger and a dexterous juggler both perform alike things to appearance, though the one be real, and the other delusory, while the evidence of the facts seems to be equal on both sides; who but those that are skilled in the one, or the other, can distinguish the one from the other? How many juggling tricks of Heathen and Popish priests are recorded in history for miracles; and other impositions for the wonderful works of their Gods and Saints, all for the honour and glory of religion, and sometimes to subdue men's minds to virtue: Are they capable of the same evidence as other historical facts? How easy is it for a pious soul to be induced to believe notorious frauds, that have the face of piety, and seem done to promote it; are the reports of strange things, which they are not in a condition to make a true judgment of, equal to those of other historical facts? Tho' all historical facts recorded are not true, yet there is a vast difference between the probable and improbable. If a man tells me he came over Westminster bridge to day, it may be true, though a little objection may be against it, because it is not quite finished, which may occasion some further questions, in order to be better satisfied of the truth of it; but if he tells me he took a running jump, at low tide, and leapt it over just by the bridge, I know it to be impossible, therefore a lie, and enquire no more about it. Is this latter story as credible as the former? no sure, though I may know the relater, and know him to be an honest man, that is not used to lye; and tho' it be attested by many others, I ought to have extraordinary evidence, to induce me to believe extraordinary things, that are supernatural, which cannot be so credible as ordinary things which are natural. In cases where there is difficulty and danger in trusting to ones own senses and judgment, there is much more in trusting to the senses and judgment of others, and confiding in their report: therefore such reports are not as capable of the same evidence, nor as fit to be believed as other historical facts. Since we are warned against the impositions of false miracles, we have certainly a right to enquire what are true, and whether any? And therefore we should be most careful of trusting those that are most capable of deceiving. Not only the histories of miracles should be cautiously received, but the performer of them; for as a man possessed of uncontrollable power is not a proper person to be trusted with any property, neither is such a person proper to be the director of my judgment, who can by his power play upon my weakness, by his art impose upon my understanding, and by his tricks deceive my senses: a miracle worker has it in his power to do all these things. Men are often deceived without a wonder, but wonders are very capable of deceiving; and therefore a wonder-working man may be a powerful deceiver; he that can alter things, or the nature of them in any case, can also alter the appearances of things, by either of which the rules of truth and certainty are destroyed; because either the observer is deceived, or there is no trace left for his judgment; for what confounds the order of nature must confound man's judgment. When a point is to be proved by miracle, we give up reason to authority, and by the same means, if it can be done, it may raise any sort of deity, or establish any doctrine. Suppose but the power and possibility of deception in a miraculous operator, which I think may be reasonably supposed, and then there is not the same reason to believe a miracle, as in cases, where no possibility of such power is; for the appearances of things are more easily changed, than the reality of them. Therefore miracles are not capable of the same evidence, nor have an equal right to be believed as other historical facts, let the evidence be reputed ever so credible. Both a miracle-worker and the reporters of miracles, are of all mankind the least fit to put confidence in, and the most to be guarded against; because we ought always to be on our guard against the appearance and possibility of deception; therefore the miracle-worker, the work, and reporter have not an equal right to be believed, nor are as credible as other common facts, by those that would neither be imposed upon, nor impose on others. Common sense teaches us, that stories probable and improbable are not on the same foundation, nor have or deserve equal credit. Besides, an easy belief upon hearsay, a surprise, incurious enquiry, the fondness of novelty, and of telling a surprising tale, loving that others should believe as we do; add to these downright fibbing for pleasure or profit, render the stories of miracles, not so credible as other historical facts. It is certain, that nothing has been more pernicious and deadly to the reason, freedom and happiness of mankind, than men's giving up their understandings to the faith of wonderful stories. It has introduced and established spiritual tyranny in teachers, and slavery in believers.

Revelation (7 April 1804)

If we examine the component parts and the structure of human existence, it will not be difficult to perceive the source and inlets of all our ideas and all our knowledge. The powerful agents that surround us, the universe which we behold, act with constancy and with force upon the senses of men. It is the relationship subsisting between sensitive and intelligent life on the one part, and the material world on the other, that forms the natural basis of all science, and the diversified improvements which society has been capable of exhibiting. Religious fanaticism, is, however, never contented to see things as they are, but possesses an eternal desire for moral and theological distortions. Bigots always pretend to hate the world in which they live, they sigh and groan for some unknown paradise, of which, however, they can give but an imperfect account, but where, however, according to their dreams and visions, they are to live in a continual state of idleness, and sing loud Hallelujahs to the Lord forever. This enthusiastic spirit by which supernaturalists are so much influenced, blinds the human understanding to all clear views of the nature of man, and the causes by which his faculties are expanded. The maxim in the scripture, *set your affections on things above and not on things upon the earth*, has turned the heads of thousands and withdrawn the human attention from those objects to which it ought to have been devoted. Whoever lives perpetually in the clouds will never do any good upon earth. Wherever the holy ghost absorbs all the tender and sympathetic affections, it is not to be expected that such a being will be capable of benevolent emotions to his species. If man would study his own nature, and understand his true predicament in life, he would cease to wander after phantoms, he would reject with just indignation religious impositions, whether they came in the name of Jesus or Mahomet, whether they were sanctioned by the bible or the koran, the Sadder or the Zendavesta. Revelation is a system of juggling, in which each dexterous imposter plays off a game of folly or fanaticism to accumulate interest, or gratify the enthusiastic feelings of the heart. Among inspired idiots there is also more of pride than is generally imagined, he who elevates himself to the third heavens, and there holds divine conversation with God himself, must have no contemptible opinion of his own dignity; but sometimes in the delirium produced by religious enthusiasm, he sinks as much below the standard of manhood, as his fancy had taught him to believe he had been raised above it. There is an intellectual insanity attached to those who run after religious ideas of a supernatural kind. . . .

If the matters contained in the old and new testament be brought to the true criterion, it would be found that they do not partake at all of the character of revelation. An excellent writer, (Paine) has more than once observed in his writings, that history is not revelation, for as he very justly observes, if a man has said or done a thing, it requires no revelation to tell him that he has said or done it; if the knowledge of the fact be communicated to others down through successive generations, this transmission can never be considered in the light of revelation from God,—it is mere historical detail, and however dignified with the name of holy writ, must forever remain at the standard of its own true character.

The greater part of the Old Testament, is a mere jumble of stories, bloody stories, too many of them by far too bloody, to possess the sanction of the most high God; intermingled with these scenes of human carnage, are several love intrigues, such as those of David and Solomon. These two royal wretches, these splendid debauchees of antiquity, have been dignified by the christian church with appellations of the most honorable nature, the one is said to be the wisest man, and the other a man after God's own heart; their transactions, however, with their female companions, are destitute of all the features of divine revelation. In short, the whole class of facts and of falsehoods contained in the old testament, sinks into nothing, when we reflect that a revelation is something communicated from the Creator to man, by means of divine or supernatural power.

The precepts contained in the bible, whether immoral or moral, are surely not entitled to the name of revelation; no one will contend in favor of the first class, that is the bad precepts, and as to the second class, that is the good precepts; these are also destitute of all the characteristic features of a supernatural communication from the creator.

Moral principles are plain, simple rules, by which the conduct of man ought to be regulated; they grow out of the powers and relationships of human beings, they are deducible from the structure of man's existence, and reason is the power by which they are discovered and applied to the important purposes of human life. But there is a third class of ideas contained in the christian religion, to which believers especially annex the name and character of revelation; in this are included all the mysterious doctrines of the new testament, such as atonement, regeneration, doctrine of the trinity, etc. The answer to those who contend us in this ground is very short and easy. The doctrines are all either unjust or unintelligible, and in either case they cannot be called divine revelation. God will not reveal that which is unjust, and to reveal that which is unintelligible would be of no use—it would be a revelation unrevealed, it would be a revealed mystery which is no revelation at all. But it will perhaps be said that the position which has been laid down is wrong, that these doctrines are neither unjust, nor unintelligible; but we affirm that the doctrine of the atonement is unjust, because it sacrifices innocence at the shrine of vice; the doctrine of the trinity, christians themselves do not pretend to understand, they only pretend to believe it, because they think it is heresy not to believe it; the doctrine of regeneration is as little capable of being understood, it is a mysterious change that nobody can give any account of; Jesus himself was puzzled with it, for when Nicodemus asked him how a man could be born again, he evades the enquiry, by saying, the wind bloweth where it listeth. . . .

Laws of Nature (28 April 1804)

It is by long observation, that man discovers the true character of the laws, by which the world is governed, the united experience of nations and ages bears such ample testimony, to a general, universal and immutable establishment, that doubts in the present case, seem tantamount to a willful attack upon the mass of evidence, which is calculated to work general conviction in the human mind; where Phenomena are constant and uniform, they ought most undoubtedly to become the basis of the highest confidence. If it were possible for a single individual, to possess all the rational powers, with a knowledge of one solitary fact, that the sun has risen in the Eastern hemisphere, he could not affirm that there existed a certainty of his ever beholding the same phenomenon again: from a single case, no general deduction can be drawn, but from thousands and thousands of cases, conclusions may be made, against which nothing but folly and fanaticism could be induced to make any opposition. When the Bible asserts that the sun stood still, or that the regular operations of the laws of nature were suspended in the planetary system, the universal observation of mankind, the experience and the testimony of ages are against the assertion: to say that it is a lie, is perfectly consistent with all those rules of judging, by which the reason of man ought to be regulated; nay, further, in all other cases where religion is not concerned, men of common understanding would be ashamed to acquiesce in decisions of a similar nature. When the New Testament affirms that Jesus turned water into wine, we know or ought to know, that the assertion is false; first, because the practicability or possibility of such a thing is denounced by the nature of the case,—by the reason and experience of mankind; secondly, because the science which man has acquired, has exposed innumerable impostures of this kind, and so many detections have thrown a coloring of suspicion over all the rest. Credulity, however, and especially religious credulity, seems to be a leading property to which the imbecility of man has exposed his existence. In proportion as the human mind becomes improved and enlightened, it becomes less credulous, less disposed to swallow absurd and marvellous doctrines. The sublime and elevated power of contemplation excludes all credulity, and surveys with steadiness, the character of different beings or objects; it enquires with patient perseverance, and never suffers itself to be thrown off from that well balanced position, which takes in all the points and bearings of any given portion of Physical existence. Intellectual precipitancy leadeth to error; it is the character of the mind in search of truth, to move in an easy and happy medium of doubt—always disposed to be influenced by the greatest opacity of evidence which the nature of the case presents to view, when a man in a state of intellectual finity reads in *holy writ*, the story of Jonah and the whale, or in other words the big fish; it is scarcely possible to refrain from a burst of laughter. If religious superstition were not blinded by the inherent nature of her own character, she would be ashamed of the gross attempts to impose upon men, such miraculous tales, for a system of truth and genuine theology; but nothing will tend to destroy superstition, more than a persevering attention to the laws of nature; no man who understands these laws, and who perspicuously surveys the immutable properties which they possess, can possibly believe in the hobgoblin stories of antiquity. It may be objected here that Newton was a good philosopher;—that he understood well the laws of nature, and yet, that he was a believer in the christian religion; in the first place, it is uncertain in what respects he was a believer, or how far in his own mind he might have rejected certain absurd and ridiculous parts of the Old and New Testament: It is well known, that he did not believe in the doctrine of the Trinity, and his knowledge of the solar system, must have elevated him above any kind of credence in the following declaration in *holy writ, Sun stand thou still upon Gideon, and thou moon in the valley of Agalon*; but if we concede what has generally been considered as a fact, that he was a christian upon a graduate scale, it will prove nothing in the present case. A correct knowledge of the laws of nature, includes something more than mere mathematical calculation, or demonstration; it includes something more than planetary revolutions, eccentricity of comets or magnitude of celestial bodies; that important and useful science, which embraces all the operations of the human mind, and on which in fact the welfare of the intelligent world depends, was not well understood by Newton; he understood physical nature, but with the moral science he was much less conversant; he had not compared the operations of the understanding, with the doctrines and opinions contained in the Bible. From such a comparison made without prejudice, deductions must have followed hostile to the sentiments of the church, and to that system of religion, from which the church has drawn its tenets; these tenets must eventually give way to a thorough knowledge of moral and physical existence.

On Christian Faith (12 May 1804)

The nature of human credence as it relates to common objects, is a matter extremely clear and intelligible, it is an assent of mind to the truth of a proposition when that proposition is supported by sufficient evidence; but christian faith assumes quite a different character: it is wild extravagance and pretends to a thousand things, to the performance of which it is totally incompetent. In the

New Testament it is said if a man have faith like a grain of mustard-seed, he shall say to yonder mountain, remove hence and it shall be removed! Now every christian that has common sense knows, that there is not a word of truth in this declaration. I say to one, do you believe in the christian religion? he answers in the affirmative, speak then to the Allegheny Mountain to march beyond the Mississippi and I will believe too. The mountain does not move—I press him for the evidences of his faith. He stands and either looks like a fool or grows angry. Will you start the mountain?—I cannot. Then you have no faith—I have. Then the book tells a lye, and so you must either prove the truth of the book by your faith, or I will prove the book is not entitled to credit. Believer how canst thou escape from this dilemma? The signs or evidences of christian faith are specifically stated in the last chapter of Mark, verse 17, 18. And these signs shall follow them that believe: in my name shall they cast out devils; they shall speak with new tongues; they shall take up serpents; and if they drink any deadly thing it shall not hurt them; they shall lay hands on the sick and they shall recover. Now we challenge the whole phalanx of christian believers to verify the scriptures by exhibiting the above mentioned signs. They know that they cannot do it, and yet they say they believe every word contained in the Old and New Testament. It is a pity that the Reverend the Clergy, of all denominations, who make so much noise about infidels and infidelity, will not be so very obliging as to give at least one of these signs as proof of the sincerity of their faith. Take, for instance, that which would be most useful in yellow fever times—they shall lay hands on the sick and they shall recover. Surely if they had faith they would have humanity enough to exercise that faith in behalf of their distressed friends and neighbours destined to death by the raging influence of Yellow Fever. But no, they can give us no such testimony—they make false *the sacred word of God* in which they pretend to believe. They have faith that the country air is purer than that of the city—away they run, in this they are right enough, but how does this conduct comport with their pretended faith in divine revelation and the signs which this revelation ascribes to their faith. Such inconsistencies denounce the divinity of the book, and prostrate it in silence before the throne of reason.

More of Human Reason (28 July 1804)

"Reason," says a believer to an infidel, "is a deceitful and blind guide, and in spiritual concerns will infallibly lead to destruction." "How are you assured of it?" says the other—"to which of my faculties is this addressed? Does reason by exercising its own powers discover its own treachery? If so, does it not in the act of communicating give the lie direct to the sentiment? If your reason can so clearly discern that it is obscured, it cannot surely be that very blind guide you would represent it— If it cannot so discern, the assertion is evidently made at random, and requires examination."—"I am enabled (replies the believer) to see spiritually, and you only carnally—your mind is not yet endued with divine grace, and until an inward change is effected, which cannot be wrought but by God himself, you cannot perceive the force of what is addressed to you. —Be not however led astray by the subtle and specious arts of sophistry; but believe, and trust in God to work the change in your heart at his own good pleasure."

Now one of these beings makes a serious and solemn assertion which the other verily disbelieves and denies. —Supposing them both equally honest and sincere (for the unbeliever cannot surely be censurable for not using that which the believer tells him he has not and cannot have till God sends it) how is their difference of opinion to be canvassed, and the error corrected? With what mental powers are they respectively to set about the inquiry? Is the truth of the question to be on both sides—examined by the help of reason or without it, or with some other and what faculty? Or is one party (who has nothing better) to exercise his single talent on the occasion, while the other opposes to it a power which to reason is declared incomprehensible. If the carnal man and the spiritual are conveying their thoughts through a different medium, how can they ever come to a point? and where is the utility of the latter's sowing where nothing can be reaped, or in other words, of casting pearls before swine? For the spiritual man says, the carnal one cannot understand him when he speaks the truth spiritually, though according to his own account, he is at the same moment opposing to a mere human faculty, one that partakes of the divine.

If a book called profane be put into the hands of a stranger, it will be admitted that he is to examine it with his natural understanding; but how is he to act when the bible is produced to him, particularly when informed by the human producer, that it is a divine communication and not to be examined like productions merely human? How is he to set about considering that to the proper examination whereof his reason is declared incompetent? Is he with his unassisted faculties to examine and judge of it as well as he can until he hears express from heaven with better, or is he to rely implicitly on human intelligence which accompanies it, and lay down or lock up the book till celestial optics are given for the purpose? The contents of the bible being first received through the same channels as those of any other work, can the reason of a believer, like the stops of an organ, be shoved aside and the faculty fitted for this occult study introduced at pleasure into its room?—The canonical books of the Old and New Testament must no doubt be read with the spiritual faculty and the uncanonical apocrypha with the natural, but how suddenly to convey the matter of these respective works through the eyes and ears of their readers to the appropriate powers of the mind is the difficulty. —Is there in the bible (dictated as is said by God) any passage signifying that the understanding of its readers shall not take cognizance of its sentiments, and if such should (upon spiritualizing something for the purpose) be found in it how can reason, while it reads, avoid controverting the position and refusing to knuckle to a usurper? —To what faculty of the human mind is the bible supposed originally to have been addressed? How can it be a revelation to man, if it must steer clear of his reason as a ship avoids a shoal? If it be not intended to be examined by the faculty which distinguishes man from brute, why is it not as fit to be addressed to brutes as to men? If the prime and essential quality of man is not to meddle with it, why is it addressed to man in particular? —We are not it is said, to examine a divine communication with a human and imperfect understanding. How then must it be examined? We cannot do it with any thing divine, and if not cognizable by human reason, why must it be examined with something inferior to reason which is still human? —If there be any fault in examining a divine present with human powers, with whom do believers contend that such fault originates? It is said to have been revealed for the benefit of human sinners, who nevertheless are declared incapable of reading it to any purpose until they can send to Heaven for spectacles. —If the book is not to be examined by unassisted human faculties, why has the supposed revelation been made to human beings, or why did not a divine key or glossary accompany it?

The truth is, that this same thing called a revelation, is, according to the believer's own account of it, not a thing revealed or made plain; but something placed by God in the sight of man requiring abundance of explanation, which nevertheless cannot be had—without further supernatural assistance. This same supernatural assistance, too, of which (though said to be given for the important purpose of expounding God's word to his creatures) no proof has ever been exhibited, causes its pretended possessors to put different and contradictory constructions upon the same divine passages (thereby increasing the difficulty) and in effect to charge each other as madmen or imposters. — They are unanimous only (where they cannot help it) in failing to produce evidence of their authority, and yet arrogantly claim from their fellow mortals a blind and passive assent to all their jarring and inconsistent assertions, taking fire even at the expression of a doubt. A system of religion thus aiming to subvert Heaven's best gift to man, and involved in such a budget of absurdity, is at war with every attribute of divinity and deserves the solemn reprobation of every upright mind.

Superstition (24 November 1804)

It is by the slow progress of the human understanding that the evils of human life can be diminished or destroyed. Superstition presents a formidable obstacle to the diffusion of science and the augmentation of human happiness. Nothing important can be done for the benefit of man, without a development of the moral energies of his nature; but superstition holds him fast, tells him it is a crime to think, and frightens him almost out of his senses with spiritual spectres that have no real existence. Thousands of gods, ghosts and devils have been fabricated with vast variety of characters on purpose to terrify weak and deluded man. A subordinate class of spiritual lackeys have also been created and sent as Missionaries over the whole earth to frighten women and children. Of this sort were the witches, the fairies and the sprights of former days, and which, even now, form the basis of universal terror in many countries. The Bible sanctioned these incongruous ideas, and gave to nonentity the form, character and effect of real existence. The clergy declare to the people that this is the best book in the world; they found their discourses upon the incoherencies therein contained, and the people are swallowed up in a gulph of superstition from which they know not how to escape. Ye spiritual instructors of a lost and wicked world! read over once the Books of Genesis and Exodus, and ask yourselves the question, whether you would think it any honour to yourselves to be the authors of such a production? Would you not blush for many of the sentiments therein contained, and do you imagine that such composition would render your names illustrious in the great republic of letters? Superstition and interest have combined to create and perpetuate an attachment to the sacred writings of the Jews and Christians. The age of happiness must be that in which all theological conceptions shall be concentered in the Theism of Nature, or the belief of one God. This God must be destitute of all irascible passions and malignant attributes of every kind; he must be a very different being from the God of the Old Testament, for the belief in such a God produces the most destructive consequences. Superstition has always ascribed to the divinities in whose existence she has placed confidence, a surplus of properties, and these properties were generally of a pestilential and contagious kind. The disease thus caught was worse than the yellow fever; it spread desolation and death to all around; it carried conflagration and carnage over the whole earth; it shook to the foundation the tranquility of the world. Man, cultivate thy reason and truth; virtue and happiness will be the necessary consequences.

The Indian Student; or, Force of Nature
(24 November 1804)

From Susquehanna's farthest springs
Where savage tribes pursue their games,
(His blanket tied with yellow strings,)
A shepherd from the forest came.

Not long before, a wandering priest
Express'd his wish, with visage sad—
"Ah, why," he cry'd, "in Satan's waste,
Ah, why detain so fine a lad?

"In white man's land there stands a town
Where learning might be purchas'd low—
Exchange his blanket for a gown,
And let the lad to college go."

From long debate the council rose,
And viewing Shalum's tricks with joy
To Cambridge Hall, o'er wastes of snows,
They sent the copper-colour'd boy.

One generous chief a bow supply'd,
This gave a shaft, and that a skin:
The feathers, in vermillion dy'd,
Himself did from a turkey win:

Thus dress'd so gay, he took his way
O'er barren hills, alone, alone,
His guide a star, he wander'd far,
His pillow every night a stone.

At last he came with foot so lame,
Where learned men talk heathen Greek,
And Hebrew lore is gabbled o'er,
To please the Muses,—twice a week.

A while he writ, a while he read,
A while he conn'd their grammar rules—
(An Indian savage so well bred
Great credit promis'd to the schools.)

Some thought he would in law excel,
Some said in physic he would shine;
And one that knew him, passing well,
Beheld, in him, a sound divine.

But those of more discerning eye
Even then could other prospects show,
And saw him lay his Virgil by
To wander with his dearer bow.

The tedious hours of study spent,
The heavy moulded lecture done,

He to the woods a hunting went,
Thro' lonely wastes he walk'd, he ran.

No mystic wonders fir'd his mind;
He sought to gain no learn'd degree,
But only sense enough to find
The squirrel in the hollow tree.

The shady bank, the purling stream,
The woody wild his heart possess'd,
The dewy lawn, his morning dream
In fancy's gayest colours dress'd.

"And why (he cry'd) did I forsake
My native woods for gloomy walls;
The silver stream, the limpid lake
For musty books and college halls:

"A little could my wants supply—
Can wealth and honour give me more
Or, will the sylvan god deny
The humble treat he gave before?

"Let seraphs gain the bright abode,
And heaven's sublimest mansion see—
I only bow to Nature's God—
The land of shades will do for me.

"These dreadful secrets of the sky
Alarm my soul with chilling fear—
Do planets in their orbits fly,
And is the earth, indeed, a sphere?

"Let planets still their course pursue,
And comets to the centre run—
In him my faithful friend I view,
The image of my God—the Sun.

"Where nature's ancient forests grow,
And mingled laurel never fades,
My heart is fixed;—and I must go
To die among my native shades."

He spoke, and to the western springs,
(His gown discharg'd, his money spent,
His blanket tied with yellow strings,)
The shepherd of the forest went.

Remarks (26 January 1805)

The subject of Blasphemy has been viewed in different points of light, in different countries; and the opinions of individuals in the same country have been so diversified, that an enquiry into the nature of the case, and the character of Blasphemy, seems to have become extremely necessary. The ignorance, the timidity, and the superstition of man, have created a thousand spiritual phantoms which have no positive or real existence in nature; these frightful productions of the human imagination are, however, very highly estimated by their legitimate progenitors. The more distorted the object of adoration is, the more it seems to excite the pious affection of its devoted victim. Fanaticism and folly are always the concomitants of false religions; and when once the human mind is subjugated and placed completely under the dominion of superstition, reason loses all the energy of its character, and the moral world becomes a chaos of ignorance, vice, and misery. It is amidst this general darkness that hot-headed, religious enthusiasm sets about the business of protecting the phantoms of its own creation. This must be done either by civil or ecclesiastical law, annexing a terrifying penalty to each violation. But who is this law to protect? The answer to this would be different in different countries; and even among the sectaries professing substantially the same religion. Among the Christians, the Trinitarians would contend for a law which should cover over the sublime and mysterious doctrine of the Trinity, and guard the Father, Son, and Holy Ghost against human outrage and profane obloquy. Among Arians and Socinians, the law would go only to protect Jehovah himself, leaving the Son and Holy Ghost to shift for themselves, and defend their character in the best manner they can. We do not mean to insinuate here that the Arians and the Socinians have no regard to the character of Jesus; on the contrary, it is true that the Arians ascribe to him a superangelic nature; and the Socinians consider him as a mere man, endowed with extraordinary gifts and graces, and both view him as an agent from God, to restore a lost world to Divine favour. These sectaries do not wish for a law to protect the character of Jesus against Blasphemy, and as to the Holy Ghost, they have dismissed him entirely and thrown him out of their spiritual service. Thus Christians themselves would be unable to agree upon the persons or beings whose character the law of Blasphemy ought to protect. The most numerous and ruling sectaries, however, regulate this matter as they please; and subjecting, at the same time, all other sectaries to the unjust criminations of their spiritual tyranny. In countries not professing the Christian religion, another and distinct class of spiritual idols are set up as objects of adoration, and of course, all these *Blasphemous laws*, as they ought to be called, go to the point of guarding their character, such as it is, against the slanderous insults of all those who come under their jurisdiction. The character of Mahomet is as sacred in Turkey, as that of Jesus is among the Christians. Zoroaster commands the adoration of the Persian world, and his character there is profoundly sacred. Penetrate into the Indies, and you will find the sacred name of Fot, commanding the adoration of millions, and it would be blasphemy there to speak against his Divinity. The same remark, in spirit and principle, will apply to all the sublime and dignified phantoms of all the other nations of the earth. But the advocates for the laws of Blasphemy will say, that there is one supreme God, and that his character ought to be protected, whatever may be said concerning the inferior Divinities. But it may be answered, who gave to legislators on earth, the right and the power of making laws concerning the character of the Creator? Is he not fully competent to protect his own character, without recourse to the malignant and persecuting arm of human flesh? Yes, and there is no man, or set of men, on earth, that has a right to make laws respecting the religious opinions of individuals—let those opinions be what they will. The laws should take cognizance only of immoral actions, leaving to each individual the absolute right of modifying his theological ideas according to the best judgment which human reason can form upon the subject. Whoever is not sufficiently civil to the Divinity he adores, must look to that matter himself, and settle the dispute in the best manner he can. Let legislators look to the morals, the science, and the virtues of society—with theology they have nothing to do; it is beyond the sphere of their jurisdiction.

Enthusiasm (2 February 1805)

Immediate revelation being a much easier way for men to establish their opinions and regulate their conduct than the tedious and not always successful labour of strict reasoning; it is no wonder that some have been very apt to pretend to revelation, and to persuade themselves that they are under the peculiar guidance of heaven in their actions and opinions, especially in those of them which they cannot account for by the ordinary methods of knowledge and principles of reason. Hence we see, that in all ages, men in whom melancholy has mixed with devotion, or whose conceit of themselves has raised them into an opinion of a greater familiarity with God, and a nearer admittance to his favour, than is afforded to others, have often flattered themselves with a persuasion of an immediate intercourse with the Deity, and frequent communications from the Divine Spirit. God, I own, cannot be denied to be able to enlighten the understanding by a ray darted into the mind immediately from the fountain of light. This they understand he has promised to do; and who then has so good a title to expect it as those who are his peculiar people, chosen by him, and depending on him?

Their minds being thus prepared, whatever groundless opinion comes to settle itself strongly upon their fancies, is an illumination from the Spirit of God, and presently of Divine authority; and whatsoever odd action they find in themselves a strong inclination to do, that impulse is concluded to be a call or direction from heaven, and must be obeyed; it is a commission from above, and they cannot err in executing it.

This I take to be properly enthusiasm; which, though founded neither on reason nor divine revelation, but rising from the conceits of a warmed or over-weening brain, works yet, where it once gets footing, more powerfully on the persuasions and actions of men, than either of those two or both together: men being most forwardly obedient to the impulses they receive from themselves; and the whole man is sure to act more vigorously, where the whole man is carried by a natural motion. For strong conceit, like a new principle, carries all easily with it when got above common sense; and freed from all restraint of reason and check of reflection, it is heightened into a divine authority in concurrence with our own temper and inclination.

For the Prospect (30 March 1805)

The Law of this State, the Constitution of which professes to secure the *free* exercise and *enjoyment* of religious *profession* and worship, without *discrimination* or *preference*, to *all* mankind, declares, in regard to oaths, that any person who believes in a Supreme Being, and a future state of rewards and punishments, shall be admitted to give testimony in its courts, and in order to discover (when occasion requires it) whether a person produced as a witness be or be not competent to be admitted, it has been the practice of Judges to propound to the individual, questions relative to his or her belief, for the express purpose of ascertaining by answers, given when not under oath, whether such witness will speak the truth when sworn. The same law, by annexing a penalty to perjury, virtually admits the possibility of false swearing, and the uncertainty of an oath. If, then, it be evident that a person after swearing, can yet violate the oath which he has taken, and declare what is false, by what reasoning is it inferred that the answers of the same person, before he is sworn, to questions relating to his right to be examined, can be a correct or infallible standard, whereby to regulate its exercise? Is a simple promise to execute an obligation, more sure and sacred than the instrument itself, when sealed? Or, can the preliminary engagement be held inviolable, while the final query is insecure? As well might the effect of a muzzle upon a mastiff be tried, by first turning the animal loose amongst crows, or Jupiter's belts be looked for, with the naked eye, in order to ascertain whether they be discoverable by a telescope, as the bare word of a man, under such circumstances, be taken as a criterion whereby to measure his attachment to an oath. If two Universalists, or other unbelievers, are called as witnesses on the same occasion, one of whom in obedience to the law professes to believe what in reality he thinks false, while the other honestly declares his disbelief, what is the consequence? The testimony of the latter, who, by his scrupulous adherence to truth, has proved himself deserving of the highest credit, is rejected, with a stigma into the bargain, upon his candour; while that of the timid or time-serving hypocrite is received without hesitation, and even with comparative applause. The character of this law . . . savours highly of spiritual domination. The true definition of the word *ortho-dox*, as it respects religion, when simplified and examined, will in every country be found to be neither more nor less than *uppermost*; and the law in question, framed by legislators whose individual bible opinions might for the time being have the ascendency, operates as far as it goes as a religious establishment or direct preference of one sect over others, and so far from leaving to each the free exercise and *enjoyment* of its own profession, as intended by the constitution, leaves only the *exercise*, but robs and deprives some of their most valuable and inherent *rights* and *enjoyments*, viz. the benefit of a good name and reputation, until lost or strained by immoral conduct. Shame! that a republican legislature should attempt thus to domineer in affairs of conscience, and prove themselves incompetent to discriminate between the different duties owing to their Creator and their constituents. A person of the strictest integrity and veracity may, by operation of this law, have his credit impeached without fault of his own, if he does not happen either to embrace a creed chalked out for him by his neighbours, or in default consent to play the hypocrite; while a profligate and abandoned wretch, who for interest or convenience can make and alter his professions at pleasure, may raise his reputation upon the other's misfortune. Such a proceeding is both in principle and practice in direct and open violation of the constitution, and iniquitously aims to usurp to man prerogatives pertaining exclusively to God.

The Theophilanthropist
The Love of God and Man

The nineteenth century's first decade witnessed the final and rather pathetic convulsions of Enlightenment deism in the United States. Palmer, the leader of American deists, died in 1806; Paine, the grand old man of free thought, in 1809. A new generation of rational religionists, including such figures as Abner Kneeland and Robert Owen, would emerge in midcentury. But they were of a different stripe from their colonial and Early Republic predecessors, influenced less by Enlightenment rationalism than by Spencerism and social utopianism. Deism as an offshoot of the eighteenth century's New Learning, then, fizzled out with a whimper by the end of 1811. The short-lived and anemic *Theophilanthropist* was its swan song.

Following Palmer's death, the Deistical Society of New York and its kindred societies in Maryland, Pennsylvania, and elsewhere tended to break apart and dissolve. In a last-ditch effort to salvage something of the movement's earlier vitality, the New York Society of Theophilanthropy was organized shortly before Paine's death. *The Theophilanthropist* was launched in January 1810 as the society's official organ. Originally intended as a monthly, only the first five issues appeared on schedule. Four more followed, irregularly and undated, between June 1810 and late 1811.

As financially precarious as *The Temple* and the *Prospect* had been, *The Theophilanthropist* was even more straitened. Its money problems illustrated in part the decline of popular interest in deism; subscriptions by and large were limited to the sparse membership of the society. But the obvious lack of quality, imagination, and fervor in *The Theophilanthropist*'s pages probably also contributed to its lack of appeal. Its articles, quite frankly, made for dull reading. There was certainly nothing original in either the topics covered or the way in which they were approached. Unlike its two sister periodicals, *The Theophilanthropist* had no intrinsic philosophical merit, and its value today is primarily historical.

Even the periodical's title was secondhand. Theophilanthropy as a "system" was first introduced in September 1795, when a small work appeared in Paris entitled *Manual of the Theoantropophiles*. Although the somewhat barbarous name was soon amended, for obvious reasons, its message remained the same. A theophilanthropist was a lover (philos) of both God (theos) and man (anthropos). The original Parisian fraternity, of which Paine was a member, had but two creeds, both expressed in the 1795 *Manual:* "Les Théophilan-tropes croient à l'existence de Dieu, et à l'immortalite de l'âme." [The Theo-philanthropists believe in the existence of God and the immortality of the soul.] But the way in which these two tenets were spelled out in the *Manual* revealed them to be thoroughly deistic in nature. Paine himself admitted that the principles of the Parisian society were identical to those defended in his *Age of Reason.* The word *theophilanthropy* presumably was adopted first by the Parisians and later by the descendants of the New York Deistical Society be-cause it had more benign connotations than *deism,* which smacked too much in the popular mind of infidelity and atheism. The very fact that the last American periodical devoted to deism chose to style itself in this fashion indi-cates the extent to which the movement had shed its earlier unashamed mili-tancy.

Most of *The Theophilanthropist* was devoted to reprinting previously pub-lished essays by Paine. Occasionally, however, there were original pieces. As can be seen from the selections included here, none of them evoke the vitality of either *The Temple* or the *Prospect.* Both the "Prospectus" and "Introductory Address" are predictable statements of deistic principles which deplore super-naturalist superstition and insist on the primacy of reason and science. The "Character of Jesus Christ" repeats a favorite theme of American deism: the original purity of Jesus' religious teaching and its subsequent corruption by metaphysical nonsense. Of all the pieces to appear in the periodical, "Inter-course between Intelligent Beings" is the most interesting. In it, the author appeals to the Great Chain of Being metaphor to dismiss the possibility of revelatory knowledge. Just as human capacities render the race incapable of communicating with "inferior" species, so they likewise preclude direct inter-course with "superior" ones—including God. Consequently, the scriptural claim of direct communication between humans and the divine is logically unacceptable: "All direct and immediate communications must be made be-tween beings in some degree, and in some circumstances, respectively conso-nant and equal to each other; but what degree of equality, or relationship, or consonancy or correspondence, can there possibly be between a limited and an unlimited being; between finite and infinite?—None."

The final selection, "Humanity," reiterates American deism's faith in the liberating effects of popular education. If ignorance and fear breed oppression, it follows (at least for *The Theophilanthropist*) that universal education will encourage open-minded tolerance as well as the desire to promote the welfare of all members of the human family. This argument, of course, had been as-serted by earlier American deists (and, indeed, by the entire Enlightenment tradition) time and again. The tragedy of *The Theophilanthropist* was its as-sumption that merely echoing that tradition, instead of aggressively pursuing its actualization, was sufficient.

Prospectus (January 1810)

The object of this publication is, to present to the public such critical, moral, theological and literary essays, as may tend to correct false opinions, promote the progress of reason, and increase the sum of human happiness.

Truths, which we deem important, will be boldly advocated, and pernicious errors exposed in all their deformity. Bigotry and superstition, those tyrants, which have so long held the world in bondage, and destroyed the peace and repose of man, will meet with merited chastisement; and the mild, tolerant religion of virtue, which the Creator has wisely revealed to the consciences of all mankind, will be asserted and maintained.

Of all subjects, correct religious opinions are the most important to the happiness of man; but, unfortunately, there are none in which deceit and imposture have been more successfully practised.

Theologians, by their contempt of virtue, and by substituting in its place puerile, nonsensical creeds, have bewildered the mind of man, and involved it in darkness, mystery and terror.

The sincere enquirer after truth, checked in his progress by contradictory opinions, called orthodox by their respective votaries, and claiming divine authority under the cabalistic term mystery, finds himself under the necessity of making a choice of absurdities, or of retiring from a pursuit which promises so little satisfaction. "The dreams of the timid and whimsical—the cheats of the cunning—the suborned villainies of the wicked—every tale, folly and contradiction huddled together, are called religion!—What violence to language!"

How a system, where never-ending and excruciating torments are pronounced the doom of the wicked, and according to which, all have been criminal can be benign and consolatory, outdoes all the labyrinths and repugnances of theology. When it is observed that men, the dreams of a shadow, believe they may suffer immortal punishment, who can refrain pronouncing with Pliny, "that man is at once the most vain, and miserable of all animals."

To have faith in a system which preaches torments infinite in excess and duration, is to stand on a precipice with closed eyes, that you may fling yourself into immeasurable destruction.

The last and consummate effort of the soul, is the religion of philosophy: whose only dogma is, that one God superintends the universe; whose mysteries are the means most conducive to human happiness; whose ceremonials are acts of charity, benevolence, generosity, and public spirit; whose discipline and designs are to refine the sympathies, direct the passions, strengthen and enlarge the mind, and facilitate the communication of wisdom and science.

Our feeble talents shall be exerted to establish these holy principles, so natural, and so consoling to the human mind; and from which nothing but the most villainous imposture could have deluded it.

We shall avail ourselves of the works of those luminaries of thought, whose lives have been devoted to humanity, and whose writings are little known by the public in general; and we solicit the co-operation of all who may be disposed to volunteer in this cause.

Biographical sketches, and critical reviews of modern literary productions, will form a part of this publication.

Improvements in agriculture; the advancement of American manufactures; useful discoveries; and new invented machinery for lessening labour, will be duly noticed.

Occurrences, important to the future historian; political essays upon general, and liberal principles; and articles of mere amusement, will occasionally find admittance in this work.

Communications on any of the above subjects will be gratefully received.

Introductory Address (January 1810)

It is highly proper, at the threshold of this work, to develop the views and motives of the publishers more particularly than has been done in the Prospectus. This we shall do with that candid frankness, which is at all times the companion of truth, and the handmaid of reason. Although the principles indicated by the title of the work, are as ancient as philosophy, and, in fact, co-existent with man, the term *Theophilanthropist* has but lately been introduced into our language. It may, therefore, be pertinent accurately to define its meanings, in order to silence ignorant fanaticism, and interested priestcraft; whose clamorous declarations we expect to encounter, for our exposition of the frauds, which have been, and still are practised on the great majority of mankind. Unappalled, however, by these clamours, we shall march straight forward in the path, to which truth and reason point.

Theophilanthropist is of Greek origin, and is compounded of three of the strongest words in that refined and sonorous language, viz. *Theos*, God; *philos*, a lover, and *anthropos*, man. It therefore means *a lover of God and man*; or one who not only entertains a profound respect for his Creator, but unites therewith, kind and benevolent affections towards his fellow creatures, not merely on account of human sympathies, but from a conviction of the relative situation they stand in, along with himself, to "the great first cause of all."

From this definition it is easy to comprehend the creed of the *Theophilanthropist*. His dogmas are contained in the name he bears. He believes in *one* supreme and incomprehensible *Deity*, and with pious reverence acknowledges his power and perfections. He adores and venerates him as the Creator and conservator of the universe. Hence his devotion partakes not of that debasing servility which characterizes Christian and Mahometan worshippers, but is merely the spontaneous and genial effusion of the soul.

From his relative situation in the scale of being in which he is placed, he readily learns the duties he owes to his fellow men. He at once perceives that the nature of these are simple, and are in unison with the best affections of the human heart, and may be comprehended under the general titles of *justice and benevolence*. From his very nature, he with equal ease perceives that the duties he owes to himself, consist in the due regulation of his passions. His, therefore, may emphatically be styled the *religion of nature*. His creed and his duties are imprinted on every leaf of its vast volume. When he contemplates the planets as they roll; the variety, the order, the economy and the harmony of the little globe he inhabits: he is fired with devotion, and penetrated with astonishment at the sublimity, and grandeur of the scene, and his mind is naturally elevated to contemplate the all perfect Deity, by whose wisdom the wonderful system of nature is preserved, and by whose power it was originally created.

In reviewing the beautiful perspective, he painfully perceives that man has not profited as he ought by the superior reason with which he has been endowed. Tracing him through every state of society, he observes that the greatest portion of the species have been the ready dupes of the crafty, or the willing slaves of superstition; that the image of the incorruptible God has been defaced, the empire of reason overturned, and the horrors of Cimmerian darkness permitted to brood over the human mind. He perceives that though civil tyranny carries along with it the elements of its own destruction, that, which is founded on religion, is strengthened by age, and entailed on its unfortunate victims from generation to generation. From this picture of debased reason he turns with disgust, and truly and sincerely pities the condition of the votaries of superstition. With these impressions we shall not hesitate to expose the cheats practised on degraded man, under the pretended sanction of religion; and shall endeavour to uproot from the social garden, those prejudices, which like noxious weeds are destructive to the soil, and pestiferous to the atmosphere. We are aware of the extent of the task, which we have voluntarily imposed on ourselves; but we shall not shrink from the irksome duty, for if we did, we should be unworthy the name of *Theophilanthropists*.

It is time that man return to reason, which he has so ungratefully abandoned; that he relinquish his chimerical fears; that he at length place confidence in the justness and goodness of that God, who is not the patron of any particular sect or nation, whether Jew or Gentile, but the Creator and preserver of all nature and of all worlds; "of whose existence no mind can doubt, without being involved in the most inextricable absurdities; but in search of whom, o'erstretched idea bursts, and thought rolls back on darkness." This God, to whom the speculative opinions of mankind must be sovereignly indifferent, punishes naught but crimes, and those in proportion to their magnitude. What a consoling reflection to the moral man! He sees the path of salvation and happiness open before him, which he cannot mistake without doing violence to that best gift of God to man, his reason: to which all Bibles, Korans and

Vedams, must eventually make their final appeal.

We shall urgently press upon our readers the importance of this subject; the necessity of discharging those puerile prejudices, which they imbibed with their mother's milk, which their nurses have copiously infused, and which their spiritual guides still continue through interested motives, to rivet upon them. We by no means wish to wound the feelings of theological teachers, they do exactly the same as other men would do in their situation. The people oblige them to preach the stupid doctrine, which they have inherited from their forefathers. Let the people change, and their teachers will soon follow. Let the people build temples of reason, and they will soon find priests to officiate at their altars. This fact has been proved in France, where formerly monkish priestcraft reigned triumphant. The sun of reason arose; it was permitted to shine; its rays spread like lightning throughout the nation; priests and people became illumined, and chanted together the funeral dirge of superstition. But in that country, unfortunately, the monster despotism, which cannot flourish in the meridian sun of reason, is again nursing and invigorating the decrepit hag, superstition. So much light, however, had been shed abroad in France, that its tyrant dare not attempt to stifle it wholly at once. He has therefore only declared that the government is Catholic; intending thereby to render that religion fashionable, knowing that the greatest portion of mankind are governed by fashion.

In fine, America is the only country in which "reason is left free to combat error." If we do not profit by this privilege, the fault will lie at our own door. Let us then think freely, and express our thoughts like freemen. We shall on our part endeavour to demonstrate the genial influence of *true religion* upon the morals and social happiness of men; and, at the same time, shall warn our readers against the baneful effects of fostering ignorance and superstition, those deadly enemies to all the joys of life; which, having broken down all the barriers established by Deity, between virtue and vice, right and wrong, and not content with robbing man of the little happiness which this world might afford, insultingly threaten him with an eternity of misery in the world to come.

Character of Jesus Christ (February 1810)

Much as we esteem Mr. Volney, and highly as we prize his literary productions, we cannot agree with him in doubting the existence of Jesus Christ. Although much mythological fable has been artfully interwoven into his biography, by his interested followers, yet we fully believe that such a person lived in Judea, about two thousand years ago. Tacitus, who, by the way, is the only historian that says any thing that can be supposed to relate to Jesus Christ (the passage in Josephus respecting him having been proved to be an interpolation) observes, that a sect arose at this time, (the period in which Christ is supposed to have lived) which made some disturbance in Judea. The Jewish tradition, although no doubt interlarded with fable, is at least some evidence of the fact; which acknowledges that such a person actually sprang up amongst them, and after, as they say, deluding many, suffered an ignominious and cruel death. We therefore have no more doubt on our minds that there was such a man, than we have that there existed such legislators as Moses and Mahomet.

In that age it appears that the Mosaic superstition, which, from its commencement, was a grievous burthen on the Jewish nation, had been shamefully corrupted, and that the priests possessed unbounded power over the property and consciences of the people—hence they increased the rituals of worship to such a pitch as to render them an intolerable tyranny. The Romans also, at that period, had partially subdued the Jewish nation, and left them but the shadow of their ancient independence.

At this important crisis, this obscure *reformer*, whose youth had been spent in the mountainous parts of Palestine, daringly attacked their national prejudices, and attempted to uproot that corrupt system of religious mummery, with which they were oppressed.

His political principles were those of a republican, for he taught the lessons of political equality.

His religious dogmas were those of the *Theophilanthropist*, for he inculcated reverence to the deity, and benevolence towards the whole human family. It is true that his tenets have since been veiled and enshrouded in the robes of impiety by the knavery and craft of some of his fanatical disciples;—but we shall, in future numbers, endeavour to sift and separate the wheat from the chaff, and show that the morality which he preached to his followers was the same as that taught by Plato, Socrates and Epictetus, who lived before him.

In that rude and barbarous age, it was the practise of men who wished to govern the passions of the ignorant, to pretend to be messengers sent from heaven; it is therefore probable that Jesus Christ, like many of his contemporaries, made use of this stratagem, more powerfully to enforce his doctrines upon the minds of the vulgar. However that may be, we find that the Jewish Sanhedrin became alarmed at this growing popularity; for, from his obscure retreat, we find him advancing into their very capital, and in their very temple bearding their authority; ridiculing their ridiculous superstitions, and assuming a controul over the pettifogging retailers of offerings in the porches, and also over the horde of usurers that infested the temple. After numerous expedients had failed, they at length hit upon one, which they hoped would be effectual, to take off their dangerous rival. They therefore denounced him as a traitor, and an enemy to Caesar.

The Roman governor, to gratify the revenge of the infuriated priests, whose power he had shaken delivered him over to their will, after a mock trial; at the same time declaring that he found him guiltless. They therefore doomed him to suffer crucifixion, the common punishment for heinous offences.

Thus the man who had humanely endeavoured to ameliorate the condition of his countrymen, and to rescue them from civil despotism and religious tyranny, prematurely fell a victim to the bigotry and superstition of the age in which he lived, and became a martyr in the cause of philanthropy. His character was adorned with an assemblage of amiable virtues, and his ethics were calculated to render his fellow-creatures individually happy, and socially benevolent.

Such, in our opinion, are the true characteristics of Jesus Christ. But, several centuries after his death, interested and fanatical men founded a monstrous and impious system of religion in his name. —It is not pretended that he wrote a single line of this himself. His expositors however, to suit their own purposes, taking the heathen mythology as their guide, first deified him, and then intermixed with his rational ethics the most abominable frauds that were ever imposed upon human credulity.

Intercourse between Intelligent Beings (March 1810)

The intercourse between intelligent beings depends entirely on their capacity for reciprocating intelligence. This faculty in man is improved by education: it is also improvable, and by the same means, in dogs, horses, and other quadrupeds. The congeniality, in some particular points, of their natures with ours, appears indispensably necessary to this intercourse. With fish and fowl, the ability to correspond is, on both sides, very inadequate: but it is in exact proportion to the disparity of their several natures. Descend still lower on the scale of existence, and man, though surrounded by myriads of sentient beings, finds society totally at an end. 'Tis the same if he attempts to ascend the scale. The reports of the existence of such beings as angels, it is difficult to conceive. We necessarily conclude that as the exercise of power and intelligence universally indicate *mind*, the infinite power and intelligence manifested in the organization of vegetables, animals, and the world, must have proceeded from an infinitely powerful and wise being; and these conclusions are the only possible intercourse that we are capacitated ever to have with such a being. For if neither our physical, nor our moral powers, qualify us for corresponding with the beings the next below, or the next above us, on the great scale of existence, how is it possible that we should hold communication with beings a great many degrees higher? And if such intercourse with finite beings is impossible, how much more impossible must it be to correspond *viva voce*, with the highest and first of all beings, viz. with the Infinite and Eternal Mind? It also must appear, from the great disparity between the infinite mind and the effects of its operations, that the infinite being cannot, in our present circumstances, communicate, or hold correspondence with us, in any other manner, or by any other means, than through the medium of the vast creation, or, its operations on matter. The small degree of power and intelligence in the being called man, is not sufficient, as yet, to comprehend the organization of even a blade of grass, or a grain of wheat; and for such a being to pretend to hold a direct, spontaneous, and immediate intercourse and correspondence with the great creating and sustaining cause of grass and grain, an intercourse he is not capacitated for, and therefore cannot be benefitted by, is a pretence that can be founded only on extreme ignorance and presumption—or worse.

In tracing the manifestation of power and intelligence, whether in a solar system, a man, or a grain of wheat, we find that they all, universally and necessarily lead to the same conclusions, and the same source; i.e. to a perfectly intelligent and powerful cause, that must have designed, and made them all exactly what they are, consequently must have had this perfect power, intelligence and design, before they had existence; and that without the aid of *such a cause* it is not possible to account for their existence, organization, or nature, at all.

I am led to say, "that the infinite and eternal mind cannot correspond with a limited and finite mind, except through the operations of the creation, or of what is, in other words, commonly called nature," from the necessary impossibility of such a correspondence. Let us not start at the supposition. All direct and immediate communications must be made between beings in some degree, and in some circumstances, respectively consonant and equal to each other; but what degree of equality, or relationship, or consonancy or correspondence, can there possibly be between a limited and an unlimited being; between finite and infinite? —None.

The marks of the perfections of the eternal mind, or intelligent cause of that most great and complete effect which we call nature, are, to us, so manifest and so numerous, that we cannot suppose any thing imperfect, or absurd, in that cause; for it follows, that if we did, we should suppose a manifest contradiction.

Circumscribed as our knowledge is of the vast creation, we know, however, finite and frail as we are, and it is a great deal for us to know, that infinite power and wisdom cannot contradict itself; cannot cause a greater number to be taken from a less; cannot cause two hills without a valley between them; cannot cause a thing to be, and not be, at the same time; cannot cause a part to be equal to the whole. The laws that govern the universe, appear to have been the offspring of an infinitely powerful, wise, and immutable mind. All *viva voce* correspondence, therefore, between this mind and man, for any particular purpose whatever, suggests a mutability which all nature loudly contradicts; and all such reports and pretensions, must consequently be founded on ignorance, presumption, policy, or imposture.

Humanity (April 1810)

HUMANITY is the child of sensibility, the parent of charity, and the companion of philosophy; the possessor of this inestimable attribute can never be truly unhappy, for he is in the constant enjoyment of a quiet conscience. The recollection of the past, and the anticipation of future acts of benevolence, so absorb his reflections, that no vacuum remains to be filled by the gloomy meditations of the niggardly, or the plodding designs of the monopolist.

Like the light of heaven, humanity dispenses its favours with impartiality; the wretched and desponding seek her castle, and there find an antidote and a home; the houseless beggar, the widow and the orphan, the lame and the blind all claim kindred with this angel of beneficence, and "have their claims allowed."

Our city has produced many charitable institutions, where the humane citizen may give his aid to suffering humanity, and to the great work of forming and reforming the rising generation. Education is a principal and almost indispensable source of morality; it is the best security for liberty, the greatest boon of freemen; as its suppression by the tyrants of Europe constitutes their only safety against the just vengeance of their insulted subjects. Education in a free country, conducted on the principles of sound philosophy prepares the mind for those great efforts of genius, which render society useful and happy; it tends to substitute wholesome and just laws, in the place of those tyrannical and oppressive systems of Europe, which are the bane of social felicity. It lessens labour by the ingenuity of artificers, erects comfortable mansions in the place of miserable thatched hovels, and converts a howling wilderness into fruitful fields and populous cities.

Whilst on the subject of education it would be unpardonable not to bestow a tribute of praise on the establishment of the New-York free-school, which if not the most important institution of the city, promises to become a nursery of morals and useful knowledge.

Happy the individual, who, considering himself one of the great family of mankind, knowing and acknowledging the necessity of reciprocal dependence and mutual protection, the happiness of extending and receiving alternate benefits, contributes his aid to the promotion of education, of moral virtue, and the enaction of humane laws. Such an individual fulfils the duties of humanity, and feels thrilling through his heart the indescribable pleasure of *doing good*.

How different the selfish worldling, who, concentrating all his hopes and wishes in the gratification of sordid passions, without sensibility, pines, dissatisifed in the midst of plenty and luxury, because his inordinate wants cannot be supplied, or his unbounded avarice satiated. How basely mean is the man in office, who exercises power but to extort and torment! How cruelly unjust the pawn-broker, who demands the usurious interest of one dollar weekly for the loan of twenty, and reimburses himself by the sacrifice of ten dollars worth of the borrowers property! How void of humanity must that creditor be, who can consign to a loathsome prison, where no provision is made for his sustenance, an unfortunate but honest debtor!

How doubly unfeeling and brutal is that landlord, who, at quarter day can wrest the bed from under a sick woman, to remunerate himself for an exorbitant rent!

Such beings unfortunately exist; they belong to the numerous family of evils that afflict this world, which otherwise might have continued a paradise of bliss.

But with all their ill-gotten gains they are not happy; thrice more happy, in most instances, are the objects of their cruelty, their perfidy and injustice.

The image of a reproaching conscience continually haunts them and disturbs their repose.

The blush of guilt, suffusing itself through the paleness of a tortured visage, leaves to the sight, nothing but the horrid picture of *inhumanity.*

Sources and Permissions

Benjamin Franklin

A Dissertation on Liberty and Necessity, Pleasure and Pain (1725), *The Papers of Benjamin Franklin*, edited by Leonard W. Labaree and Whitfield J. Bell, Jr. (New Haven, Conn.: Yale University Press, 1959–), 1:59–71. Reprinted by permission.

Articles of Belief and Acts of Religion (1728), *The Works of Benjamin Franklin*, edited by Jared Sparks (Boston: Charles Tappan, 1844), 2:1–8.

Doctrine to be Preached (1731), *The Papers of Benjamin Franklin*, edited by Leonard W. Labaree and Whitfield J. Bell, Jr. (New Haven, Conn.: Yale University Press, 1959–), 1:213. Reprinted by permission.

On the Providence of God in the Government of the World (1732), *Works*, 2:525–32.

Self-Denial Not the Essence of Virtue (1735), *Works*, 2:63–66.

Dialogue between Two Presbyterians (1735), *The Papers of Benjamin Franklin*, edited by Leonard W. Labaree and Whitfield J. Bell, Jr. (New Haven, Conn.: Yale University Press, 1959–), 2:28–33. Reprinted by permission.

Letter to Josiah and Abiah Franklin (13 April 1738) and Draft of a Letter to His Father, *The Papers of Benjamin Franklin*, edited by Leonard W. Labaree and Whitfield J. Bell, Jr. (New Haven, Conn.: Yale University Press, 1959–), 2:202–4. Reprinted by permission.

The Lord's Prayer (1768?), *The Writings of Benjamin Franklin*, edited by Albert Henry Smyth (New York: Macmillan, 1907), 7:427–30.

Selections from Franklin's *Autobiography*, *Works*, vol. 1: 74–77 (selection 1); 102–8, 114–16 (selection 2); 119–20 (selection 3); 136–38, 139 (selection 4); 155–56 (selection 5).

370   *The Levée* (1779?), *Works*, 2:164–66.

Letter to Joseph Priestley (8 February 1780), *Works*, 8:418.

Letter to _____ (?) (3 July 1786[?]), *Works*, 10:281–82.

Motion for Prayers in the Convention (28 June 1787), *Writings*, 9:600–601.

Letter to Ezra Stiles (9 March 1790), *Works*, 10:423–24.

Thomas Jefferson

"On Freedom of Conscience," from *Notes on the State of Virginia* (1785), *The Writings of Thomas Jefferson*, edited by Albert Ellery Bergh (Washington, D.C.: Thomas Jefferson Memorial Association, 1903), 2:217–25.

"An Act for Establishing Religious Freedom, Passed in the Assembly of Virginia in the Beginning of the Year 1786," *Writings*, 2:300–303.

Letter to Peter Carr (10 August 1787), *Writings*, 6:257–61.

Letter to the Rev. Isaac Story (5 December 1801), *Writings*, 10:298–99.

Letter to Joseph Priestley (9 April 1803), *Writings*, 10:374–76.

Letter to Benjamin Rush (21 April 1803), *Writings*, 10:379–85.

Letter to John Adams (12 October 1813), *Writings*, 13:388–92.

Letter to John Adams (28 October 1813), *Writings*, 13:395–97, 399–400, 401–2.

Letter to Thomas Law (13 June 1814), *Writings*, 14:138–44.

Letter to Charles Thomson (9 January 1816), *Writings*, 14:385–86.

Letter to Francis Adrian Van der Kemp (30 July 1816), *Jefferson's Extracts from the Gospels*, edited by Dickinson W. Adams (Princeton, N.J.: Princeton University Press, 1982), 374–75. Reprinted by permission.

Letter to Margaret Bayard Smith (6 August 1816), *Writings*, 15:59–61.

Letter to Ezra Stiles Ely (25 June 1819), *Writings*, 15:202–4.

Letter to William Short (4 August 1820), *Writings*, 15:257–62.

Letter to Jared Sparks (4 November 1820), *Writings*, 15:287–88.

Letter to Benjamin Waterhouse (26 June 1822), *Writings*, 15:383–85.

Letter to John Adams (11 April 1823), *Writings*, 15:425–30.

Letter to Alexander Smyth (17 January 1825), *Writings*, 16:100–101.

Ethan Allen
Reason the Only Oracle of Man, or a Compenduous System of Natural Religion (Bennington, Vt.: Haswell & Russell, 1784).
 I.1. The Duty of Reforming Mankind from Superstition and Error and the Good Consequences of It, 23–25
 I. 2. Of the Being of a God, 25–35
 III.1. The Doctrine of the Infinite Evil of Sin Considered, 110–14
 III.2. The Moral Government of *God* Incompatible with Eternal Punishment, 114–29
 V.1. Speculations on the Doctrine of the Depravity of Human Reason, 177–85
 V.2. Containing a Disquisition of the *Law of Nature* . . . , 186–99
 VII.5. Miracles Could Not Be Instructive to Mankind, 267–69
 IX.1. Of the Nature of *Faith* and Wherein It Consists, 330–35
 X.3. The Imperfection of Knowledge in the Person of Jesus Chrsit . . . , 352–56
 XII.6. The Person of *Jesus Christ*, Considered in a Variety of Different Characters . . . , 411–22
 XIV. 2. Morality Derived from Natural Fitness, and Not from Tradition, 466–72.
 XIV.3. Of the Importance of the Exercise of Reason . . . , 472–77

Constantin François Chasseboeuf, Comte de Volney
Volney's Ruins; or, Meditation [sic] on the Revolutions of Empires (1791), no translator cited (Boston: Charles Gaylord, 1835).
 Problem of Religious Contradictions, 93–112
 Solution of the Problem of Contradictions, 170–74
The Law of Nature and Condition of Man in the Universe, 175–86, 199–201, 206–8

Thomas Paine
The Age of Reason (New York: D. M. Bennett, 1878). (Headings mine.)
 The Author's Profession of Faith, 5–6
 Of Missions and Revelations, 6–8, 13
 Of Jesus Christ, 9–10
 Of Scripture, 19–21
 Of Redemption, 22–23
 Of Miracles, 49, 50–51, 52
 Of the Immorality of Christianity, 143–46

Of Christian Theology and True Theology, 28, 29–32
Of True Revelation; and of God, 24–27
Conclusion, 146–51

"The Existence of God: A Discourse Delivered to the Society of Theophilan-thropists at Paris," *The Great Works of Thomas Paine* (New York: D. M. Bennett, 1878), 280–87.

My Private Thoughts on a Future State, in *Great Works*, 270–71.

Elihu Palmer

Principles of Nature; or, A Development of the Moral Causes of Happiness and Misery among the Human Species, 3d ed. (New York: 1806). (Headings mine.)
    Critique of Christianity
        Ignorance and Christianity, 18–19
        Sacred Scripture and Revelation, 25–29
        Original Sin, Atonement and Faith, 35–48
        Eternal Damnation, 175–77
        Miracles, 79, 81–85
        The Immorality of Christianity, 52–56, 110, 115–18
    Natural Morality
        The Origin of Moral Evil, 126–30, 134—36
        Morality Is Not Based on the Divine, 191–94
        Universal Benevolence, 194–99
        Moral Principle, 212–20
    The Religion of Nature, 240–44, 178–80

"Principles of the Deistical Society of the State of New York," *Posthumous Pieces. By Elihu Palmer, being three chapters of an unfinished work intended to have been entitled "The Political World." To which are prefixed a Memoir of Mr. Palmer by his friend Mr. John Fellows of New York, and Mr. Palmer's "Principles of the Deistical Society of the State of New York,"* edited by John Fellows (London: R. Carlile, 1828), 11–12.

Philip Freneau

Poems Written and Published during the American Revolutionary War . . . (Philadelphia: Lydia Bailey, 1809).
    "On the Powers of the Human Understanding"
    "Reflections on the Constitution, or Frame of Nature"
    "Science, Favourable to Virtue"
    "On a Book Called Unitarian Theology"

A Collection of Poems, and a Variety of Other Subjects, Chiefly Moral and Political; Written between the Year 1797 and the Present Time (New York: David Longworth, 1815).

"On False Systems of Government, and the Generally Debased Condition of Man-
kind"
"The New Age: or, Truth Triumphant"
"On Superstition"
"On the Abuse of Human Power, as Exercised over Opinion"
"On the Uniformity and Perfection of Nature"
"On the Universality, and Other Attributes of the God of Nature"
"On the Religion of Nature"
"On the Evils of Human Life"
"Belief and Unbelief: Humbly Recommended to the Serious Consideration of Creed Makers"
"On Happiness, as Proceeding from the Practice of Virtue"
"The Millennium—To a Ranting Field Orator"

"Letter 13" (originally appeared in the 8 August 1799 issue of the *Aurora*), *Letters on Various Interesting and Important Subjects . . . by Robert Slender* (Philadelphia, 1799).

"The Voyage of Timberoo-Taho-Eede, an Otaheite Indian," *The Miscellaneous Works of Mr. Philip Freneau, Containing His Essays, and Additional Poems* (Philadelphia, 1788), 211–12, 213–14.

The Temple of Reason
"To the American Reader" (8 November 1800)

"The Deists Creed" (8 November 1800)

"A Demonstration of the Being and Attributes of God" (8 and 15 November 1800)

"An Ode to Reason" (8 November 1800)

"Christian Morality Compared with That of the Pagan Philosophers" (29 November 1800)

"A New Hymn for the Temple of Reason" (16 September 1801)

"Natural Ideas Opposed to Supernatural" (30 December 1801)

Prospect; or View of the Moral World
"Competency of the Human Powers" (10 December 1803)

"Explanation of the Principles of Deism" (17 December 1803)

"Aphorisms" (17 December 1803)

"Moral Philosophy" (31 December 1803)

"Religious Self-Conceit" (21 January 1804)

"On the Christian Religion" (28 January 1804)

"Communication on Science from 'A Subscriber' " (25 February 1804)

"Miracles" (31 March 1804)

"Revelation" (7 April 1804)

"Laws of Nature" (28 April 1804)

"On Christian Faith" (12 May 1804)

"More of Human Reason" (28 July 1804)

"Superstition" (24 November 1804)

"The Indian Student; or, Force of Nature" (24 November 1804)

"Remarks" (26 January 1805)

"Enthusiasm" (2 February 1805)

"For the Prospect" (30 March 1805)

The Theophilanthropist
"Prospectus" (January 1810)

"Introductory Address" (January 1810)

"Character of Jesus Christ" (February 1810)

"Intercourse between Intelligent Beings" (March 1810)

"Humanity" (April 1810)

All three deistic newspapers are available on microfilm in Lamont Library, Harvard University.

Bibliographic Essay

The bibliographical information here is not intended to be exhaustive. Instead, it lists and discusses those titles that may be of most use to the reader interested in exploring further American deism, its intellectual background, and its immediate aftermath. Most of the works cited contain excellent bibliographies. There are also three general bibliographical resources which are extremely helpful. *Freethought in the United States: A Descriptive Bibliography* (Westport, Conn.: Greenwood Press, 1978), edited by Marshall G. Brown and Gordon Stein, is an excellent guide to both primary and secondary literature. Less detailed is *A Critical Bibliography of Religion in America* (Princeton, N.J.: Princeton University Press, 1961), edited by Nelson R. Burr; sources on American deism are listed and annotated on pages 184–210. *The Encyclopedia of Unbelief* (Buffalo, N.Y.: Prometheus Books, 1985), edited by Gordon Stein, provides succinct articles on deism as well as its individual proponents.

For those interested in comprehensive histories of religious thought in America, the two best works are unquestionably Winthrop S. Hudson, *Religion in America* (New York: Scribner's, 1965), and Sydney E. Ahlstrom's encyclopedic *A Religious History of the American People* (New Haven, Conn.: Yale University Press, 1972). Both contain extensive bibliographies.

The New Learning and the Enlightenment

The three luminaries of the Enlightenment were Francis Bacon, John Locke, and Isaac Newton; Jefferson admired them so much that he hung their portraits in his Monticello study. Complete editions of their works as well as anthologies are readily available, and the interested reader is referred to citations in the Introduction for specific titles.

The secondary literature on all three men is encyclopedic, but a few titles are especially pertinent to the subject of their influence on Enlightenment philosophy and religion. Benjamin Farrington's *Francis Bacon: Philosopher of Industrial Science* (London: Lawrence & Wishart, 1957) focuses on the instrumental bent of Bacon's new logic. In *The Philosophy of Francis Bacon* (Chicago: University of Chicago Press, 1948), F. H. Anderson provides an exhaustive treatment of Bacon's philosophy of science as well as his criticisms of the Aristotelian system, as does Peter Urbach more recently in *Francis Bacon's Philosophy of Science: An Account and Reappraisal* (LaSalle, Ill.: Open Court Press, 1987). Paolo Rossi, *Francis Bacon: From Magic to Science*, translated by Sacha Rabinovitch (Chicago: University of Chicago Press, 1968), and John C.

Briggs, *Francis Bacon and the Rhetoric of Nature* (Cambridge, Mass.: Harvard University Press, 1989), explore Bacon's style of discourse and its relation to the investigation of nature. Charles Whitney's *Francis Bacon and Modernity* (New Haven, Conn.: Yale University Press, 1986) argues that Bacon is best viewed as the prophet and founder of the modern scientific temperament.

James Gibson's *Locke's Theory of Knowledge and Its Historical Relations* (Cambridge: Cambridge University Press, 1960) examines the epistemology of the *Essay* and discusses its relation to the thought of Locke's contemporaries. A convenient overview of Locke's entire philosophical project, including his religious attitudes, is presented by John W. Yolton in *Locke: An Introduction* (London: Basil Blackwell, 1985). Yolton, who is probably the preeminent modern Locke scholar, also discusses the influence of Lockean philosophy on the continental savants in his recent *Locke and French Materialism* (New York: Oxford University Press, 1991). The metaphysical implications of Locke's epistemology are the subject of John L. Kraus's *John Locke: Empiricist, Atomist, Conceptualist, and Agnostic* (New York: Philosophical Library, 1968). R. S. Woolhouse, *Locke's Philosophy of Science and Knowledge* (New York: Barnes and Noble, 1971), provides an interesting discussion of Locke's account of natural or scientific laws.

Newton's methodology is the centerpiece of two excellent essays: Alexandre Koyré, "Concept and Experience in Newton's Scientific Thought," in *Newtonian Studies* (Cambridge, Mass.: Harvard University Press, 1965), and N. R. Hanson, "Hypotheses Fingo," in *The Methodological Heritage of Newton*, edited by Robert E. Butts and John W. Davis (Oxford: University of Toronto Press, 1970). Frank E. Manuel analyzes Newton's religious beliefs in *The Religion of Isaac Newton* (London: Oxford University Press, 1974), and an especially fine collection of essays on the same topic is to be found in *Essays on the Context, Nature, and Influence of Isaac Newton's Theology*, edited by James E. Force and Richard H. Popkin (Dordrecht, Netherlands: Kluwer Academic, 1990). Of particular interest in this collection are Popkin's "Polytheism, Deism, and Newton" and Force's "The Newtonians and Deism." The *Principia* as a "verification" of eighteenth-century empiricism is discussed by Ernan McMullin in "The Significance of Newton's *Principia* for Empiricism," in *Religion, Science, and Worldview: Essays in Honor of Richard S. Westfall*, edited by Margaret J. Osler and Paul Lawrence Farber (Cambridge: Cambridge University Press, 1985). Westfall's *Never at Rest: A Biography of Isaac Newton* (Cambridge: Cambridge University Press, 1980) is modestly titled. Much more than just a biographical study, it is an exhaustive treatment of Newtonian natural philosophy and its impact on eighteenth-century thought. Finally, the collection of essays in *Let Newton Be!*, edited by John Flauvel et al. (New York: Oxford University Press, 1988), is a richly illustrated discussion of

Newton's scientific and religious thought. Especially interesting is John
Brooke's contribution, "The God of Isaac Newton."

A number of studies focus on the intellectual foundations of the Enlightenment ethos. Richard S. Westfall's *Science and Religion in Seventeenth-Century England* (Ann Arbor: University of Michigan Press, 1973) is a masterful
study of natural religion, faith, and reason in pre-Enlightenment Britain.
Herbert Butterfield, *The Origins of Modern Science, 1300–1800* (New York:
Macmillan, 1959); E. A. Burtt, *The Metaphysical Foundations of Modern Science* (Garden City, N.Y.: Doubleday, 1955); and E. J. Dijksterhus, *The Mecha-
nization of the World Picture*, translated by C. Dikshoorn (New York: Oxford
University Press, 1969), all discuss the impact of the scientific revolution on
subsequent European and British thought. Nature and optimism in Enlightenment thought are examined in chapters 6 and 7 of Arthur O. Lovejoy's *The
Great Chain of Being* (Cambridge, Mass.: Harvard University Press, 1936);
also see Basil Willey's *The Eighteenth-Century Background: Studies on the Idea
of Nature in the Thought of the Period* (London: Chatto & Windus, 1940). The
Enlightenment's drive to subdue and manage natural forces is treated by William Leiss, *The Domination of Nature* (Boston: Beacon Press, 1974), and
Carolyn Merchant, *The Death of Nature: Women, Ecology, and the Scientific
Revolution* (San Francisco: Harper and Row, 1980). The scientistic consequences of this endeavor for the study of humans and society are explored in
Floyd W. Matson, *The Broken Image: Man, Science, and Society* (New York:
George Braziller, 1964), and in my *The Sane Society Ideal in Modern Utopian-
ism* (Lewiston, N.Y.: Edwin Mellen Press, 1989).

There are several good studies of Enlightenment thought as a whole. Most
comprehensive is probably Peter Gay's *The Enlightenment: An Interpretation*
(New York: Alfred A. Knopf, 1966–69). His companion volume, *The Enlight-
enment: A Comprehensive Anthology* (New York: Simon and Schuster, 1973),
offers almost one thousand closely printed pages of texts from the European,
British, and American Enlightenment. Less inclusive but still useful is *The Portable Age of Reason*, edited by Crane Brinton (New York: Viking Press, 1956).
Two histories of Enlightenment thought have acquired the status of classic:
Carl Becker, *The Heavenly City of the Eighteenth-Century Philosophers* (New
Haven, Conn.: Yale University press, 1932), and Ernst Cassirer, *The Philosophy
of the Enlightenment*, translated by Fritz C. A. Koelln and James P. Pettegrove
(Boston: Beacon Press, 1965). Two studies that focus on the Enlightenment's
impact on religious sensibilities are Ernest Campbell Mossner, *Bishop Butler
and the Age of Reason: A Study in the History of Thought* (New York: Macmillan, 1936), and Margaret C. Jacob, *The Radical Enlightenment: Pantheists,
Freemasons, and Republicans* (London: George Allen & Unwin, 1981). In the
latter, chapters 3 ("The Newtonian Enlightenment and Its Critics") and 7

("Pantheistic Religion, Revolution, and the New Science") are particularly pertinent.

The American Enlightenment has received less attention than its European counterpart, but there are still several good historical studies. Among the best are Henry May's *The Enlightenment in America* (New York: Oxford University Press, 1976), Donald H. Mayer's *The Democratic Enlightenment* (New York: G. P. Putnam's Sons, 1976), and Daniel Boorstin's *The Lost World of Thomas Jefferson* (Boston: Beacon Press, 1964). Boorstin's study suffers, however, from a total disregard of the influence of Scottish common sense philosophy on American Enlightened thought. May and Meyer discuss the issue, as do Mark A. Noll in *Princeton and the Republic, 1768–1822* (Princeton, N.J.: Princeton University Press, 1989) and Elizabeth Flower and Murray G. Murphey in the first volume of their *History of Philosophy in America* (New York: G. P. Putnam's Sons, 1977). Less comprehensive treatments of the American Enlightenment include Ernst Cassara, *The Enlightenment in America* (Lanham, Md.: University Press of America, 1988), and Garry Wills, *Cincinnatus: George Washington and the Enlightenment* (Garden City, N.Y.: Doubleday, 1984). John Corrigan's essay, "The Enlightenment," in the *Encyclopedia of American Religious Experience*, vol. 2), edited by Charles H. Lippy and Peter W. Williams (New York: Charles Scribner's Sons, 1988), is an excellent short introduction. The impact of the Enlightenment on American political thought is dealt with by Bernard Bailyn, "Political Experience and Enlightenment Ideas in Eighteenth-Century America," *American Historical Review* 67 (1962); Henry Steele Commager, *Jefferson, Nationalism, and the Enlightenment* (New York: George Braziller, 1975); Morton White's masterly *The Philosophy of the American Revolution* (New York: Oxford University Press, 1978); and Garry Wills, *Inventing America: Jefferson's Declaration of Independence* (Garden City, N.Y.: Doubleday, 1978). In *The Empire of Reason* (New York: Anchor Press, 1977), Henry Steele Commager argues that the American experiment "realized" by enacting in public and social policy the ideals of the European Enlightenment. Adrienne Koch discusses Franklinian pragmatism and the Jeffersonian concept of happiness in *Power, Morals, and the Founding Fathers: Essays in the Interpretation of the American Enlightenment* (Ithaca, N.Y.: Cornell University Press, 1961). Paul Merrill Spurlin examines the influence of French thought on the American Enlightenment in *The French Enlightenment in America: Essays on the Times of the Founding Fathers* (Athens: University of Georgia Press, 1984). Finally, American science in the Enlightenment period is explored by John C. Greene, *American Science in the Age of Jefferson* (Ames: Iowa State University Press, 1984), and Brooke Hindle, *The Pursuit of Science in Revolutionary America, 1735–1789* (Chapel Hill: University of North Carolina Press, 1956).

Deism

Garland Press recently has issued facsimile editions of the works of a few of the British deists—John Toland, Matthew Tindal, and some of the lesser figures—but most primary texts from the British tradition remain long out of print and generally inaccessible. Two anthologies, neither of them very good, collect a few selections from the British deists: Peter Gay, *Deism: An Anthology* (New York: Van Nostrand, 1968), and E. Graham Waring, *Deism and Natural Religion: A Source Book* (New York: Frederick Ungar Publishing Co., 1967). Gay's anthology reproduces a meager selection from Palmer. Waring concentrates on British deism but also includes selections from eighteenth-century critics such as William Law. For a general introduction to Enlightenment deism, see "The Religion of Nature," chapter 13 of John Herman Randall, Jr.'s *The Making of the American Mind: A Survey of the Intellectual Background of the Present Day* (Boston: Houghton Mifflin Co., 1926), which covers the period between 1650 and 1800; and also Alfred Owen Aldridge's "Deism" in *The Encyclopedia of Unbelief.*

A good treatment of liberal Christianity and the rise of deism in Britain may be found in John Redwood, *Reason, Ridicule, and Religion: The Age of Enlightenment in England, 1660–1750* (Cambridge, Mass.: Harvard University Press, 1976). For readers who can locate it, John Leland's *View of the Principal Deistical Writers* (1754), covering Toland to Hume, is still a good resource, although Leland sometimes grinds a sectarian ax. Its 1837 reprint (London: T. Tegg and Sons) is available in many research libraries. The first volume of Leslie Stephen's *History of English Thought in the Eighteenth Century* (New York: G. P. Putnam's Sons, 1908) gives four comprehensive and well-documented chapters to the British deists; Stephen divides deism into two functional camps, "constructive" and "critical." E. Royston Pike's *Slayers of Superstition: A Popular Account of the Leading Personalities of the Deist Movement* (London: Watts & Co., 1931) is a highly readable account but lacks documentation. Rather biased is the treatment by John Orr, *English Deism: Its Roots and Fruits* (Grand Rapids, Mich.: W. B. Eerdmans Publishing Co., 1934). Three works dealing with specific British deists are worthy of note: James O'Higgens, *Anthony Collins: The Man and His Works* (The Hague, Netherlands: Martinus Nijhoff, 1970); Stephen H. Daniel, *John Toland: His Methods, Manners, and Mind* (Montreal: McGill-Queen's University Press, 1974); and Robert E. Sullivan, *John Toland and the Deist Controversy: A Study in Adaptations* (Cambridge, Mass.: Harvard University Press, 1982). The works of O'Higgens and Sullivan are especially fine, painstakingly researched and documented. An account of early French deistic thought, ending with Voltaire's *Lettres philosophiques* (1734), is C. J. Betts, *Early Deism in France* (The Hague, Netherlands: Martinus Nijhoff, 1984).

The two standard works devoted to American deism proper, as opposed to the American Enlightenment in general, are G. Adolf Koch, *Republican Religion: The American Revolution and the Cult of Reason* (New York: Henry Holt, 1933), and Herbert A. Morais, *Deism in Eighteenth-Century America* (New York: Russell & Russell, 1960). Koch's work sheds some interesting light on American deism's tenuous historical association with Freemasonry and has a good chapter on Palmer. Morais covers much of the same ground but also provides a discussion of the influence of French thought on American deism. Neither work, however, is analytical or critical. Instead, both offer descriptive historical accounts.

The Infidel: Free Thought and American Religion (Cleveland, Ohio: World Publishing Co., 1961) is one of Martin E. Marty's earlier works and does not demonstrate the sophistication of his later books. Although its initial chapters cover the high points of American deism, they tend to be sloppily general and uncritically negative in tone. More judicious accounts of American deism may be found in I. Woodbridge Riley, *American Philosophy: The Early Schools* (New York: Dodd, Mead, 1907), and "Early Freethinking Societies in America," *Harvard Theological Review* 11 (1918): 247–84, as well as Ernest Sutherland Bates, *American Faith* (New York: W. W. Norton, 1940), chapter 20, "The Rise of Deism," and Edwin Scott Gaustad, *Dissent in American Religion* (Chicago: University of Chicago Press, 1973). Gaustad discusses, *inter alia*, the deism of Franklin and Jefferson in his more recent *Faith of Our Fathers* (San Francisco: Harper and Row, 1987), and Norman Cousins excerpts selections from Franklin, Jefferson, and Paine in *The Republic of Reason: The Personal Philosophies of the Founding Fathers* (San Francisco: Harper and Row, 1988; reprint of the 1958 *In God We Trust*). Cousins's selections are not always astute or accurate. Finally, I have discussed the rise and fall of American deism in my *Rational Infidels: The American Deists* (Wolfeboro, N.H.: Longwood, 1992).

For treatments of post-Enlightenment, nearly nineteenth-century American infidelity, Albert Post's *Popular Freethought in America, 1825–1850* (New York: Columbia University Press, 1943) is the best documented, but James Turner's *Without God, Without Creed: The Origins of Unbelief in America* (Baltimore, Md.: Johns Hopkins University Press, 1985) must be regarded as definitive. Turner's book also contains a good discussion of American deism. Herbert Hovenkamp, *Science and Religion in America, 1800–1860* (Philadelphia: University of Pennsylvania Press, 1978), explores the effect of eighteenth-century natural philosophy on early nineteenth-century styles of theologizing.

Two recent studies, both ground-breaking and extensively documented, deal with postdeistic Christianity in the nineteenth century: Charles D. Cashdollar's *The Transformation of Theology, 1830–1890* (Princeton, N.J.: Princeton University Press, 1989) and Nathan O. Hatch's *The Democratiza-*

tion of American Christianity (New Haven, Conn.: Yale University Press, 1989). Cashdollar traces the influence of positivism on Christian theology, and Hatch examines the "popular religion" of evangelism in the Early Republic.

Benjamin Franklin

The definitive edition of Franklin's collected works, *The Papers of Benjamin Franklin*, edited by Leonard W. Labaree and Whitfield J. Bell, Jr. (New Haven, Conn.: Yale University Press, 1959–), has now published twenty-eight volumes, running through early 1779. The Labaree edition is the only one that contains Franklin's early *Dissertation on Liberty and Necessity, Pleasure and Pain*. Curiously, both the Sparks and Smyth editions mention but do not reproduce it. These two earlier editions of Franklin are neither as comprehensive nor scholarly as Labaree's but are still useful: *The Works of Benjamin Franklin*, edited by Jared Sparks (Boston: Charles Tappan, 1844), ten volumes, and *The Writings of Benjamin Franklin*, edited by Albert Henry Smyth (New York: Macmillan, 1907), ten volumes. Of historical interest is the early edition that Franklin's grandson William Temple Franklin helped prepare: *Memoirs of the Life and Writings of Benjamin Franklin*, second edition (London: Henry Colburn, 1818), six volumes. This edition, needless to say, is quite incomplete. Two good anthologies of Franklin's writings are also available: *Benjamin Franklin: Representative Selections*, edited by Chester E. Jorgenson and Frank Luther Mott (New York: Hill and Wang, 1962), and *Writings* (Library of America series), edited by J. A. Leo Lemay (New York: Viking, 1987). Jorgenson and Mott's anthology is an especially fine piece of work, with generous annotations to the texts and an excellent 150-page introduction containing an extremely able analysis of Franklin's religious beliefs.

The publishing of Frankliniana has been a major industry for two centuries, and titles run in the thousands. Biographical treatments are numerous, but one of the best documented is still Carl van Doren's *Benjamin Franklin* (New York: Viking Press, 1938). Three recent biographies deserve mention: Ronald W. Clark, *Benjamin Franklin* (New York: Random House, 1983), David Freeman Hawke, *Franklin* (New York: Harper and Row, 1976), and Esmond Wright, *Franklin of Philadelphia* (Cambridge, Mass.: Belknap Press of Harvard University Press, 1986). While each of them is competent and contains extensive bibliographies of the secondary literature, Wright's is the most scholarly. Hawke's, however, is the most readable and is a nice companion piece to his *Paine* (see below). Unfortunately, all three focus primarily on Franklin the statesman and only briefly deal with his religious or ethical thought.

Fortunately, there are a number of solid discussions of Franklin's religious perspective. James Madison Stifler's *The Religion of Benjamin Franklin* is unimaginative but provides a decent introductory overview. A. Owen Aldridge examines Franklin's early dogmatic materialism in "Benjamin Franklin and

Philosophical Necessity," *Modern Language Quarterly* 12 (1951): 292–309, his connections with the European Enlightenment in *Franklin and His French Contemporaries* (New York: New York University Press, 1957), and his empiricist approach to religious inquiry in "Franklin's Experimental Religion," in *Meet Dr. Franklin*, edited by Roy N. Lorren (Philadelphia: Franklin Institute, 1981). Especially noteworthy is Aldridge's *Benjamin Franklin and Nature's God* (Durham, N.C.: Duke University Press, 1967), acknowledged as the best single study of Franklin's religion. Unfortunately, Aldridge's treatment is flawed by his bizarre argument that Franklin advocated an eighteenth-century religious polytheism, a thesis partially inspired by David Williams's "More Light on Franklin's Religious Ideas," *American Historical Review* 43 (1938): 803–13. The polytheistic thesis, at least in my judgment, simply does not hold up, and a fresh look at Franklin's rich religious thought is badly needed. More acceptable but still somewhat tainted by the polytheism thesis is Aldridge's *Benjamin Franklin: Philosopher and Man* (New York: Lippincott, 1965).

Several other treatments of Franklin's religious views deserve mention. Charles L. Sanford maps their permutations in "An American Pilgrim's Progress," *American Quarterly* 6 (1954): 297–310. I. Bernard Cohen traces the impact of Franklin's empiricism on his moral system in *Benjamin Franklin: His Contributions to the American Tradition* (Indianapolis: Bobbs-Merrill, 1953). Two studies focus on the ambivalence in Franklin's deism: Donald H. Meyer, "Franklin's Religion," in *Critical Essays on Benjamin Franklin*, edited by Melvin H. Buxbaum (Boston: G. K. Hall, 1987), and David L. Parker, "From Sound Believer to Practical Preparationist: Some Puritan Harmonics in Franklin's Autobiography," in *The Oldest Revolutionary: Essays on Benjamin Franklin*, edited by J. A. Leo Lemay (Philadelphia: University of Pennsylvania Press, 1976). I likewise deal with Franklin's religious ambivalence in chapter 2 of my *Rational Infidels: The American Deists*. Finally, Melvin H. Buxbaum entertainingly and painstakingly examines Franklin's tolerant attitude to sectarian allegiances as well as his dislike of religious bigotry in *Benjamin Franklin and the Zealous Presbyterians* (University Park: Pennsylvania State University Press, 1975).

Thomas Jefferson

Twenty volumes, running through the year 1792, of the comprehensive *Papers of Thomas Jefferson*, edited by Julian P. Boyd (Princeton, N.J.: Princeton University Press, 1950–), have appeared to date. The edition does for Jefferson what Labaree's does for Franklin: It provides an exhaustive and scholarly access to the complete works of a major American thinker. Until the Boyd edition is completed, readers will find useful the still respectable *Writings of Thomas Jefferson* (Monticello edition), edited by Albert Ellery Bergh (Washington, D.C.: Thomas Jefferson Memorial Association, 1903), twenty volumes, and the sometimes risky *Writings of Thomas Jefferson*, edited by Paul L. Ford (New York: G. P. Putnam's Sons, 1892–99), ten volumes. Merrill D. Peterson has edited a convenient anthology of Jefferson's essential writings, *The Portable Thomas Jefferson* (New York: Viking Press, 1975). Peterson's introduction is rather cursory, but his selections are judicious. His edition contains all of Jefferson's *Notes on the State of Virginia*, several of Jefferson's public papers and addresses, and over two hundred pages of correspondence. Especially invaluable to the student of Jefferson's religious and ethical thought are two collections: *The Adams-Jefferson Letters*, edited by Lester J. Cappon (Chapel Hill: University of North Carolina Press, 1959), and *Jefferson's Extracts from the Gospels*, edited by Dickinson W. Adams (Princeton, N.J.: Princeton University Press, 1982). Cappon's collection contains all of the extant correspondence between Adams and Jefferson, running from 1771 to 1826. The selections from 1813 on, after the two men had retired from public life and thus could afford the luxury of unhurried philosophizing, provide a wealth of information concerning Jefferson's views on religion, ethics, and Christianity. Adams's volume has Jefferson's "The Philosophy of Jesus" and "The Life and Morals of Jesus," prefaces them with thoroughly researched introductions, and concludes with one hundred pages of Jefferson's correspondence in which he specifically deals with religious issues. These two collections are arguably the most important references for anyone interested in Jefferson's religion and ethics.

As in the case of Franklin, there is a seemingly inexhaustible mine of secondary literature on Jefferson the man and thinker. Among biographies, Dumas Malone's massive *Jefferson and His Times* (Boston: Little, Brown, 1948–81), six volumes, is unquestionably the most comprehensive. Noble Cunningham's *In Pursuit of Reason: The Life of Thomas Jefferson* (Baton Rouge: Louisiana State University Press, 1987) takes a look at Jefferson the Enlightenment thinker, and Edwin Thomas Martin's *Thomas Jefferson: Scientist* (New York: H. Schuman, 1952) focuses on Jefferson's interests in natural philosophy. Karl Lehman emphasizes Jefferson's social thought in *Thomas Jefferson: American Humanist* (New York: Macmillan, 1947), and Fawn Brodie offers a sometimes unsympathetic look at Jefferson the man in *Thomas Jefferson: An Intimate Biography* (New York: W. W. Norton, 1974).

Jefferson's religious thought, and particularly his admiration for the moral teachings of Jesus, have fascinated a long line of commentators. Two older pieces which attempt short overviews are J. Lesslie Hall, "The Religious Opinions of Thomas Jefferson," *Sewanee Review* 21 (1913): 164–76, and William D. Gould, "The Religious Opinions of Thomas Jefferson," *Mississippi Valley Historical Review* 20 (1933): 191–208. More recently, Henry Wilder Foote explored the issue in *Thomas Jefferson: Champion of Religious Freedom, Advocate of Christian Morals* (Boston: Beacon Press, 1947) and *The Religion of*

384   *Thomas Jefferson* (Boston: Beacon Press, 1960). Two works in particular examine Jefferson's views on religious liberty and freedom of conscience: Robert M. Healy, *Jefferson on Religion in Public Education* (New Haven, Conn.: Yale University Press, 1962), and Frank Swancara, *Thomas Jefferson vs. Religious Oppression* (New York: University Books, 1969). The most informative book to date on Jefferson's religious convictions is Charles B. Sanford's *The Religious Life of Thomas Jefferson* (Charlottesville: University Press of Virginia, 1984). Sanford's study draws on the entire Jeffersonian corpus and is generous in its use of quotations. Its major drawback, however, is that it is more compendium than analysis: Sanford fails to weave his rich textual expertise around an interpretation. Still, his study is an invaluable resource guide.

To my mind, Adrienne Koch's *The Philosophy of Thomas Jefferson* (New York: Columbia University Press, 1943) is still the best study of Jefferson's epistemology, ethics, and political thought, although there is some merit to the conventional charge that she anachronistically paints a too positivistic portrait. Her *Jefferson and Madison: The Great Collaboration* (New York: Oxford University Press, 1969) examines, *inter alia*, the relationship between Jefferson's political and religious views. Stuart Gerry Brown examines Jefferson's ethical theory in "The Mind of Thomas Jefferson," *Ethics* 73 (1963): 79–99, as I do in chapter 4 of my *Rational Infidels: The American Deists*. Charles A. Miller, in his recent *Jefferson and Nature: An Interpretation* (Baltimore, Md.: Johns Hopkins University Press, 1988), provides an intriguing look at Jefferson's metaphysical and ethical thought that may well replace Koch's earlier treatment. His opening chapter, "Jefferson, Nature, and the Enlightenment," analyzes the importance for the Enlightenment of the concept of nature.

Ethan Allen

Most of the first edition of Allen's *Reason the Only Oracle of Man, or a Compenduous System of Natural Religion* (Bennington, Vt.: Haswell & Russell, 1784) was destroyed by fire while it sat in the printer's warehouse, but pirated editions, some of them abridged, appeared through the middle of the nineteenth century. A facsimile republication of the first edition (New York: Scholars Facsimiles and Reprints, 1970), appeared recently, but it is difficult to read in certain places, probably because of photographic difficulties. Most of Allen's other publications, mainly political pamphlets, are of little interest to the nonspecialist. But his memoirs, *A Narrative of Colonel Ethan Allen's Captivity . . .* (Philadelphia, 1779), still make for lively if not always reliable reading. Several modern editions have appeared.

There are four standard biographies of Allen: Henry Hall, *Ethan Allen* (New York: D. Appleton & Co., 1892), Stewart H. Holbrook, *Ethan Allen* (New York: Macmillan, 1944), Charles Jellison, *Ethan Allen: The Frontier Rebel* (Syracuse, N.Y.: Syracuse University Press, 1969), and John Pell, *Ethan*

Allen (Boston: Houghton Mifflin Co., 1929). Jellison's is clearly the best of the four, although sparse on specific documentation. But none of them provides more than a cursory sketch of Allen's deism or its relationship to the broader American Enlightenment.

B. T. Schantz's "Ethan Allen's Religious Ideas," *Journal of Religion* 18 (1938): 183–217, gives an informative although somewhat dated overview of the pertinent literature. Discussions of Allen's *Reason the Only Oracle* may be found in Dana Doten, "Ethan Allen's Original Something," *New England Quarterly* 11 (1938): 361–66, and 'Ethan Allen's Philosophy,'" ibid.; Clarence Gohdes, "Ethan Allen and His Magnum Opus," *Open Court* 43 (1929): 148; and chapter 3 of my *Rational Infidels: The American Deists.* An intriguing discussion of the problem of authorship of the *Oracles* is provided in George Pomeroy Anderson, "Who Wrote 'Ethan Allen's Bible'?" *New England Quarterly* 10 (1937): 685–96. Finally, Darlene Shapiro draws connections between Allen's religious and political thought in "Ethan Allen: Philosopher-Theologian to a Generation of American Revolutionaries," *William and Mary Quarterly,* 3d ser., 21 (1964): 236–55.

Constantin François Chasseboeuf, Comte de Volney

Les Ruines, ou méditations sur les révolutions des empires; par M. Volney, Député à l'Assemblée Nationale de 1789, appeared in Paris in 1791. Thomas Jefferson began a translation of it subsequently completed by Joel Barlow and published as *Ruins; or Meditations on the Revolutions of Empires* (New York, 1799). The *Ruins* went through numerous editions in the nineteenth century and has recently been reissued in France (Paris: Éditions d'Aujourd'hui) and retranslated into English by Burton Feldman and Robert Richardson (New York: Garland Press, 1979). Nineteenth-century editions often printed along with the *Ruins* translations of Volney's *La Loi naturelle* (Paris, 1793), which first appeared in the United States as *The Law of Nature, or Principles of Morality Deduced from the Physical Nature of Mankind and the Universe* (Philadelphia, 1796). The impact of these two works on late American deism was profound, as was Volney's defense of deism in *Answer to Dr. Priestley, on a Pamphlet Entitled Observations on the Increase of Infidelity* (Philadelphia, 1797). Both of these works, along with Volney's *Voyage en Égypte et en Syrie* (1787), are in his posthumous *Oeuvres completes* (Paris, 1821), eight volumes.

Secondary literature on Volney is scarce. Gilbert Chinard edited and discussed Volney's correspondence with Jefferson in *Volney et l'Amérique d'après dès documents et sa correspondance avec Jefferson* (Baltimore, Md.: Johns Hopkins University Press, 1923), and Jean Gaulmier's *Volney* (Paris: Hatchette, 1959) is the only recent biography. Mouza Raskolnikoff, in "Volney et les Idéologues: Le Refus du Rome," *Revue d'Histoire* 267 (1982): 357–73, discusses a 1795 series of lectures by Volney in which he unfavorably compares classical Roman culture to the eighteenth-century Enlightenment. Discussions of Volney's influence on American deism may be found in Koch's *Republican Religion*, Morais's *Deism in Eighteenth-Century America*, and Leon Howard's *The Connecticut Wits* (Chicago: University of Chicago Press, 1943), chapter 9.

Thomas Paine

Paine published his major deistical treatise *The Age of Reason* in 1794–95. Since that time, scores of editions have appeared. Four standard collections of his writings are especially comprehensive: *The Writings of Thomas Paine*, edited by Moncure Daniel Conway (New York: G. P. Putnam's Sons, 1894–96), four volumes; *The Life and Works of Thomas Paine*, edited by William M. Van der Weyde (New Rochelle, N.Y.: Thomas Paine Historical Association, 1925), ten volumes; *The Complete Writings of Thomas Paine*, edited by Philip S. Foner (New York: Citadel Press, 1969), two volumes; and *The Life and Writings of Thomas Paine*, edited by Daniel Wheeler (New York: V. Park & Co., 1915), ten volumes. Foner's edition includes a chronological table of Paine's writings and substantial editorial notes. *Thomas Paine: Representative Selections*, edited by Harry Hayden Clark (New York: Hill and Wang, 1961), offers a less comprehensive selection but has the advantage of a closely argued introduction dealing with the influence of the New Learning on Paine's thought. It also contains a helpful bibliography.

Biographical studies of Paine abound. Moncure Daniel Conway's two-volume *Life of Thomas Paine* (New York: G. P. Putnam's Sons, 1892) is the best from the nineteenth century but offers little documentation and probably overstresses the influence of Quakerism on Paine's thought. Alfred Owen Aldridge's *Man of Reason: The Life of Thomas Paine* (New York: Lippincott, 1959) is a carefully documented study of Paine's life and work. A more popular but well-researched treatment is David Freeman Hawke, *Paine* (New York: Harper and Row, 1974). Two recent studies are generally unreliable. David Powell's *Tom Paine: The Greatest Exile* (New York: St. Martin's Press, 1985) contains a wealth of factual errors, and British philosopher A. J. Ayer's *Thomas Paine* (New York: Atheneum, 1988) is uncritically derivative in its history and more Ayeresque than Paine-ish in its philosophy. More trustworthy is Audrey Williamson, *Thomas Paine: His Life, Work, and Times* (New York: St. Martin's Press, 1973), as well as the excellent updated version of Jerome D. Wilson and William F. Ricketson, *Thomas Paine* (Boston: Twayne Publishers, 1989). Wilson and Ricketson include a brief but helpfully annotated bibliography.

Works dealing primarily with Paine's radical republicanism include A. Owen Aldridge, *Thomas Paine's American Ideology* (Newark: University of Delaware Press, 1984), S. M. Berthold, *Thomas Paine: America's First Liberal* (Boston: Meader Publishing Co., 1938), Mary A. Best, *Thomas Paine, Prophet and Martyr of Democracy* (New York: Harcourt, Brace & Co., 1927), and Eric Foner, *Tom Paine and Revolutionary America* (New York: Oxford University Press, 1976), Aldridge's study is the best, and Foner's, which approaches Paine's thought from a Marxist perspective, is the most original, even if not entirely convincing.

Studies dealing solely or in large part with Paine's religious views are numerous. After *The Age of Reason* appeared, a rash of contemporary replies were published. Two of the best that are still of interest to the modern reader are Joseph Priestley, *An Answer to Mr. Paine's Age of Reason* (1794), and Richard Watson, *An Apology for the Bible in a Series of Letters, Addressed to Thomas Paine* (1796). Unfortunately, both are out of print and difficult to locate. More accessible is Ira M. Thompson, Jr., *The Religious Views of Thomas Paine* (New York: Vantage Press, 1965), a published thesis somewhat short on analysis. Arnold Smithine in his *Natural Religion in American Literature* (New Haven, Conn.: College and University Press, 1966) offers more trenchant insights into the relationship between Paine's thought and American natural religion, but it is not devoted to Paine alone. Chapter 5 of my *Rational Infidels: The American Deists* discusses Paine's deism as well as its relation to his radical republicanism. No definitive book-length study of Paine's deism exists, but a handful of articles examines specific points. Of these, the most useful include Harry Hayden Clark's "An Historical Interpretation of Thomas Paine's Religion," *University of California Chronicle* 35 (1933): 56–58, and "Toward a Reinterpretation of Thomas Paine," *American Literature* 5 (1933–34): 133–45. Both stress Paine's reliance on the New Learning. Robert P. Falk, "Thomas Paine: Deist or Quaker?" *Pennsylvania Magazine of History and Biography* 62 (1938): 52–63, is a valuable counterweight to M. D. Conway's overzealous argument that Paine's religious thought is largely an offshoot of his youthful Quakerism. Jack Fruchtman, Jr., examines an aspect of the Priestley-Paine debate in "The Revolutionary Millennialism of Thomas Paine," in *Studies of Eighteenth-Century Culture*, vol. 13 (Tempe: University of Arizona Press, 1984). Henry Leffmann's "The Real Thomas Paine, Patriot and Publicist," *Pennsylvania Magazine of History and Biography* 46 (1922): 81–99, and Franklin K. Prochaska's "Thomas Paine's *The Age of Reason* Revisited," *Journal of the History of Ideas* 33 (1972): 561–76, examine the origins and subsequent misreadings of Paine's deistic treatise. Finally, two comparative studies are interesting: Michael Payne's "Priestley, Paine, Blake, and the Tradition of English Dissent," *Pennsylvania English* 10 (1983): 5–13, and Margaret M. Vanderhoar's "Whitman, Paine, and the Religion of Democracy," *Walt Whitman Review* (March 1970): 14–22, trace the connections between Paine's religious thought and, respectively, eighteenth-century British liberalism and nineteenth-century American romanticism.

Elihu Palmer

In spite of his blindness and hectic pace of activities, Palmer's literary output was respectable. It includes three published speeches: *Extracts from an Oration, Delivered by Elihu Palmer, the 4th of July, 1793,* in *Political Miscellany,* edited by G. Forman (Philadelphia, 1793); *An Enquiry Relative to the Moral and Political Improvement of the Human Species. An Oration Delivered in the City of New York on the Fourth of July*... (New York, 1797); and *The Political Happiness of Nations; an Oration. Delivered at the City of New York, on the Fourth of July*... (New York, 1800). In keeping with the spirit of their delivery dates, these pieces discuss the blessings of liberty and decry the "double despotism" of church and state which seeks to curtail freedom of conscience. Palmer's magnum opus, *Principles of Nature; or, A Development of the Moral Causes of Happiness and Misery among the Human Species,* first appeared in 1800 or 1801. It went through three revised editions before Palmer's death in 1806 and continued to be reissued in England as well as the United States well into the nineteenth century. In addition to the work published under his name, Palmer contributed scores of articles, some of which found their way into the *Principles,* for *The Temple of Reason,* and the *Prospect.* Indeed, most of the latter's contents are from his pen. Palmer left unfinished a treatise on republican politics that his friend John Fellows published along with his speeches a few years later: *Posthumous Pieces. By Elihu Palmer, being three chapters of an unfinished work intended to have been entitled "The Political World." To which are prefixed a Memoir of Mr. Palmer by his friend Mr. John Fellows of New York, and Mr. Palmer's "Principles of the Deistical Society of the State of New York"* (London: R. Carlile, 1828).

The sad obscurity into which Palmer has fallen is suggested by the almost complete lack of secondary literature. Although he is at least mentioned in most histories of the American Enlightenment, few studies are devoted to him. One notable exception is Roderick S. French's fine "Elihu Palmer, Radical Deist, Radical Republican: A Reconsideration of American Freethought," in *Studies in Eighteenth-Century Culture,* vol. 8 (Madison: University of Wisconsin Press, 1979). French also contributed the article on Palmer in *The Encyclopedia of Unbelief.* I discuss Palmer's life and thought, as well as its Enlightenment background, in the introduction to my *Elihu Palmer's "Principles of Nature": Text and Commentary* (Wolfeboro, N.H.: Longwood, 1990), chapter 6 of *Rational Infidels: The American Deists,* and "Elihu Palmer's Crusade for Rational Religion," *Religious Humanism* 24 (Summer 1990): 113–29, 146. A full-length treatment of Palmer's thought and his pivotal role in the deist movement is sorely needed. American deism, especially its later, militant period, cannot be adequately understood except in comparison to Palmer's contributions.

Philip Freneau

Freneau was one of the more prolific of the lesser American deists, and his journalistic essays and poetry were collected and published during his lifetime in many volumes. Philip M. Marsh provides an exhaustive survey in *Freneau's Published Prose: A Bibliography* (Metuchen, N.J.: Scarecrow Press, 1970) and *The Works of Philip Freneau: A Critical Study* (Metuchen, N.J.: Scarecrow Press, 1968). The most significant of Freneau's works are: *The Poems of Philip Freneau* (Philadelphia: Francis Bailey, 1786); *The Miscellaneous Works of Mr. Philip Freneau* (Philadelphia: Francis Bailey, 1788); *Poems Written between the Years 1768 and 1794* (Monmouth, N.J.: By author, 1795); *Letters on Various Interesting and Important Subjects . . . by Robert Slender* (Philadelphia: D. Hogan, 1799); *Poems Written and Published during the American Revolutionary War* (Philadelphia: Lydia Bailey, 1809), two volumes; and *A Collection of Poems . . . Written between the Year 1797 and the Present Time* (New York: David Longworth, 1815), two volumes. Of particular interest for the student of Freneau's deism are the *Miscellaneous Works*, the *Letters*, and the 1809 and 1815 editions of poetry. In addition to his bibliographies, Philip M. Marsh has rendered large portions of Freneau's poetry and prose accessible to the modern reader in two collections: *The Prose of Philip Freneau* (New Brunswick, N.J.: Scarecrow Press, 1955), and *A Freneau Sampler* (Metuchen, N.J.: Scarecrow Press, 1963). The second of these is especially invaluable because it reproduces a good quantity of the deistic poetry omitted in Fred Lewis Pattee's three-volume *The Poems of Philip Freneau* (Princeton, N.J.: Princeton University Press, 1902). Pattee's otherwise fine collection neglects to include Freneau's religious and philosophical poems because the editor curiously judged them uninteresting.

Lewis Leary's *That Rascal Freneau*, a title Washington ungraciously bestowed on the poet, is the best available biography (New York: Octagon Books, 1964), nicely documented and with insightful reflections on Freneau's intellectual development. Other biographical treatments of slightly less caliber include Mary Stanislas Austin's *Philip Freneau: The Poet of the Revolution* (Detroit: Gale Research Co., 1968) and Mary Weatherspoon Bowden's *Philip Freneau* (Boston: Twayne Publishers, 1976).

Critical studies are rather sparse. One of the best, and the only one that focuses on Freneau the deist, is Nelson F. Adkins's *Philip Freneau and the Cosmic Enigma: The Religious and Philosophical Speculations of an American Poet* (New York: New York University Press, 1949). Adkins's study examines Freneau's fidelity to natural religion without losing sight of its protoromantic undercurrents, and he makes an interesting case for the claim that Freneau was significantly influenced by the Roman materialist Lucretius; however, the volume is too slender to do more than cut a rather impressionistic swath. Still, it points the reader in the right direction, and I flesh out Adkins's cursory treatment in chapter 7 of my *Rational Infidels: The American Deists*. Jacob Axelrod examines Freneau's social and political views in *Philip Freneau: Champion of Democracy* (Austin: University of Texas Press, 1967). Although not directly interested in Freneau's deism, Richard C. Vitzthum's *Land and Sea: The Lyric Poetry of Philip Freneau* (Minneapolis: University of Minnesota, 1978) explores the romantic element in Freneau's thought.

Deistic Periodicals

No work devoted to an examination of eighteenth-century deistic journalism in America exists, but interesting discussions of the issue may be found in Koch's *Republican Religion* and Morais's *Deism in Eighteenth-Century America*. Morais's bibliography contains an extensive listing of pertinent journals and periodicals, as does an appendix to the second volume of *The Encyclopedia of Unbelief*.

Index

Alcott, Bronson, 42
Alembert, Jean Le Rond, d', 6
Allen, Ethan (1737–1789)
  on faith, 169–71
  francophilia of, 24
  on God, arguments for existence of,
    146–50
  on Jesus, character of, 171–72, 172–77
  on miracles, 167–69
  on natural law, 148, 162–67
  on punishment for sin, 152–54, 158
  on reason, 158–62
  on sin, 150–52
  on superstition, 145–46
  on virtue, 162–67
  on virtue, origin of, 156–57
  on virtue and reason, 179–81
Ames, William, 14
Aquinas, Thomas, 308
Aristotelianism in colleges, 14
Arminianism, 17, 20, 22. *See also*
  Calvinism in America
Autobiography (Franklin)
  Articles of Belief, 93
  Dissertation, 92
  on habituation to virtue, 94–96
  on Presbyterian doctrine, 92–93
  on Quakers, 98–99
  on Whitefield, George, and revivalism,
    96–98
  youthful reading of deistic tracts, 91

Bacon, Francis, 7–8, 11, 14, 23
Barlow, Joel, 182, 279
Becker, Carl, 5
Beecher, Lyman, 1, 43
Benezet, Anthony, 98
Bentham, Jeremy, 307
Blackmore, Richard, 70n
Bliss, William, 15
Blount, Charles, 141
Bolingbroke, Henry Saint-John, Viscount,
  25
Bradstreet, Anne, 278
British deism, 12–13, 26–27
Burke, Edmund, 26
Burtt, Edwin, 37

Calvin, John, 16
Calvinism in America, 16–23
  and covenant of grace, 18
  and depravity of reason, 17, 20–21
  Five Points of, 17–18
  introspection of, 20–21
  and scheme of salvation, 19–20
  and war of self against self, 19–20
Campbell, Alexander, 43
Cassirer, Ernst, 6
Channing, William Ellery, 1
Cheyne, George, 11, 15
Christianity
  and angels, 365–66
  and atonement, 249–51
  and faith, 251–53, 269–71, 347–48
  intolerant attitude of, 83–87, 88–89,
    111–14, 115–16, 130, 145–46, 185–
    92, 193–96, 206–7, 244–45, 263–64,
    298–99, 302–5, 309, 327, 331, 350–
    51, 354–57, 363
  and Jesus, 29, 105, 118–19, 120–22,
    129–30, 131, 132, 136, 215–16,
    324–26, 363–65
  and miracles, 29–30, 123, 133–34, 135,
    137–39, 140, 220–21, 254–57, 339–
    41, 342–44
  morality of, 31, 221–23, 257–60, 261–
    62, 324–26
  and revelation, 30–31, 140, 185–86,
    188–92, 213–15, 223, 226–27, 245–
    46, 344–46
  and scripture, 30, 117, 120–22, 216–
    18, 221, 245, 258, 259, 260
  and sin, 150–58, 246–49, 253–54
  See also under individual authors
Churches, reactions of to deism, 2–3
Clap, Thomas, 1
Clarke, Samuel, 11, 15
College of New Jersey (Princeton), 1, 14
College of William and Mary, 1, 107
Collins, Anthony, 12, 15
Copernicanism in colleges, 14

Dartmouth College, 1, 240
Declaration of Independence, 107
Deism. *See* British deism; Rational
  Religion

Deistical Society of New York, 241, 307, 359
  principles of, 276–77
Diderot, Denis, 6
Driscoll, Dennis, 306, 307
Dudleian Lectures, establishment of, 15
Dummer, Jeremiah, 14

Edwards, Jonathan, 13, 15, 20–21. *See also* Calvinism in America
Emerson, Ralph Waldo, 42
Enlightenment, characteristics of, 5–7
Ethics in deism, 33, 57–59, 64–65, 78–79, 80–82, 94–96, 105, 124–26, 127–29, 156–57, 162–67, 177–81, 203–4, 205–6, 210, 264, 265–67, 268–71, 285–86, 297–98, 299–300, 338, 366–67. *See also under individual authors*

Faith, Christian. *See* Christianity
Fénelon, Archbishop of Cambrai, 70n
Five Points, 17, 18
Franklin, Benjamin (1706–1790)
  conversion to deism, 15
  francophilia of, 24
  on free will and necessity, 57–59, 78–79
  on God, 56–66, 67–68, 73–74
  Great Awakening, reaction to, 22
  on immortality, 64–65, 105
  on Jesus, 105
  on Job story, 99–100
  on Lord's Prayer, 89–91
  motion for prayers in convention, 103–4
  on pain and pleasure, 60–63
  on providence, 64–65, 75–79, 104
  on Scottish philosophy, 14
  on subordinate gods, 67
  on tolerance, 83–87, 88–89
  on virtue, 80–82
  See also Autobiography
French enlightenment, 23–24, 44
French revolution, 24–26
Freneau, Philip (1752–1832)
  on *Age of Reason*, 3
  on Christian practices, absurdity of, 304–5
  on ethics, 285–86, 297–98
  on freedom of conscience, 298–99
  on happiness and virtue, 299–300
  on hypocrisy, 302–4
  on liberty, 287–90, 291–92, 293–95
  on natural law, 283–85
  on rational religion, 286–87, 296–97, 300–301

  on reason and superstition, 282–83, 292–93
  on science, 285–86
Fuller, Margaret, 42

Galileo (Galileo Galilei), 335
Gay, Ebenezer, 20
Gibbon, Edward, 2, 25
God, 4, 29, 56–66, 67–68, 73–74, 96, 146–50, 162–67, 188–92, 227–29, 232–38, 273–75, 276–77, 295–96, 310, 311–13, 314–22, 365–66. *See also under individual authors*
Goodwin, George, 19
Great Awakening, 20–23. *See also* Calvinism in America
Green Mountain Boys, 141

Hall, Robert, 25
Hamilton, Alexander, 106
Hargrove, John, 206, 332
Harvard College, 1, 2, 14, 15
Hawley, Joseph, 15
Helvetius, Claude, 182, 307
Hobbes, Thomas, 294, 331
Holbach, Paul Henri Thiery, Baron d', 41, 187, 307
Hume, David
  on miracles, 30
  on skepticism, 14, 25, 32, 35–36, 38, 39, 307
Hutcheson, Francis, 14, 23

Infidelity, post-deistic expressions of, 42, 358
Intolerance, doctrinal. *See* Christianity

Jefferson, Thomas (1743–1826)
  on ancient philosophers, 119, 120–22, 133
  on Book of Revelations, 140
  on Christianity, Platonic corruptions of, 123, 133–34, 135, 137–39, 140
  francophilia of, 24
  on freedom of conscience, 111–14, 115–16, 130
  free-thinking table talk of, 2
  on natural aristocracy, 124–26
  on natural law, 118
  on reason, 116–18
  and Scottish philosophy, 14
  on scriptural exegesis, 117, 120–22
  on virtue, 127–29
Jesus. *See* Christianity
Kant, Immanuel, 6, 36, 39

Kneeland, Abner, 358

Laplace, Pierre Simon, Marquis de, 9
Laws of Nature. *See* Natural Law
Leland, John, 15
Leslie, Charles, 15
Liberal Christianity, 11–13, 15
Locke, John, 6, 7–11, 14, 23

Macquarrie, John, 44
Mather, Cotton, 15, 52
Mechanism, Newtonian, 36–39. *See also*
   Newton, Isaac
Miller, Perry, 19
Milton, John, 70
Miracles. *See* Christianity
Mitchell, John, 19
Montesquieu, Charles de Secondat, Baron
   de, 183
Morality. *See* Ethics

Napoleon, 182
Natural law, 118, 124–26, 156–57, 163–
   67, 177–79, 180–81, 196–206, 223–
   26, 264, 265–67, 268–71, 283–85,
   287–90, 291–92, 293–95, 360, 366–
   67. *See also under individual authors*
Natural religion. *See* Rational religion
New Learning, 5–11, 15–16, 20, 23
Newton, Isaac, 7, 8–11, 14, 23

Ogden, Uzal, 3
Owen, Robert, 43, 358

Paine, Thomas, (1737–1809)
   on God, 227–29, 232–38
   on immorality of Christianity, 221–23
   on immortality, possibility of, 238–39
   on Jesus, 215–16
   on miracles, 220–21
   on natural religion, 212–13, 223–26,
      229–32, 233–38
   on New Testament, 216–18
   on Old Testament, 221
   personal credo, 212–13
   on redemption, 218–20
   on revelation, 213–15, 223, 226–27
Palmer, Elihu (1764–1806)
   on the atonement, 249–51
   on despotism, 263–64
   on evil, 261–62
   on immorality of Christianity, 257–60
   on natural religion, 273–75, 276–77
   on original sin, 246, 253–54
   on reason, 244–45, 263
   on reciprocal justice (ethics), 33, 268–
      71
   on revelation, 245–46

on scripture, 245, 258, 259, 260
on superstition, 244–45
on universal benevolence (ethics), 33,
   264, 265–67
Pascal, Blaise, 38, 39
Pope, Alexander, 9, 15
Priestley, Joseph, 55
Prospect
   on Christianity, 339–41, 347–48, 355–
      56
   on ethics, 338
   on miracles, 342–44
   on natural law, 346–47
   on natural religion, 336–37, 351–54
   Palmer's contributions to, 332, 333–34
   on reason, 334–36, 348–50
   on revelation, 344–46
   on science, 341–42
   on tolerance, 338–39
   on tolerance and blasphemy, 354–55,
      356–57
Rational religion, 1, 3, 4, 15, 25–28, 195,
   212–13, 223–26, 229–32, 233–38,
   273–75, 276–78, 286–87, 296–97,
   300–301, 327–31, 336–37, 351–54,
   360–61, 366–67. *See also under*
   individual authors
Ray, John, 70n
Reason, 31–33, 116–18, 145–46, 158–62,
   196–206, 244–45, 263, 282–83,
   285–86, 292–93, 309, 322–23, 334–
   36, 348–50, 362–63. *See also under*
   individual authors
Reciprocal justice. *See* Palmer, Elihu
Reid, Thomas, 14, 23
Religion of Nature. *See* Rational religion
Revelation. *See* Christianity
Rousseau, Jean-Jacques, 6
Royal Society (British), 11
Rush, Benjamin, 241

Scottish common sense school, 14–15
Scriptures, Christian. *See* Christianity
Second Great Awakening, 42, 43. *See also*
   Calvinism in America
Sin, original. *See* Christianity
Small, William, 106
Stewart, James, 244
Stiles, Ezra, 1, 2, 16, 20, 24, 43, 53, 105,
   143
Synod of Dort, 17, 18

Taylor, Charles, 5
Temple of Reason, The
   on Christian morality, 324–26
   on deism, 309–10

394 *Temple of Reason, The (continued)*
on God, 310, 311–13, 314–22
on Jesus, 324, 325, 326
on pagan philosophy, 325–26
on reason, 309, 322–23
statement of purpose, 309
on supernaturalism, 309, 327–31
tolerance, defense of, 309, 327, 329–30
Tennent, Gilbert, 20, 21
Theophilanthropist, The
on angels, 365–66
on God, 365–66
on humanity, 366–67
on Jesus, 363–65
on liberty, religious, 363
on rational religion, 360, 366–67
on reason, 362–63
theophilanthropy, meaning of, 361
Thoreau, Henry David, 42
Ticonderoga, Fort, 142
Tillotson, John, 15
Tindal, Matthew, 12, 15
Toland, John, 12, 15, 141
Tolerance, religious, 83–87, 88–89, 98–
99, 111–14, 115–16, 130, 193–96,
206–7, 263–64, 298–99, 302–4, 309,
327, 329–30, 338–39, 341, 354–55,
356–57. *See also under individual
authors*
Trumbull, John, 2

Universal benevolence. *See* Palmer, Elihu
Universal Society (Philadelphia), 240

Virtue. *See* Ethics
Volney, Constantin, Comte de (1757–
1820)
on diversity of religious doctrines, 195
on intolerance, religious, 193–96, 206–
7
on martyrdom, 186
on miracles, 185
on natural law, 196–206
on religious contradictions, 185–92
on religious doctrines, 188–92
on revelation, 185–86, 188–92
Voltaire, François Marie Arouet de, 182

Watson, Richard, 2
Westminster Confession, 52. *See also*
Calvinism in America
Whitefield, George, 20, 21, 96–98
Wollaston, William, 15, 55
Woods, Leonard, 43
Woolston, Thomas, 12
Wortman, Tunis, 3

Yale College, 1, 14, 20
Young, Thomas, collaboration with Ethan
Allen, 142